PATTERN AND REPERTOIRE
IN HISTORY

Pattern and Repertoire
in History

Bertrand M. Roehner

Tony Syme

HARVARD UNIVERSITY PRESS

Cambridge, Massachusetts

London, England · 2002

Library of Congress Cataloging-in-Publication Data

Roehner, Bertrand M., 1946–
Pattern and repertoire in history / Bertrand M. Roehner, Tony Syme.
p.   cm.
Includes bibliographical references and index.
ISBN 0-674-00739-5 (alk. paper)
1. History—Methodology.   2. Forecasting—History.   3. History—Historiography.
4. Social sciences and history.   I. Syme, Tony.   II. Title.

D16 .R68 2002
907'.2—dc21   2001051915

It may be that to some my History will not make agreeable reading because of the absence in it of fanciful stories. I shall be satisfied if what I have written is useful to those who wish to know what happened in the past and, human nature being what it is, may well happen again.

Thucydides, *History of the Peloponnesian War*

Having gathered these facts, Watson, I smoked several pipes over them, trying to separate those which were crucial from others which were merely incidental.

Sir Arthur Conan Doyle, "The Adventure of the Crooked Man"

Contents

Preface

The history of a country is like a river. As we walk along its banks, our attention is drawn to the river's sparkling, ever-changing surface, with its swirls and sudden directional changes. But watching from a safe distance we find that the picture becomes more orderly. One may observe that whenever the river becomes narrower the speed of the stream increases, or that a rocky riverbed produces more turbulence at the surface. If such observations are intended to be more than just casual remarks, they have to be confirmed by studying not just one but several rivers. That, in a nutshell, encapsulates our approach in this book. The rationale for such a project lies in the obvious fact that there can be no scientific explanation for unique events. Unique events can only be described and, as pointed out by Veyne (1984), this is precisely what history does. In this book we consider historical events from a comparative perspective. In the past the comparative approach has been pioneered either by comparative historians, such as Clausewitz, Marx, Bloch, Braudel, and Snooks, or by sociologists, such as Durkheim, Pareto, Connor, Goldstone, Hechter, Lieberson, and Tilly. But in recent years the field of historical sociology has experienced a rapid development. Many innovative ideas have been put forward that have provided the impetus to explore new directions.

Recent research has mostly concentrated on what can be called macrosociology or macrohistory. One notable exception is the work of Tilly, who has extensively explored popular disturbances; in a similar way this book is mainly concerned with microhistorical events. Our primary objective is to show that the concepts of historical pattern and repertoire introduced by Tilly have a fairly large scope of application. We show that by breaking up complex historical phenomena into simpler "modules," it becomes possible to study the latter from the point of view of sociology. In this way, historical sociology can aspire to bridging the long-standing gap between history and sociology. Sometimes, especially when we want to refer to the decomposition of a historical episode into simpler components, we use the expression "analytical history"; the field of analytical history should be seen as a branch, a ramification, of historical sociology.

This book focuses on a few, but fairly different, historical phenomena. They range from the French Revolution to the Pacific War. Clearly a separate book could be written on each of these events. But in focusing on one specific topic we would miss our main objective; we do not want to write yet another book about the French Revolution or the Pacific War, but to show that both phenomena can be studied (and better understood) using the methods of analytical history. In other words, we would like to convince the reader that the approach we propose has a wide applicability. The first chapter explains the methodology, then in the subsequent chapters a number of case studies show how it can be implemented. "A tree is judged by its fruits" goes the popular saying; similarly we wish this book to be judged on the basis of the new connections that it suggests, on the unexpected regularities that it discloses, and on the basic historical mechanisms that it highlights.

At this point a word of caution may be useful to emphasize that the satisfactions to be procured from this book are of a different nature than those expected from standard historical works. The chapters that follow contain (in Thucydides' words) few "fanciful stories"; instead they provide sequences and fragments of stories that are considered from a comparative perspective. The gratification one gets from the comparison of these partial accounts, we hope, is an understanding of the deep similarities between seemingly unrelated sequences. In short, behind the confounding complexity of historical events a hidden order will be seen to emerge. In Chapter 6, for example, we recount how in September 1914 Von Kluck's army suddenly turned away from Paris and marched eastward contrary to orders received from the General Staff. But we stop the narrative at this point without relating subsequent events, such as the battle of the Marne and how the German advance was checked. Instead, in order to better understand Von Kluck's conduct, we set out to examine the behavior of other German generals in the Franco-Prussian and Austro-Prussian wars. Thus the reader will find that we shift from one country at a given time to other countries and to other periods. Instead of reading just another story, the reader will be able to see connections between seemingly unrelated events. Realizing that German generals acted similarly at the battles of Sadowa (1866) and Gravelotte (1870), he will no longer be surprised by Von Kluck's attitude. Taken alone, Von Kluck's behavior is nothing more than an anecdote; considered in conjunction with similar situations, it tells us something about how the German High Command functioned as an organization. In the first case it is a record in military history, in the second it is a contribution to the sociology of organizations.

Writing this book has been an exhilarating journey in the course of which we have roamed through many periods and events. In some places we may have erred; that is almost inevitable if one considers the extent and the diversity of the data that needed to be processed. We welcome notification of possible errors or omissions. It may also be that in some places our statements appear a little too categorical; we fully realize that the problems that we deal with are multifaceted, but to surround each argument in a multitude of reservations would make the text difficult to read without adding anything to our purpose.

A first draft of this book was written in 1993. Although the main lines of the project have remained the same since then, many of our ideas have become more precise thanks to a number of discussions and email exchanges with colleagues. It is a pleasure to acknowledge those who have encouraged us and offered their advice. Pierre Chaunu, Francesco Galassi, and Charles Tilly were among the first to believe in this undertaking; we are grateful for their unfailing support. In 1998 one of us spent three months at Harvard as an invited scholar. Lectures on "pattern and repertoire" were given at Harvard, the State University of New York, the University of Arizona, and the University of California–Davis; many thanks to Stanley Lieberson, Immanuel Wallerstein, Michael Hechter, Dane Archer, Jack Goldstone, and John Hall for their interest and their advice. While we were pursuing this project Graeme Snooks reactivated and renewed the field of comparative history by publishing an impressive trilogy. Many thanks to him for leading the way.

As is often the case for new ideas, a primary difficulty was to get our approach accepted (to some extent) by other social scientists; Stanley Lieberson, our reviewers, and Michael Aronson of Harvard University Press played an instrumental role in that respect. Without their insight this book would not have been published in its present form; our sincere thanks to them. Through her apt queries and suggestions, Elizabeth

Gilbert helped us to improve the manuscript in many respects; it was a pleasure and a privilege to work with her.

Our colleagues, both in Paris and at Warwick and Oxford, have been of great assistance on many occasions, and we are particularly grateful to Laurent Baulieu, Bernard Diu, Jean Letessier, and Ahmed Tounsi.

The book is dedicated to our wives and children, who have patiently put their faith in us; their cheerful encouragement and stimulating support have been invaluable.

PATTERN AND REPERTOIRE
IN HISTORY

Analytical History:
Where History and Sociology Meet

"Where History and Sociology Meet," the title of a paper by John R. Hall (1992), refers to an appealing but rather problematic encounter. Indeed from Marx and Pareto up to the present time, several attempts have been made to marry history and sociology. Such a field, commonly referred to as sociohistory or historical sociology, would combine the potentialities of its parent disciplines; history would bring its extensive and detailed knowledge of particular events, and sociology, thanks to its theoretical insight, would enable us to structure and organize that vast amount of empirical evidence. The agenda is a fascinating one. Needless to say, that marriage can be arranged in a number of different ways. Currently historical sociology is a mosaic of various approaches developed by a number of distinguished scholars, including Connor, Goldstone, Hechter, Laitin, Flora, and Tilly, rather than being a unified field. That diversity attests to the field's vitality and rapid development. Hall in his 1992 paper makes a perceptive and penetrating analysis of the different strategies that can and have been used.

In the second section of this chapter we discuss these different options, after giving a quick overview of our approach in the first section. In the third and fourth sections we delineate our approach in more detail. Its most important feature is its focus on "simple" phenomena; many of its other characteristics derive from this requirement. For such simple phenomena it becomes possible to consider several historical manifestations; this in turn leads us to a discussion of recurrent events. Finally, in the fifth section, in order to give the reader some sense of the kind of understanding provided by this approach, we briefly describe several of the patterns that will be discovered in later chapters. In a general way the observation of

1

a definite pattern is a good starting point for the search for a theory. In this chapter we also introduce a number of general concepts, including modularization, paronymy, parsimony, and collective historical memory, which will be used throughout the rest of the book.

Not Because It Is Important but Because It Is Simple

There has been only one French Revolution; but, as we shall see in Chapter 3, there have been three stormings of the Bastille (1560, 1588, and 1789), about twenty meetings of the Estates-General, and, throughout Europe, more than fifteen episodes involving a confiscation of Church estates. In other words, by breaking down a complex phenomenon into simpler ones, one is able to study many instances instead of just a single one. What is to be gained from this? The approach makes a considerable difference, for, as is well known, there can be no scientific explanation for unique events; only descriptions are possible. Another way to put it is to say that by considering sets of events, one shifts from history to comparative history and sociology. Decomposing a complex phenomenon into simpler ones also has other advantages, as is made clear by the following analogy.

A "Not So Simple" Experiment

Consider the following experiment. A person takes a bottle of cola from the refrigerator, fills a paper cup, and, perhaps because he or she does not like drinking ice-cold cola, leaves the cup in the sun on the kitchen table. Slowly the cola will warm up. This experiment, which is schematized in Figure 1.1a, can be labeled "the warming of a cup of cola." However simple the label sounds, the experiment itself is by no means simple, at least if we look at it from the eyes of a physicist (Table 1.1). First the sunlight has to be transformed into heat, either on the surface of the cup or in the upper layer of the cola. The transformation of radiation into heat (following Wien's law) has been fully understood by physicists only since the beginning of the twentieth century. Then the heat has to travel through the paper cup and be transmitted to the liquid. The phenomenon of thermal conduction is fairly complex and was modeled satisfactorily only by the late nineteenth century. Finally the fact that the cola becomes warmer on the side exposed to the sun gives rise to convection streams within the liquid. The equation describing such streams are well known in hydrodynamics (Navier-Stokes equations), but they are highly complicated; solving

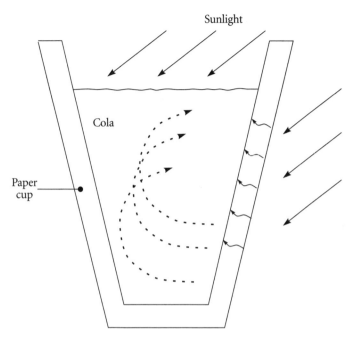

Figure 1.1a The warming of a cup of cola. The figure schematically represents an experiment in which a cup is filled with ice-cold cola and is left to warm up in the sun. One may be tempted to consider this a simple phenomenon; yet from the perspective of a physicist, it is in fact very complicated. Its understanding draws upon four different branches of physics: optics for the transformation of light into heat, statistical mechanics for the propagation of heat through the cup, hydrodynamics for the creation of convection streams between points that are at different temperatures, and thermodynamics for the diffusion of the heat throughout the volume of the liquid. This example calls into question the usual belief that social phenomena are inherently more complicated than those of the natural sciences.

them, even in an approximate way, would require hours on a high-speed computer.

What does this story tell us? (1) It is often claimed that social and economic phenomena are far more complex than those considered in the natural sciences. This is a questionable statement, as our example shows; the warming of a cup of cola turns out to be an incredibly complicated phenomenon even though our description was simplified in many ways (we did not, for example, take into account the role of the bubbles). (2) How then can we explain why physics has been so successful in the last few cen-

Table 1.1 Decomposition of a complex phenomenon into modules

Warming of a cup of cola	Field
Transformation of sunlight into heat	Optics
Propagation of heat in a solid/liquid	Statistical mechanics
Convection created by a temperature differential	Hydrodynamics
Diffusion of heat in the cola	Thermodynamics

French Revolution	Number of occurrences in France	Number of occurrences in Europe
How indebtedness weakened the power of the monarchy	10	30
Tactical alliance between the bourgeoisie and the clergy	5	15
Confiscation of Church estates	1	20
Insurrection in the capital city	5	25

Note: For France, the number of occurrences is based on a detailed enumeration; for the whole of Europe, the numbers should rather be considered as loose approximations.

turies? The answer is easy: physicists have restricted themselves to simple problems. Nobody has ever tried to give a complete theory for the warming of a cup of cola. Instead physics has concentrated its attention on the different subphenomena involved in that experiment, that is, the transformation of light into heat, the conduction of heat in a solid, and so on. Each of these phenomena has first been studied under the simplest possible conditions. The conduction of heat, for instance, is easier to study in copper or aluminum than in a heterogeneous material such as paper or cardboard. In a general way physics leaves aside all questions that turn out to be too difficult, even if they are of fundamental as well as practical importance. For example, why does water boil at 100°C and not, say, at 120°C, or why is iron ferromagnetic while copper or aluminum is not? Such questions are never touched upon in textbooks.

Simplicity, a Basic Requirement of the Human Mind
Decomposing complicated phenomena into simpler ones is an approach that has been used not only in physics but also in other fields. In astron-

omy, the laws of celestial mechanics were first established for Mars. Although basically governed by the same laws, the orbits of comets or asteroids are more difficult to decipher. In the same vein one can mention Pareto's (1917) perceptive remark that the discovery of the laws of gravitation was favored by the fact that the mass of the sun is much larger (about one thousand times) than the mass of the largest planets; under other circumstances, for instance, with a lighter sun or with a double star in place of the sun, the movements of the planets would be considerably more complicated; this would have made the discovery of Newton's law much more difficult. In chemistry, as well, the fundamental concepts were laid down by analyzing simple chemical elements rather than products such as wood, steel, or wine; the latter, though undoubtedly more useful, are also much more complex. Similarly, the basic laws of genetics were first established for Mendel's garden peas and for Morgan's drosophilia.

In fact the rule that a problem should be divided "into as many parts as would be required for a better solution" was stated more than three centuries ago by the philosopher and scientist Descartes (1965 [1637]). Subsequently the term "modular approach" has been used to refer to the decomposition of a complex phenomenon into simpler ones.

Nowadays this approach is used extensively in computer science, because it helps to economize "on the most scarce resource in nature, the intellect" (Snooks 1997). Suppose a computer programmer wants to write a software program for airline reservations. He will design different modules: one for schedules, another for fares, a third for reservations, and so on. Moreover each of these programs will itself have a modular structure. In that way, if a change has to be made, only one submodule has to be modified. In contrast, if the program is not structured into modules, any small change at one place may require substantial alterations in the rest of the program. In short, the modular approach has two distinct advantages: it saves a considerable amount of work, and, most important, it makes possible a cumulative development of human knowledge. In the next section we discuss the latter aspect from another perspective.

Limitations of the Phenomenological Approach

Coming back to the warming of a cup of cola, one may object that a much simpler approach can be used. By repeating the observation under sunlight of varying intensity, it is possible to estimate, for instance, the correlation between the intensity of light and the velocity of the convection streams or the temperature in the upper layers of the cola. Doing this bypasses the various complicated phenomena that we mentioned above; in physics such an approach would be called a phenomenological model, by which one means that it is purely empirical and established by statistical methods. Basically this is the approach used in econometrics; it is also used in sociology by those researchers who have adopted the techniques of econometricians.

This approach indeed looks very appealing because of its simplicity, but here the simplicity is rather illusory. The phenomenon still remains complicated; it is only the model that looks simple. The shortcomings of such an approach are obvious. If one replaces the paper cup with a glass, the whole study has to be resumed anew; similarly if the cola is replaced by milk (which is white) or by water (which is transparent), none of the previous correlations will hold. In other words, if even a single parameter is changed the whole study has to be restarted from the beginning. On the contrary, once the physicist has understood the transformation of light into heat he will know how the results have to be adapted if the color or the reflection index of the liquid is changed.

It has often been deplored (see Summers 1991 for an economist's view) that in the social sciences knowledge does not seem to grow cumulatively. This "Sisyphus syndrome" can be attributed to the lack of interest in breaking down complex phenomena into simpler ones. In the next section we examine how the modular approach can be applied in history.

The Modular Approach in History

Let us come back to the example of the French Revolution in order to examine how our ideas about simplicity and modularity can be adapted to history. We have already mentioned three possible modules, namely, the meetings of the Estates-General, the confiscation of Church estates, and the Parisian insurrection. Needless to say, these three episodes are only a part of a larger sample, which is illustrated in Figure 1.1b. In this book we sometimes use the term "analytical history" to refer to the study of the modules composing a complex phenomenon. A similar approach was proposed by Veyne (1976) in his opening lecture at the Collège de France; unfortunately he did not have the opportunity to carry out his research agenda in subsequent years.

It remains to show how these different modules can be studied separately and to examine what can be learned from such a modular approach. For purposes of illustration, we consider the meeting of the Estates-Gen-

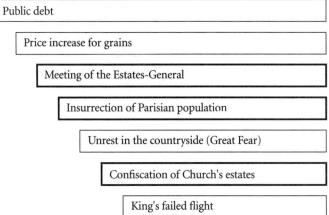

Selected Components of the French Revolution

| Public debt |
| Price increase for grains |
| Meeting of the Estates-General |
| Insurrection of Parisian population |
| Unrest in the countryside (Great Fear) |
| Confiscation of Church's estates |
| King's failed flight |

Figure 1.1b The French Revolution can be broken up into a number of separate episodes much in the same way that the warming of a cup of cola can. The components with a thick border are examined in detail in Chapter 3. Needless to say, other episodes could be added to this list, such as the civil war in Vendée or Brittany. Usually these components can be further decomposed into smaller subcomponents. In its principle this decomposition of a complex phenomenon into building blocks is similar to the approach advocated by Lieberson (1992); in his words, such an approach would permit knowledge to (cumulatively) build on knowledge.

eral. In the centuries before 1789, the Estates-General and parliaments (before the eighteenth century the two words are almost interchangeable) were summoned repeatedly not only in France but also in Britain, the German states (for example, Bavaria, Hesse, Prussia, Saxony, and Württemberg), Spain, Sweden, and in many other European countries. A cross-national comparison of such meetings discloses a number of regularities; for instance, it helps us to understand the conditions for a tactical alliance between the bourgeoisie and the clergy, or shows to what extent the authority of the monarch was weakened and undermined by indebtedness (see, in this respect, Goldstone 1991); one also realizes that the vote for a Bill of Rights was a crucial step for the bourgeoisie in its power struggle with the monarchy. In short, all these events that played an essential role in 1789 can be observed in earlier meetings of the Estates-General either in France or in other European states. A number of studies have already been concerned with similar issues; for example, Carsten (1959) has studied the parliaments in the German states, Picot (1872) has written a detailed history of the meetings of the French Estates-General. But so far such studies have been conducted in an unsystematic and haphazard way. There have thus been a number of important comparative historians, but as a field, comparative history still lacks a sound and coherent basis.

Applications

Three examples suggest ways in which the decomposition of a complex phenomenon into modules can be of practical relevance.

HOW LOUIS XVI COULD HAVE SAVED HIS THRONE IN 1789

Louis XVI could (perhaps) have saved his throne and his head in 1789 by carefully studying the course of action taken by his ancestor Charles V when confronted with a similar situation in February–March 1358.

Charles V faced the opposition of both the Estates-General and the Parisian population. His position was all the more difficult since he was only the dauphin while King John II was held captive in Britain. Yet not only did Charles V save his throne, but within a year he was able to curb the Parisian uprising. His plan was to leave Paris, gather support from the provincial capitals, and isolate the Parisian rebels. His first attempt to flee Paris failed, but a week later he managed to find refuge among his supporters in Senlis, a city about 40 kilometers to the north of Paris. As we know, Louis XVI also tried to leave Paris, but his plan had little in common with Charles's strategy. First, he waited too long; by the end of June 1791 the new regime was already firmly established. Second, instead of seeking refuge in a major provincial city he headed for a small town, Montmédy, on the Belgian border (Figure 1.2). Belgium at that time was part of Austria; seeking refuge under Austrian protection was seen as a betrayal by the French public. At Varennes-en-Argonne Louis XVI was recognized and arrested. Of course we cannot take for granted that a more clever plan would have saved him, but at least studying Charles's experience would have suggested to him a more sensible course of action.

Incidentally, a third episode of this kind occurred in France in the twentieth century. In May 1968, challenged by social and political unrest, President Charles de Gaulle left Paris. Using Charles V's strategy would have been unthinkable; instead, de Gaulle came back to Paris the next day. His

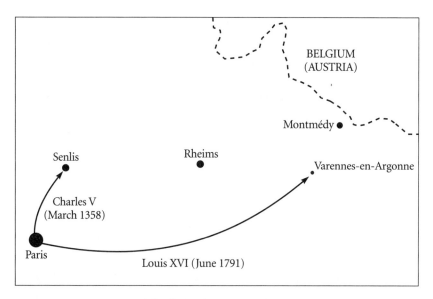

Figure 1.2 Comparison of the flights from Paris of Charles V (1358) and Louis XVI (1791). Charles V did not go far; Senlis, where he found refuge among his supporters, is only 40 kilometers away from Paris. Louis XVI, on the contrary, made for a small town, Montmédy, on the Belgian border, 240 kilometers away from Paris. Belgium at that time was part of Austria and in June 1791 the relations between France and Austria were already strained; war was to break out less than a year later. At Varennes-en-Argonne Louis XVI was recognized, his guards were disarmed, and he was put under arrest.

departure, however, had created a psychological shock; within a few days the situation was again under control.

Sometimes even a careful analysis is not sufficient to change the course of history. An example is provided by Napoleon's campaign in Russia. Napoleon was not in the habit of trusting his fate to luck; before the campaign he ordered a careful analysis of Charles XII's 1709 campaign in Russia. Yet this did not save his army; Russia was probably just too vast. But at least he did not repeat Charles's errors.

STRATEGIC PLANNING IN WORLD WAR II

Like the French Revolution, World War II was of course unique; but some of its modules were not. Such is the case for the war in Europe. Strategically the problem was fairly simple. In 1942 one country, Germany, and its allies occupied almost the whole of continental Europe. The United States along with Britain had control of the seas (at least after mid-1942), and they had an important ally, Russia, in Europe. Replace "Germany" with "France" and "United States and Britain" with Britain alone, and the description will apply to the Napoleonic Wars. This is more than a superficial similarity. In Chapter 6 we show that there is a striking parallelism between many strategic or tactical episodes of the two wars, including the war in Libya (versus Egypt), the war in Italy (versus Spain), the resistance and uprisings in occupied countries, the submarine war in the Atlantic (versus privateers).

THE FRENCH GENERAL STRIKE OF DECEMBER 1995

On November 23, 1995, a strike of railway workers began in Tours in protest against a plan to raise the retirement age. On November 25 the strike spread to other railway centers, and on November 28, the workers of Electricité de France (a power utility) joined the strike. At this point it became clear that the strike belonged to the class of what we call in Chapter 5 "mushroom strikes." Strikes of this sort had previously occurred in 1936, 1953, 1960, and 1968. All lasted about one month. Thus by the end of November 1995, it was possible to predict that the strike would first spread to the whole country but also that it would be over by the end of December. This is precisely what happened. In Chapter 5 we report how this prediction was made publicly and how it was indeed confirmed by subsequent events.

Comparative Approaches in Historical Sociology

The idea directs the experiment.
Claude Bernard (1865)

An anecdote is relevant here. In September 1995 one of the authors participated in the Quantitative Economic and Social History Conference organized by James Foreman-Peck at St. Catherine's College, Cambridge. The contributions fell into two distinct categories. The first category, which represented the overwhelming majority, was concerned with the description of a single episode of social or economic history and included presentations on topics such as "Retracing the social structure of late Weimar unemployment" or "Danish unemployment, 1845–1901." A small number of participants took a different approach; they began their talk by asking a question and then went on to analyze whatever observations could help to answer that question. At the time of the conference the difference between these two viewpoints passed almost unnoticed by the participants. Yet the difference is considerable. In the first case past events were the primary object of study, in the second they were considered as a pool from which observations could be selected in order to answer a specific question. The latter is the hallmark of a genuine comparative approach; in Claude Bernard's words, the idea then directs the experiment.

The comparative approach was introduced in economic history, particularly by Marc Bloch (1886–1944) and the so-called Annales School. Yet it is still used by only a small minority of economic historians.

In sociology the situation is different. Sociology came into being as a separate field only in the mid-nineteenth century and, thanks to the contributions of scholars like Durkheim (1858–1917) and Pareto (1848–1923), the comparative approach quickly assumed a central role. But since that time there has been an ongoing debate about methodological issues.

The Debate over Comparative Methodology
In the last few decades a number of important contributions attest to the vivacity of the debate over comparative methodology. Of special significance are Abbott (1998), Abrams (1982), Burke (1992), Dogan (1994), Goldstone (1982, 1997, 1999), Lieberson (1985, 1991, 1994), Lloyd (1993), Monkkonen (1994), Ragin (1987, 1997), Rule (1997), Skocpol (1984), Stinchcombe (1978), and Tilly (1985, 1997). At a more philosophical level, Bunge (1996, 1998) has analyzed explanation in the social sciences in comparison with physics.

A recent book edited by Mjöset (1997), containing contributions from a number of authors who have played an essential role in the development of historical sociology, provides a lucid account of the main issues. In many respects the approaches developed in the past three decades are complementary, as detailed in Figure 1.3 and Table 1.2. Although the micro-macro distinction is standard in economics, it is only occasionally made in sociology (and even less often in history). In some cases the qualitative/quantitative distinction is clear-cut; for instance, Pareto's analysis of superstitions is undoubtedly of a qualitative character. But in some works qualitative and quantitative analysis are used hand in hand; one example is Laitin's work, another is the present book. One distinct advantage of quan-

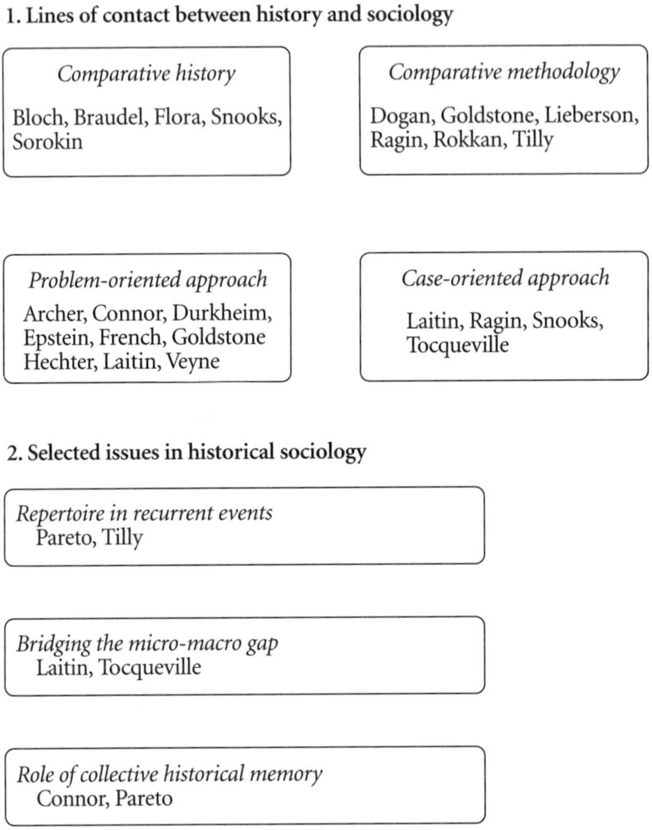

1. Lines of contact between history and sociology

Comparative history	*Comparative methodology*
Bloch, Braudel, Flora, Snooks, Sorokin	Dogan, Goldstone, Lieberson, Ragin, Rokkan, Tilly

Problem-oriented approach	*Case-oriented approach*
Archer, Connor, Durkheim, Epstein, French, Goldstone Hechter, Laitin, Veyne	Laitin, Ragin, Snooks, Tocqueville

2. Selected issues in historical sociology

Repertoire in recurrent events
Pareto, Tilly

Bridging the micro-macro gap
Laitin, Tocqueville

Role of collective historical memory
Connor, Pareto

Figure 1.3 Where history and sociology meet. History and sociology can be brought together in a number of ways. The first part of the diagram lists some of the lines of contact between history and sociology along with the names of some of the scholars who have explored them. The second part refers to more specific aspects of historical sociology.

tification is that it greatly facilitates comparison. The why/how distinction is an important one and will be discussed below.

At this point it may be of interest to examine to what extent our approach follows well-established procedures for social inquiry. In their book *Designing Social Inquiry* (1994), King, Keohane, and Verba discuss scientific requirements in the social sciences. Their approach has important points of contact with ours. First, the simplicity condition, which is central to our argument, is also strongly emphasized by King and his colleagues.

Table 1.2 Complementary approaches in historical sociology

Situations	Authors
Microhistory/Macrohistory	
Microhistory	Archer and Gartner, Bloch, Connor, Deutsch, Durkheim, French, Hall, Hechter, Laitin, Pareto, Tilly, Tocqueville, Veyne, *R&S*
Macrohistory	Braudel, Flora et al., Goldstone, Hechter, Laitin, Lieberson, Snooks, Tainter
Qualitative/Quantitative	
Qualitative	Bloch, Connor, Hall, Laitin, Pareto, Skocpol, Tainter, Tocqueville, *R&S*
Quantitative	Archer and Gartner, Braudel, Durkheim, Flora, Goldstone, Laitin, Lieberson, Tilly, *R&S*
Why?/How?	
Why?	Goldstone, Hechter, Laitin, Skocpol, Tainter, Tocqueville
How?	Braudel, Durkheim, French, Hall, Laitin, Pareto, Snooks, Tilly, *R&S*
Number of cases	
1–3 (small *N*)	Bloch, French, Hall, Hechter, Skocpol, Tocqueville, Veyne
4–10	Connor, Durkheim, Laitin, Pareto, Snooks, Tainter, *R&S*
More than 10 (large *N*)	Archer and Gartner, Flora et al., Tilly

Notes: For the sake of clarity we have not indicated years of publication; they can be found in the reference list. This table includes few references to works in cultural sociology, an omission related to the fact that cultural aspects are not considered in this book. *R&S* indicates the present book.

They note: "Systematic simplification is a crucial step to useful knowledge. As an economic historian [E. Jones] has put it, if emphasis on uniqueness is carried out to the extreme of ignoring all regularities the very possibility of social science is denied and historians are reduced to the aimlessness of balladeers" (p. 43). Second, King and his colleagues recommend (p. 10) that in studying complex and in some sense unique events, one should consider them as members of a larger class of events; they can thus be studied in a "systematic and comparative fashion." Such a methodology will indeed be applied extensively in the case studies in later chapters.

Third, *Designing Social Inquiry* stresses that there is no substantial methodological difference between qualitative and quantitative inquiries. In our book qualitative and quantitative evidence similarly complement each other.

In brief, our methodological options are in line with those advocated by King and his colleagues. Not surprisingly, there are also some points where our approaches diverge. For example, consider the following rule set forth by these authors for the selection of research questions: "A research project should pose a question that is important in the real world, one that significantly affects many people's lives" (p. 15). As explained elsewhere in this chapter, we favor simplicity even at the cost of significance in terms of policy implications. Our objective is to find stable and accurate regularities, independently of their immediate usefulness.

The Search for Patterns and Repertoires

In *The Mind and Society* (1935), Pareto comments that "it is enough for us to know that social facts reveal certain uniformities." What Pareto calls uniformities are also commonly referred to as regularities or patterns. Finding regularities is an important step; it is a prerequisite before one can think of building a model, for the regularities are precisely what the model should try to explain.

Drawing upon a formidable array of empirical evidence, Tilly (1986) introduced the concept of a people's repertoire of action: "Any population has a limited repertoire of collective action . . . People tend to act within known limits, to innovate at the margins of existing forms . . . People know the general rules of performance and vary the performance to meet the purpose at hand" (p. 390). In the pages that follow, Tilly proposes a classification of the forms of collective action before and after the industrial revolution and carefully studies the transition from one repertoire to the other. He points out that new forms of action are not introduced all at once; they result from many attempts and counterattempts spread over time.

Pareto (1935) drew a similar conclusion from his investigation of superstitions, noting: "It is a curious fact that the ties [between a number of elements] so imagined persist in time. It would be easy enough to try some new combination every day; instead there is one combination, fantastic though it be, that tends to prevail over all competitors."

In all areas it is easier to make variations on a theme than to create new themes. Thus biological evolution, if it has indeed created here and there new forms and functions, has above all put together a few basic patterns to create an incredible diversity of living forms. Jacob (1970) referred to this as the great tinkering of evolution: nothing is thrown away, innovations are shelved for future use in a different context. This is one of the major themes of this book. The creation of new forms of organization or action takes place in history in an extremely parsimonious manner. A structure that "works" will be used again many times, and even when one believes that it has outlived its usefulness one will notice decades later than some elements have been reused in a different context. This point is emphasized in the fascinating work that Jenkins (1986) has devoted to Jurassian separatism in Switzerland.

Why versus How
Whereas it is fairly easy to show that there is a correlation (or more generally a connection) between two phenomena, A and B, it is much trickier to assess the direction of the causality; is it $A \rightarrow B$ or $B \rightarrow A$? In some special cases the question has an obvious answer. For instance when Durkheim (1951) observes that suicides are most frequent on Sundays, there can be little doubt about the direction of the causality. But when Tainter (1988) notes that fiscal revenue diminishes in times when the state is weak, it is not obvious which is the cause and which is the effect.

There are two main difficulties with causality in the social sciences; one is technical, the other of an epistemological nature. The first is the multifactorial character of most phenomena. The fact that a phenomenon cannot be explained by a single cause does not mean, of course, that the very notion of causality should be rejected; but the simultaneous action of a great number of factors means that causality tests pertaining to one of these factors have to be carried out very carefully. The matter has received considerable attention in recent decades on the part of econometricians. Ever since the pioneering papers of Granger (1969), several multifactorial causality tests have been developed. Even in a field like modern economics, however, where accurate time series are available, the results of several decades of causality testing have been rather disappointing. In a review paper written in 1988, Zellner observes: "With all the work in the past two decades on definitions of causality and tests for causality, it may be asked 'How many new causal economic laws have been produced by this work?' I believe that an honest answer is: 'Not a single one.'"

The reason for these difficulties could be ascribed to the fact that, in Zellner's words, models are either too broad or too narrow. If they are broad, that is, if they involve many variables, then causality tests become technically very tricky and hazardous even when performed on fairly long time series. If the model is rather narrow, it may well overlook one (or several) significant variables, and this omission may lead to incorrect conclusions.

We may also look at the question of causality from a more general viewpoint. Here we will essentially follow the analysis of Veyne (1984). Concerning the symbolic example of the fall of an apple, Veyne stresses that one would search in vain for a reply to the question: why did this apple fall at this particular moment? In fact, depending on the perspective adopted, many replies are possible. The apple had become too heavy; the stem of the apple had by drying become brittle; there has been a gust of wind and the branch has been shaken, and so on. One would try in vain, concludes Veyne, to give a detailed account of the fall of the apple, but never discover the attraction that is the common cause not only of the fall of apples but also of the fall of pine cones or of water drops. At most one would reach the truism that unsupported objects fall. But if one passes from the question "why?" to the question "how?" then the way is opened that can allow one to discover that there is a universal law behind the fall of various objects.

In addition to these fundamental difficulties there are also practical obstacles. For multifactorial phenomena there is usually no objective criterion to decide whether one cause is more important than another. What were the causes of the Civil War in the United States? There are an infinite number of answers to such a question; whether one prefers one set of answers to another is just a matter of personal taste.

Bridging the Gap between Micro- and Macrosociology

Sometimes it is possible to identify mechanisms at the microlevel that have implications at the macrolevel. As an illustration consider the following problem. As far as state formation is concerned, the nineteenth century has seen two opposite movements. On the one hand, a number of empires and kingdoms have disintegrated: the Spanish, Ottoman, Austro-Hungarian empires, and the Danish kingdom. On the other hand, a number of separate entities have coalesced into new states, for example, Germany and Italy. How can we explain those opposite changes? There is an interesting explanation at the microsocial level, namely, the shift from religion to language as the defining principle of a state. The empires and kingdoms that disintegrated were multilinguistic entities held together by a common religion: Catholicism for the Spanish and Austro-Hungarian empires, Protestantism for the Danish kingdom, Islam for the Ottoman Empire. The new states, on the contrary, had a single language and, in the case of Germany, had long been deeply divided by religious issues.

We have here an example of a change at the microsociological level that brought about macrohistorical transformations. Such explanations are particularly attractive because microsociological phenomena often are not restricted to just one country; they thus present ideal opportunities for comparative analysis. But while there has been a sustained interest for comparative methods in the past decades, actual progress has been slow. It is the purpose of the next paragraph to examine why.

Obstacles to the Development of Comparative Analysis

In our opinion the main obstacle to the development of comparative analysis is the lack of adequate sources. Let us illustrate this point by an example. In 1997 there were riots in Indonesia between ethnic Chinese and Javanese. The clashes were by no means the first of that sort. Similar riots have occurred repeatedly in Indonesia since 1945 and even before independence. Suppose we want to make a precise study of such incidents. On which source can we rely? On the *Times* or on the *New York Times?* Clearly these papers had no reason to report small-scale riots in Indonesia. Since the country is a former Dutch colony, we have a better chance of finding the information in a Dutch newspaper. But then one has to be able to read Dutch or to find a Dutch collaborator. Even assuming that this practical problem has been solved, without the help of an index it will take a considerable amount of work to extract these events from the daily press.

From this example one can better understand why so many microsociological studies undertaken in the United States focus on either Britain or the United States, two countries for which there are convenient newspaper indexes. Generally there are few sources arranged in a cross-national perspective; chronologies are almost the only systematic sources of this sort.

In history there has been even less comparative work than in sociology. Academic and psychological obstacles seem to play an important role here. Currently one of the main criteria with which to judge the value of a piece of research in history is the number and variety of the archival sources used. Such a criterion constitutes a considerable barrier to the development of comparative studies to the extent that it is hardly possible, if only because of the difficulties of language and time, to work on the archival sources of, say, ten countries. It is a little as if one asked an economist to carry out personally the surveys and statistical studies on which his mathematical model is dependent. Comparative history will be hampered unless it is recognized as a separate discipline, with its own criteria for evaluation. In sociology, the situation is a little more favorable, but the conclusions of Archer and Gartner (1984) show that much ground still needs to be covered. Concerning the psychological obstacles, we think especially of the almost emotional bond that often exists between a historian and his subject of study. For example, if an American or English historian chooses northern Italy as his subject of study, that supposes a familiarity with the Italian language as well as frequent sojourns in the country to work in libraries and archives. There is nothing similar in comparative research. The researcher will be faced with ten, perhaps twenty cases distributed across different countries and various historical periods. Personal familiarity with the languages, the cultures, or the people is impossible. Note, however, that in this respect the situation also occurs in the natural sciences; when a chemist chooses to study organic-phosphoric compounds, this is most likely not because he feels a particular affinity for these products.

The Best Predictor for Tomorrow Is Yesterday

In this section's title, the term "predictor" is used in the sense defined by Tilly. It does not refer to a prediction "ex nihilo"; rather, if a sequence of events (a strike or an uprising, for instance) starts then we claim that we can more or less predict the form it will take. Two other qualifications have to be made. First, the statement "the best predictor for tomorrow is yesterday" applies only to modules, that is to say, to simple phenomena. In a general way the simpler the event the better the prediction. Second, the statement does not apply if there is a major change in the social or political environment. For example, in New Zealand the Maori resistance to colonization, though still active, cannot assume the forms (that is, open warfare) it had in the nineteenth century; in this case what has changed dramatically is the firepower of the army. These qualifications should be kept in mind throughout this section.

Once a phenomenon has been decomposed into simpler episodes, it usually appears that there is a strong similarity between episodes of the same sort. Why? This is the first question that we have to discuss. It will lead us to examine the notion of imitation (at an individual or collective level), the constraints imposed by tradition, and the role played by collective historical memory.

Paronymy, Imitation, Repertoire

History never repeats itself exactly. Even for simple episodes, an event *A* and an event *B* are never identical but only similar. To describe this form of similarity we use the word "paronymic," a technical term taken from the field of linguistics. Two words are paronymic if their spellings differ only by one or two letters; for example "collision" and "collusion" are two paronymic words, "graduation" and "gradation" is another example. Notice that the meaning of the words is of no matter.

The expression "paronymic episodes" implies two notions that are well suited to our purpose. First, as already mentioned, it means that the episodes are not completely identical but only similar. Second, it conveys the idea that we are not interested in the political meaning of an episode but only in its form. In recent years the notion of paronymic events has been introduced through a number of case studies (Roehner 1993, 1997a,b). It differs from the notion of imitation introduced by Snooks (1996, 1997) mainly by the fact that it refers to *collective* (and more or less unconscious) forms of imitation.

IMITATION

Imitation is one of the main notions on which Snooks's powerful trilogy (1996, 1997, 1998) is based. To our knowledge it is the first attempt of such scope and magnitude to use that concept in a systematic way. He writes: "Imitation is the major shaping force in life" (1997, p. 124); "The great majority of individuals make decisions through imitation of those who are demonstrably successful" (p. 4); "This decision-making mechanism has its origin in earlier animal forms" (p. 11); "If members of a group are feeding on a new food source without suffering any ill effects, then follow their lead . . . We prefer to make choices that economize on the most scarce resource in nature, the intellect" (p. 112).

A telling illustration of imitation behavior in the animal world is provided by the Antarctic tern. This gull pulls almost all of its food from the sea; it swallows fishes after having picked them up by the head, a method that makes sense because the fish's head is the largest part of its body.

These gulls also attack small penguins after their birth. If one closely observes such a scene, one notices that the gull tries to apply to the penguin the method that succeeds so well with fish; but because the body of a penguin is larger than the gull's head, the bird is obliged to release its prey. To overcome this problem the gulls work in twos, one on either side, and even then they are obliged to peck at the meat with their beaks; their clumsiness is glaring. The point we will retain is that, confronted with a new situation, the animal's first reflex is to apply methods that have been well tried in the past. It is only in the case of obvious failure that these will be renounced, but in this case the development of an efficient and new procedure will in general be a long-term affair. Notice that in this example the animal imitates not other members of its group but rather its own former behavior. In other words it is closer to the notion of paronymy. Compared with Snooks's imitation concept, the latter notion adds a social dimension. To explain the similarity between the general strikes in France in 1936 and 1968, imitation at an individual level seems inadequate. Before examining the sociohistorical forces that shape paronymic behavior at the level of a community, we want to discuss the question of collective behavior in more detail.

INDIVIDUAL CHOICE VERSUS COLLECTIVE BEHAVIOR

Individual choice theories are attractive for at least two reasons. First, since everybody has to make decisions, the process of individual choice has a strong intuitive appeal. Second, rational choice models can be formulated in a clear and well-defined way. Economics has a century-long tradition in this respect; in recent decades there has also been impressive progress along this line in sociology, as in Hechter's work (1994, 1997, 1999).

In contrast the analysis of collective behavior is hindered by the fact that, as individuals, we do not have a clear perception of the many collective factors that affect our decisions. Furthermore, when it comes to mathematical formulation one faces a difficult challenge. Satisfactory mathematical models are available only for the simplest forms of interaction. Yet these models (for example, the models for phase transition in physics) have shown convincingly that the behavior of a group can be dramatically different from what could be expected at an individual level. The transition from water to ice specifically is a collective behavior; it does not make any sense at the level of individual molecules.

That the framework of individual choice theory is too narrow has been demonstrated by several influential sociologists. First it can be recalled that all of Durkheim's work stressed the importance of group representation and collective consciousness; both develop through the interaction of many minds.

In a 1999 paper Goldstone provides a compelling argument pointing in the same direction. Let us recall it briefly. Tullock (1971) showed that if individuals made separate choices as to whether to join a revolutionary movement, and if (as is usually the case) the benefits of the revolution went to everyone and not just to those who rioted, then revolutions would be impossible. Individuals would not have any incentive to incur risks by taking an active part if they could enjoy the benefits of the revolution whether or not they participated; if every individual calculated in this fashion, revolutionary mobilization could not occur. Not surprisingly, economists championed Tullock's result as a triumph of logic. Yet, since revolutions do in fact occur, one has to find out what is wrong in Tullock's argument. Goldstone (1994) showed that one of his premises was faulty. "Individuals do not decide to join, or not join, revolutionary movements as isolated individuals." Instead, they decide "as part of groups to which they have prior commitments" (Goldstone 1999). This leads us to analyze the role of social constraints.

THE WEIGHT OF SOCIAL CONSTRAINTS

Snooks is also well aware of the many connections between an individual's mind and his social environment. This is especially clear in his case studies; thus about ancient Greece he writes, "Greek religion was an ordered and rational social activity that supported the merchant's desire for peace and prosperity. It can be contrasted with the religions of conquest societies that emphasize the darker and more chaotic forces in human imagination . . . The Olympic games also helped to imprint the commerce strategy on the community consciousness" (Snooks 1997, p. 230). This indeed is a very "Durkheimian" perspective.

To sum up, there is a permanent osmosis between the human mind and social influences such as tradition, religion, geographical and institutional constraints, and so on. Here we shall just give two microsociological examples. Although of minor importance by themselves, they are quite revealing of the role played by tradition and collective historical memory. The first example concerns the meeting of the Council of Ministers in France; it takes place on Wednesday mornings. Is it not surprising that under the ancien régime the king's council also met on Wednesday mornings (Marion 1976 [1929]). Notwithstanding several revolutions and changes of constitutions a three-century-old custom has survived. As another example of the homeostasis of institutions, consider the tax on playing cards in France. Like so many others this tax was abolished in 1790. Yet it was reestablished in stages, first in 1797, then in 1804. What is interesting to note is that the new regulation was almost an exact copy of the ancien régime regulation of 1751: a requirement that the manufacturers use only paper provided by the administration, a requirement to make castings in the offices of the administration, the same formalities for the packaging of each game by the manufacturer, and so on; other details are given in Stourm (1885, 2:121). Note that the images on the cards themselves were modified by the Revolution, kings and queens being replaced by figures from ancient times; thereafter there was a return to the traditional images.

We now discuss a factor that helps us understand why societies are reluctant to innovate.

A COMPLEX TASK MADE EASIER THROUGH REPETITION

So far we have highlighted the role of social representations in individual behavior; because of their permanence, social representations certainly contribute to the paronymic character of recurrent events. Now we describe another factor which, though often overlooked, establishes a link between paronymic repetition and the principle of least effort; as we know from Zipf's (1972 [1949]) work this principle most likely plays a great role in human behavior. In short, a complex task can be executed faster, better, and with less effort when it is repeated several times. What do we mean by a "complex task"? Moving an army across the Atlantic is no doubt a complex task. But our present argument also applies to microsociological tasks that look far less impressive. For instance, organizing a large demonstration is by no means a simple business. It involves steps that include (1) obtaining the required authorization from municipal authorities; (2) writing, producing, and distributing pamphlets; (3) getting in touch with the parties, unions, or local committees that may support the demonstration; and (4) calling on the people, for example, through cars with loudspeakers, to demonstrate. For an inexperienced group this amounts to an almost impossible mission. Frequent repetition, however, can bring about a high level of competence; a spectacular illustration is given by the French colonists in Algiers, a case discussed later in this chapter. It is important to note that, once again, the competence is a collective one; not only must every participant know his own task, but, above all, participants must be able to work together.

Repetition is the basic principle in the training of armies. Here we have one of the best examples of a complex task involving a large organization. This, incidentally, is why much this book is devoted to an analysis of warfare. In military matters, while exercises and maneuvers are obviously important, the best training is provided by the repetition of real operations. Thus between March 1938 and May 1941, the German invasion of Russia was preceded by a series of "repetitions," by which we mean invasions on a smaller scale: Austria (March 1938), Czechoslovakia (March 1939), Poland (September 1939), Denmark-Belgium-France (June 1940), and Yugoslavia-Greece (May 1941). Each repetition improved the army's performance. Similarly the Allied landing in Normandy in June 1944 was preceded by a series of repetitions: North Africa (November 1942), Sicily (June 1943), Calabria (September 1943). There is no doubt that these repetitions in increasingly difficult terrains substantially improved the technique of the operation.

The expected benefit from successive repetitions can be estimated quantitatively. In the field of operations research it is well known that, at least in the start-up phase, the completion of a complex task requires less time as it is performed again and again. Typically it takes only half as much time to perform a task for the tenth time as it took for the first (Figure 1.4). On average, the time required decreases as $1/n^{0.3}$, where n is the number of times the task has been performed. Repetition also has important psychological implications. The first time one has to perform a given task one is rather reluctant to undertake it, perhaps for fear of failing. Then after a number of repetitions, fear and reluctance disappear and are replaced instead by a feeling of pleasure and confidence. The feeling of confidence is quite understandable in so far as, even before settling down to the job, one is mentally able to review its successive steps; it is almost as if the job were already done.

"MEN GAIN LITTLE PROFIT FROM THE LESSONS OF HISTORY"

Snooks and others have emphasized that individuals have a tendency to imitate those "who are demonstrably successful." But at a collective level, strange as it may seem, groups have a marked tendency to repeat even unsuccessful episodes. This can be demonstrated by using examples from separatist struggles; the Algerians, Hungarians, Irish, Maoris have recurrently fought losing battles, and arguably they had little choice. Yet even in

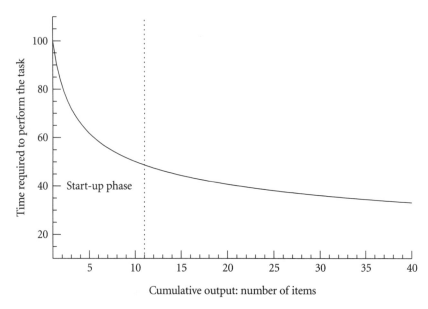

Figure 1.4 The learning curve. When the manufacturing of a new and complex item (for example, an airplane) begins, the time required for its production decreases steadily as more and more items are produced; from the beginning of the so-called start-up phase to the end, production time can be divided by four. This graph shows a case where the production time is inversely proportional to a power function of the number of items produced; the exponent is taken as equal to 0.3, a figure commonly observed in the aeronautical industry (Baloff 1971).

cases where one could expect fairly rational decisions, the same errors are repeated over and over again; in Aldous Huxley's words, "the fact that men gain little profit from the lessons of history is the most important lesson that history teaches us." This can be illustrated by Hitler's strategic choices in World War II. On April 17, 1923, in a speech in Munich, he analyzed Germany's errors during the course of the World War I in the following manner: "Even on 3 August 1914 it was thought that England would remain neutral. What enormous damage Germany suffered from that mistake. Then there was the illusion about Russia; it was said that Russia was a corrupt state and was in no position to wage a war. One blow and it would collapse. Thirdly there was the illusion about Italy. Ludendorff had already in 1912 pointed out that Italy was of no value at all as an ally" (Baynes 1942). However, the perceptiveness of his analysis would still not prevent him from committing point by point the same errors less than twenty years later: England's entry into the war; misjudgment of Russia's potential

for struggle and, as its corollary, a war on two fronts, the worst nightmare
of the German General Staff, and finally the defection of Italy.

In Search of Fossils

"In search of recurrent events" would have been a more conventional title
for this section. Yet we believe that the parallel with paleontology can be a
valuable guide.

A PARALLEL BETWEEN PALEONTOLOGY AND HISTORICAL SOCIOLOGY

A paleontologist's work can be said to have two separate steps. For the
purposes of illustration let us consider the case of the evolution of the
modern horse. The first step is to break up the problem of the horse's evolution into a number of subproblems: the evolution of the skull, the jaw,
the teeth, and so on. The second step is to investigate the evolution of these
elements and to find adequate fossils.

As a historical event the French Revolution is unique in the same sense
that the horse is unique as an animal species. But horses did not appear all
of a sudden; they had ancestors: Eohippus, Mesohippus, Merychippus. In
the same way historical events can be traced back to a number of precedents and forerunners. A complex event such as the Revolution of 1789 is
of course made up of a number of components and strata. In much the
same way that a paleontologist would study the evolution of the horse's
skull or teeth, we can consider a number of separate elements of the Revolution: the storming of the Bastille, the meeting of the Estates-General, and
so on. These building blocks are the analogues of the horse's skull or teeth.
What we want to discover is whether there are earlier fossils and what they
look like.

What can be gained from such a perspective? Let us say right away that it
will not necessarily give us better insight into the future. After all, the fossils of the horse do not give us any indication about its future evolution.
But at least these social "fossils" will make these events appear more plausible, more natural. Instead of being "creationists," historians will become
"evolutionists." The parallel with paleontology will now help us to explain
why the objectives of analytical history are far less ambitious than those of
"standard history."

THE MODESTY OF ANALYTICAL HISTORY'S GOALS

It may seem that studying the previous meetings of the Estates-General
without connecting them to other events is a fairly artificial and unrealistic

approach. Yet this is precisely what the paleontologist does. He reconstructs sequences showing the evolution of specific elements, for example, the molars, the jaw, the forefeet. Certainly there is a connection between the evolution of the molar and the evolution of the jaw or even of the forefeet. Obviously for the molar to become bigger in the course of evolution, there has to be a parallel growth in the size of the jaw. There is probably also a relationship between changes in the size of the molar and the evolution of the forefeet; but this relationship is by no means an obvious one. Questions of this kind are structural problems and usually very difficult ones. It is precisely because these questions are largely out of his reach that the paleontologist concentrates his attention and efforts on an easier problem, namely the reconstruction of separate sequences.

In contrast, one of the main purposes of history is to study the connections between separate elements, such as the impact of street riots on the power struggle in the Estates-General, or the consequences of the king's execution on the subsequent development of the Revolution. These are structural questions and they are very difficult to answer satisfactorily. To answer them one needs nothing less than a theory of revolution. In the same way, in order to answer his own structural questions the paleontologist will need a global model of the horse's evolution.

Far from being overly ambitious, the objective of analytical history is quite within our capabilities. In contrast, when "traditional" history tries to explain (instead of just describing) a succession of events, it embarks upon an almost impossible task.

SMALL VERSUS BIG EVENTS

"Small" events are likely to recur more frequently and in more identical forms than "bigger" ones. Let us illustrate this idea with a riddle. Where and when did the following episode occur? "He was killed by an angry crowd, and his head, stuck on a pike, was paraded in triumph through the city." That description could well apply to the scene that followed the storming of the Bastille, when the governor of the Bastille was killed and his head paraded through the streets. Yet that excerpt in fact refers to an episode that occurred in Kosovo almost a century after the storming of the Bastille; the person killed was an Ottoman marshal (Malcolm 1998, p. 223). Indeed, parading the head of a vanquished enemy was a common practice throughout Europe, from Britain to Albania. Not only are such episodes very similar but they have also happened fairly frequently (Figure 1.5a,b).

How often did it happen?

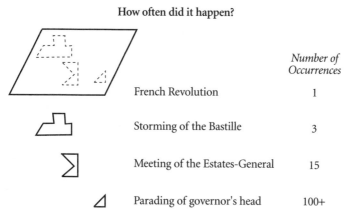

	Number of Occurrences
French Revolution	1
Storming of the Bastille	3
Meeting of the Estates-General	15
Parading of governor's head	100+

Figure 1.5a How often did it happen? The French Revolution can be seen as a complex assemblage of different elements. As a whole, it happened only once, but some of its modules have occurred several, and sometimes many, times. Generally speaking, the smaller a module the more frequently it will be observed. For instance, parading the head of a vanquished enemy was common practice in Europe and may have been observed hundreds of times.

The preceding example has a noteworthy consequence for analytical history. Suppose I want to write a book about the way people paraded the heads of their enemies. From the point of view of comparative analysis, one would be in an ideal situation; with about a hundred occurrences this indeed would be a "large N" analysis. But it is doubtful whether such a topic would interest many readers; most likely it would be difficult if not impossible to find a publisher for such a book. In other words, a reasonable compromise has to be found for selecting the modules. They should not be too microscopic, but at the same time there should be a fairly large number of occurrences.

If the search for fossils has so far received only little attention from academic historians, it has been used extensively in politics, as we shall see.

Use and Abuse of Historical Analogies in Politics
Reasoning by analogy and comparison turns out to be common practice in the making of political decisions. Political leaders are tempted to scan the past for situations bearing some similarity to those with which they are confronted. In so doing they implicitly recognize that the past can be an acceptable predictor for the future. Several twentieth-century world leaders (for example, Winston Churchill, Charles de Gaulle) have had an ex-

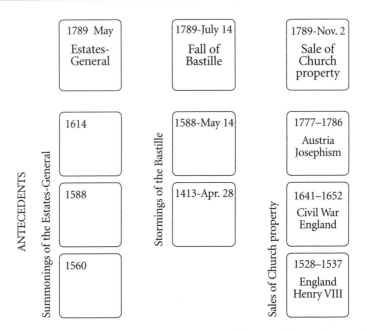

Figure 1.5b Antecedents of some of the modules of the French Revolution. The chart displays three events that occurred in 1789, along with some of their antecedents. The dates for the meetings of the Estates-General refer to France, but there were similar assemblies in other countries throughout western Europe. The confiscation and sale of Church estates had not previously occurred in France, but had taken place repeatedly in other European countries, particularly at the time of the Reformation.

tensive knowledge of history. But using historical analogies is a tricky business. While the tool may have been used effectively by a few masters, in the hand of other leaders it has proved deceptive and misleading; this has been shown in a pioneering study by May (1973) and subsequently in two other studies by Neustadt and May (1986) and Khong (1992).

As an illustrative example let us consider the decisions leading to the Korean, Vietnam, and Gulf wars. In his memoirs, President Harry Truman explains the American intervention in Korea in the following way: "I remembered how each time that the democracies failed to act, it had encouraged the aggressor to keep going ahead. Communism had acted in Korea just as Hitler, Mussolini and the Japanese had acted 10, 15 or 20 earlier" (Neustadt and May 1986). Subsequently the Korean analogy was invoked to justify the intervention in Vietnam. Khong (1992) made a precise count of the number of times specific analogies had been used both in public speeches and in private reports by the Johnson administration (Table 1.3). On both counts Korea ranks first. The private reports are of special interest, since they show that analogies were not used only for communication purposes; they were used in the decision-making process itself. The analogy with the French Vietnam war (a war that ended in disaster for the French) was employed almost exclusively in private reports. Even in these it was only used half as often as the analogy with Korea, in spite of the fact that it could certainly be expected to prove more accurate than any link to Korea, a country more than 4,000 kilometers away. A similar example is provided by the Gulf War (January–February 1991). For President Bush the appropriate analogy was Hitler in the late 1930s, the Rhineland, Austria, and Czechoslovakia (Yergin 1991).

In the previous cases both the selection of the analogies and the way they were used were fairly unsophisticated. First, these analogies were drawn exclusively from the recent history of Western countries. The history of the conflicts between Korea and Japan or between Vietnam and China was completely ignored. Second, one may wonder if it made sense to compare North Korea or Iraq to Germany. In 1949 North Korea had a population of only 9 million, and Iraq had 16 million in 1990; in 1939 Ger-

Table 1.3 Analogies most frequently used in preparing the Vietnam decisions of 1965

In public speeches	Number of times used	In private reports	Number of times used
Korea	63	Korea	46
1930s	42	French Indochinese War	26
Greece	33	Malaysia	12
Malaysia	22	1930s	10
Berlin blockade	19	Greece	8
Philippines	15	Philippines	6
Cuba	14	World War II	5
Turkey	10	Berlin blockade	4
World War II	9	Cuba	3
Germany	8	Turkey	2

Source: Khong (1992).

many, in contrast, had a population of over 70 million, and a GNP that was surpassed only by that of the United States.

A closer examination shows that if politicians have managed poorly in using analogies it is in fact because only poor information has been available to them. As a case in point let us consider the Vietnam War. If one makes the reasonable assumption that the best analogies for the Vietnam War were the wars waged previously by the Vietnamese people themselves, one is led to wonder about the quality of the information provided on this subject by American historians. An examination of the resources of a large American university library (Harvard's Lamont Library) reveals that only a small proportion (on the order of 5 percent) of the books relating to the Vietnam War granted the slightest attention to the successive wars that the Vietnamese waged against the French, the Japanese, and then the French again; as for the numerous struggles that they sustained against China in the sixteenth, seventeenth, and eighteenth centuries not more than a few lines were found. It is therefore highly likely that the information that should have been put at the disposal of policymakers was simply not available.

That foreign policy is not the only area in which comparative analysis is used poorly is illustrated by the following example. In the area of public health, the question of the decriminalization of so-called soft drugs recurs from time to time. The question is whether or not decriminalization can lead to a reduction in the consumption of drugs, whether soft or hard. Usually the public authorities set up a commission of experts comprising physicians, jurists, police officers, and so on; these people then discuss the various facets of the problem as they see it. An alternative approach consists in noting that for the last twenty years or so, soft drugs have been decriminalized in a number of countries, for instance in Spain and the Netherlands. It is therefore possible to observe the response to decriminalization. Such a comparative approach is used only infrequently.

To What Extent Does History Repeat Itself? Some Examples

So far we have assumed the existence of historical fossils; or, stated differently, we have supposed that, at least to some extent, history repeats itself. It is one of the main purposes of the subsequent chapters to examine that question in detail. Here a few examples are considered in order to give the reader a quick overview. The study of recurrent events uses both historical (longitudinal) and cross-national (transversal) analysis, as illustrated in

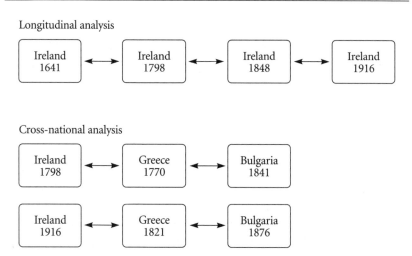

Figure 1.6 Chronological (longitudinal) and cross-national (transversal) analysis. The chart refers to the example of separatist uprisings in Ireland. Longitudinal analysis compares events that happened at different moments in the history of a given country: 1641, 1798, 1848, 1916 are the dates of successive Irish uprisings. In cross-national analysis, one compares similar events that occurred in different countries. For instance, 1798, 1770, and 1841 were three "failed" uprisings in Ireland, Greece, and Bulgaria, respectively; 1916, 1821, and 1876, in contrast, are the dates of three "successful" uprisings in the same countries in the sense that these events led to the nation's independence within a few years.

Figure 1.6. Roughly speaking, three levels of growing sophistication can be distinguished: enumerative studies, qualitative studies, and quantitative studies. An enumerative study simply lists a number of events of the same kind. What can be the value of such a review? To know that an event, far from being exceptional or unique, in fact has a number of antecedents can make a significant difference. By way of illustration, one can observe that the assassination of Archduke Francis Ferdinand on June 28, 1914, in Sarajevo was not, despite its immense consequences, an exceptional event in this period; on the contrary, political assassinations were very much in fashion: 1911 had seen the assassination of the prime minister of Russia, 1912 that of the prime minister of Spain, while in 1913 the prime minister of Salvador, the president of Mexico, and the king of Greece were assassinated (*World Almanac and Book of Facts* 1925, p. 693). A more ambitious objective is to try a comparative analysis of the recurrent events in the hope of finding a number of regularities. At the third level quantitative analysis allows the investigation of definite correlations between various factors. In this chapter, and indeed in most of this book, we restrict ourselves to the two first levels. We turn now to the examination of a number of recurrent events.

THE REVOLTS OF THE KRONSTADT SAILORS

Kronstadt was an important Russian naval arsenal situated several kilometers to the northwest of St. Petersburg (renamed Petrograd at the start of the 1914–1918 war) at the base of the Gulf of Finland. The march on Petrograd of the sailors of the arsenal played an essential role in the revolution of October 1917. This successful intervention in the course of history was nevertheless preceded by several other mutinies, all suppressed with varying degrees of severity (Wieczynski 1988). These events are summarized in Table 1.4; note that the same episode repeated itself even though previous attempts had not been successful. As discusses earlier, this phenomenon contrasts with the pattern of imitation at individual level. Yet the bloody repression of 1921 seems to have discouraged further uprising attempts.

DISTURBANCES BETWEEN HINDUS AND MUSLIMS IN KASHMIR

In the Kronstadt case all the events occurred within a short period of only two decades. This is fairly exceptional in the analysis of recurrent events; usually one has to scan a much longer period. A case in point is provided by the historical roots of the Kashmir conflict. In an article entitled "The Historical Roots of the Kashmir Conflict" (Mohan 1992), the author pays little attention to the period before 1945; this is typical of political scientists, who are often reluctant to look at the more distant past. This omission can lead to serious errors; thus Mohan's comment that the "communal riots which occurred in 1931 and 1932 came after a period of 80 years of communal harmony" is not true (see Table 1.5). The demands put forward by Muslim people in a memorial addressed in 1924 to the viceroy of India to a large extent paralleled those of the Irish people in the nineteenth century: (1) property rights of the land should be given to the peasants; (2) the system of forced labor should be abolished; and (3) all Muslim mosques in government possession should be handed over to the Muslims. These claims reveal that, like the Catholics in Ireland, the Muslims in Kashmir faced economic as well as religious oppression.

In October 1951 the people in the Kashmir Valley massively boycotted

Table 1.4 Precursors and replicas of the revolt of the Kronstadt sailors in October 1917

	Date	Description	Number of deaths	Success (S) or failure (F)
1.	1905, Oct. 26	On October 26 a sailor was killed in a clash; by the end of the day the rebellion had been joined by 3, 000 sailors and 1, 500 soldiers. Two days later, ships with specially selected crews arrived at Kronstadt and the sailors were disarmed. A powerful wave of solidarity strikes in St. Petersburg, however, prevented the crackdown.	>1	S-F
2.	1906, July	On July 19 there was a rebellion of the First and Second Fleet divisions that was joined by 400 workers. The next day the rebellion was defeated by government forces; 43 men were tried and shot.	43	F
3.	1917, Feb.	On February 28 a new rebellion broke out; sailors were released from jails and disciplinary units by the insurgents. Admiral Viren and several other high-ranking officers were murdered.	about 10	S
4.	1917, July	Premature and abortive uprising against the government of Kerensky. Ten thousand men, of whom about 3, 000 were armed sailors, arrived in Petrograd. After a short armed conflict they were disarmed; most were allowed to return to their base.		F
5.	1917, Oct.	The march on Petrograd of the Kronstadt sailors ensured the success of the Bolshevik revolution.		S
6.	1921, Mar.	An uprising took place that was vigorously suppressed by Trotsky. On February 28 a resolution was adopted that became the political basis of the rebellion. A first assault by 25, 000 troops was a failure. Finally, on March 18 a second attack by 50, 000 men succeeded: the rebel losses were 600 dead. Some 8, 000 were able to escape to Finland.	600	F

Source: Wieczynski (1988).

Table 1.5 Conflict between Muslims and Hindus in Kashmir before 1945

	Date	Description
1.	18th century	Severe restrictions imposed on the religious observance of the Hindus by the Afghan governors.
2.	19th century	Muslim people were considered the lowest class during the Sikh domination. During the great famine of 1871, the Sikh Maharaja failed to rescue them.
3.	1921	Insurrection of Muslim tenants against Hindu landlords and money lenders.
4.	1924	Uprising by the workers of Srinagar's silk factory and occupation of a plot of land by the Muslims. A memorial is submitted to the Viceroy of India.
5.	1931, June	Widespread communal riots occurred in Srinagar and in the rest of the Jhelum Valley. Shops and houses of Hindus were looted and burnt. Many Hindus were killed.
6.	1931, July 13	The central jail in Srinagar was attacked to free an imprisoned Muslim leader. The police opened fire; 21 were killed.
7.	1931, Sept.–Oct.	Political demonstrations by Muslim crowds.
8.	1932, Oct.	Riots in Srinagar.

Sources: Bazaz (1954); Koul (1972); Rahmat (1933).

the election to the constituent assembly; such a reaction cannot be surprising if one realizes that the situation in 1951 was the result of a long-standing conflict.

ANTECEDENTS OF THE FRENCH DEFEAT OF DIEN BIEN PHU

On May 7, 1954, the encircled French troops of the entrenched camp of Dien Bien Phu in Tonkin (North Vietnam) were forced to surrender to the forces of the Viet Minh. This defeat created a considerable stir in public opinion. It was written that this was the first military defeat of a Western power by a colonized people, a statement that was patently incorrect, as shown by Table 1.6. That such an assertion could be made at all testifies to the fact that nations prefer not to keep track of painful events. Even if we restrict ourselves to Indochina, there have been at least two major forerun-

Table 1.6 Western army defeats by colonized people prior to Dien Bien Phu (1954)

	Date	Western country	Colonized people	Number killed in Western army	Reference
1.	1791, Nov. 4	United States	Ohio Indians	900	Debo (1970)
2.	1824, Jan. 21	Britain	Ashantees (Ghana)	1,000	Vincent (1898)
3.	1842, Jan. 6	Britain	Afghans	3,500	Vincent (1898)
4.	1879, Jan. 22	Britain	Zulus (South Africa)	1,300	Vincent (1898); Clammer (1973)
5.	1883, Nov. 5	Britain	Mahdists (Sudan)	11,000	Vincent (1898)
6.	1884, June 22	France	Vietnamese	800	Teulières (1978)
7.	1896, Mar. 1	Italy	Abyssinians (Ethiopia)	9,000	Vincent (1898)
8.	1921, July 21	Spain	Moroccans		Martin (1990)
9.	1950, Oct.	France	Vietnamese	4,000	Teulières (1978)

ners, in 1884 and 1950. In 1884 a column of 800 men was ambushed on the route that follows the frontier between Indochina and China. In October 1950 two columns under the command of colonels Charton and Lepage were annihilated on the same route. Approximately 4,000 men were killed or captured.

DEMONSTRATIONS IN ALGIERS BEFORE AND AFTER MAY 13, 1958

In the preceding cases we contented ourselves with listing precursors without addressing the question of why these recurrent events looked so similar. The purpose of the present case is to suggest how a more detailed analysis can be carried out. The political demonstrations in Algiers raise a number of interesting questions. First, the demonstration of May 13, 1958 brought about the end of the Fourth Republic and the return to power of General de Gaulle. This is a rare instance in French history where a significant political change was caused by an event that occurs on the periphery, rather than in Paris. Second, the fact that large demonstrations involving more than 50,000 people took place so frequently is a puzzle in itself if one remembers that Algiers had a population of only about 500,000. No similar phenomenon has been observed in cities of that size either in France or in the rest of Europe. How did the people in Algiers manage to stage such large demonstrations? This is a useful illustration of what repetition can achieve.

A typical episode comprised the following steps. (1) First the demonstration was decided on and planned by a number of organizations: the patriotic leagues, vigilance committees, and territorial units. These groups made up an unusually large proportion of the population of Algiers. (2) Through the distribution of pamphlets and by loudspeakers, the population was urged to demonstrate. (3) Shops and even a number of public utilities were closed during the demonstrations. (4) Usually the demonstration began with the laying of wreaths in front of the war memorial. (5) Then the procession would climb to the Plateau des Glières, the largest esplanade of the city. (6) Once gathered there, the crowd would listen to speeches and sang the national anthem as well as other patriotic songs. Note on this subject that, as confirmed by sound recordings, the level of execution of the "Marseillaise," the French national anthem, was very much above what it was in metropolitan France in terms of, for example, number of verses sung. Even for a crowd, repetition is the key factor for a successful performance.

Table 1.7 shows that by and large the demonstrations were successful before May 1958, with a climax reached on May 13. But that month was also a watershed; after this all demonstrations were failures. Unable to stop the march of Algeria toward independence, the extremist elements within the European population increasingly resorted to violence.

PARONYMIC REPETITIONS OF THE OPERATION OF DIEN BIEN PHU

We have shown that the Dien Bien Phu defeat had a number of forerunners. But that argument can be extended to the planning of the operation itself.

After the departure of the Japanese army that had occupied Indochina during World War II, the Viet Minh of Ho Chi Minh took virtual control of the country. Between 1949 and 1954, encouraged by the United States, the French tried to bring the situation back under control. In that strategy a key element was the occupation of fortified positions from which the enemy's supply lines could be threatened and the movements of its troops checked. This was basically the pattern of all the operations mentioned in Table 1.8. Yet in order to demonstrate the strong similarity between these operations one has to describe them in some detail.

Hoa Binh (November 1951–February 1952)   On November 14, 1951, a parachute drop enabled the French occupation and fortification of the position of Hoa Binh (180 kilometers to the west of Haiphong); this was

Table 1.7 Political demonstrations and uprisings in Algiers, 1870–1962

	Date	Description	Success (S) or failure (F)
1.	1870, Oct.	On October 24, at the height of the Franco-Prussian war, the French Ministry of War appointed General Walsin Esterhazy as governor of Algeria. The appointment of a soldier deeply displeased the colonists. At the call of the municipal council, the crowd invaded the governor's palace, where the troops offered no resistance. Under popular pressure the general had to resign his office. To a chorus of boos he was driven by carriage to the frigate *La Gloire,* to be returned to Marseilles.	S
2.	1956, Feb. 2	There was an enormous demonstration to mark the departure of the former governor-general Jacques Soustelle, who had known how to win over the Algerians.	S
3.	1956, Feb. 6	The visit of the French prime minister, Guy Mollet, led to a number of important demonstrations of hostility. As a result the Algerian French were able to force the replacement of General Catroux as governor-general by the civilian Robert Lacoste. Once again the colonists had been able to make their will prevail.	S
4.	1956, Dec. 29	The burial of Amédée Froger, the president of the Algerian Federation of Mayors, who had been assassinated, gave way to a large demonstration with shouts of "French Algeria" and "The army to power."	
5.	1958, Apr. 26	A demonstration took place that served as a dress rehearsal for that of May 13. It was intended to affect the negotiations that were then taking place in Paris to form a new government.	S
6.	1958, May 13	The demonstration of May 13 was organized, not without ulterior political motives, following the execution by the National Liberation Front of three French soldiers. After the laying of wreaths at the War Memorial, the demonstration headed toward the seat of the government on the Plateau des Glières. At 5:30 P.M. the crowd forced open the doors of the building; the paratroopers of General Massu did not intervene. After May 13, other mass demonstrations took place; but because of the installation of a strong government in Paris, the French Algerians could no longer impose their views.	S

Table 1.7 (continued)

	Date	Description	Success (S) or failure (F)
7.	1958, May 15	In front of 50, 000 people gathered under the balcony of the government building, General Salan, commander in chief of Algeria, gave (not without hesitation) his endorsement to General Charles de Gaulle by closing his speech with "Long live General de Gaulle."	S
8.	1958, June 4	During the visit of General de Gaulle, a new mass demonstration took place. The crowd waited for him to pronounce the words "French Algeria"; this he did not do.	F
9.	1960, Feb.	During the so-called insurrection of the barricades, a demonstration of support was organized. A shoot-out left several dead among the security forces who had tried to disperse the crowd with the help of tear-gas grenades.	F
10.	1962, Mar.	The last, and most tragic, demonstration took place on March 26. It was organized by the Organisation de l'Armée Secrète (or OAS) that three days earlier had led a fierce battle in the quarter of Bab-el-Oued against the regular army of General Ailleret. During the demonstration a shoot-out on the corner of rue d'Isly left 46 dead.	F

Table 1.8 Paronymic antecedents of the operation of Dien Bien Phu

	Began	Duration (month)	Number of troops	Location	Success (S) or failure (F)
1.	1951, Nov.	4		Hoa Binh	S-F
2.	1952, Oct.	10	8, 000	Na San	S
3.	1953, Mar.	3	6, 500	Plain of Jars	S
4.	1953, Nov.	7	12, 000	Dien Bien Phu	F

Source: O'Neill (1969); Teulières (1978).

supposed to cut the lines of communication of the Viet Minh. Deciding against making a direct attack on this well-defended position, General Giap concentrated his forces on the French supply lines, the Black River and Route 6. By January 1952, the passage of French river convoys on the Black River became too hazardous to attempt in the face of Viet Minh artillery. Thus the battle shifted to Route 6. The Viet Minh temporarily cut the route, and it took a force of twelve battalions to reopen it. On February 22, 1952, General Salan ordered the French withdrawal from Hoa Binh (O'Neill 1969).

Na San (October 23, 1952–August 1953)   Around a small airfield, the French organized a fortified camp with blockhouses, foreshadowing what would be Dien Bien Phu. All the troops (twelve battalions, or approximately 8,000 men) and all the equipment as well as the artillery were conveyed by airlift. Against this fortified position General Giap committed nineteen battalions. The heavy artillery division 351 could not be committed for lack of adequate roads. The main attacks, at night as usual, started on November 30 and December 1, 1952. But the means of the Viet Minh were insufficient in the face of the aviation and the artillery that were under Colonel Gilles's command. It is estimated that the Viet Minh lost 4,000 men (Teulières 1978). The garrison of Na San was brought back by air to Hanoi in August 1953, and this operation was achieved in the face of the Viet Minh. No Viet Minh attack was mounted and the last plane escaped without incident.

Plain of Jars (Spring 1953)   An airfield was installed in the Plain of Jars in Laos to counter the Viet Minh offensive that had already taken the outposts above Luang Prabang. An airlift dropped troops there (ten battalions) as well as tanks. Although it was situated 800 kilometers from Hanoi and 1,600 kilometers from Saigon, the camp's supply could be assured. On April 21 the camp succeeded in repelling an attack of the Viet Minh. The beginning of the rainy season forced Giap to withdraw his troops.

Dien Bien Phu (November 20, 1953–May 1954)   The French High Command seemed to be misled by the success of the defense of Na San into the overconfident notion that they could challenge Giap from a divisional-sized fortress anywhere in Tonkin. The operation of Dien Bien Phu was mounted in the same way as that of Na San. Six battalions of parachutists under the command of Colonel Gilles occupied the terrain and built the airfield and fortifications. But in contrast to what had happened at Na San, thanks to continual porterage, Giap could bring in the heavy division

351. Furthermore, almost 350 kilometers of trenches and tunnels were dug. In so doing the Vietnamese were applying to the art of war an ancient tradition in the construction of dikes that had allowed them for centuries to master the Red River and the North River.

The defeat of Dien Bien Phu led to the signing of the Geneva Accords in 1954. A dozen years later a new conflict erupted in which the United States found itself more and more involved. During that war fortified positions were used by the American troops. In 1968 (January to April) General Giap tried to repeat his success at Dien Bien Phu by surrounding Khe Sanh, which was located 50 kilometers south of the North Vietnamese border and about 10 kilometers east of the border with Laos. The weight of Vietnamese troops in this region produced a result similar to that achieved by Giap in the early stages of the battle of Dien Bien Phu, in that the Americans became unable to support patrol activity over a wide area. In particular, the besieged could observe that Khe Sanh was entirely surrounded by a complex system of tunnels and blockhouses. On February 6, the Special Forces camp of Lan Vei (10 kilometers southwest of Khe Sanh) was overrun despite heavy air support. Its garrison consisted of 1,000 soldiers, mainly Laotians plus a few Americans. All told 10,800 shells hit Khe Sanh in seventy-seven days; Dien Bien Phu, in contrast, was struck by 103,000 Viet Minh shells in fifty-five days; twenty-two American airplanes and helicopters were destroyed as compared with sixty-two aircraft lost by the French air force during the siege of Dien Bien Phu (Clodfelter 1995). The availability of American air power over Khe Sanh ensured sufficient supplies and fire support to enable the defenders to hold out. For example, on February 15, 1968, 50,000 tons of napalm were dropped around Khe Sanh (O'Neill 1969, p. 195; Mangold and Penycate 1986; Welsh 1991).

The preceding case studies provide a first illustration of our method of investigation. First we select a number of events, then we put them under the "microscope," adjusting the magnification until the element we are interested in appears with maximum sharpness. We use the word "microscope" intentionally to emphasize the similitude of our approach with that used in the natural sciences, to which we now turn.

Social versus Natural Sciences

As the reader will have understood, this book aims to bridge the methodological gap between the social and the natural sciences. It turns out that most of the objections to such a program rely on an outdated conception of the natural sciences. The idea that there is a radical difference between the social and the natural sciences usually relies on the following arguments: (1) in the natural sciences an experiment can be repeated; (2) in the social sciences the phenomena are too complicated to apply John Stuart Mill's canons of logic; and (3) individual will and human liberty are not compatible with theoretical models. We now turn to the examination of these points. The position we defend is close to the one advocated by Goldstone (1997, 1999) and by Tilly (1997).

Is It Possible to Repeat an Experiment in the Natural Sciences?
In natural sciences such as astronomy, meteorology, and geodynamics it is of course not possible to make experiments; only observations are possible. But it would be inappropriate to limit ourselves to such cases for the obvious reason that the basic concepts used in astronomy, meteorology, or geodynamics are derived from physics. We argue that even in physics, however, it is not possible to repeat an experiment. To make this point we do not consider a complicated situation involving random perturbations or chaos; instead we consider what is probably one of the simplest experiments: the swing of a pendulum. Suppose we want to measure the vibration period of the pendulum. Suppose further that two successive measurements turn out to be 2.37 seconds and 2.35 seconds. If we are satisfied with an accuracy of 0.1 second, we can conclude that the period is 2.3 seconds. This corresponds to what can be called the textbook representation (Figure 1.7a). In such a representation the only exogenous force affecting the pendulum is the gravitational force of the earth; under such conditions the experiment is reproducible.

Now suppose one wants to measure the period to an accuracy of 0.01 milliseconds. Then one can no longer ignore the numerous perturbations that affect the movement of the pendulum, such as the people walking in the same building and the vibrations due to vehicles in the street or to planes flying over the building (Figure 1.7b). These are mainly high-frequency perturbations. But there are also low-frequency perturbations due to the gravitational influence of the sun, the moon, and the largest planets (Figure 1.7c). As the earth turns on itself the direction of these forces change; in other words it is no longer possible to repeat the experiment under the same conditions.

To sum up, experiments in the natural sciences can be considered repro-

Earth gravitational force

Figure 1.7a Swing of a pendulum: textbook representation. A pendulum consists of a mass hung from a pivot by an arm. In this ideal representation (Main 1978, p. 17) the only exogenous force acting on the pendulum is the earth's gravity (along, of course, with the reaction of the supporting frame). Yet through its pivot, the pendulum is connected to the ceiling (or floor) of the laboratory, and the ceiling itself is part of the structure of the building. Vibrations from outside are thus transmitted to the pendulum as shown in Figure 1.7b; moreover, as shown in Figure 1.7c, the mass of the pendulum also experiences gravitational attraction from other celestial bodies.

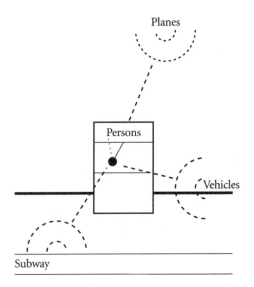

Figure 1.7b Swing of a pendulum: high-frequency perturbations. Movements that occur either inside or outside the building, such as people walking, vehicles, subways, and airplanes, induce vibrations that are transmitted to the pendulum and affect its oscillations.

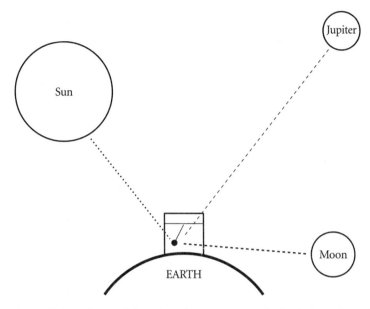

Figure 1.7c Swing of a pendulum: low-frequency perturbations. Apart from the attraction of the earth, the mass of the pendulum is also subject to the gravitational fields of the sun, the moon, and the largest planets (Jupiter, Saturn). Although these gravitational forces are much smaller than the gravity of the earth, they play a role in high-accuracy measurements. For instance, if the pendulum's period is on the order of 5 seconds, the corrections due to the moon and to the sun would be on the order of 2 and 0.7 microseconds, respectively. Thus at the accuracy level of microseconds, the measurement will produce different results at different moments; in other words, the experiment is no longer reproducible in the standard way. One should notice that the figure gives a fairly schematic representation; technically speaking, the driving force is the difference between the gravitational and centrifugal forces, that is, the so-called tidal force.

ducible only if one has a clear understanding of the forces that affect the system and of their relative orders of magnitude. This is precisely what is often lacking in the social sciences, as can be illustrated by the following two examples, chosen at random among many others. The first case is taken from a history of the oil industry (Yergin 1991). The author quotes several causes of the abrupt explosion of prices in 1974: the nationalistic demands made by the Arab countries towards Anglo-American oil companies; the delays in the development of Alaskan oil deposits; the Watergate scandal that deprived the American president of his freedom for action.

The main link between these events and the price hike is a certain synchronism. However, the geographical origin of the author has without doubt biased his judgment; the "causes" that he cites are all in connection with the Western world. It is curious to touch on Alaska, whose production never, even at its maximum at the end of the 1980s, exceeded 3.5 percent of the world's production, and to be silent on the situation in the Soviet Union, a country that was in the 1970s the world's largest producer (20 percent of the world total) and the second-largest exporter. The second example is a quotation from Hallgarten (1961) about the coming to power of Napoleon III in France in 1851: "The international situation created by the discovery of gold mines in California eradicated first of all the difficulties caused by the coup." Certainly, there is between these two events a certain synchronism, since the discovery of the first Californian gold mine dates back to September 1847 (Vincent 1898, p. 188). It is doubtful, however, that this discovery had noticeable effects on the internal political situation in France. In this respect, the price of wheat surely had a far more determining influence; between 1848 and 1850 the average price of wheat in France fell from nearly thirty francs per hectoliter to fifteen, before rising again to thirty in 1855. Presumably Hallgarten mentions the discovery of gold in California because he knows that region well, having been a professor at Berkeley for several years. Transposed to the case of the pendulum it amounts to taking into account the influence of Jupiter while ignoring the attraction of the earth.

Mill's Canons of Logic
Using the simple example of two automobile incidents, Lieberson (1991, 1994) showed that deductive reasoning using J. S. Mill's canons of logic becomes inadequate for small N comparative studies, that is to say when only a few observations are available. Furthermore it has been pointed out by Goldstone (1997) that in the social sciences, because of the huge number of factors, Mill's logic will be of little use whether for small N or large N comparative studies. This problem, however, is not specific to the social sciences, as we show now. Above we saw that the pendulum is affected by a large number of exogenous forces. We have not thus far mentioned factors within the laboratory itself. Yet for a high-accuracy measurement, one has to take into account possible changes in temperature (which affect the length of the pendulum), in pressure, or in the hygrometry of the air; clearly this list of factors could be expanded further. This makes the application of Mill's methodology very difficult; it can be applied only once one

has acquired an intuitive and operational knowledge of what the most important factors really are.

Analytical History and Human Liberty

What action better symbolizes human liberty than the choice made by an individual who decides to commit suicide? Yet in any nation, the percentage of the population committing suicide remains relatively stable over the course of time. In the United States the suicide rate was 10.2 per 100,000 in 1900 and 11.2 in 1970. The means a person uses to commit suicide is yet another manifestation of his (or her) free choice. Yet again the rates are remarkably stable over the course of time; suicide by poisoning, for example, accounted for 30 percent of the suicides in 1900 and for 28 percent in 1970 (*Historical Statistics*, 1975, p. 414). These and other regularities were pointed out in Durkheim's celebrated study that marked the beginning of quantitative sociology. The relation between individual action and group behavior was given a modern and elegant formulation in a 1997 paper by Goldstone in the following terms: "We may be unsure about how any given individual react, and with small groups (up to a few dozen or so) we cannot have certainty about macro-outcomes because stochastic variations will be large. But if we have a pool of thousands, or millions, it really doesn't matter much what particular individuals do; the standard deviation of the expected group outcome will be minuscule" (p. 117).

But one important qualification is in order. The above conclusion does not apply to a succession of different actions. This leads us to an important distinction between what Lieberson (1985) called "doable" and "undoable" problems.

Undoable Problems and Chaos

Why did the century-long Irish struggle for independence unfold the way it did, and why did it eventually succeed in 1921? This is an example of an undoable problem. That struggle consisted in a succession of actions; after each step there are a number of possible options for the next step, as schematized in Figure 1.8. If we assume that at each step there are two equally likely options (which is certainly a conservative estimate) the likelihood of a path comprising 8 steps will be $(1/2)^8 = 0.004$. In other words, the probability of observing one of the many possible trajectories is close to zero. Consequently, trying to predict that trajectory is an impossible task, and an undoable problem in Lieberson's terms.

Figure 1.8 represents a chaotic system. This notion was introduced in

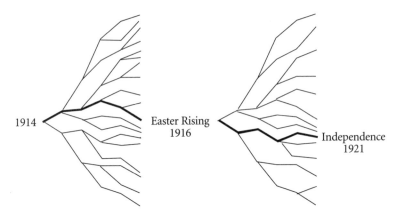

Figure 1.8 Predicting the successive stages of the Irish struggle for independence is an "undoable problem" in the sense Lieberson (1985) gave to this expression. It took a number of steps to get from 1914 to the Easter Rising; at each, depending upon a huge number of factors, history had to select one of several possible options. The same argument applies to the steps that lead from the Easter Rising to independence. If we assume that there were eight steps and two equally likely options at each step, the actual trajectory (schematized by a thick line) has a probability of $0.5^8 = 0.004$. We have here a chaotic system. The presence of too many bifurcations frustrates prediction.

the 1980s, when mathematicians and physicists began to realize that even for fairly simple (and deterministic) systems the future evolution can be unpredictable. The existence of too many bifurcations (as in Figure 1.8) generates an extreme sensitivity to initial conditions. With his celebrated stardom paradigm, Lieberson (1985) was able to capture that characteristic at a time when the scientific community was just beginning to recognize the importance of chaos. The decomposition of a historical episode into simpler modules can be seen as a way to get around the problem of chaotic systems.

The previous paragraphs were devoted to the discussion of epistemological options. There is another crucial factor whose importance is often underestimated, namely, the availability of reliable data.

An Essential Condition for Progress: The Availability of Reliable Data
Either in the natural or the social sciences a crucial condition for progress is the availability of extensive and reliable data. Even the best methodological options are useless if one cannot rely on adequate data. This point can

be illustrated by two examples from the history of science. The first example is taken from Jacob (1970). A British physician, William Harvey (1578–1657), studied two important topics, blood circulation and the rules governing heredity. As we know, he was able to solve the first question but could hardly make any progress on the second. Why? In Harvey's days much attention was given to the notions of pressure and fluid velocity, to pumps, to compressors, to the movement of liquids in pipes, and so on. Able to rely on a dependable set of knowledge and data in fluid dynamics, Harvey was in a good position to tackle the question of blood circulation. On hereditary mechanisms, in contrast, there was only scant new evidence. The second example is even more revealing. In his "Discourse on Method, Optics, Geometry, and Meteorology," Descartes (1596–1650) proceeded in two steps. In the first chapter he introduced a new methodology, then in the second part of the book he set out to apply it to several case studies. He sought to understand the rainbow, for example, and a number of meteorological phenomena, such as thunder. He was able to solve the first question but was unable to progress on the second. Why? As we know the phenomenon of the rainbow is caused by the refraction of sunlight by droplets of rain. In Descartes's time much experimental work had been devoted to the question of refraction, either by Descartes himself or by other scholars. Able to rely on firsthand knowledge about refraction, Descartes was in a good position to solve the problem of the rainbow. On the contrary there was no new evidence about sound propagation; thus, for all his insightful views about methodology, Descartes was unable to explain the origin of thunder.

Similarly, future progress in historical sociology is conditioned by the availability of comparative historical data. So far progress has been slow in that direction, the work of Tilly being a noteworthy exception. In the concluding chapters of this book we discuss this issue in more detail and make a number of practical suggestions.

Presentation of Subsequent Chapters

In this section we explain how the basic methodology developed in the earlier part of this chapter will be applied to the different case studies considered in the rest of the book. The book is divided into three parts: Revolutions, Wars, and Prospects. In this chapter we have explained the philosophy and methodology of our comparative approach; Parts I and II are illustrative case studies that show how this methodology can be implemented. We concentrated on revolutions and wars because the comparative approach for these topics is already far more advanced than for many others. For wars, for instance, reliable comparative statistical data are available for almost all major countries in the world, a situation that is extremely useful from the perspective of comparative studies.

To begin Part I with the French Revolution of 1789 was an obvious choice, because it is in a sense the archetype of revolutions. At the same time the American Revolution, because it was so unique, represented an obvious challenge for comparative analysis. In Western countries, after the revolutionary era, which ended in 1848, came the era of the general strike; some general strikes (for example, in 1918 in Switzerland or in 1968 in France) even nearly ended in real revolutions. Therefore it was natural to close Part I with a chapter on general strikes.

In our approach to wars in Part II, we seek to show how the constraints of tradition and logistics provide a unifying perspective for a variety of conflicts ranging from the Seven Years' War (1756–1763) to World War II. As in Part I, we are interested in the course of wars rather than in their causes.

Because this book's ambition is to explore a new avenue in historical sociology, in Part III we discuss how our approach can be widened, deepened, and developed.

Determining Modules

How can we know which historical analogies will reveal significant patterns and which are merely trivial? What criteria can be used to identify truly important comparisons? Some sensible rules that we have already mentioned are (1) to consider a sharply defined phenomenon that (2) has occurred several times (the standard "large N" condition) and for which (3) there are accurate and possibly quantitative historical sources. Taken together, these criteria provide valuable, practical guidelines and narrow the field of research. Any study conducted along such lines will produce useful and non-trivial results.

Yet from a theoretical perspective, these criteria fail to answer the real question, which is: how can one produce results that not only are useful but provide a new perspective? Let us once again resort to the example of the fall of an apple. Although at first sight an apple's fall may seem to be a well-defined phenomenon, a little reflection shows that in fact it has many facets. Consider the following investigations that might be undertaken. (1) One could analyze the rupture of the link between the stem (the peduncle, in botanical terms) and the branch. This kind of study would touch upon the science of materials and the breakage of bodies. In this case a cluster of similar events would consist in the rupture of the peduncle for different sorts of fruits (cherries, chestnuts, and so on). (2) One could study the shock of the apple as it hits the ground. According to the hardness of the soil, the apple will be more or less damaged. This phenomenon is of obvious economic interest for, as every gardener knows, a bruised apple cannot be kept for a long time. In this second case the cluster of similar events would include the fall of fruits that are softer (or harder) than apples, such as pears, peaches, and tomatoes (or oranges and lemons). (3) One could also look at the (free) fall of the apple. In this case a cluster of similar events would include the fall of rain, hailstones (of different sizes), leaves, or cannon balls.

If conducted carefully the first two studies will certainly yield useful results, but none of them will be path-breaking. As we know, it is by studying the third phenomenon that Newton was led to a genuinely staggering discovery; and that discovery came when he had the intuition to include the fall of the moon toward the earth into the class of falling objects. Thus it was by enlarging the cluster of similar events that the theory of gravitation emerged. Needless to say, there is no recipe for such intuitions; but the identification and analysis of clusters of similar events can pave the way for such epoch-making advances.

From a more technical perspective there are basically two ways to decompose complex historical phenomena into simpler modules. First, the decomposition can be made on a chronological basis. Thus a complex sequence of events can be decomposed into separate episodes. Second, the decomposition can be accomplished by breaking up a large class of events (for example, strikes) into smaller subsets, as shown in Figure 1.9. In the subsequent chapters both methods will be used, as indicated in Table 1.9.

Comparison can be carried out either on a cross-national basis (spacelike comparison) or on a longitudinal basis (timelike comparison). The two approaches are illustrated in Figure 1.6. Both methods are used alternatively in the case-study portion of this book. Cross-national comparisons will be found in Chapters 2, 3, 4, 5, and 7. Longitudinal comparisons are made in Chapters 3, 5, 6, and 7.

1. Decomposition into separate episodes

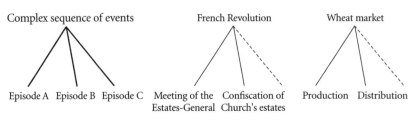

2. Decomposition into subsets

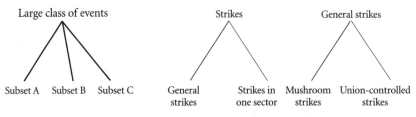

Figure 1.9 Two methods for decomposing a complex phenomenon into modules. The first method is the chronological decomposition already illustrated in Figures 1.1b and 1.5b. It leads to the definition of a number of separate episodes. Two illustrative examples are given on the right-hand side; the wheat market case has been considered in a previous study (Roehner 1995). In the second method a large class of events is broken up into a number of subsets; a similar taxonomic approach is used by botanists and naturalists. To make sense such a classification must be based on objective criteria; for example, the decomposition of the set of all strikes into general strikes versus strikes in one sector is based on the extension of the strike; the second decomposition is based on the role played by the unions: weak unions lead to "mushroom strikes," whereas strong unions lead to union-controlled strikes. General strikes and mushroom strikes are studied in Chapter 5.

Summary of Subsequent Case Studies

The main objective of this book is to show that seemingly unrelated events in fact follow common patterns, so that behind an apparently chaotic collection of events there is in fact a hidden order. In this section we provide a number of examples.

SOME RESULTS

Consider the (failed) revolution of 1356 in France and the Revolution of 1789. In Chapter 3 we show that they followed the same logic in terms of

Table 1.9 Implementing modularization in subsequent chapters

Chapter	Complex phenomenon or large class of events	Modules (episodes)
1. Decomposition into separate episodes		
Chap. 2	Struggle of the bourgeoisie for political power	Fight against nobility / Church / Crown
Chap. 3	First year of the French Revolution	Estates-General / Parisian insurrection / Confiscation of Church estates
Chap. 4	American Revolution	Logistic aspects / Unification versus fragmentation
Chaps. 6–7	Wars for territorial expansion	Logistic aspects / Strategical aspects / Tactical aspects / Submarine warfare
2. Decomposition of a large class of events into subsets		
Chap. 5	Strikes	General strikes / Mushroom strikes
Chap. 6	Wars	Wars for territorial expansion / etc.

the tactical alliance between the Third Estate and the clergy, the affirmation of the bourgeoisie's rights, and so on (see Table 3.2 for more detail).

Consider the uprisings that took place in Paris in 1789, 1830, February 1848, July 1848, and 1870; in Chapter 3 we prove that they followed the same scenario. These events involved the same actors—the National Guard, the people from the eastern suburbs, and some liberal bourgeois—and their repertoire comprised similar episodes: confrontation with the army, meeting at the Hôtel de Ville, processions through the streets, and so on.

The general strikes that took place in France and Belgium in 1936, 1953, 1960, 1968, and 1995 are seemingly unrelated events. Yet in Chapter 5 we show that they followed the same dynamic (that is, a diffusion process), the same timing, and the same repertoire. For instance the buildup phase of the strike lasted about two weeks; an agreement was usually reached during the week when the strike had its maximum extension; it then took two or three weeks for work to resume in every sector (for a quantitative description, see Figure 5.2a, b).

Consider the invasion of Portugal and Spain in the decade 1805–1815 by a British expeditionary force under Wellington and the invasion of Italy by the Allies in World War II. In Chapter 6 we show that these seemingly unrelated events are in fact two parallel strategic steps in the struggle between a maritime power and a continental power. Chapter 6 more generally analyzes the similarities between the Napoleonic Wars and World War II in Europe—for example, the blockade, the role played by the campaign in Russia, and the part played the patriotic awakening in occupied countries.

As has been emphasized by a number of historians, including Winston Churchill, Japan's decision to attack the United States can hardly be explained on a rational basis. Remember that at the time America's GNP was about ten times larger than the Japanese GNP. In Chapter 6 we show that Japan's course of action becomes clear when it is interpreted as a paronymic repetition of previous wars. Indeed in the fifty years before Pearl Harbor Japan repeatedly waged war against countries (for example, China and Russia) whose population and/or national income were several times larger than its own. Furthermore, the tactical planning of the attack on Pearl Harbor was in many ways a paronymic repetition of the raid on Port Arthur in February 1904.

Much has been written about Von Kluck's "insubordination" in August 1914 when he ignored Moltke's order to proceed toward Paris. In Chapter 6 we show that, far from being exceptional, Von Kluck's elastic interpretation of the General Staff's orders was in fact a common attitude among German generals. Again the principle of paronymic repetition provides a natural explanation.

SUMMARY

Finally we give a brief overview of the case studies. Chapters 2 and 3 are devoted to a longitudinal and cross-national analysis, respectively, of the French Revolution. The cross-national analysis shows that similar attempts took place in other European countries: in Geneva (1781), the Netherlands (1785), Belgium (1787), and Hungary (1848). It also highlights a number of factual similarities between the Revolution of 1789 and the Puritan Revolution in England. The study also shows that the strategy of the different actors and the pace of reforms were very different from one country to another. In France the monarchy was on the side of the nobility, while in some German and Scandinavian states the monarchy sided with the bourgeoisie. The longitudinal analysis shows that in several respects the events of May-August 1789 were the "heirs" to movements that had already occurred at other times in French history.

Chapter 4 attempts a comparative analysis of the American Revolution. This objective presents a significant challenge, given the singularity of the event, the first of its kind in world history. Our analysis shows that if a war of independence was to break out somewhere in British, French, or Spanish colonies, then the thirteen colonies were the very place where this was most likely to happen. It also shows that the decade of the 1770s was very timely for waging a successful war of independence. The chapter ends with a comparative analysis of the struggle for independence in Latin America, on the one hand, and in the United States, on the other. Why did the former bring about fragmentation instead of unity?

Chapter 5 is devoted to general strikes. It is related to the previous chapters in the sense that in the nineteenth and early twentieth centuries a general strike was considered a prelude to revolution. Not only were the objectives of general strikes often openly political, but the army was frequently called in to check demonstrations. The chapter first provides a general overview of general strikes in Western countries and insists in particular on the fact that each country had its own "tradition." In France and Belgium, general strikes took the form of what we call mushroom strikes; such strikes start and spread despite directives from the unions recommending moderation. For this reason they are especially observed in countries where the rate of unionization is low. The strike of May 1968 in France was of this type; similar episodes occurred in 1936, 1953, 1960 (Belgium), and 1995.

Chapter 6 is devoted to a study of wars; but in contrast to other sociological inquiries (for example, Bouthoul 1970, Singer and Small 1972), it is concerned not with the causes of war but with its forms. The field of sociological history is thus extended to cover a ground so far occupied only by historians. It is precisely because the forms of wars display definite patterns that their study makes sense from a sociological point of view. In this chapter we examine the wars of territorial expansion that have marked the history of a number of nations since the seventeenth century, in particular in Sweden, England, France, Germany, Japan, and the United States. These episodes have many common features with regard to strategy as well as to tactics. There is a deep parallelism, for example, between the Seven Years' War (1756–1763) and the Napoleonic Wars (1796–1815), on the one hand, and World War I and II, on the other hand. All these wars were world wars and opposed a continental power to a maritime power.

Chapter 7 complements Chapter 6 by analyzing the financial and logistical requirements for waging war. For instance, we examine how war expenditures affected national economies in terms of debt and inflation. At the level of logistics we show that the speed of advance of an army rarely has exceeded 20 kilometer per hour and that it has hardly increased since the time of Napoleon.

Part III discusses an agenda for future research, exploring in particular the possibility of prediction and the improvement of comparative data sources. It will be seen that some amazingly exact forecasts have had almost no impact on the march of history simply because contemporaries had little confidence in them.

Writing Comparative History

Before we close this introductory chapter a word of caution is in order. In comparing historical events a basic difficulty arises. All the events mentioned in this book cannot possibly be described and recounted in detail, first because the writer does not have the space for that and secondly because only few readers would have the time and patience to read such a lengthy book. Therefore the writer must assume the reader to have some knowledge of the events he considers. Failing that, fruitful comparison becomes difficult. This obstacle is inherent to qualitative comparative analysis. Clausewitz (1976 [1836], p. 173) encountered it in his study of military campaigns; he studied no less than 130 campaigns and it was of course out of question to recount all of them in detail.

In this book we have tried to overcome this difficulty in two ways. First, bearing in mind that the historical backgrounds of American, European, African, or Asian readers are fairly different, we tried not to restrict our examples to only one continent. Yet we are conscious that Asian and African history is underrepresented. Second, we have supplemented the qualitative description of events with a number of figures and tables. The latter are particularly appropriate for comparison purposes.

Needless to say, there is another obvious way to bypass the problem, which is to use quantitative data. Very often, unfortunately, this could not be done, either because quantification was impossible or because no data were available.

Revolutions

2

European Variants of the French Revolution

The American Revolution was without a doubt a work of genius, and the founding fathers deserve the tributes they have received over the centuries. History gave them the unique opportunity to write on a blank sheet; America was a new society that, thanks to migration and the mixing of the population, had torn itself away from the weight and tradition of European societies. Within a few decades effective institutions had been created and put to work. Western Europe, in contrast, was not a blank sheet, and the transition from the ancien régime to political democracy had to overcome many obstacles; as a result the process would take much longer, lasting typically between one and two centuries. Among the countries who took an active part in World War I there were still only two republics, France and the United States; the other countries, that is, Austria-Hungary, Belgium, Britain, Germany, Italy, and Russia, were either kingdoms or empires, and the aristocracy continued to play an important role in many of them. It is the purpose of this chapter to analyze some of the salient features of the transition to political democracy in western Europe.

In a sense the problem is fairly simple. Two and a half centuries ago all European societies were dominated by the aristocracy and the clergy and ruled by a (more or less) absolute monarch. Let us call this situation state *A*. In the France of 1789, for example, the nobility and the clergy represented less than 2 percent of the population (Soria 1987, p. 43); from a democratic perspective, their domination of political, administrative, judicial, and military life was therefore an anomaly.

Today the bourgeoisie is firmly in power in all the European countries, and a political system based on universal suffrage prevails. Let us call that second situation state *B*. While all the states *A* can be seen as being fairly

Table 2.1 Types of democratic transitions

Type of transition	Countries
Revolutionary	China (1911), France (1789), Hungary (1848), Switzerland (1847)
Gradual and fairly smooth	Britain, Germany, Sweden
Recurrent revolutionary disturbances	Portugal, Spain, Mexico
Belated	Denmark, Poland

Note: This is a very schematic classification; its main purpose is to emphasize the great variety in the forms assumed by the transition to political democracy.

similar throughout western Europe, and similarly the states *B*, there is a great variety in the trajectories that led each country from state *A* to state *B*: different transition steps, a different pace, different forms. This is schematically illustrated in Table 2.1.

Trying to "explain" the numerous peculiarities of each national transition would be an overwhelming task. Moreover such an objective would be completely at variance with the methodological goals outlined in Chapter 1. Our ambition is rather to show that a small number of factors can account for several important regularities observed in European revolutions. Among these factors three are of particular significance: (1) the size of the country, (2) the power of the Church, and (3) the weight of the nobility. Their respective roles may be outlined as follows.

(1) Observation shows that social revolution almost never succeeds in small countries. This is illustrated in this chapter by several examples of revolutionary movements that were broken up by foreign military intervention. (2) The Reformation resulted in the Church's losing most of its economic power. The confiscation of Church property will be examined both in this and in the next chapter. This loss of economic prestige widened the gulf between the nobility and the Church, and both classes lost part of their influence in the process. (3) The nobility, simply by virtue of its size, varied greatly in importance from one country to another. As a percentage of total population it ranged from 0.6 percent in Sweden to roughly 10 percent in Poland, a ratio of 1 to 18 (see Table 2.2). Needless to say, in seeking to overthrow the power of the nobility such a discrepancy made a difference.

Our claim that these three parameters can help us to find some kind of order in the bewildering diversity of revolutionary transitions may seem

Table 2.2 European nobility: Population estimates

Country	Nobility (thousands)	Total population (millions)	Nobility as a percentage of the population
Poland (1760)	750 ± 50	7	10.7 ± 0.7
Spain (1768)	722 ± 50	10	7.5 ± 0.5
Hungary (1784)	416 ± 60	9	4.6 ± 0.3
Russia (1762)	550 ± 80	30	2.2 ± 0.3
Germany (c. 1750)	300 ± 50	22	1.4 ± 0.2
Italy (c. 1750)	200 ± 50	16	1.3 ± 0.3
France (1789)	300 ± 70	28	1.1 ± 0.3
Britain (1690)	(?) 60 ± 15	6	(?) 1.0 ± 0.3
Sweden (1718)	12 ± 2	2	0.6 ± 0.1

Sources: Meyer (1973); Mitchell (1978).

Note: For the sake of simplicity and because it is generally much smaller than the relative error on nobility figures, the margin of error on populations has been ignored. The question mark on Britain's data highlights the fact that in this country the nobility had no well-defined boundaries.

rash, or at least overdone, to many historians; it is therefore appropriate to repeat the defense made by distinguished scholars whose approach has been similar. At the beginning of his path-breaking study about internal colonialism, Hechter (1975) noted: "I am well aware that this kind of model-building is frowned upon in historical circles. This study may not pay sufficient attention to microscopic details for some readers. The great advantage of using models is that they can be falsified whereas descriptions can only be amended." Hechter's attempt belonged to a tradition that has also been advocated by economists. In his *Essays in Positive Economics* (1953), Friedman emphasized that "a hypothesis is important if it explains much by little, that is if it abstracts the common and crucial elements from a mass of complex and detailed circumstances surrounding the phenomena and permits valid predictions on the basis of them alone." This is precisely what Goldstone (1991) tried to do in his study of revolutions, pointing out that a similar set of conditions is to be found at the origin of many revolutions. His study is complementary to ours. In the following pages the reader will not find the slightest attempt to explain why a particular event occurred at a given moment. Instead we are interested in overall patterns. Goldstone, in contrast, shows convincingly why the French Revolution could be expected in the decade after 1785 or the English Revolution in the

1740s. His study stands out for the very reason mentioned by Hechter: it is quantitative and thus can be falsified; to our knowledge it is the first investigation of revolutions of that sort.

There is an extensive literature on the emergence of political democracy; this chapter has the following distinctive features. First, the main emphasis is on the decay of the ancien régime and on the resistance put up by its supporters rather than on the emergence of new democratic ideas. Second, as far as possible the study tries to offer quantitative evidence. In this respect we should mention the handbook by Flora, Kraus, and Pfenning (1987), an indispensable source for any comparative study on this subject; Markoff's (1994) brilliant essay, a truly comparative historical study, very much in line with our approach in this chapter; and a study by Palmer (1959), which, though older, is still of great interest.

The chapter proceeds as follows. First we examine movements that took place in the decades before 1789 and can be considered forerunners of the events to come. They show that the pressure for revolution was increasing; yet because they occurred in small countries, they were doomed to failure. In 1786 the Patriots' movement in the United Provinces, for example, was broken by the Duke of Brunswick; but six years later, when trying to repeat the same operation in France, he was defeated at the battle of Valmy.

In the second section we highlight a number of intriguing similarities between the revolutionary movements in Britain and in France. Our objective is to show that, once started, revolutionary movements to some extent follow the same dynamic. Of course, for two countries such as Britain and France such a demonstration is facilitated by the fact that their histories are closely connected and, despite obvious differences, share many common features. Yet the same argument can also be applied to more distant examples, such as the Russian Revolution of 1917 or the Ethiopian Revolution of 1974.

In the third section we estimate how solidly the ancien régime was entrenched in various European countries. First, we present four examples—Denmark, Poland, Portugal, and Ethiopia—in order to illustrate the great diversity of situations. Then we define a number of criteria that can be used to assess the privileged position of the nobility and clergy or the degree of absolutism of the state. As a case in point, we examine more closely the role and evolution of the Church. Finally, a concluding section summarizes the regularities revealed by the chapter and briefly discusses possible implications for the present time.

Forerunners of Revolutionary Movements

In the two decades before 1789 there were many attempts to shake off the shackles of the nobility and the clergy in Europe. They all failed. However, despite their failure, these attempts are full of lessons; one will find in them most of the ingredients that made up the explosive cocktail of the French Revolution.

Revolutionary Attempts

GENEVA

Geneva is one of the smallest Swiss cantons; in 1780 its population bordered on 100,000 residents. Then as now, Geneva had a well-established reputation for expertise in the areas of banking and watchmaking. Although formally having a high degree of local autonomy (it was a Swiss allied territory but was not yet one of the thirteen cantons in the Swiss Confederation), this small territory was under the supervision of its powerful neighbors: the canton of Bern, France, and the kingdom of Piedmont-Sardinia established in Savoy. Being prince of the neighboring city of Neuchâtel, the king of Prussia also had an eye on what was going on in Geneva. With regards to politics its institutions were similar to those of the republic of Venice: a Great Council of 200 members, a Small Council of several dozen members (analogous to Venice's Council of Ten), and a General Council gathering 1,200 people (analogous to the Venetian Senate). Members of the Great Council and the Small Council were essentially selected by co-optation. The elections often attracted only a minimal number of voters; those of January 1783 attracted less than 300. Just as in Venice, the power was essentially in the hands of a narrow oligarchy. In the eighteenth century it seems to have been particularly impervious to the entry of the new bourgeois, who provoked frequent disturbances (Guerdan 1981): in 1707 the agitator Pierre Fatio was executed; in 1737 there were ten fatalities from shooting between soldiers of the government and the militia. By 1781 there were three different competing groups: the government, that is to say the patricians who dominated the councils; the bourgeoisie; and the so-called natives, that is to say the most recent residents who did not have the status of bourgeois.

On February 6, 1781, there were, as in 1737, battles for control of the streets between government soldiers and bourgeois militias; the latter got the upper hand. The bourgeois and the natives then had the General

Council adopt an edict that granted a certain professional equality between natives and patricians. At this point the king of Prussia demonstrated his concern by asking in a letter that the old constitution be maintained. France urged the same thing. On April 7, 1781, to the sound of the alarm, armed groups of bourgeois militia took possession of the artillery depot, seized the arsenal, and forced the garrisons posted at the three entrances to the city to surrender. In the days that followed the Small Council was purged of eleven of its members and the Great Council of thirty-two of its members. Bern, Zurich, and Piedmont-Sardinia as well as France refused to recognize the new regime. On July 1, 1781, a Sardinian army arrived at the entrances to the city. At their first vote the besieged pronounced themselves in favor of fierce resistance, but in a second vote they more realistically opted for surrender. The Geneva revolution had lasted one hundred days. It was followed by a period of restoration and purge: many of the rebels were exiled, some for life, others for ten years. About 1,000 Genevese applied to the lord-lieutenant of Ireland for permission to settle in that country; in July 1783 many of the fugitives indeed came to Ireland. Subsequently, however, most of them left and settled in England (Keller 1934).

The General Council lost a great part of its power; the bourgeoisie was disarmed and its militia dissolved. It is significant, however, that in 1787, after a food shortage had resulted in popular troubles, the bourgeois militia was reestablished.

What can be retained from this episode? First of all the crucial role played by the bourgeois militia, which is similar to that of the National Guard in the French Revolution. Second, at the tactical level, the fact that the rebels had the primary objectives of taking the artillery depot and the arsenal foreshadows the taking of the arms deposit at the Invalides (July 14, 1789) and the gunpowder stores of the Bastille. It also shows that in this period cannons had become easy enough to handle to be dragged into the streets and sufficiently safe to be fired by semiprofessionals.

THE PATRIOTS' REVOLUTION IN THE UNITED PROVINCES

After their war of liberation (1565–1600), the United Provinces became the main commercial and maritime power of Europe. In the seventeenth century two-thirds of the ships that crossed the Sound (the strait between Denmark and Sweden) belonged to the United Provinces. During the first two Anglo-Dutch wars (1652–1654 and 1665–1667) the Dutch fleet achieved dazzling victories. But a century later, although Amsterdam had preserved its role as a great financial center, England had succeeded in imposing its commercial and naval supremacy. The fourth Anglo-Dutch war (1780–1784) was a naval walkover for England, during which it gained important advantages on the commercial front. Faced with this decline, in part a result of the weakness and lack of centralization of the oligarchic government, the United Provinces experienced several outbursts of revolt. The country had a loose federal structure. The stadholder played the role of a lieutenant-general either at a provincial level or at the level of the whole country. After 1751 the function of stadholder became hereditary in the Orange-Nassau dynasty; in 1766 William V of Orange-Nassau became stadholder (Langer 1968, p. 476).

Under the influence of the American War of Independence, a movement took place in 1786–1787 that relied largely on the citizens' militias. In June 1785 an act of association was concluded between the various citizens' militias to request a "true republican constitution" and the end of the co-optation of the nobles. Their intransigence and the secret interventions of the English ambassador radicalized the movement, whose members called themselves the Patriots. In 1786 the Dutch states withdrew from the stadholder the command of the troops of the province. In May 1787 the Patriots' militia routed a small army of the stadholder near Utrecht. On September 8, 1787, the king of Prussia, Frederick William II, delivered an ultimatum. On September 13, approximately 26,000 Prussians entered Holland under the direction of the Duke of Brunswick. On September 20, Utrecht and the Hague fell. Amsterdam surrendered on October 10. There followed a period of repression and restoration. The stadholder had his rights reestablished, while the Patriots were imprisoned and their houses looted. A large number of them escaped to France.

What can be retained from this episode? Again the Patriot militias played an essential role and again it was foreign intervention that broke the movement. The next case is interesting precisely because the insurrection succeeded, at least for a time, in countering the foreign intervention.

THE BRABANT REVOLUTION

Brabant is a district situated in the center of Belgium (at that time called the Austrian Netherlands) near the cities of Brussels and Louvain. The north of Brabant is Flemish and the south is French speaking. At the end of the eighteenth century Belgium was still part of the Habsburg Empire, as had been the case for the United Provinces before their independence. On January 1, 1787, Emperor Joseph II introduced a wide-ranging reform of the province's traditional institutions (Dumont 1977), provoking deep discontent. The opposition was led by two leaders, both attorneys, but very different politically. Jean-François Vonck was an upholder of the philosophy of the Enlightenment, while Henri van der Noot was a supporter of regionalism and a return to a system of traditional government in which the privileged dominated. It was the rather conservative van der Noot who finally gained the upper hand among the rebels. On May 30, 1787, the Archduchess Maria Christina (sister of Joseph II) suspended the execution of the main reforming edicts. Disavowing his sister, Joseph II sent Count von Trauttmansdorff there with very extensive authority. On December 17, a clash between troops and demonstrators who threw pebbles and potatoes left six of the demonstrators dead. The revolt calmed for a time. But in the autumn of 1788, the provincial states of Hainaut and Brabant refused to approve the taxes requested by the government. Joseph II responded by dissolving the provincial states. On July 22, 1789, following the example of Paris, the cities of Tirlemont, Mons, Louvain, and Tournai rebelled and a troop of patriots defeated the small Austrian army in the city of Turnhout (October 24, 1789). Plagued with desertions, the Austrians evacuated the country. On January 7, 1790, the Estates-General of Belgium met for the first time since 1630 and adopted at the urging of van der Noot the Act of Constitution of the Belgian States. It was inspired by the Articles of Confederation of 1777; but whereas the Americans innovated the Belgians only restored the past. On July 27, 1790, England, the United Provinces, and Prussia committed themselves to guaranteeing Leopold II (the successor to Joseph II) the reestablishment of his authority. Van der Noot ordered an uprising. But the Austrian troops made short work of the 20,000 badly equipped and little-trained volunteers. On December 2, the Austrians retook Brussels.

Note that there was also a somewhat independent revolt in the principality of Liège, situated 80 kilometers to the east of Brussels. On August 18, 1789, the bishop prince signed his abdication and withdrew to Trier, leaving a progressive bourgeoisie in power in the principality. Division and chaos followed, however, with bloody riots in several quarters of the city. Shortly afterward the king of Prussia sent troops. Reestablished in his functions, the bishop prince hunted down the rebels, of whom a great number fled to France.

DISCUSSION

What to retain from these episodes? First, in the revolutions in the United Provinces and Brabant, the influence of the American Revolution is clear. Second, there is what can be called a federalist temptation, that is to say an attempt by regions to gain their autonomy. In the Belgian case it was inherent from the start in the movement against the centralizing decrees of Joseph II. Note, however, that the temptation of federalism accompanies all revolutions, for the simple reason that the transition from one type of power to another is accompanied by a temporary eclipse of the central power. Such centrifugal movements are perceptible in the English Revolution of 1641–1660, the French Revolution (the federalist movement of 1793), the Mexican revolution of 1830, the Austrian revolution of 1848, the Chinese Revolution of 1911, and the Russian Revolution of 1917. A third recurrent feature is the role played by Prussia in opposing revolutionary movements.

Reform Attempts

The preceding examples concerned popular revolts. However, even in certain leading circles anti-aristocratic and anti-autocratic ideas have gained ground. Here are three illustrations.

STRUENSEE: THE DANISH TURGOT

Struensee became prime minister in Denmark in 1770, four years before Turgot in France. Their programs were astonishingly similar and their falls similarly were provoked by palace intrigues of the privileged. In contrast to Turgot, who simply quit his function as comptroller general of finances, Struensee was executed. Again a period of aristocratic reaction ensued. For instance, whereas Struensee had restricted compulsory labor obligations on the basis of 144 days per year for a tenancy of average size, a new ordinance of August 12, 1773, stated that the obligations were again to be determined by former usage and custom (Barton 1986).

THE DEADLOCK BETWEEN THE KING AND THE ESTATES IN SWEDEN

In 1719–1720 the Swedish parliament (Riksdag) brought an end to the king's absolutism. The Riksdag was composed of four estates: the nobility, the clergy, the burghers, and the peasants. In 1771 a conflict arose between the aristocracy, which was allied to the king, and the demands of the bourgeoisie and the peasants. The bourgeoisie asked in particular for equal access to the higher offices of state. On February 11, 1772, King Gustav III wrote to his mother: "There is the nobility on the one side and the other three orders on the other. We have reached the point where civil war may emerge from these disorders" (Barton 1986). A compromise was finally found, but a second conflict took place at the time of the convocation of the Riksdag of 1786. This time the noble estate was followed by the peasants. For seven weeks the tension continued, and the situation remained at a standstill. Finally Gustav III dissolved the Riksdag. Drawing a lesson from this failure, Gustav III undoubtedly convinced himself that only strong-arm tactics could make the nobility give in. On February 20, 1789, he presented to the Riksdag an "Act of Union and Security" which amended the constitution to increase the king's power. Faced with the opposition of the nobility, he placed in detention nineteen leaders of the noble opposition. The act was accepted by acclamation by the three other estates.

In this case, by abandoning his role as arbiter, the king actively contributed to the eviction of the nobility. The example of Joseph II in Austria constitutes an even more spectacular example. Nevertheless, as we shall see, the latter found himself faced with a much more numerous opposition and eventually had to renounce his program.

JOSEPH II'S REFORM ERA IN AUSTRIA

Both the ecclesiastical institutions and the privileges of the nobility were the object of the reforming zeal of Joseph II in Austria between 1765 and 1790. An Edict of Toleration of 1781 (extended to the Jews in 1783) made official the policy of multireligious coexistence in the Habsburg Empire. Most religious congregations, with the exception of hospital and teaching orders, were abolished: nearly 700 convents were thus transformed into schools. A decree of 1789 introduced a uniform tax on the lands of the nobility as well as on those of the bourgeoisie. The corvée was suppressed and replaced by a monetary contribution. The traditional institutions of Brabant were abolished practically overnight; this was the cause of the Brabant revolution, and this wave of reform came up against strong opposition more generally as well. The failure of the reform attempt was in a way made official when, on the eve of his death in January 1790, Joseph II rescinded most of his decrees except the Edict of Tolerance and a few others favorable to the peasantry.

THE REFORMISM OF THE MARQUIS OF POMBAL IN PORTUGAL

The Marquis of Pombal was prime minister in Portugal from 1750 to 1777. He implemented a program of economic modernization and tried to limit the power of the clergy. Jesuits were expelled and the traditional institution of the Inquisition was abolished. But here too the resistance of the aristocracy and the Church got the better of the reformer and his reforms. Nevertheless the very existence of these attempts shows that the old state of equilibrium was at breaking point.

Conclusion: The Nobility on the Defensive

The image that emerges from the preceding examples is one of a nobility which is on the defensive but remains powerful. This interpretation is certified by the failure of all the attempts at change, whether they were reformist or insurrectionary. The retreat of the nobility concerned the aristocracy of the royal court as well as the established landed nobility. The erosion began in those countries in which the nobility was less numerous (see Table 2.2) and where the bourgeoisie had been able to develop. If most of the preceding movements were failures, it is largely because of the military intervention of conservative monarchies. It is this deadlock that the French Revolution would break.

Parallels between the English Revolution and the French Revolution

Are there any parallels between the English Revolution and the French Revolution, and if so, are they more than coincidences? First, one can note that the principal actors were the same: the king, the queen, the parliament, the aristocracy, and the foreign powers. Second, the immediate problems were often similar: how to obtain funds or, failing that, estates that could serve as guaranty for obtaining loans; how to avoid the atomization of the movement, which could only lead to chaos and failure. Before exploring the details, we summarize the main events. For more details about these and other episodes, consult Charles Tilly's *European Revolutions* (1993), which constitutes a worthy companion volume to this chapter.

Chronology

THE REVOLUTIONARY PERIOD IN BRITAIN

The religious policy of Charles I exposed him to the hostility of the Parliament, and he dissolved this body on March 10, 1629 (according to the dates of the Roman calendar in operation in England until 1751; to convert to the Gregorian calendar it is necessary to add approximately ten days). The next Parliament, the so-called Long Parliament, was not sum-

moned until eleven years later, under the pressure of financial needs stem-
ming from the war against Scotland. On January 3, 1642, faced with the
hostility of this Parliament, the king attempted a coup de force by trying to
arrest five delegates. On June 1 the Parliament presented to the king a set of
radical demands, the Nineteen Propositions. The civil war began in August
1642. During the first three years few decisive battles took place. Having
withdrawn to Oxford, the king organized his government there. On June
14, 1645, Oliver Cromwell won a decisive victory over the royal troops at
Naseby; on September 10, Bristol fell. In April 1646 the king fled to Scotland, where the Stuart dynasty had originated. Negotiations took place between the king and the Parliament. The occupation of London by Cromwell's army on August 6, 1647, cut short these talks, and the king was
delivered to Parliament in return for a payment of £200,000. Sentenced to
death by the High Court, Charles I was executed on January 30, 1649.

During the period that followed, Parliament was dissolved several times:
on April 20, 1653; in December of that year; on January 22, 1655; on February 3, 1658; on April 22, 1659; and on October 13, 1659. Its role was
more nominal than real, power resting in the hands of Cromwell and the
army. On December 16, 1653, Cromwell received the title of lord protector
of the Commonwealth. He died in 1658. On December 29, 1660, the monarchy was restored, bringing Charles II to the throne (1660–1665). The
conversion of his successor, James II (1685–1688), to Catholicism precipitated a conflict with Parliament that had been latent for several years.
James was deposed in November 1688 by a Parliament allied to William of
Orange.

THE REVOLUTIONARY PERIOD IN FRANCE

On May 6, 1788, Louis XVI ordered the arrest of two members of the
Parlement of Paris. In protest, insurrections burst out in the provinces and
especially at Grenoble (June 7). With the state facing budgetary pressures,
the Estates-General were convened on May 4, 1789. On June 20 the delegates of the Third Estate took an oath (the so-called Tennis Court Oath)
not to disband before having given a constitution to the kingdom. On July
13–14 the insurrection seized the Invalides, which provided it with arms,
and then took the fortress of the Bastille, both a symbol of royal absolutism and an important reserve of ammunition. On October 5 a procession
led by market women set out for Versailles, followed by detachments of the
National Guard under Lafayette. Early the next morning a minority of the
crowd who had spent the night outside the palace broke into the royal

apartments. They and the rest of the protesters were not appeased until the royal family agreed to accompany them back to Paris to take residence in the Tuileries. On June 20, 1791, the king attempted to escape to the Austrian Netherlands, but was stopped near the border and returned to Paris. A constitution was promulgated in September 1791. From this date until August 10, 1792, the king played his role of constitutional sovereign while maintaining contacts with counterrevolutionary forces abroad, that is, with noble émigrés and the Austrian government. On August 10, after the taking of the Tuileries, Louis XVI was removed and the royalty was abolished. Sentenced to death, Louis XVI was executed on January 21, 1793. From 1795 to 1799 power was in the hands of five directors, who formed the so-called Directory. The coup d'état of Bonaparte (November 9, 1799) inaugurated the period of the Consulate. In 1804 Bonaparte took the title of emperor. After the fall of the empire the monarchy was restored (June 4, 1814, and November 1815) under Louis XVIII (1814–1824). During the reign of his successor, Charles X (1824–1830), an aristocratic reaction took place that lead to the revolution of June 27–29, 1830 ("Les Trois Glorieuses"), and the advent of a bourgeois royalty. In 1848 another revolution abolished the monarchy.

Parallels in the Overall Chronology of the Events
Table 2.3 provides a parallel chronology of the two revolutionary periods. One could object that this parallelism is fictitious to the extent that it depends on the choice of events selected. It is difficult to deny, however, that most of the retained events mark major stages in the development of the movement. In our opinion this parallelism reflects certain deep mechanisms of revolutionary dynamics. Until these mechanisms are identified, deciphered, and formalized our thesis will remain a working hypothesis. It is possible to support it by several qualitative arguments, however, as shown below.

FINANCIAL PROBLEMS

As was convincingly shown by Goldstone (1991), revolutions are often triggered by public indebtedness. In the case of England it is known that financial difficulties led to the reunion of the Long Parliament; similarly in France the king's prime objective in convening the Estates-General was to solve the financial crisis. How serious was the situation? Was it a banal problem of the management of public debt or was the credit of the state truly at stake? It was, it seems, the latter in both countries. In England in

Table 2.3 Parallel chronologies of the revolutionary periods in England and France

Event	England			Event	France		
	Date	Years after beginning of the revolution			Date	Years after beginning of the revolution	
Financial difficulties	1638–1640			Financial difficulties	1785–1789		
Convocation of the Long Parliament	Nov. 1640	0		Convocation of the Estates-General	May 1789	0	
Sale of Church property	1641–1652	1–12		Sale of Church property	1790–1796	1–6	
Flight of the king	1646	6		Flight of the king	1791	2	
King's execution	Jan. 1649	9		King's execution	Jan. 1793	4	
Phase of military conquest	1649–1652	9–12		Phase of military conquest	1793–1805	4–16	
Cromwell becomes Lord Protector	1653	13		Coming to power of Bonaparte	1799	10	
Restoration	1660	20		Restoration	1815	26	
Change of dynasty: Glorious revolution	Nov. 20, 1688	48		Change of dynasty: "Les Trois Glorieuses"	June 27–29, 1830	41	

Note: The term "Les Trois Glorieuses" refers to the June 27, 28, and 29, 1830; it is probably more than just a coincidence that the term is similar to the one used in England 150 years before for a change of a similar nature.

July 1640, when asked to lend to the government the necessary subsidies for the war against Scotland (Second War of the Bishops), the City refused the loan. Similarly in France, on the eve of the Revolution, interest payments on the public debt absorbed almost 50 percent of the state budget. This debt came from loans contracted at the time of the Seven Years' War (1756–1763) and after the American War of Independence (1778–1783), as shown by the following figures giving the share of the budget devoted to the payment of interest on the public debt (*Atlas historique* 1968, p. 284).

1683	1715	1722	1739	1763	1774	1789
10%	39%	22%	16%	28%	30%	45%

In this sense one can say that the American War of Independence was a direct cause of the French Revolution. Both the European and the American wars had already necessitated an increase in taxes in France, so the French government's room to maneuver had become greatly reduced. Already in 1770 the comptroller general of finances had been forced to suspend the payment of short-term interest.

SALE OF CHURCH ESTATES

For every revolutionary government the financial situation is necessarily a crucial preoccupation; during troubled periods tax returns are low while the needs are immense, particularly because of military expenses. There is therefore a strong temptation to expropriate opponents, in this case the noble royalists, and to draw from the immense "kitty" constituted by the goods of the clergy. The sale of these goods, moreover, increases the loyalty of the buyers to the new regime. It is therefore not surprising that the two revolutions had recourse to this device.

THE EXECUTION OF THE KING

From the moment that the conflict between the Revolution and the king became irrevocable, his execution became almost a political necessity. Can one imagine a king imprisoned for life? And what a tremendous capacity for nuisance a monarch in exile would represent. This is illustrated in England by the recurrent Jacobite disturbances led by the supporters of James II after his exile, or in France by the repeated calls from the Vendée leaders to the heir of the throne (compare Montagnon 1974). The fact that a dethroned absolute monarch has to be eliminated in order to guarantee the success of a revolution is further confirmed by the examples of Tsar Nicholas II, executed in 1918, and Emperor Haile Selassie, (very probably) executed in August 1975 one year after the revolution in Ethiopia. Yet an obvious objection comes to mind: the often repeated claim (see, for instance, the *Encyclopaedia Britannica* 1967) that Louis XVI was condemned to death by a majority of one (361 against 360) makes his execution seem a rather random event rather than a historical necessity. Patrick (1972), however, convincingly shows that throughout the trial (which lasted from December 11, 1792, to January 20, 1793), in approximately ten different votes, there was a consistent majority in favor of the king's execution. For instance, in the last vote (January 20), a reprieve proposal was rejected by 380 to 310.

THE COMING TO POWER OF CROMWELL AND BONAPARTE

The monarchy had made the leading elites as well as the population accustomed to a strongly personalized power. From a psychological point of view, the transition to a form of collegiate and parliamentary power undoubtedly would require a long delay, on the order of several decades. Thus it is not surprising that after ten years of "republican chaos," we find a return to personalized power. It was Cromwell in England (after thirteen years) and Bonaparte in France (after ten years). Other cases illustrate the same phenomenon: Stalin in Russia (after ten years); Salazar in Portugal (after ten years), Hitler in Germany (after fourteen years), Franco in Spain (after twenty years), Mao Tse-tung (after thirty-five years). An indirect confirmation is further provided by the fact that the above effect is not observed in "new" countries (America, Australia).

Microanalogies

In this section we discuss a number of similarities of a more specific character.

A DETESTED QUEEN

In England, Queen Henrietta Maria was Catholic and of French origin (she was the daughter of Henry IV and Marie de Medici). She was suspected of having an ominous influence on Charles I. The situation was very similar in France. Queen Marie Antoinette was the sister of Leopold II, who was emperor of Austria from 1790 to 1792. Opposed to reforms, she was suspected of supporting the party of the nobility and the cause of absolutism. That these queens were both of foreign origin was not by

chance, of course; it resulted directly from the tradition of marriages between reigning courts, a tradition that has survived to the present day.

THE ABOLITION OF THE REMAINS OF FEUDALISM

In England in February 1646 an ordinance abolished the Court of
Wards and Liveries and freed many land tenures of their feudal character.
Similarly in France, the decree of August 11, 1789, codifying the resolu-
tions of the night of August 4, abolished seigniorial justice, the rights of
hunting and serfdom, and rendered other feudal rights redeemable.

EXECUTION "CUSTOMS"

Among the popular representations of the French Revolution, there are
two images that often appear in book illustrations: that of the executioner
raising the head of Louis XVI to show it to the public and that of the crowd
trailing on the end of a pike the head of Launay, the governor of the Bastille. In fact, such behavior was not in the least specific to the Revolution;
on the contrary it was, at that time, a well-established tradition to show the
head (or even the limbs) of victims after their execution. The scene was
very similar for Charles I: "The executor separated with one cut the head
from its body; then raising it in the air, he showed it to the people saying
'This is the head of a traitor'" (Whitelocke 1963 [1682]). In the case of the
more infamous crimes, as for example the execution of ten regicides (people who voted for the death of the king) in October 1660, not only the
heads but the limbs of the victims were exposed on pikes. Such practices
persisted up to the end of the nineteenth century, especially in colonial
wars (for example, in Sudan and Tanzania).

Parallels between the English Civil War and the Insurrection of
the League

It would be wrong to conclude that the parallels between the English and
the French Revolution are the only ones possible. An episode as complex as
the English Revolution comprised many facets. To illuminate some of
them it is useful to put them in parallel with other similar episodes. Consider, for example, the period in England from 1642 to 1645, when the king
and his entourage had withdrawn to Oxford, 100 kilometers from London
where the Parliament was sitting. During these years the king tried to operate not only a government but also courts independently of Parliament.
The latter similarly had to substitute itself for the executive power held by
the king. This situation, in which two powers both proclaimed themselves

sovereign, has no analogy in the turbulent history of the French Revolu-
tion, but it touches another episode in French history, the period of the
League (1588–1594). Here is a broad outline. On May 12, 1588, King
Henry III was driven from Paris by the uprising of the Parlement and of
the population supported by a conspiracy of Catholic hard-liners, the Holy
League. After the assassination of Henry III (August 1, 1589), the two authorities came into conflict with each other. On one side there was the
Holy League, which was supported by the Parlement of Paris and had proclaimed the cardinal of Bourbon as king under the name of Charles X; in
1593 there was even a meeting of the Estates-General called to legitimize
his power. On the other side, facing the League, was the party of the legiti-
mate heir to the throne, Henry IV, who was Protestant. He installed his
government at Tours (200 kilometers southwest of Paris), where he was
joined by members of the Parlement of Paris. One then has a picture very
similar to that of the civil war in England: a conflict that is largely based on
a religious difference with foreign interference (Scotland in one case, Spain
in the other); two powers opposing each other, one comprising the legiti-
mate king and the other the most important parliament in the kingdom;
the armies of both parties clashing intermittently and trying to occupy the
greatest number of cities and fortified towns.

Struggles against the Established Powers

In the two preceding sections, we have presented a comparative analysis
limited to the short term. To see how various countries have succeeded in
liberating themselves from the tutelage of the monarchy, the nobility, and
the clergy, it is necessary to adopt a long-term perspective. What is most
surprising when studying the political evolution of the European states is
the extreme diversity of situations and cases. In certain societies such as
Poland or Venice, a parliamentary regime functioned very early (from the
thirteenth or fourteenth century) but to the exclusive benefit of one social
class. In other cases, as in Denmark, royal absolutism remained until a very
late date (1901). In some countries the transition was peaceful; elsewhere it
brought about civil wars. Before we describe particular cases, a few general
remarks will be helpful.

First, because the king and the royal court constituted only a very small
group, royal absolutism had necessarily to find support in the two privileged classes, the nobility and the clergy. This gave rise to a game of complex alliances and reversals of alliances. For example, in Denmark in 1660

the king ruled in close union with the nobility to the point that all twenty members of the royal council came from its ranks. This situation lasted until 1666 when the king, leaning on the bourgeoisie and the clergy, led a coup de force against the nobility and withdrew their power to elect the sovereign during dynastic changes. Denmark thus passed from an oligarchic to an absolutist state.

Second, the numbers of the nobility varied greatly from one country to another and even within a given country, from one region to another. In France on the eve of the Revolution it is estimated that (depending on the criterion used) the nobility represented between 0.4 percent and 1.4 percent of the population. In Poland, in contrast, the nobles represented roughly 10 percent of the population. Table 2.2 summarizes this data for a number of countries. Two groups are evident: countries of strong nobility density—Poland, Spain, and Hungary; and countries of low nobility density—Italy, France, Great Britain, and Sweden, though in Great Britain the very notion of nobility is difficult to define; between these two groups are Russia and Germany.

Third, as for the importance of the clergy, the situation is very different in Protestant and Catholic countries. In the former, the economic and political weight (as property owners) of the clergy is clearly weaker than in the latter. This is linked less to a question of doctrine than to the "nationalization" of goods of the clergy that took place in an almost systematic manner during the changeover of these countries during the Reformation. This point carries some weight because the solidity of the ancien régime structure was largely assured by the symbiosis between its three constituent elements (see Figure 2.1). When the clergy lost its lands, an ecclesiastical career was no longer attractive to the sons of the nobility; gradually the Protestant churches allied themselves to the bourgeoisie from whom they stemmed. This element weakened the ancien régime in Protestant countries.

Four Typical Cases
We first consider three cases from the north, the east, and the south of Europe. The case of Ethiopia has been added in order to show that similar events took place even in the second half of the twentieth century.

DENMARK
The Church in Denmark essentially lost its political weight when it became Protestant with the institution of the Reformation in 1536. All the

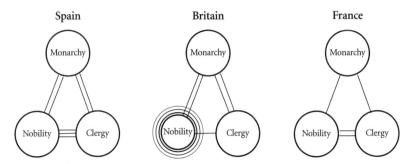

Figure 2.1 The monarchy, nobility and clergy, the three entities on which the ancien régime was based, mutually supported one another, but the strength of the links differed from one country to another. In Britain, for example, the link between the high aristocracy and the high clergy was weaker than in France. Whereas in Britain many bishops came from the gentry or the bourgeoisie, in 1780 in France, 97 percent of them came from the aristocracy (that is, wealthy noble families); there was, however, a deep rift between low and high clergy, which played a crucial role in the first stages of the French Revolution.

goods of the churches and convents were confiscated by the crown. The archbishopric disappeared, and bishops answered directly to the king. At the time of the sale of the clergy's goods, moreover, the nobility was able to strengthen its role as property owner. The institution of an absolute monarchy dates from the "royal revolution" of 1665. The monarchy then became hereditary, and the monarch was deemed responsible only to God (King's Law, 1665). At the same time, through the institutionalization of a titled nobility, the nobles became more dependent on royal power; this was accomplished in 1671 when King Christian V created a new high nobility of counts and barons to serve largely as an ornamental court as at Louis XIV's Versailles. At the same time, the top positions in administration and the officer and diplomatic corps were monopolized by the nobility. The bourgeoisie, however, had access to property ownership, and between 1730 and 1766 the number of farmsteads owned by bourgeois proprietors increased from 33 percent to 42 percent (Barton 1986). The subjection of the peasantry worsened during the eighteenth century with the institution of the *stavnsbaand* (which means "place bound") in 1733; this ordinance forbade the male peasant to leave the manor where he resided from his fourteenth to his thirty-sixth year without the proprietor's permission.

A brief period of reform took place from 1770 to 1772 thanks to Struensee, who played a similar role in Denmark to that of Turgot in

France, but in very particular circumstances. King Christian VII became affected by mental illness, which poses a serious constitutional problem in an absolute monarchy. Queen Caroline Matilda fell passionately in love with the doctor Struensee called to the bedside of the king; this affair allowed Struensee to play a major political role. He removed the tariff barriers, reduced the monopolistic privileges of the artisan guilds, and established a commission for the gradual abolition of the *stavnsbaand*. But on January 17, 1772, he was brought down by a palace revolution. Sentenced to death, he was beheaded after his right hand was struck off. As another instance of execution "customs" it may be mentioned that his body was drawn and quartered and remained on public display on the edge of Copenhagen for the next four years (Barton 1986). After the period of reaction that followed, the situation remained deadlocked until the enormous revolutionary movement of 1848, which forced the king to grant a constitution. In 1865, however, the landowners succeeded in imposing a revision of the constitution, allowing them, in collaboration with the king, to again dominate political life. In the new Upper Chamber (the Landsting) twelve delegates were chosen by the king, twelve others by the most important taxpayers, and the remaining twelve by the rest of the voters. From 1865 to 1901, the Upper Chamber succeeded in hoarding all the power at the cost of the Lower Chamber, the Folketing. In protest the Lower Chamber blocked the vote on the budget, so that for nearly forty years the country was governed by provisional finance laws. It was on July 24, 1901, that the king finally consented to follow normal parliamentary rule by calling on the majority of the Lower Chamber to form the government.

To summarize, his example suggests the following mechanisms. The loss of its landed goods excluded the Protestant Church from the political game from 1536. The bourgeoisie, because of their ability to buy land, could gradually eat away at the position of the nobility—particularly at the expense of the small nobility, who were often obliged to mortgage their land. The weak progress of industrialization before 1900 created the risk of an alliance between the aristocracy and the high landowner bourgeoisie; that is indeed what happened between 1865 and 1901, blocking any real democratic reform until the beginning of the twentieth century.

POLAND

Poland constitutes an interesting example because of its extreme character. At a very early date it was governed by a system of assembly that was both decentralized and hyperdemocratic in the sense that the rights of the individual noblemen were very extensive, perhaps exorbitantly so. This regime eventually resulted in a complete paralysis of government. Not surprisingly this system of government was actively supported by its neighbors, Austria-Hungary, Prussia, and Russia.

As we have seen, the nobility in Poland made up roughly 10 percent of the population, by far the greatest proportion in Europe. From 1454 the Privilegium of Nieszawa allowed the nobility to escape royal justice almost completely. The king was in principle elected by a direct vote of the nobility, a rule that was indeed applied in practice from 1572, that is to say after the death of the last representative of the Jagiello dynasty. For this election several thousand nobles assembled near Warsaw. All nobles were eligible, and this was not merely a theoretical possibility, as the elections of Kings Sobieski (1674–1694) and Wisniowiecki (1669–1673) testify (Labatut 1978). Each king had to "buy" his election with new concessions to the nobility, which resulted in a slow erosion of royal power. The system was further decentralized to the extent that the representatives of the national diet were in fact elected by eighteen local assemblies. The king's signing of the Henrician Articles (1573) is an important event in the development of a true parliamentary regime; while the diet had previously been summoned at the king's pleasure it was now to be reconvened in a regular manner every two years. In 1635 the possession of land became an exclusive privilege of nobility. This blocked almost all development of the bourgeoisie—especially before the advent of the industrial revolution, which in Poland occurred quite late. What paralyzed the diets were the exorbitant powers attributed to each of its members: the right of veto, on the one hand, and the so-called liberum veto, on the other. The right of veto imposed decision making by unanimity, and this forced many diets to break up without having decided anything; between 1600 and 1650 this happened six times. After 1652 the liberum veto allowed any delegate to dissolve the diet: between 1650 and 1700 this happened fifteen times out of forty-four, and between 1733 and 1763 this happened thirteen times out of fourteen; often the dissolutions were encouraged by foreign backing. All the attempts to suppress the rule of the liberum veto came up against foreign interventions; thus at the diet of 1766, Prussia and Russia threatened Poland with war if the liberum veto continued to be queried. It must be added that this parliamentary regime was accompanied by real religious tolerance, a relatively rare occurrence in Europe in the seventeenth century. Even if the toleration deteriorated a little toward the end of the century (after 1668, all Catholics changing their religion were liable to the death penalty), it is no less remarkable especially considering the important role of the Catholic Church; in 1931 it still possessed 400,000 hectares, or 2.5 percent of arable land. As for the peasants, their condition worsened over the course of time; for example, if around 1520 the corvée was only one day per week and per plow, it gradually increased thereafter.

On May 3, 1791, a constitution was proclaimed. Its dispositions, however, were largely unrelated to the ideas that were shaking France at the time. Article 2 confirmed the exclusive right of the nobility to possess land; each order, furthermore, preserved its own courts. The great novelty was the abolition of the liberum veto. As might be expected this provoked a Russian military intervention in 1794. After this date the Polish state essentially lost its independence for 124 years. The country was shared between Austria-Hungary, Prussia, and Russia, with Russia receiving by far the largest part. Becoming independent again after World War I, Poland endowed itself with a democratic constitution in March 1921. The agrarian reform of July 10, 1919, however, remained very timid; and after 1926 the constitution was increasingly ignored as the country slipped toward an authoritarian regime.

The Polish example suggests the following conclusions. First, the monopoly of the landed nobility considerably slowed the birth of a bourgeois class that would have been able to break the domination of the nobility. Second, the absence of a central power had two perverse effects: on the one hand, it left a free hand to the dominant class; on the other, it ultimately resulted in a system of chaotic and helpless government.

PORTUGAL

The example of Portugal differs from the two preceding cases essentially in the important role played by the Catholic Church. Another interesting aspect is the country's lengthy and troubled transition from an absolute monarchy to a democratic constitutional regime.

Traditionally the Cortes, the Portuguese parliament, played a significant part in the designation of the king. Furthermore, in April 1581 it was the Cortes that made official the uniting of the country to Philip II's Spain. After the country had regained its independence in 1640, it slipped increasingly into absolutism. From 1640 to 1656 there were two convocations of the Cortes per decade, from 1656 to 1698 there was only one, and after 1698 there was none at all until 1820. It was John V (1706–1750) who

gave the monarchy its absolutist form. Inevitably this brought it into conflict with the other great component of Portuguese society, the Catholic
Church. Thus in 1726 following a dispute with the Jesuits, the king came
within an inch of expelling them; John V had additionally clashed without
success with the Inquisition when he wanted to submit its judgments to
royal control. This program was resumed by the Marquis of Pombal, who
was prime minister from 1750 to 1777. The Inquisition was removed from
the clergy and transferred to a royal court; the Jesuits were expelled in
1759. More generally Pombal imprisoned all those within the Church who
opposed his program of modernization of the state; at the time of his fall
in 1777, nearly 2,000 ecclesiastics were in prison. Trials were also started
against members of the high nobility on various pretexts. Portugal
emerged from absolutism in 1820, thanks to a military uprising that bears
some resemblance to Portugal's "Captains' Revolution" of April 25, 1974.
The constitution of July 1821 introduced a constitutional monarchy. The
Inquisition, reestablished after the disgrace of Pombal, was now abolished.
Unfortunately the new constitution was hardly applied; this was the beginning of an extremely chaotic period that came to an end only on October
5, 1910.

During this period the Catholic Church was undoubtedly an obstacle in
the transition to a liberal regime, although it is difficult to quantify this
judgment. Despite numerous laws to that effect its power was reduced only
gradually. In 1834 religious orders were abolished and their goods were
sold; with the passing of the years, however, various congregations were
discreetly reinstalled; by 1910 there were thirty of them. The clergy outside
the religious orders, meanwhile, had not been touched by the measures of
1834, and they continued to enjoy a huge fortune in property. On October
8, 1910, three days after the proclamation of the republic, a decree reestablished the main anticlerical measures taken at the time of Pombal. In particular, the Jesuits were again expelled; their return had been facilitated by
a law of 1901 that had authorized congregations of an educational or charitable character. In April 1911 a law was passed that separated church and
state and gave the real estate of the clergy to nonreligious associations. Not
surprisingly, 80 percent of the priests refused to go along with this reform.
Just as had happened during the French Revolution 120 years earlier, the
rural classes followed their priests while the urban middle classes ap-
plauded the anticlerical measures. Nevertheless the Catholics rallied to the
new constitution in 1915 and to the monarchists in 1918. But until the

coming to power of António Salazar in 1926, the regime was marked by great instability; there were on average three governments per year.

In the case of Poland it is quite easy to put one's finger on the blockages caused by aristocratic domination. In the case of Portugal it is more difficult to define the pressures and obstacles attributable to the Catholic Church; these are by definition more hidden since they are of a religious, cultural, or psychological nature. What we know of Portugal, however, and of Spain and Mexico, which are similar, leads us to think that these forces were considerable.

ETHIOPIA

Before concluding this section, in order to stress the similar nature of problems in diverse locales, we examine briefly the case of Ethiopia. Until the occupation of this country by Italy in 1935, the Coptic Church was a great slave owner; nearly 500,000 slaves were liberated by the Italians. This institution was considered an economic necessity, because the Church possessed immense estates totaling approximately 30 percent of all land (*Combat*, January 18, 1973). In the early 1970s there were still 800 monasteries (*Herald Tribune*, March 15, 1979). Allied to the clergy, the absolute monarch Haile Selassie had reigned since 1930. The peasantry remained in an archaic state and, as in France during the ancien régime, the country was periodically weakened by famines (1973, 1984) or shaken by peasant revolts (1942–1943, 1962, 1967–1968; *Times*, March 2, 1974). On March 12, 1974, the emperor conceded a constitution, but in September of that year he was deposed by the army. Then in March 1975 the monarchy was abolished; on March 17, a radical agrarian reform redistributed the property of the Church and of the large landowners: from that time forward no one could possess more than ten hectares (*Liberation*, May 2, 1977). On February 20, 1976, soldiers deposed the leaders of the Coptic Church. In May 1977, despite the death of the emperor (which had occurred, probably by execution, in August 1975), fighting broke out between the monarchist and republican militaries.

Of the four cases that we have reviewed, the Ethiopian revolution is without a doubt the one which in its timing is closest to that of the French Revolution. As in 1789, absolutism, the aristocracy, and the clergy were swept aside almost simultaneously. Furthermore, as in revolutionary France, there was an acceleration of the movement in the three years following the beginning of the revolution.

The Privileges of the Established Powers

In the preceding section our analysis was purely qualitative. Although such an approach can be satisfactory for the study of a small number of cases, it becomes impracticable if one wishes to extend the analysis to ten or more instances. In this case, before comparison is possible, the information has first to be standardized and condensed. For example if one wants to measure and compare the progressive erosion of the power of the nobility, it is necessary to rely on a set of uniform criteria. The definition of such criteria is one of the objectives of this section.

ABSOLUTISM

Before establishing the criteria that will allow one to gauge the degree of absolutism within a monarchy, it is necessary to stress that, in the framework of the ancien régime, whether in France or Scandinavia or Portugal, absolutism did not mean tyranny or dictatorship. We can illustrate this idea by referring to the case of France, whose absolute monarchy has served as a model for many European monarchs from Christian V or Gustav III in Scandinavia to John V in Portugal. Without even touching on the Fronde (1648–1649), the disputes that Louis XV and Louis XVI had with the Parlement of Paris are well known; Marion (1976) notes that all the conflicts that brought the parlements and the crown into opposition after 1750 sooner or later ended with the defeat of royal power. Even Louis XIV had to have his royal texts registered by the parlements. In the process, they could present reproofs, suggest modifications, or even recommend the abandonment of the text. The authority of the thirteen parlements of the kingdom covered the police, the finances, the organization of the regencies during the king's minority periods, and ecclesiastical discipline. The king could take no direct action against the parliamentary magistrates, because since 1467 they had been irremovable. The interpretation here is confirmed by the detailed analysis that Hamscher (1976) made of the role of the Parlement during Louis XIV's reign. "In order to reduce Parlement to a mere ornament," he tells us, "Louis XIV would have had to capture the control of magisterial appointment, break the social bonds between the judges, diminish their conception of themselves as a privileged elite in state and society. He did none of these things however."

Each camp took advantage of fluctuations in the power struggle to erode the positions of its adversary. The evaluation of absolutism thus cannot be reduced to a theoretical, judicial problem; one has to examine how the laws were actually enforced. For that purpose the following criteria can serve as initial guidelines.

1. What share did the assembly of the nobility or the Estates-General have in the designation of the king? This point is crucial, because at the time of an election the king was in general obliged to make concessions to the assembly that designated him. Examples range from the case of Poland, where the king was truly elected, to the case of France, where the Estates-General were consulted only in situations involving dynastic controversies.
2. Were the assemblies or parliaments convened at fixed dates, or did their reunion and dissolution depend upon the good will of the king?
3. Was the king obliged to register laws with the parliaments and under what conditions?
4. For how long were tax revenues granted to the king? In Britain, for example, some taxes were voted on at the beginning of the reign for its entire duration.

If one reviews the European examples it is noticeable that in many cases the powers of the monarch were limited by a system of assembly, notably in Britain, Hungary, Poland, the United Provinces, some Swiss cantons, Sweden, and Venice and other Italian city-states. Often, as in Hungary and Poland, this evolution began in the sixteenth century or even, in the case of Venice, well before. These countries thus continued the tradition of the Middle Ages where the monarch had only very limited power. Poland, for example, experienced only a brief interlude of monarchical regime in the period of the Jagiello (1410–1580), preceded and followed by two long periods dominated by the government of magnates. Very often these systems of assembly resulted in a paralysis of power; this happened in a particularly clear manner in Poland, Hungary, and Venice and equally, though in a less spectacular manner, in the United Provinces. In truth, the real challenge was to marry the assembly system with efficient management. It is this problem that Britain solved in a masterly manner from the end of the seventeenth century, well before the institution of a truly representative system at the end of the nineteenth century. Sweden too had a constitutional monarchy allying efficiency and permanent control of the parliament, apart from an absolutist episode of quite short duration from 1680 to

1718. Still other examples are analyzed in a very stimulating study by Gershoy (1966).

THE POWERS OF THE NOBILITY

The ancien régime was characterized by the supremacy of the nobility and the clergy. But what did this supremacy consist of, and what are the criteria that allow us to define it? These are fundamental questions for whoever wishes to study either the slow erosion of this supremacy or its sudden suppression. The following criteria can facilitate an initial evaluation:

1. Did the nobility have the sole right to designate a successor to the king, particularly in the case of a dynastic change?
2. Did the nobility have supremacy within the king's council?
3. Did the nobility have the sole right to occupy the high administrative, diplomatic, or military functions?
4. Did the nobility have an exclusive right to the possession of land?
5. Did the nobility enjoy fiscal privileges?
6. Could the nobles escape royal justice?
7. What feudal duties (corvée, seigniorial tithe) had the nobility preserved by the end of the eighteenth century?
8. Did the nobility have judicial rights within its estates?

Each of these criteria can be illustrated by a concrete example.

1. It has already been seen in the preceding section that in both Denmark and Poland the nobility had the right, by the vote of its representatives, to choose the king. In Denmark the nobility was dispossessed of this right in 1666. In Poland it preserved it until the abolition of the monarchy; its last enactment, on January 25, 1831, consisted of deposing the somewhat nominal king of Poland, Czar Nicholas I.

2. In eighteenth-century Denmark, the members of the national council all belonged to the nobility.

3. In Sweden, an ordinance of 1723 specified that all the high state offices from the first to the eleventh rank (there were forty ranks in all) were reserved to the nobility (Labatut 1978, p. 103). In France, the nobility was able to win back some of its former privileges in the decades that preceded the Revolution. This resulted in the reservation of positions for the nobles that had previously been open to the bourgeoisie. Thus for the positions of intendants and of officers in the navy, for example, one had to hold four

nobility quarters, which meant that a candidate had to have four generations of nobles on either the maternal or the paternal side (Soria 1987, p. 59).

4. In Poland the nobility retained the sole right to possession of the land practically until the country regained its national independence in 1918.

5. The nobility had fiscal privileges in practically all the states. In France the main tax was the *taille*. This appeared under two forms, according to the region: the *taille personnelle* and the so-called *taille réelle*. The *taille personnelle* was a sort of income tax. Nobles were exempted from it, but they were not the only ones: saltpeter miners and gamekeepers, to give only two examples, were equally exempt. One of the problems of the tax system of the ancien régime was simply that the number of exempt persons increased regularly. The *taille réelle* was imposed not on people but on property; again the lands of the nobility were exempt (Marion 1976 [1929], p. 526).

6. In France the nobles had no specific courts (if we disregard those institutions without great importance such as the courts of point of honor, the *tribunaux du point d'honneur*, whose role was to pacify quarrels between nobles and thus prevent duels). However, nobles were judged by jurisdictions that normally intervened only on appeal; in a period when the quality of justice was quite mediocre, this was a non-negligible guarantee. In Poland, as has been seen, the nobles could to a large measure escape justice.

7. Duties in kind and in cash assigned by the lords to their tenant farmers were many and strongly variable, not only from one country to the other but even within a country, from one region to the other. We touch here on only two: the corvée, or labor extracted in lieu of taxes, and serfdom, or the prohibition on the tenant farmer's leaving the estate. In the France of 1789, as with most other feudal duties the corvée was, if not in the process of extinction, at least in regression. When it existed it was estimated at twelve days per year (Marion 1976, p. 155). This contrasts with countries such as Poland or Hungary, where the corvées were on the increase compared with their levels in the sixteenth century: 50 days per year in Poland around 1550, 104 days per year in 1767 in Hungary. If serfdom was in France nothing more than a relic (it affected approximately 200,000 people, Soria 1987, p. 154), it was not the same in the countries that experienced what has been called a "second serfdom," such as Hungary, Poland, Russia, and to a smaller extent Denmark.

8. Subjected for three centuries to the competition of both royal and parliamentary justice, seigniorial justice was reduced to almost nothing in France on the eve of the Revolution. Since the Blois Ordinance (1579), seigniorial courts were no longer in the hands of the lords themselves but were entrusted to a judge. Badly remunerated, they generally carried out their task poorly and the *Cahiers de doléances* (Books of Grievances) swarmed with complaints on this subject. In sum, after having been a privilege, seigniorial justice had rather become a burden for the nobility.

THE POWERS OF THE CHURCH

Concerning the preferential position of the clergy within the state, one can make evaluations on the basis of the following criteria.

1. What place did the Church hold in leading institutions: the king's council, parliaments, Estates-General?
2. What was the Church's share in the nation's wealth?
3. What was the importance of the taxes appropriated for the benefit of the clergy?
4. What were the fiscal privileges enjoyed by the clergy?
5. In what measure could the members of the clergy escape secular justice?
6. Did the clergy have its own courts?
7. In what measure was teaching in the hands of the clergy?

Before illustrating these criteria by examples, we note the profound difference between reformed and Catholic countries. In the former the goods of the Church had been seized by the prince at the time of the Reformation; this point is discussed in more detail in the following chapter. At the same time the taxes appropriated by the clergy were abolished or transferred to the crown, the clergy being thereafter remunerated by the state. The reform thus essentially removed from the Church its political influence. Just as we have done for the nobility, we will seek to identify the powers of the Church by citing some examples.

1. For France it is difficult to estimate the political weight of the clergy separately from that of the nobility, so great was the identification between the high clergy and the high nobility. Thus around 1780, of 139 bishoprics, 135 were in the hands of the great noble families; they were also prevalent in the positions of canons attached to cathedrals.

2. The question of the economic weight of the Church can be divided

Table 2.4 Real property of the Church in different countries

Country	Date	Percentage of total area	Reference
Britain	1530	25	Moreau, Jourda, and Janelle (1950)
China	1700	14	Wolf (1969)
Ethiopia	1970	30	*Combat,* Jan. 18, 1973
France	1780	13	Lecarpentier (1908)
Romania	19th century	20	Damé (1900)
Sweden	1450	20	Andersson (1973)

Note: In the case of France, the figure is a percentage of cultivated land. In terms of total area the figure would be about 7 percent; that percentage varied greatly from one region to another and was highest in the richest parts. The table lists a sample of countries for which data could be found. Church estates probably were of comparable importance in other countries. A systematic comparative study would be of great interest.

into two: its wealth and its income. In most of the Catholic countries the Church possessed a notable proportion of the arable land (see Table 2.4). In France around 1780 the proportion was approximately 12 to 15 percent of cultivable land (Lecarpentier 1908, p. 35); in Poland at a date as late as 1930 the proportion was approximately 3 percent. In Great Britain there were two important waves of expropriation of the property of the Church: in 1524–1538 it was essentially monasteries that were affected; in 1641–1652 it was mainly the goods of the secular clergy, bishops, and chapters. In Portugal the main expropriation movement took place in 1834; a peculiarity of the Portuguese case was the subsequent ennoblement of the main buyers of ecclesiastical goods, which strengthened the nobility; from 1834 to 1879, forty-two titles of barons were thus distributed.

3. According to various estimates quoted by Marion (1976), approximately half of the income of the Church of France came from taxes (essentially tithes), the rest coming from its property. The tithe was applied to the harvest produce, and its rate is estimated at approximately 8 percent. Together with the *casuels* (occasional payments for services such as baptisms or marriages) the tithe was probably the most detested of all taxes because it was known that instead of serving to maintain the priests it would enrich the high prelates (for details on peasant complaints, see Markoff 1996b).

4. Until the last days of the ancien régime, the French clergy succeeded in holding in check the royal tax system. The Church of France provided

the state a "free gift" every five years that had been consented to and fixed by the clergy assemblies; it is estimated that the clergy contributed 3.8 percent of the receipts of the state in 1789, a percentage much inferior to the share of its patrimony (Bourgain 1890).

5, 6. In France, over the course of time both royal and parliamentary justice increasingly reduced the attributes of ecclesiastical justice. The latter only retained the sentences linked to religion: excommunication, deprivation of benefit, fast, prayer; for crimes, the members of the clergy were systematically brought before a secular jurisdiction. Similarly, during the period of the English Revolution, in February and July 1641 the ecclesiastical courts lost the right to enforce corporal sentences as well as a great part of their most important ecclesiastical attributions. In southern Europe it was the Inquisition that was the most important ecclesiastic court of law. In Portugal, the Marquis of Pombal tried to put it under the control of the state at the end of the eighteenth century. After the disgrace of Pombal it began to function again, though slowly, up to 1881.

7. The weight of religion in cultural life was immense. In France, instruction was in practice under the control of the clergy (Marion 1976, p. 208). The nomination of the instructors had to be approved by the bishop or the priest (edict of April 1695). In 1710 in Paris, more than half of the colleges were run by Jesuits, and a good part of the others depended on other congregations. Even in the United States at the time of independence all universities (except the University of Pennsylvania) were religious institutions (Lacour-Gayet 1976).

TOWARD A QUANTITATIVE COMPARATIVE ANALYSIS

Table 2.5 provides some relative chronological indications, following the three themes explored in this section, of the dates at which the bourgeoisie succeeded in freeing itself from the domination of the Church, absolute monarchy, and the nobility. In many cases, however, the evolution was more gradual than sudden, which renders the fixing of a single date difficult. This attempt is very preliminary. To obtain truly quantitative estimations it would be necessary to introduce for each of the envisaged criteria a numerical scale in a manner analogous to the Richter scale for earthquakes. This would be a large-scale project that would necessitate collaboration between scholars of various countries. Although such a project extends beyond the objectives of this book, in the next section, as an intro-

Table 2.5 Dates at which the bourgeoisie succeeded in freeing itself from the domination of the Church, absolute monarchy, and nobility

Country	Church	Absolutism	Nobility
Britain	1641–1652	1685	
Denmark	1536	1901	1901
Ethiopia	1975	1974	1975
France	1789	1750	1789
Hungary	1785		1848
Netherlands	1530	1473	
Poland	1919	1573	1921
Portugal	1911	1834	1820
Russia		1917	1917
Spain	1975	1873	
Sweden	1527	1719	1789
Turkey	1924	1909	
Venice		751	

Sources: Beauvois (1995); Dulphy (1992); Durand (1992); Helle (1992); Morris (1992); Mousson-Lestang (1995); Norwich (1986); Soria (1987); Voogd (1992).

Note: Quite often the transitions were progressive rather than clear-cut; furthermore backward evolutions were not rare. Therefore the dates shown in the table are meant to indicate a period rather than to fix an exact time.

duction to such an agenda, we consider more closely a specific case, the achievement of religious freedom.

The Achievement of Religious Freedom

"All Men Are Equally Entitled to the Free Exercise of Religion"
The title of this section is taken from article 16 of the Virginia Bill of Rights, June 1776 (*Der Aufbau* 1945). At the time, with 700,000 residents, Virginia was by far the most populous state in the United States. Pennsylvania, which was in second position, counted some 434,000 residents (Mitchell 1983). Note that neither the Declaration of Independence (July 4, 1776) nor the Constitution of the United States (1787) touched on the religious question. This was mentioned only in the ten amendments to the Constitution voted on November 3, 1791: "Congress shall make no law respecting an establishment of religion or prohibiting the free exercise of

thereof." In France the assertion of the liberty of religion was the object of article 10 of the Declaration of the Rights of Man and Citizen (August 26, 1789); remember that this declaration was to serve as a preamble to the constitution that would be promulgated in September 1791. Although nowadays the right to religious freedom may appear fairly obvious, it is necessary to stress that the above proclamations represented a break with a situation that had prevailed in the principal countries of Europe for several centuries. The current situation in certain Islamic countries allows us to better appreciate the importance that this question could have at the time.

SOCIAL IMPORTANCE OF RELIGION

It is difficult today to realize how pervasive the presence of the Church and of religion generally was before the nineteenth century in every aspect of social life. To begin with, it was the parish minister who kept the register of baptisms, marriages, and burials. As already mentioned, education was largely controlled by the clergy. Religion also permeated the whole of intellectual life. One of the ways to gauge to what extent this was true is to estimate the percentage of published books that dealt with religion. Table 2.6 provides some information on this topic. The percentages for the first half of the eighteenth century were indeed considerable. In a modern classification of the branches of knowledge, theology is only one domain among, say, twenty others, and therefore a "normal" percentage would be on the order of 5 percent, which is indeed the order of magnitude that we observe after 1900. Before the eighteenth century the very idea of religious freedom was almost inconceivable. While this is fairly obvious for the Catholic countries of southern Europe, it is no less true in the Protestant countries of northern Europe. For instance, in Britain by the various Acts of Uniformity of 1549, 1552, 1559, and 1662, every person not having a lawful excuse was required to be present at church services every Sunday (after 1581 the penalty was 20 pounds per month, Lingard 1829). In Denmark-Norway and in Sweden, the civil rights of the Catholic minority had been severely curtailed by successive laws throughout the seventeenth century. In other words, even in countries where the Church had already lost most of its estates, its influence remained. It would take centuries to progressively bring into being the rights proclaimed by the Virginia Bill of Rights and by the Declaration of the Rights of Man and Citizen. In what follows we briefly examine some of the major steps in that evolution. Before we pro-

Table 2.6 Percentage of books published relating to religion

1645	1700	1720	1740	1760	1780	1800	1813	1907	Reference
44							10	4	D'Avenel (1909)
	44	38	33	22	15	6			Bendix (1978)

Note: The first row concerns books about religion published in France, the second concerns books on theology listed in the catalog of the Leipzig book fair. As a matter of comparison, the percentage of medical books remained more or less stable between 1700 and 1900 at a level between 5 and 8 percent.

ceed, however, an important distinction has to be made between one-religion countries and multireligion countries.

ONE-RELIGION COUNTRIES VERSUS MULTIRELIGION COUNTRIES

As shown in Table 2.7, some European countries possess sizable religious minorities. Is this not in obvious contradiction with the thesis presented in the previous paragraph? First of all, it is of interest to notice that among either the one- or multireligion countries, some are majority Catholic while others are majority Protestant. Therefore one can expect that the solution of the paradox has nothing to do with religion. Indeed it can be observed that most of the multireligion regions belong to countries that were, or still are, weakly centralized. This is obvious for Germany (Prussia excepted), for Hungary, and for Switzerland; indeed, Germany and Hungary came to existence as unified states only in the second half of the nineteenth century. Even the Netherlands was a loose confederation (the United Provinces) until 1815. Hence the only case still unexplained is Prussia; it is a special case in the sense that, between 1760 and 1814 (that is, at a time when the role of religion was already somewhat eroded), the country had absorbed regions like the Rhineland, which had a substantial Catholic population. Religiously and culturally these regions were very different from Prussia's eastern regions, which were predominantly Protestant.

In short, the line of division between one-religion and multireligion countries corresponds neither to a north-south distinction (for instance, Poland is Catholic while Geneva is Protestant) nor to a distinction between Protestant and Catholic countries. It is the degree of efficiency and centralization of the state that appears to be the determining factor. The natural

Table 2.7 Population by religion

Country	Protestants (%)	Roman Catholics (%)
One-religion countries		
Denmark (1840)		0.1
France (1962)	1.6	
Great Britain (1851)		3.5
Portugal (1962)		91
Spain (1962)		99
Sweden (1870)		0.1
Multi-religion countries		
Germany (1871)	62	36
Bavaria (1871)	28	71
Prussia (1871)	65	33
Hungary (1910)	22	50
Netherlands (1849)	59	38
Holland (1849)	60	26
Switzerland (1860)	59	41

Sources: Flora, Kraus, and Pfenning (1987); Molnar (1996).

tendency for strongly centralized states was to follow the *cuius regio, eius religio* rule, which implies that the religion of the country should be the same as the religion of the ruler (and vice versa).

Toward Religious Pluralism in the One-Religion Countries

The religious climate in the seventeenth and eighteenth centuries has been excellently summarized for the case of England by Patrick Collinson: "One has to remind oneself that towards the end of the Elizabethan reign (1600) the Church is the same thing as the nation; it embraces the whole nation. This was deeply rooted in official thinking, and not only in official thinking but it was also the expectation of most people." As we shall see, this was the prevalent opinion in most European countries.

FRANCE

At first glance one might think that France is the exception to the rule associating centralized government with a single religion. Did France not experience a regime of religious liberty for nearly a century from the Edict of Nantes (1598) to its repeal (1685)? In fact, it is necessary to stress that the edict granted by Henry IV resulted as much from his spirit of personal tolerance as from the military power balance. Following a war that had lasted fifty years, the Protestants had a firm hold on a hundred cities and fortified towns, and it was necessary to compromise with them. With the passing of the decades these fortified towns fell one after the other, (La Rochelle, for example, fell in 1628) and France naturally rejoined the group of one-religion countries. In order to show to what extent religion permeated the social body and in particular education, it is interesting to quote the words of a contract passed in 1772 between a municipality and a schoolmaster who was not a cleric: "He will be obliged to raise children in the Catholic religion, to do the catechism twice a week, to supervise his schoolboys when he makes them attend mass, to say the prayers with his schoolboys in the church after having announced them to the sound of the bell every night according the usual custom" (Marion 1976, p. 206). Even in secondary education the part played by the religious colleges was considerable.

The Protestants recovered their civil rights in 1787, but it is only following the Revolution that they obtained freedom of worship. The emancipation of the Jews was achieved at the same time (1791).

BRITAIN

Legislation concerning religion in Britain is abundant. We will content ourselves with touching on a few representative acts that indicate the climate of the period. In 1709, when the Whigs gained a clear majority in Parliament, they passed an act that provided a simple procedure for the naturalization of foreigners. Aliens only had to swear allegiance to the Crown, prove that they had received a Protestant sacrament in the preceding three months, and declare in open court against the doctrine of transubstantiation (Thernstrom 1980). Similarly, since the Test Act of 1673 every civil servant had had to declare against the doctrine of transubstantiation as well (Mourre 1978, vol. 1, p. 246). The Catholics experienced a gradual emancipation, especially after the Catholic Emancipation Bill (April 13, 1829); 1829 saw the first Roman Catholic member of Parliament since 1689. In 1836 the first Roman Catholic judge was appointed. In the course of this evolution a late episode occurred in 1891, when Gladstone's bill enabling a Catholic to become lord chancellor (the highest judge in England) was rejected by the Commons. But in fact before being formally abrogated, the anti-Catholic laws fell progressively into disuse with the exception of Ireland where, mainly for economic reasons, they continued to be applied (compare Gwynn 1928). Early in the twenty-first century the rules governing the succession to the English crown still maintained that the heir to the crown can not marry a Catholic.

SCANDINAVIA

In Denmark-Norway the civil rights of the Catholic minority had been severely curtailed by successive laws enacted in 1613, 1624, and 1643. These were confirmed and strengthened by Christian V after his succession to the throne in 1660. In Sweden-Finland the discrimination against Catholics introduced by Charles X was extended by Charles XI (1660–1697): conversion to the Catholic religion was forbidden under penalty of deprivation of all possessions (Daniel-Rops 1958). In 1810 it was out of the question that the heir to the crown could be Catholic; thus before setting foot on Swedish soil for the first time, Marshal Bernadotte was received in the Lutheran faith (October 19, 1810); three days later he was proclaimed Karl XIII's adopted son (Barton 1986). Complete religious freedom was achieved in 1859 (Langer 1968).

VENICE: A BACKWARD EVOLUTION

The case of Venice deserves to be cited, as it is unique. Here is a city that for centuries had a policy of tolerance: Greek Orthodox, Armenians, and Jews were tolerated provided that they showed discretion in their religious practices. In 1475, when a wave of anti-Semitism swept through Italy, many Jews found refuge in Venice. Yet a reaction took place in 1516 and became more pronounced with the passing of the centuries; in 1516 Venice invented the word "ghetto" (from the Venetian *ghetar:* to melt metals) by installing its Jews in the quarter of the New Foundry where formerly cannons had been cast. In 1739 the Jews were required to wear red bonnets. In 1777 professional restrictions were imposed that forced more than 1,000 of them (out of a total of 2,600) to leave the city (Jonard 1965).

The Role of Religion in the Definition of National Identity

From a democratic perspective, religious freedom was certainly a major accomplishment. Several important steps are summarized in Table 2.8. But it also had far-reaching consequences in terms of national unity. In short, when religion could no longer be used to define a nation, another concept

Table 2.8 Emancipation of religious minorities in selected European countries

Country	Catholics/Protestants	Jews
Austria	1781	1781
Britain	1830–1860	1866
France	1789	1791
Italy		1859
Prussia		1870
Russia		1917
Sweden	1859	1859

Sources: Grand Larousse Encyclopédique (1963); Langer (1968).

had to take over and fill the gap. With the diffusion of higher education, language and culture naturally took the role once held by religion. This shift, however, had shattering consequences in a number of kingdoms and empires whose unity was predominantly based on a common religion. Table 2.9 details the examples of the Protestant kingdoms of northern Europe, Catholic Austria-Hungary, and the Islamic Ottoman Empire. In contrast, countries long divided by religious antagonism but which possessed a common language were able to form national states. The unification of Germany provides a major illustration; another (albeit a short-lived one) was the unification in 1918 of Orthodox Serbia and Catholic Croatia.

Summary and Perspectives

In this chapter we have carried out a cross-national analysis of revolutionary movements in the eighteenth, nineteenth, and twentieth centuries which bear some similarity to the French Revolution. This perspective has enabled us to point out noteworthy regularities; some of them are summarized in what follows.

1. It should be emphasized that, however large, our perspective was quite focused. We did not consider just any kind of revolutionary movement. The American Revolution or the Chinese Revolution of 1949, for example, did not have the objective of overcoming the power of the nobility or the monarchy. Consequently such cases were left aside; the American Revolution is examined from a different perspective in Chapter 4. In that respect our study is markedly different from other sociological studies of revolu-

Table 2.9 Implications of the shift from religion to language as defining factor of national identity

A. Disintegration
   1. Disintegration of the Protestant Scandinavian kingdoms
      a. Denmark
         Separation of: Scania (southern province of Sweden, 1680), Norway (1814), part of Schleswig-Holstein (1864), Iceland (1918, 1944).
      b. Sweden
         Separation of: Norway (1905), Finland (1809, 1917).
   2. Disintegration of the Catholic Austrian Empire
      Separation of: Lombardia (1859), Venetia (1866), Hungary (1867), Bohemia (1918), Bosnia (1918), Croatia (1919)
   3. Disintegration of the Islamic Ottoman Empire
      Separation of: Egypt (1867), Syria (1918), Albania (1881, 1912).

B. Unification
   1. Consolidation of unity of the United States (1783–1865)
   2. Unification of Germany (1870)
   3. Unification of Serbia-Croatia (1919)

Note: The kingdoms and empires that fell apart had been held together by a common religion but had different national languages. In the United States, Germany, and Serbia-Croatia, on the contrary, there were different religions but a common language. Thus the shift to language and national culture as defining principles of nationality accounted for disintegration as well as unification movements. This was the general trend, but there were also national peculiarities. For instance, the unification of Italy cannot be explained in the same way as the unification of Germany; since Italy was a one-religion country unification should have occurred much earlier. The annexation of northern Italy to Austria was based on military power; similarly the annexation of Christian countries by the Ottoman Empire was based neither on religion nor on language but rather on military hegemony. It is therefore not surprising that these countries regained their independence only through costly liberation struggles and with the support of the great powers; such is the case for: Greece (1829), Serbia (1830, 1856), Romania (1859), and Bulgaria (1878, 1885).

tionary movements; for instance in *Revolutions of the Late Twentieth Century,* Goldstone, Gurr, Moshiri, and other contributors examined diverse cases such as the struggle against apartheid in South Africa and the coup against President Ferdinand Marcos in the Philippines.

2. We have stressed that a revolution aimed at overthrowing the ancien régime could only succeed in one of the great European powers of the time, namely Austria, Britain, or France. We described several revolutionary attempts in "small" countries that were defeated by the military inter-

vention of one of the great powers. Even in Spain, which can by no means be considered a small country, the revolutionary attempt of 1819–1822 was broken by foreign interference. That intervention was decided by the great powers at the conference of Verona (October 1823) and carried out, by a strange irony of fate, by French troops.

3. By comparing the revolutions in England and France we have showed that once begun, a revolution of that kind has its own dynamic and momentum. The process is marked by an increasing polarization that made the clash with the monarchy inevitable. As a rule, the revolution had to get rid of the king; in some cases (England, France) he was tried and executed, elsewhere he was executed without trial (Russia) or killed somewhat secretly as in Ethiopia. Then after a period of chaos, power was seized by a "strong man": Lord Protector, First Consul, People's Father, or in the case of Ethiopia, Colonel Haile-Maryam Mengistu.

4. Several regularities were identified in the struggle against the nobility and the Church. For example, the position of nobility and clergy is collectively much stronger in the country where they are closely connected. This proved to be true in the countries where the Church was able to keep its estates. When in addition the nobility represents a substantial fraction of the population, as in Poland, Portugal, or Spain, then it becomes very difficult indeed for a revolution to succeed. In those countries it took about two centuries to overcome the joint resistance of the nobility and the clergy. At the other end of the spectrum there is England or Sweden. In England the aristocracy was strong too, but it had the distinctive feature of not being a closed class; any wealthy member of the gentry could aspire to become a respected member of the aristocracy. That safety valve proved to be an effective guaranty against revolution. In fact there were numerous insurrections in nineteenth-century England, but none of them was able to gather sufficient momentum to endanger political stability.

5. One may think that the question of containing absolutism basically consisted, first, in transferring some of the king's prerogatives to a parliament and, second, in having the parliament elected by a large proportion of the citizens (an overall view of this process is provided in Figure 2.2). This was only part of the challenge, however. Another essential requirement was an efficient system of government. In several countries, for instance in the kingdom of Poland or in the Republic of Venice, the government eventually became powerless as a result of overextended parliamentary privileges. A similar problem still exists today: for example, the system of proportional representation undoubtedly has advantages in

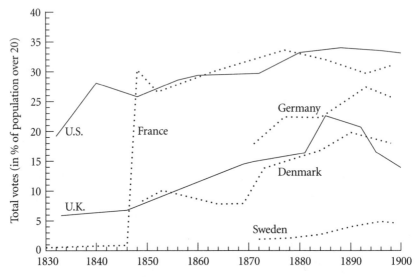

Figure 2.2 Geography of democratization in the nineteenth century. The chart shows the evolution of total votes in percentage of population twenty years old and older. As a characterization of political participation, total votes are a better indicator than the extension of franchise, for in some cases there can be a great discrepancy between electorate and actual voters; for instance, in the elections of 1886 in Britain, the electorate represented 29 percent, while the valid votes (including plural votes, meaning electors could vote several times) represented 14 percent. Apart from participation, a key element was whether or not the vote was secret; the use of secret ballots was introduced only in the second half of the nineteenth century: Germany (1848), France (1869), United Kingdom (1872), Denmark (1901). It should be noted that secrecy is a notion that depends upon various practical circumstances, a point that is illustrated for the case of Germany by Anderson (1993), who points out that envelopes to conceal the ballots from prying eyes were introduced only in 1903. Further information regarding voting rights for women and other issues can be found in the stimulating account of the ups and downs of democracy by Markoff (1996a). *Source:* Flora (1983); *Historical Statistics of the United States* (1975).

terms of democracy and minority rights, but it often leads to political instability. From a historical perspective, the real challenge is to combine political democracy and stability.

6. An essential prerequisite for the establishment of political democracy was the recognition of religious freedom. We have seen (see in this respect the overview provided by Table 2.8) that this was a very gradual process; even in the Protestant countries where the Church had already lost most of

its economic privileges, religious freedom was won only in the second half of the nineteenth century. In this matter the crucial parameter was the level of centralization of the state. Efficiently centralized states such as Britain, France, and Sweden were one-religion countries, whereas religious pluralism was accepted much earlier in loosely centralized states such as Hungary and Poland.

7. The shift from religion to language as the main factor defining national identity had major consequences. It led to the disintegration of multilinguistic states (several examples are given in Table 2.9) and strengthened the cohesion of (multireligion) monolingual states.

8. One may think that the conceptual distinction between nobility, clergy, and the Third Estate belongs to a bygone era. A little reflection, however, shows that the distance from twenty-first-century societies is not so considerable as it may seem. We can illustrate this point by considering the case of the clergy. Socially speaking, what was the role of the Church before the nineteenth century? It defined and promoted common forms of worship, it decided what was permitted and what was not, it determined what could be printed and what could not, it upheld orthodoxy against dissidents. In other words, it played a prominent role in defining the ideological basis of the society and in maintaining the unity of the social body. These are important functions in any society. In communist countries that role was played by the Communist Party. In Western societies that duty rests on the media. With the process of concentration that is under way in that industry, orthodoxy is progressively replacing pluralism. In short, the parallels between the clergy and the media become increasingly relevant, especially in Europe where the Church itself has lost much of its influence.

From Macro- to Microhistorical Perspective

In this chapter we have adopted a macrohistorical perspective. In the next one, instead of using a telescope, we use a microscope in order to identify some of the microhistorical mechanisms that led to the French Revolution of 1789. Instead of confining ourselves to strategy, we go into tactical details: where could the insurgents find arms or ammunition, how did the tactical alliance between the Third Estate and the clergy come about, and so on. Surprisingly, even at that microhistorical level we find a number of well-defined regularities. For example, the insurgents could win the day only if they had the support of the National Guard. More generally we will see that collective action has a tendency to follow well-established patterns and repertoires even at the level of microhistorical episodes.

CHAPTER
3

Building Blocks of the
French Revolution

Why is it interesting to examine the French Revolution from the perspective of analytical history? At first glance this period is so rich in innovations and upheavals that it seems to be a long series of improvisations and unexpected episodes. In this chapter we will try to show that these episodes were not as improbable as one might have thought a priori. It will be seen that even during this chaotic period, the constraints imposed by the principle of paronymy continued to apply. If this principle proves operative for a period so disturbed, it should undoubtedly be accepted all the more readily for more gradual transitions.

How does the analysis of this chapter compare with current historical research on the Revolution of 1789? Even if it is the custom among historians to assert that events of the present have their roots in the past, it must be recognized that most of the works on the French Revolution seem disinclined to search for these roots. As an example we cite two relatively recent accounts, the *Grande histoire de la Révolution française* (Great history of the French Revolution) by Soria (1987) and the *Dictionnaire historique de la Révolution française* (Historical dictionary of the French Revolution) of Soboul and his colleagues (1989). Very few of the precedents that we analyze in this chapter are mentioned in these works. Concerning the work of Soboul, this is all the more surprising as the dictionary format has the advantage of not being dependent upon the chronological account and should therefore be apt for recording historical precedents. A few isolated attempts (Godechot 1963; Doyle 1980; Bluche and Rials 1989), despite their piecemeal character, go in the direction that we propose; the work published by Bluche and Rials is especially interesting in this respect.

We concentrate our attention on three important episodes: (1) the con-

100

frontation between the royalty and the Estates-General (May–July 1789); (2) the intervention of the Parisian population (July 1789); and (3) the confiscation of Church estates (October 1789). In addition we analyze what could be called a historical accident, namely, the summary execution of prisoners in September 1792. In each of these cases we try to distinguish between actions that were paronymic repetitions of previous ones and those that truly constituted innovations. Seen from this perspective, these events will become more plausible, perhaps even to be expected.

The Confrontation between the Estates-General and the Royalty

The first meeting of the Estates-General took place in 1317. It brought together representatives of the clergy, nobility, and Third Estate, which consisted mainly of notables from the main cities. In the fourteenth, fifteenth, and sixteenth centuries the Estates were convened regularly and played an important role. Thus the Grande Ordonnance (sixty-one articles) of March 1357 constituted a sort of "Magna Carta," defining the respective roles of the royalty and the assemblies. From this point there could have been a progressive strengthening of the role of the Estates, as in England, Poland, and Sweden. But history followed another path in France. The Estates-General gradually lost their importance and it was in the parlements, and particularly in the Parlement of Paris, that a counterbalance was formed capable of restraining the power of the royalty. In this respect, the Estates-General played only a negligible role. Not only because they were no longer convened after 1614, but equally for their impotence in imposing their wishes during their last meetings in 1576 and 1614. How did these Estates-General, which were usually so unpugnacious, succeeded in a few months in 1789 in gaining the upper hand on Louis XVI and the aristocracy who supported him? In other terms, in what ways were the Estates in 1789 similar to the previous Estates and in what ways were they different? This is the object of this section.

The Well-Oiled Ritual of the Estates-General

A large part of the account that histories of the French Revolution devote to the Estates-General is not in the least specific to 1789. The writing of the *Cahiers de doléances,* the methods of electing delegates, the inaugural session of May 5, 1789, the discussions on voting by order or voting by head, the threats of dissolution were all only a repetition of the ritual and the recurrent debates that took place during the meetings of the sixteenth and seventeenth centuries. By reminding ourselves how these meetings took place, we will better see what was innovative about the delegates of 1789. Our main source will be the meticulous study of Picot (1872).

THE QUESTION OF THE NUMBER OF THE DELEGATES OF EACH ORDER

Table 3.1 gives the dates of the Estates-General with the proportion of delegates of each order where this is known. Until 1467 the Estates in northern France were convened separately from the Estates in southern France. One may also note that the tradition of compiling the *Cahiers de doléances,* which listed voters' grievances and hopes, was introduced by the end of the fifteenth century. At the outset this was without a doubt a fairly good initiative, since it allowed the delegates to gain a reasonably clear idea of their voters' concerns. However, rather quickly the work of synthesizing these *Cahiers* became such a heavy task that it paralyzed the assemblies and limited their political role.

From the point of view of numbers, two assemblies stand out: that of October 17, 1356, and that of 1789. It is probably no coincidence that these two assemblies were also particularly combative. We will return at greater length to the meeting of 1356. Concerning the representation of the Third Estate, the percentages varied relatively little from one assembly to the other. The question of the doubling of the Third Estate that attracted so much attention in the months before the 1789 meeting thus appears largely as a false debate. If the representation of the Third Estate had not been "doubled" it would have had only 289 delegates instead of 578, which out of a total number of 850 represents a percentage of 34 percent. Such an option would have given the Third Estate a much smaller representation than was traditional in the seventeenth century. In 1789 this was clearly unrealistic, especially considering the fact that since 1614 the economic weight of the Third Estate had increased a great deal.

THE ESTATES-GENERAL OF 1614

The Estates-General of 1614 is interesting on two accounts. Because it was the last meeting before that of 1789, it undoubtedly served as an organizational model for the Estates of 1789. Conversely, concerning the behavior of the delegates, it offers a striking contrast to the assembly of 1789.

In 1614 King Louis XIII was only thirteen years old, and the regency had been assumed by his mother Marie de Medici. In contrast to so many other previous cases, the Estates were not convened primarily to vote on taxes,

Table 3.1 Number of representatives at the meetings of the Estates-General

Date	Location	Total number of representatives	Bourgeoisie (%)	Nobility (%)	Clergy (%)
1355, Dec. 2	Paris				
1356, Mar. 1	Paris				
1356, Oct. 17	Paris	800	>50		
1357, Feb. 5	Paris				
1359, May 25	Paris				
1367, July	Chartres	Small			
1369, May 9	Paris				
1413, Jan. 30	Paris				
1421, May 12	Clermont				
1423–1436, several meetings					
1467, Apr. 6	Tours	192			
1484, Jan. 14	Tours	260±10			
1506, May 10	Tours				
1557, Jan. 5	Paris	Small			
1560, Dec. 13	Orleans	422	45	31	24
1576, Dec. 6	Blois	326	46	22	32
1588, Oct. 16	Blois	429	45	24	31
1614, Oct. 27	Paris	464	41	28	30
1789, May 4	Versailles	1,139	51	24	25

Sources: Picot (1872); Rathery (1845); Soria (1987); Romier (1924).

Note: For the Estates of 1560, Romier (1924) calculates that the Third Estate represented 55 percent. The tradition of the *Cahier de doléances* began in 1467; a fourth estate (justice) was represented in 1557.

but rather to establish the authority of the young king after a troubled period. As was the custom, the *Cahiers de doléances* had been written at the local level and synthesized into twelve provincial *Cahiers*. One of the main roles of the Estates was to go through these twelve *Cahiers* and draw up a final synthesis in the form of a single *Cahier* that would be given to the king. On October 14, 1614, preparatory sessions were held to rule on questions of etiquette for the inaugural session and to verify the mandates of the delegates. It was decided to bring the verification of the elections to the king's council. This approach contrasted with that of the Estates at Blois in 1588, when the delegates had energetically claimed this right for themselves; it did not augur well for the independence of the delegates from the crown.

The inaugural session in the presence of the king took place on October 20, 1614. Each of the orders had delegated a speaker, but the one from the Third Estate, in contrast to those of the other two orders, had to speak on his knees. This image could, however, give a false idea of the behavior of the delegates of the Third Estate; in fact their interventions were at times strongly energetic. Thus on February 23, 1615, in the presence of the king, Miron, delegate of the Third Estate, carried out a vigorous attack on the nobility: "The great privileges that the nobles enjoy have been granted to them to inspire their virtue . . . Today, their main actions consist of excessive gambling, debaucheries, superfluous expenses, and public and private violence."

After the first session involving all the delegates, the three Estates sat separately, a shuttle system providing a makeshift form of communication. When in mid-February the work of synthesizing the *Cahiers de doléances* came to an end, the usual question was posed: how to ensure that the king provided responses to the grievances before the Estates were dissolved? With this in mind a deputation was sent to the Louvre to obtain an extension of the assembly until the royal response was forthcoming. Here lay an inherent stumbling block to the very functioning of the Estates. The synthesized *Cahier* formed a very thick document and dealt with numerous and complex questions; it was impossible for the king's council to read it, let alone provide responses, within a few weeks. Thus the Estates repeatedly had to break up without having received anything but vague promises. In 1789 the delegates overcame this pitfall by adopting another strategy and by giving very little attention to the synthesis of the *Cahiers de doléances*. It is an irony of history that these petitions, which have received so much attention from historians, were hardly used by those for whom they had been written.

Let us return briefly to the Estates of 1614 and see how they finished. On February 23, 1615, the formal session of presenting the synthesized petition to the king took place. In addition to the delegates, more than 2,000 courtiers attended this session; many delegates were shocked by the disorder that this caused. The following day, February 24, delegates of the Third Estate, having decided to wait for the king's response, tried to meet again but were surprised to find the doors closed. Despite this, they continued to meet in small groups. On March 24 the president of the Third Estate and the presidents of the provinces were received at the Louvre where, in the presence of the king, the chancellor announced that it was impossible to reply within several days to the great number of questions contained in the

Cahiers. He made a few promises, but only on specific points. In the end, the delegates returned wearily to their respective provinces.

Combative Estates
THE ESTATES-GENERAL OF 1560

The Estates-General that met in Orléans in 1560 presents an interesting case. The situation at that time was revolutionary in many respects, which Goldstone's (1991) criteria help us to see. (1) As in 1789, the government was facing a major problem of indebtedness. (2) As in 1789, there was a growing rift among the ruling elites. The division was on religious rather than on political matters but, as we know from the previous chapter, at that time politics and religion were almost indistinguishable. (3) There was a political vacuum. Indeed after having summoned the Estates-General, King Francis II suddenly died before the meeting in December. Since the heir to the throne was only nine years old, his mother Catherine de Medici acted as regent. (4) Finally, as in 1789, there was a great agitation in the country which brought about a high level of interactivity between people (numerous demonstrations, meetings, and so on).

Yet what was to follow was not a revolution but a long period of civil war (in 1790–1795 there was a civil war as well, but of much shorter duration). In such circumstances it is interesting to investigate the attitude of the Estates-General. It comprised a substantial minority of Protestants and many of its recommendations reflected the positions both of the Third Estate and of the Protestants. In particular, as will be seen in more detail below, they offered the king permission to confiscate part of the goods of the clergy. Furthermore many delegates did not hesitate to take a bold political position by denying the queen mother any right to the regency. In short, the Estates of 1560 were far more active politically than the Estates of 1614. They could hardly aspire to the same role as the Estates of 1789, for the religious question fell outside their competence. The conflict was largely a matter of international relations, with Philip II supporting the cause of Catholicism while the Swiss, German, and Dutch states backed the Protestants.

CONFRONTATION BETWEEN THE ESTATES-GENERAL AND THE CROWN IN 1356

In order to find an assembly as militant as that of 1789 it is necessary to go back in time quite a long way, to the Estates of 1356–1357. We shall see that its actions yield some analogies with the Estates of 1789. The general situation in 1356 lent itself particularly to a Third Estate offensive. On September 19, 1356 the army of King John II had been defeated by the English at Poitiers; the king and a number of nobles were captured. The responsibility of power rested with the dauphin, the future Charles V; he was only eighteen years old. In order to pay the king's ransom and continue the struggle he needed money, and the bourgeois understood very well that their help was essential. Nor must it be forgotten that from 1348 to 1350 the Black Death had ravaged Europe, killing approximately one-third of the population and turning social structures upside down. When the Estates-General gathered in Paris on October 17, 1356, the Third Estate (or, as was said at the time, the delegates of the *bonnes villes,* or the king's cities) exceeded half the total number. The nobility was particularly small in number. Note that an Estate session for the southern provinces had been convened at the same time in Toulouse, which will be left aside in the present discussion. From the outset the delegates declared that the king had been badly served and called for the arrest of the principal councilors of the king as well as the confiscation of their property. Attacking the king through his councilors was a proven and clever tactic. In 1641 the English Parliament used it when asking for the indictment of Strafford and, a little later, for that of Laud. In France in 1356, the delegates' efforts included many delegates of the clergy, who joined their voices to those of the Third Estate. Aside from Etienne Marcel, the leader of the Third Estate, one of the most passionate speakers was Robert Le Coq, the bishop of Laon. We may recall in this connection the role played in 1789 by Talleyrand, the bishop of Autun. The tactical alliance that is found in these two cases was surely not a coincidence. In effect, even if there were some liberal nobles, the interests of the nobility were fundamentally opposed to those of the Third Estate, with the result that the only possible tactical alliance was between the Third Estate and the clergy. Either this alliance was made and the Third Estate could make its voice heard (as in 1356 and 1789), or it was not and it was reduced to impotence in the face of the alliance of the crown and the nobility; in other countries, such as the Scandinavian states, there was at times a tactical alliance between the king and the Third Estate.

Returning to our account, we note that the dauphin gave an indignant refusal to the demands of the Estates-General. But the assembly remained steadfast in its demands. The situation was deadlocked, and the assembly was adjourned. From December 11 on, revolt seized Paris. On January 14 Etienne Marcel, supported by a crowd of armed Parisians, went to talk with the dauphin. On January 20 the dauphin accepted the dismissal and arrest of the members of the king's council that the assembly had named. At the demand of Etienne Marcel the Estates-General were summoned for a new session on February 5, 1357. It resulted in March in a group of proposals known under the name of the Grande Ordonnance, which asserted the necessity of control by the Estates over the monarchy. It even authorized the recourse to insurrection in order to resist an excessive power. On March 1 the most influential members of the Estates supporting Etienne Marcel (in particular the archbishop of Rheims and the bishop of Langres) entered the king's council. As summer began, the reformers were masters of Paris and part of the kingdom, and they dominated the king's council. But the balance of power was soon to reverse. By making a tour of the provinces the dauphin succeeded in rallying a number of cities. The archbishop of Rheims changed sides and supported him; the alliance of Etienne Marcel with the peasant revolt of the so-called Jacquerie, who had gained the province of Picardy (to the north of Paris), brought him much discredit in the cities.

THE TURNING POINT IN THE MEETING OF 1789

Thus having gazed at the scenarios of 1356 and 1614 one may wonder from what moment the Estates of 1789 left the orbit of 1614 to join the trajectory of 1356 (see Figure 3.1 and Table 3.2). On the day after the inaugural meeting in 1789, the clergy and the nobility again met separately from the Third Estate. This is typical of the 1614 scenario, with separate meetings of each order. The decision to meet separately was confirmed by a vote among the nobility and the clergy; the option carried by 188 votes against 47 in the nobility and by a rather narrower majority of 133 votes against 114 in the clergy. This last vote points to the reconciliation between the clergy and the Third Estate that would take place in the days to come. Among the 291 delegates of the clergy the simple clerics were in a majority: 204 (that is to say 81 percent of the delegates) against 48 archbishops and bishops. This is in sharp contrast with the meeting of 1614, where only 10 percent of the delegates of the clergy were simple clerics (in this respect see the nice 1997 study by Tackett on the social origins of the deputies at the Estates-General of 1789). On June 13 a group of ecclesiastics belonging to the most humble part of the clergy crossed the Rubicon and joined the Third Estate. Fortified by this endorsement, the assembly of the Third Estate on June 17 proclaimed itself the National Assembly. On the morning

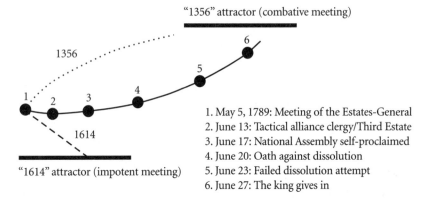

1. May 5, 1789: Meeting of the Estates-General
2. June 13: Tactical alliance clergy/Third Estate
3. June 17: National Assembly self-proclaimed
4. June 20: Oath against dissolution
5. June 23: Failed dissolution attempt
6. June 27: The king gives in

Figure 3.1 Bifurcation diagram for the Estates-General of 1789. Schematically there were two attractors, the powerless and the combative, pugnacious Estates-General. The word "attractor" comes from dynamic system theory; alternatively one could speak of two paradigms. The powerless Estates were characterized by a small representation of the Third Estate, an insignificant political role restricted to the synthesis of the Books of Grievances, and finally premature dissolution. The combative Estates were characterized by a large representation of the Third Estate, a political role that was not confined to the synthesis of the Books of Grievances, and a long duration (over six months).

of June 20 the delegates were surprised to find that their usual meeting room was locked. Here again we are in the schema of 1614. Having met in a neighboring sports hall, the delegates one by one took the so-called Tennis Court Oath: "The members of this assembly make the solemn oath not to separate until the constitution of the kingdom is established."

This was an important step, for it can be recalled from previous meetings of the Estates-General, as well as from the history of the British Parliament, that dissolution was the ultimate weapon of the sovereign. Another illustration can be found in Austria in 1849. Following the revolution of March 1848, the Austrian Reichstag was summoned in November in order to work out a new constitution. But in March 1849, as it was about to complete its constitutional work, it was dissolved by the Austrian army under General Schwarzenberg; incidentally this constitutional work (the so-called Kremsier constitution, from the name of the town in Moravia where the Reichstag met), is regarded by many historians as having offered the last real chance for a reorganization of the Austrian monarchy (Szekfu 1945).

Table 3.2 Parallels between the Estates-General of 1356–1357 and those of 1789

Features	1356–1357	1789
Large number of representatives	800	1,139
Strong representation of the Third Estate	>50%	51%
Weak position of the king	The king a prisoner of war	Financial crisis
Tactical alliance between part of clergy and Third Estate	Bishops of Laon and Rheims	Father Jallet, Talleyrand (bishop of Autun)
Bill of rights	rande Ordonnance	Declaration of the Rights of Man and Citizen
Armed support from the population of Paris	Yes	Yes
The insurgents swept into the king's apartments	Feb. 28, 1358	Oct. 5, 1789
Agitation of the peasants	Jacquerie	July 1789

Sources: Mollat and Wolff (1970); Picot (1872–1888).

On June 23, with his Declaration of Fifteen Articles, Louis XVI tried to bring the delegates back into line. The first article proclaimed that "the ancient distinction of the three orders will be conserved in its entirety." The declaration ended on these words: "I order you, gentlemen, to disperse immediately and return tomorrow morning to the chamber assigned to your own order and resume your deliberations" (Soria 1987, p. 101). Submitting to this order would have been to return to the 1614 scenario. The delegates of the Third Estate were not willing to comply. Mirabeau, one of the Third Estate's leaders, reminded them of the oath of June 20 and when they were urged to leave their place and disperse, he made this famous response: "Go and tell those who have sent you that we sit here by the will of the People, and that we shall not leave except by the force of bayonets." Bayonets, this time, were not used. But following this warning sign the Assembly voted for a motion concerning the immunity of the delegates. After his defeat of June 23, the king feigned to yield; but pushed by the royal court he was in fact preparing a second confrontation. In 1357 the dauphin Charles had similarly tried to play for time before he finally had to yield. As in 1357 the decisive endorsement of the reformers came from the Parisian population.

The Intervention of the Parisian Population

Using a vast set of observations relating to popular movements in France and England, Tilly (1986) has introduced the idea that each social group has a certain repertoire of collective actions; according to circumstances it will perform one or another of the roles of this roster. What is the repertoire of the Parisian population in the case of popular uprising? In this section we shall argue that by and large the population of Paris had to choose between two kinds of insurrection: the static, defensive insurrection and the mobile, dynamic insurrection (Table 3.3). In the first, the population tries to occupy and hold streets by the construction of barricades. In the second, armed groups move to tackle objectives that can often be found outside their original district. Historically this second type of behavior is much less common than the first. In what follows we will illustrate these two types by some examples; then we will ask ourselves what could direct the choice toward one or the other.

Static Insurrections

THE DAY OF THE BARRICADES AND THE FLIGHT OF HENRY III FROM PARIS (MAY 11, 1588)

Between 1562 and 1630 France experienced a long series of religious wars between Catholics and Protestants; Tilly (1993) counts no less than twelve. The episode that we recall here belongs to the ninth of these wars, known under the name of the War of the League. The Holy League, which we encountered briefly in Chapter 2, was formed by Catholic princes in France, supported by Spain, in response to the agreement of May 6, 1576, by which the royalty conceded important advantages to the Protestants. In May 1588 a confrontation took place in Paris between the leader of the League, Duke Henry of Guise, and King Henry III. The following brief review is taken largely from the accounts of contemporaries (Mariéjol 1904). On the evening of May 11, 1588, the companies of the bourgeois militia that appeared the most faithful were placed by the king at strategic points: the place de Grève, bridges on the Seine, and so on. They only occupied these locations while waiting to be relieved by the Swiss and French Guards, who arrived the following morning at 5 A.M. Spread by Catholic priests and hardliners, the most sinister rumors spread in the population about the intentions of the royal court. One claimed, for example, to have seen up to eight executioners called by order of the king to the town hall. Members of the Parlement, such as Brissac, got carried away by the popu-

Table 3.3 Static versus mobile insurrections in Paris

	Success	Failure
1. Static insurrections		
1588, May 11	X	
1648, Aug. 26	X	
1830, July	X	
1848, Feb.	X	
1848, June		X
1851, Dec. 2		X
1968, May		X
2. Mobile insurrections		
1356, Jan. 14	X	
1358, Feb. 28	X	
1413, Apr. 27	X	
1789, July 14	X	
1792, Aug. 10	X	
1870, Sept.	X	
1871, May		X
1944, Aug. 18	X	

Note: It can be noted that the Gordon Riots in London (1780) belong to the mobile type. Static insurrections involving the construction of barricades were fairly rare in London. Regarding eighteenth-century insurrections in London, see Lecky (1892) and Rudé (1959).

lar passions and took up arms; he put himself at the head of the university contingents. The bourgeoisie pulled chains across the streets, into which they threw anvils, beams, carts and casks filled with cobblestones. Behind these fortifications and at the house windows harquebuses were posted. The whole city was covered with barricades and soon the soldiers found themselves imprisoned; the supplies or the orders that were sent to them were stopped. The bourgeois sent a deputation to the king to request that he call back his troops. An agreement was made. During their retreat the Swiss kept the wicks of their harquebuses lighted; someone shouted at them to extinguish; they refused. A gunshot was heard and gunfire followed, leaving several dead. The following day, May 13, 1588, the king discreetly left Paris; he would be assassinated on August 1, 1589, without being able to return there. Let us add that on May 14, 1588, the Bastille, where the troops that were faithful to the king remained, was taken by the insurrection (Bluche and Rials 1989).

What can be retained from this episode? First of all we observe the role played by the bourgeois militias, who mirrored the role of the National Guard during the Revolution. We should also note the role played by popular rumor, an important component in 1789 as well. In a period without bulldozers, barricades were an efficient means of paralyzing Paris. Incidentally, it is tempting to connect this episode to a very similar scenario that took place far more recently, between May 8 and 13, 1968. There were many similar ingredients: the barricades barring almost the same roads around the Sorbonne, the role of the university, and finally the departure from Paris of the president of the Republic, General de Gaulle, on May 29.

In this connection, we mention an interesting paper by Traugott (1995). By drawing the attention to the episode of 1588, he convincingly shows that the 1827 rising is by no means the first modern use of barricades as is often claimed. Moreover, he identifies twenty-one occurrences of barricade construction in France between 1789 and 1870; at the broader European level, it was the revolution of 1848 that marked the summit of barricade construction.

EXPULSION OF THE ROYAL COURT FROM PARIS (AUGUST 26, 1648)

In order to show that the preceding example is not unique, it seems important to cite a second one, even if the account is a little repetitious. In 1648 the young Louis XIV was only ten years old. The regency was assumed by his mother, Anne of Austria, daughter of King Philip III of Spain. She was aided by the cardinal of Mazarin, who was her prime minister. Of Italian origin, he gained his rapid ascension thanks to the protection of Richelieu; but in 1648 he was extremely unpopular. The arrest of Broussel, a respected and popular member of the Parlement, gave the signal for revolt (Lavisse 1905, p. 38). The shout of "M. Broussel is arrested" left the district of Grève (alongside the Seine, the current location of the town hall), where he resided, and spread to the hundreds of boats moored to the banks as well as to the bridges lined with houses. The chains that served at night to block the street-ends were drawn. A wave of barricades rose up in the vicinity of the Royal Palace, a kilometer to the west. The following day, August 27, by order of the regent the city, the militia took up arms. With most of the militia companies under the command of the parliamentarians, it is hardly surprising that they sided with the rebels. The troops of the king's house, the French Guards, were very small in number. Billeted with the local population, they were quite bound to them (as would be true in 1789 as well). The Guards declared that they would not fire on the people.

The regent ordered Broussel to be set free. The Parlement, however, maintained the state of turmoil; waiting for the arrival of troops from Flanders, Mazarin led the royal court to Rueil situated, 14 kilometers to the west of the capital.

What can be retained from this episode? We see that periods of regency, marked by a weakening of the crown, are particularly favorable to revolts. Also evident is the important role played by the bourgeois militia, as well as its close connection to the Parlement. This militia was obviously a rather unsafe army for the government, but it was difficult to manage without it because of its ability to enforce public order; this is certified by various foreign examples (Geneva, Brabant).

To finish, it is necessary to stress that, in addition to the experience of 1968 already cited, the scenario of a barricade insurrection is repeated many times, for instance in 1830 and 1848. A contemporary observer described as follows a scene in Paris during the insurrection of February 23–24, 1848: "The whole district of the Sorbonne was aroused. Along the length of the boulevards trees were cut down, carts were reversed and heaped cobblestones completed these improvised battlements . . . The National Guards clashed courageously but in vain against the tremendous barricade of the rue du Petit-Pont. Finally that evening an attack of the regular troops overcame this terrible obstacle" (*Annuaire historique universel* 1848, pp. 83, 226).

Offensive Insurrections

By their audacity and their mobility the Parisian insurgents of 1789 differed greatly from the cases already considered. In fact, the real question one should ask is: why did they not construct barricades? They took the Invalides and the Bastille, entered the royal apartments (October 5, 1789), and brought the king back to Paris. These are actions that go far beyond the static demonstrations that we described in the preceding section. Do precedents for such bold behavior exist? The answer is yes, but in order to find them it is necessary to go quite far into the past, to a period where the royalty did not yet have the authority that it would acquire thereafter .

PARISIAN INSURRECTIONS UNDER ETIENNE MARCEL (1357, 1358)

The historical context of these events has already been described in the discussion of the Estates-General of 1356–1357. One may recall that the northwest of France was occupied by English troops who kept King John II captive (he would be set free only in 1560). Our account of the popular insurrection relies essentially upon the *Grandes chroniques de France*, written by a contemporary, Pierre d'Orgemont, and on the chronicles of Froissart; for a more detailed discussion of the sources one can refer to Mollat and Wolff (1970, p. 117).

Etienne Marcel's influence came from his membership in the high Parisian bourgeoisie; his father was a rich cloth merchant and his mother belonged to the family of a king's aide. The first example of this alliance between the bourgeoisie and the artisans seems to have taken place on January 19–20, 1357, with the return of the dauphin from a trip to Metz where a diet of the Holy Empire had been held. Paris had an appearance of a city in a state of siege; the merchants had stopped their work and the provost, Etienne Marcel, had asked everyone to arm himself. Marcel went around the city accompanied by armed people, and it was such a procession that welcomed the dauphin upon his return. In the background the struggle continued between the king of Navarre, supported by Marcel, and the royalty. Another episode of this confrontation took place on February 23, 1358. On this day the royal apartments were invaded by the crowd and two marshals were killed. It seems that their execution had been decided in advance (Coville 1902, p. 127); they were apparently suspected of wanting to side with the English. The first was executed in the room of the dauphin, the second was executed after having been chased from bedroom to bedroom. Marcel explained to the dauphin that his marshals had been executed by the will of the people, and he obtained a pardon. On February 23 the dauphin promised a new purge of the king's council in order to introduce some of the bourgeoisie there. But while having to yield to force, the dauphin was preparing his revenge. On March 14, 1358, he took the title of regent and thereafter sought to leave Paris, where he was a semiprisoner of the insurrection. A first attempt on March 19 failed, and one of his horsemen was beheaded for his participation in the plan. During a second attempt, on March 27, he succeeded in leaving the city. It must be noted that the agitation had also seized some of the provincial towns, especially Amiens, Arras, and Toulouse. But in other cities the dauphin (now regent) was sure to be able to find support, especially in Senlis, where he went after leaving Paris.

It may also be of interest to note that there were similar movements at about the same time in Bohemia, Denmark, and Italy (see in this respect Langer 1968, Macek 1984).

What to conclude from this episode? First of all it is necessary to stress that the analogies of this movement with the French Revolution have puzzled many historians (compare Mollat and Wolff 1970, p. 116). This parallel shows the extent to which the royal authority was weakened on October 5, 1789; on this day the crowd once more took up the practices that had previously only been possible in exceptional circumstances: military defeat, partially invaded territory, captive king. Next notice that once the whole population was armed, it became an extremely difficult force to control by usual police means. Finally, note that by not leaving Versailles for the provinces, Louis XVI certainly deprived himself of a card that Charles V had played skillfully in 1357.

THE REVOLT OF THE CABOCHIANS (APRIL 27, 1413)

To show that the preceding episode too is not unique, we consider another that occurred over fifty years after the 1357 insurrections. In 1413, once again the country was in chaos. King Charles VI (1380–1422) had since 1392 been subject to frequent crises of madness; and the dauphin, the future Charles VII, was only ten years old. The kingdom was torn by a civil war between the Duke of Orléans and the Duke of Burgundy, the latter allied with England. Paris was primarily under the control of the Duke of Burgundy; the royal government was torn between the two parties. This situation was comparable to that experienced in England forty years later during the Wars of the Roses (1455–1485) between the Lancastrians (who chose the red rose as their emblem) and the Yorkists (who chose the white rose).

On April 27, 1413, a crowd with the followers of the Duke of Burgundy and the leader of the butchers, Caboche, at its head appeared in front of the residence of the king and the dauphin. The doors were broken and the palace invaded. Three of the king's retinue were killed and fifteen others were taken prisoner. On May 11 the crowd once again invaded the royal apartments. On this day, with the return of the king to health, there seemed to be a moment of respite. As a sign of conciliation Charles VI wore the white chaperon (a bonnet that covers the head and shoulders) of the Parisians and which was the symbol of the Ghent revolution of 1380. But on May 22 a new deputation requested and obtained the dismissal of other royal officials. On May 24 the rebels obtained official recognition, in the form of ordinances, of the measures that they had succeeded in wresting from him. These ordinances were even, on May 26, recorded by the

Parlement. Soon after, however, the bourgeoisie became frightened and toward the end of August drew closer to the king. A reaction commenced. The May ordinances were revoked and, between December 1413 and July 1414, 107 people were banished.

What to retain from this episode? It is noticeable that, as in the preceding episode, the extreme weakness of the crown was linked to rather precise conditions: the sickness of the king, the young age of the dauphin, the alliance of the Duke of Burgundy with the English (in the autumn of 1411 he brought 1,200 English soldiers to Paris). By comparison this episode once again emphasizes the deterioration of the crown's authority in the fall of 1789, even though the king was in good health and there was no external danger threatening the nation. Can this deterioration be explained by the disturbances of the so-called Pre-Revolution?

Disturbances in the Decades Preceding the Revolution
The analysis of prerevolutionary troubles is marked by the brilliant contributions of Rudé (1959, 1964), Egret (1962), and Godechot (1963). These turmoils indisputably contributed to the weakening of the royal authority, but these were only pin-pricks in comparison with the thrusts of 1789. Table 3.4 summarizes the main insurrections that preceded July 1789. These turmoils are of various types. (1) Traditional wheat disturbances related to inflated grain prices were genuinely recurrent phenomena. The last of this sort took place in 1847; see in this respect the enlightening analysis by Louise Tilly (1992). (2) Other agitations were linked to the confrontation between the Paris Parlement and royalty. Those of August 1774 were related to the exile of the Parlement to Troyes. More serious was the turmoil linked to the arrest of two members of Parlement in May 1788. (3) Riots of the workers from the suburbs occurred in 1755 and 1789. By the number of victims these were by far the most serious of all in this period; they resulted in more victims than the storming of the Bastille. There were twelve soldiers killed, mainly from stones thrown from the roofs, because at this time the crowd was still not armed. The number of the victims on the side of the demonstrators is very uncertain: between twenty-five, according to the police report, and several hundred, according to witnesses.

Even though they were all of limited extent, these turmoils belong to the category of offensive insurrections. In none of these cases is the construction of barricades witnessed. Why? The question remains open.

Before we close this section a cautionary remark is required. Table 3.4

Table 3.4 Insurrections in Paris between 1750 and July 15, 1789

Date	Event	Type	Number of deaths	Reference
1750	Revolt of the suburbs			Soria (1987), p. 57
1774, Aug. 25–31	Riot of parlement clercs	P		Pillorget (1977)
1775, May	Food riots ("guerre des farines")	F		Godechot (1965)
1788, May	Parlement riots	P	8	Rudé (1964)
1789, Apr. 27–28	Réveillon riots	L	300 ±200	Soria, p. 76
1789, May 28–June 10	Food riots	F		Godechot (1965)
1789, June 30	Liberation of Gardes-françaises			Soria (1987), p. 111
1789, July 12	Clashes with police		~5	Soria (1987)
1789, July 12	Destruction of toll gates	F		Godechot (1965)
1789, July 13	St. Lazare monastery ransacked	F		Godechot (1965)
1789, July 14	The Invalides invaded		0	Soria (1987), p. 130
1789, July 14	Fall of the Bastille		~100	

Note: F–Food riots; L–Labor riots; P–Riots in connection with Parlement of Paris.

suggests an acceleration of the insurrection process as July 1789 approached. However it is clear that the years 1788–1789 have benefited from much greater attention on the part of historians than earlier, more "ordinary" years. The more attention one gives to the archives, the more the number of observed events tends to increase. As an example we cite the figures reported by Pillorget (1977) for Provence. By descending from the provincial archives to the level of municipal archives he found a great number of insurrectional events:

110 for the period 1660–1715, which is 2.0 per year on average
95 for the period 1715–1774, which is 1.6 per year on average
30 for the period 1774–1787, which is 2.3 per year on average

If there was an acceleration in the eighties, it appears to have been more modest than that suggested by Table 3.4; perhaps the discrepancy is simply due to the fact that the figures refer to different areas: Provence is not Paris. Nonetheless, it should be noted that Provence indeed experienced a major, early wave of antiseigniorial peasant action (for details on this question, see Markoff 1996b).

Popular insurrections certainly were one of the most spectacular and dramatic aspects of the Revolution. Other aspects, though far less spectacular, were no less important. Among them is the confiscation of Church property. Without this step, the Revolution was bound to lose its momentum like a car that runs short of gas. The next section explores this facet in some detail.

The Confiscation of Clergy Property

Are there any precedents in French history for the confiscation of clergy property in 1789–1790? To find these it is necessary to go back to Philip the Fair (1285–1314). Generally there are very few examples of this type in Catholic countries before 1750. But from 1750 onward the examples multiply themselves (Portugal, Austria), indicating the beginning of a new tendency. On the other hand, as shown by Table 3.5, the Reformation provides a long list of operations of this type, so much so that one can say that the Reformation and the confiscation of ecclesiastical property were hand in glove. To explore such confiscations and sales, several questions can be posed:

1. What was the initial share of landed property in the hands of the Church?
2. What types of property were sold? Those of the monasteries, those of the secular clergy, or both?
3. What means of retaliation were available to the clergy?
4. Who were the buyers of ecclesiastical property? This question is of course in direct relation to the size of the plots put on sale.
5. Finally, we should ask ourselves what became of the sold property during possible restorations.

Even if available sources do not allow us to answer these questions in a systematic manner, they nevertheless give an idea of the most current practices.

Confiscations of Ecclesiastical Property at the Time of the Reformation
Luther was fundamentally opposed to monastic orders. He developed his theses in his work "De votis monasticis," published in 1521 (Knowles 1959,

Table 3.5 Confiscation of ecclesiastical property

Date	Country	Type	Reference
350	Roman Empire		Stein (1959)
1314	France	Templars	Mayeur et al. (1990)
1524	Transylvania		Hergenroether (1880), p. 396
1524	Zürich	M	Knowles (1959), p. 67
1526	Hesse		Janssen (1892), p. 59; Wolff (1913)
1527	Sweden	M	Hergenroether (1880), p. 398
1531–1543	Saxe		Hilpert (1911); Kühn (1966)
1536	Denmark		
1536	Würtemberg		Janssen (1892), p. 309
1537–1538	England	M	Knowles (1959); Constant (1930)
1530	Brandeburg		Janssen (1892), p. 440
1641–1643	England		Cahen and Braure (1960); Walter (1963)
1650	Russia	M	Daniel-Rops (1958), p. 259
1770	Austria	M	Daniel-Rops (1958), p. 259
1789–1790	France		
1807–1812	Spain	M	Dulphy (1992)
1834	Portugal		Durand (1992)
1847	Switzerland	M	Keller (1934), p. 511
1837–1856	Spain		Dulphy (1992); Clarke (1906)
1870	Italy	(Vatican land)	
1902	Philippines		Keller (1934), p. 395
1910	Portugal		Durand (1992)
1914	Wales		Williams (1961)

Note: M indicates confiscation restricted to monastery property.

p. 64). True Christian life, he argued, consists of active works of mercy, not in wearing a cowl, shaving the head, scourging oneself, fasting, and repeating sets of prayers. Melanchthon and other Protestant theologians went further and made it a duty for Protestants to confiscate the property of not only the regular clergy (that is, of the monasteries) but also that of the secular clergy. In 1537 Melanchthon wrote: "Our princes are right to abolish in their territories the false cult deep-rooted in the abbeys and convents placed under their jurisdiction; they perfectly have the right to confiscate the incomes of these monasteries. As for the cathedral chapters, the town councils have the right to seize in the interest of religion everything that is necessary for its maintenance" (Janssen 1892, p. 362). Princes and kings hurried to follow this advice, as Table 3.5 shows.

What was the fate of this property during the Catholic restorations? In total the returns to the Church were very rare. In England at the time of the Catholic restoration of Mary Tudor, the three Parliaments of 1553–1554 confirmed for the most part the rights of new owners (Morris 1992, p. 70). In Germany the Edict of Restitution of 1629 claimed to impose on all Protestants having occupied Catholic property since the Peace of Augsburg, that is, for seventy-five years, the requirement that they give back what they had usurped. But this edict seems hardly to have been applied and in 1648 the Peace of Westphalia decided that ecclesiastical properties should belong to those who possessed them in 1624 (Daniel-Rops 1958, p. 163). Hungary experienced a similar restoration edict (April 10, 1560). In France, after the monarchical restoration of 1815 the nobles regained their property but ecclesiastical property remained with its buyers. Spain was one of the rare countries where the confiscations were canceled and the property was returned.

Examples of Confiscation

These episodes present some similarities. From a state perspective, the confiscation came at a time when the temporal power tended to distance itself in relation to the power of the Church. Furthermore, the confiscation could bring a radical solution to severe problems of public debt. Let us examine this latter point first.

It is generally estimated that government debt becomes preoccupying when service of the debt absorbs more than half of the budget. Such was the situation of France in 1789 (see Marion 1976 [1929], p. 60, and the figures given in the previous chapter) or the Netherlands in 1842 (Voogd 1992). At this level of debt the "ordinary" means (increase of taxes, tightening of expenses) are no longer sufficient. More radical means mainly amount to the following: (1) obligatory loans at low rates and conversion of former loans to reduced rates; (2) the creation of money; (3) confiscation of ecclesiastical property; (4) military conquest and expropriation of resources of the occupied territories.

In 1848 the Netherlands used the first means, but it is clear that such a process would not hold favor with the bourgeoisie. Because potential lenders must be placated and their aspirations fulfilled, this policy often has, as a corollary, the granting of a liberal constitution that leads to reliance on large popular support. The English revolution essentially had recourse to the last two means. The French Revolution at first had recourse to the second and the third; then after its radicalization it also had recourse to the first, and finally after 1795 it used the last. However the confiscation of ecclesiastical property constituted the cornerstone for the whole plan of action because it allowed the guaranteeing of the loans and it supported monetary creation. In this way the English Parliament could obtain from the City in October 1646 a loan mortgaged on ecclesiastical property; equally in this way the French Constituent Assembly could issue two billion assignats (paper currency) wagered on the sales of ecclesiastical estates and those of the emigrated nobles. Let us examine these experiences in more detail.

ENGLAND (1530–1540 AND 1641–1643)

In fourteenth-century England there were approximately 1,000 convents; the secular and regular clergy approached 40,000 (Mayeur et al. 1990, p. 661). Around 1530 the estates of the Church were estimated at a quarter of the property wealth of England (Moreau, Jourda, and Janelle 1950, p. 342). These holdings were therefore a potential resource of a considerable extent. Part of this property was confiscated by Henry VIII in the great movement to dissolve the monasteries that followed the Reformation. Then between 1641 and 1650 the property of bishops, chapters, and deans was confiscated. This property was sold in plots of significant size. There were very few of them for less than £900, which was far out of the reach of an average yeoman, whose annual income was around £40 (R. Marx 1971, p. 185).

FRANCE (1307–1314)

At the beginning of the fourteenth century the sovereigns in several countries were expressing their spirit of independence in the face of papal power. This explains the conflict between Louis of Bavaria and Pope John XXII (1316–1334), on the one hand, and, on the other, those between the king of France, Philip the Fair, and the popes Boniface VIII and Clement V. The policy of extension of royal power carried out by Philip the Fair required significant financial resources. A first conflict was provoked by the taxation that Philip the Fair imposed on ecclesiastical property; a second, rather more serious, resulted from the king's attack on the Knights Templars. It is estimated that the Knights had 1,170 establishments and sources of income in France. When the order was finally abolished by the pope on May 3, 1312, it was prescribed that its property be transferred to the Hospital of Saint John of Jerusalem (the future Order of Malta). It is difficult to tell in what measure this prescription was respected by Philip the Fair.

A FAILED CONFISCATION: FRANCE (1561)

In 1561, after decades of war in northern Italy against the Habsburg monarchy, France's public debt amounted to more than three times the annual revenue, with the service of the debt absorbing 16 percent of the budget (Romier 1924). The Estates-General were summoned to find a solution to the financial crisis. But instead of granting tax increases, they made the following recommendations to the king (Major 1954). First, the king should take the revenue of all ecclesiastical benefices that were not actually administered by the holder, and an income tax should be levied on the possessors of other benefices. Second, the surplus revenues of all monastic orders should be confiscated. Third, permission was granted to the king to confiscate part of the temporal goods of the clergy. The king, as it turned out, did not follow these recommendations. Instead the clergy made a "free gift" that over the next eight years represented about 8 percent of the budget.

Although there was no confiscation on a national scale, there was nevertheless a substantial wave of confiscation in the Languedoc as documented by Le Roy Ladurie (1966). In the dioceses of Agde and Montpellier, for example, the sales of confiscated property represented 3 to 5 percent of the clergy's estates.

Why did King Charles IX not follow the tempting advice of the Estates-General? The reason is obvious. In previous decades the Reformation had secured a strong position among the aristocracy and in many cities; therefore there were only two possible options: either to follow the example of England, Denmark, and Sweden and accept the Reformation, or to remain on the side of Catholicism. Since Charles IX favored the second option, it was out of the question to confiscate the Church estates at that time.

Another failed confiscation occurred in 1764, when the Society of Jesus was dissolved in France. Its property, which was estimated at 53 million livres (Crétineau-Joly 1859), was used to create a fund that allowed former Jesuits to be paid a pension of one franc per day.

FRANCE (1789)

On October 10, 1789, the bishop of Autun, Talleyrand, addressed the National Assembly in the following terms: "The state has for a long time been grappling with the greatest needs, which none of us ignores. It now needs great means to meet them. The ordinary means are exhausted, the people are squeezed from all sides. For the future it needs an immense and decisive resource. This resource appears to me entirely in ecclesiastical property" (Bourgain 1890, p. 229). His language at least had the merit of clarity. To better measure the audacity of this proposal, it is necessary to go back a little. In 1749, to prepare for the levying of a 5 percent tax on the clergy's wealth, the government had wanted to carry out a survey of Church property. This led to a two-year crisis as the Church balked, and in 1751 the project had to be abandoned. A new attempt in 1780 came up against the same resistance. Another example of this resistance is provided by the assembly of the clergy of May 1788. One of its roles was to determine the amount of the "free gift" granted to the government; this gift was a substitute for the tax to which the clergy was not subjected. The government had asked for 8 million livres; the assembly only granted 1.8 million and vigorously reaffirmed its fiscal immunities (Egret 1962). In October 1789 the amount at stake was no longer 8 million livres but a sum that bordered on 2.5 billion livres, the estimated amount of ecclesiastical property (Lecarpentier 1908, p. 113). In terms of landed property, this corresponded to approximately 6 percent of the country's total territory or 13 percent of plowable lands and meadows (*Statistique de la France* 1837, p. 98).

At the time of the sale of national property seized from the Church, the plots were put within reach of the average bourgeoisie. Drawing on polls in various departments, Lecarpentier has established that in 1790–1791 the average area of a sale was 11 hectares. In the next few years this average regularly declined and then stabilized: 1792, 4 hectares; 1793, 3 hectares; 1794, 0.75 hectares; 1796, 0.80 hectares. Four-fifths of the sales were completed before 1793.

In making the seizures, the Revolution only followed the example of the Protestant countries during the Reformation. Without the confiscation of ecclesiastical property the Revolution would have rapidly sunk into bankruptcy.

SPAIN

It was Charles IV (1788–1808) who took the first measures of confiscation in Spain. He used the property of the banished Jesuits to reduce the national debt; he also expropriated charitable institutions and religious guilds. Rome's assent was solicited only after the deed was done. After 1808 large sales of church property were carried out by Joseph Bonaparte. At the restoration in 1814, the measures were rescinded (Clarke 1906). Later, in 1820, when the liberals suppressed half of the tithe, the pope withdrew his nuncio. In 1835 (July 20), as soon as it was known that the government had broken with the Church and had decreed the suppression of all religious houses of less than twelve persons, the Radicals led the mob to assault the convents; ecclesiastics were killed at Saragossa. Following this turmoil, however, the government was thrown out of office. When on March 22, 1836, the Cortes decided to expel the regular clergy and confiscate their property, the House of Notables voted that the plan's execution be suspended at least for some time.

By 1843 only about half the property (worth 60 million pounds) was still to be sold. A new law stated that it should be sold by auction in small parcels so that the poorer people would be able to buy them. There was much resistance: the pope broke off diplomatic relations; the bishops who protested were exiled; attempted riots had to be suppressed. In 1856 the sales were still not finished, and it is highly likely that the support brought by Queen Isabella II (1843–1868) to the party of O'Donnell against the progressives was motivated by a concern to save what remained of the property not sold. On September 23, 1856, the decree of confiscation was suspended.

CONCLUSION

The preceding examples provide insight into the mechanism of the confiscation process. At the onset the clergy, which represented on the order of 1 to 2 percent of the population, held approximately one-fifth of landed property. When the confiscation of this property took place in the framework of a powerful movement such as the Reformation or the Revolution of 1789, it raised less resistance than in countries such as Spain or Portugal where it was stretched out to nearly a century. The sales essentially profited whichever social class whose support was the most necessary to the movement: the landowner aristocracy in England, the average bourgeoisie in France, the peasantry in the middle of the nineteenth century in Spain. Our analysis has left out the case of Italy, which is unique to the extent that the question of ecclesiastical property was coupled with that of the papal estates. The question was not settled until the Lateran Treaties of 1929.

We now turn to the last episode of the Revolution to be analyzed in this chapter. Together with the Terror (1793–1794) it is one of the darkest pages in the history of the Revolution.

The Summary Executions of September 1792

Why have we chosen to study the summary executions of September 1792? In contrast to the three other episodes examined, this one does not in the least constitute a major stage of the Revolution, but rather a tragic chapter. The events rapidly became a point of obsession with which partisans and adversaries of the Revolution confronted each other. The former tended to minimize what happened, the latter tended to amplify it and to put the blame on the Parisian population, the revolutionary leaders, and the revolution itself. Our objective is twofold here. We seek, on the one hand, to show that only a patient and systematic study of the sources can settle this type of debate; on the other, to stress, as Bloch (1974 [1949], p. 119) said so well, that the historian should avoid any expression of blame, praise, and generally any moral judgment. "History," says Bloch, "by preferring the compilation of honor rolls to that of notebooks, has given itself the appearance of the most uncertain of disciplines." More specifically, we show that the circumstances of September 1792, namely (1) a vacancy of power, (2) a climate of civil war and a thirst for reprisals, and (3) an external peril, have in the course of history often aroused the same tragic acts elsewhere. First we briefly recall the events, then we mention the misrepresentations to which they have given rise. Finally we draw a parallel with events that have occurred in similar conditions.

What Happened?

HISTORIANS' CURRENT VIEW

In September 1792 the Revolution had more than three years behind it. Despite his escape on June 22, 1791, Louis XVI had made a pretense of playing the role of constitutional monarch reserved to him by the constitution of 1791. However the danger of an external intervention was becoming clear. The troops of the Duke of Brunswick approached from the East. On August 1, 1792, the duke published his declaration demanding the submission of all Frenchmen to their king and threatened Paris and the rest of France with severe reprisals if this were not the case. On August 10 the Tuileries were taken and the king deposed. The assault left 400 dead among the assailants and more than 1,000 in the king's guard. Executive power was placed in a provisional council, but with the constitution no longer able to function, there was a legal vacancy of power. There were several opposing decision centers: the Legislative Assembly, at the end of its course (it would be replaced on September 21 by the National Convention) and no longer possessing great power; the provisional council that had no legality; and finally the council of the insurrectionary Paris commune. On August 30 the Assembly tried to quash the council of the commune, but the latter entered into open rebellion. At the same time, at the end of August the external threat approached. On August 23 Longwy (260 kilometers northeast of Paris) was taken; on September 2 it was the fall of Verdun (220 kilometers from Paris). Therefore at the beginning of September the three elements that we have cited—vacancy of power, climate of civil war, and external peril—all combined.

Between September 2 and September 5 approximately 1,300 convicts were executed in ten Parisian prisons after sentences whose summary character varied from one prison to another. The percentage of convicts killed varied from 97 percent for the prison of Les Bernardins to 12 percent for that of La Salpétrière, or 1 percent for that of La Petite Force. Among the victims the largest category was that of common criminals (70 percent): assassins, grain monopolizers, forgers of assignats, and so on. Among the political prisoners the most targeted category was that of refractory priests. Few women were killed (3 percent), a notable exception being the Princess de Lamballe, an intimate friend of Marie Antoinette and considered the moving spirit behind her treason (for more detail, see the 1933 biography of Marie Antoinette by Stephan Zweig).

HISTORIANS' EARLIER VIEWS

From the point of view of historiography, this episode constitutes an excellent case and deserves a detailed discussion. In many popular disturbances it is almost impossible to know the number of the victims, even in an approximate way. Consider the Gordon Riots that took place in England in June 1780. In protest against the measures of partial tolerance with respect to Catholics, large crowds looted and burnt buildings for six days; these assaults were not limited to Catholic targets, for even the Bank of England building was attacked. On June 7, the last day of the riots, there were approximately thirty-six fires in London (Godechot 1965). Probably most of the wounded and the dead were carried away by the rioters so as to avoid subsequent prosecutions (after the events twenty-five people were condemned to death and hung). Thus the official toll of 285 dead (Rudé 1964) can only be very partial. This is confirmed by the fact that most recent accounts report higher figures: Burne (1989), Palmer and Palmer (1992), and Carruth (1993) give 500, 850, and "over 800" persons killed, respectively (unfortunately in none of these books is there any indication of the source). Thus there is a 1:3 margin of uncertainty. Considering the fact that the riots lasted almost a week and, as is made clear in Lecky's (1892) vivid description, involved a large number of people, such uncertainty is not surprising. In fact, if it were available, the number of soldiers killed in action would probably be the only reliable figure. The indication of 285 deaths comes from a report issued by General Amherst shortly after the suppression of the revolt; for lack of adequate sources the actual figure will probably never be known.

In the case of the events of September 1792 the situation regarding the evidence is not at all the same. The persons killed were prisoners whose names figured on prison registers. In particular the number of victims could not be greater than the total population of the prisons, which was on the order of 2,500 (Bluche 1986). Furthermore, for a great number of prisons, the registers also mentioned the fate of the prisoners. This allows the establishment for each prison of a relatively precise statistic for the number of victims.

As shown by Table 3.6, fairly realistic figures were published in the first few years following the episode. Despite this, estimations exceeding ten times these figures were published thereafter. Let us make it clear that these estimations have not appeared in controversial documents but in the works of historians. A particularly illuminating case is the publication of Berville and Barrière in 1823. These two historians had acquired a certain notoriety by publishing the memoirs of important actors in the Revolution: Dumouriez, Fréron, Bailly, and so on. Their work relative to September 1792 is of the same type; it concerns the memoirs of a convict, Jourgniac de Saint Méard, who witnessed the executions but was liberated himself. Although his text published in 1792 contained no estimate of the numbers of persons killed, Berville and Barrière have reported it as having quoted a precise assessment for each of the prisons; these figures exceed the real figures (as well as the total numbers of prisoners) by a factor varying from five to sixty (Carron 1935; Bluche 1986). Generally, it is interest-

Table 3.6 Estimates for the number of deaths in the executions of September
1792

Date of publication	Number of deaths reported	Reference	Page
1792	No figure given	Jourgniac de Saint Méard	
1793	12,000	Barruel (Abbé)	298
1794	1,089	Maton de la Varenne	460
1797	9,000 ± 1000	Des Odoards	28
1796–1797	1,433	Prudomme	108
1799	15,000	Crommelin	198
1801	4,000	Lacretelle	411
1802	6,000	Molleville	298
1823	13,000	Berville and Barrière	
1827	2,500	Montgaillard (Abbé)	
1840	966	Maurice	
1860	1,458	Granier de Cassagnac	487
1863	1,368	Mortimer-Ternaux	548
1907	10,000	Boysson	175
1935	1,242 ± 150	Carron	
1986	1,327 ± 80	Bluche	254

Sources: Caron (1935), p. 77; Bluche (1986).

ing that the publication of inflated figures came either from ecclesiastics or coincided with periods of restoration (1799–1802, 1823, 1827). One might despair of historical objectivity if there were not several noteworthy exceptions. Thus Maton de la Varenne (1794), for example, arrives at an estimate of excellent quality, despite the passionate character of his work; his antirepublican political affinities are clearly revealed by the title of his book.

In French historiography the events of September 1792 are known under the name of the "September massacres." We purposely avoided using the term "massacre" here. In three prisons it was indeed a matter of massacres, but in the other seven, summary judgments would be a more appropriate term. In support of this assertion there are two types of evidence: the proportion of prisoners killed and the duration of the operation. In three prisons the proportion is greater than 80 percent and the duration less than a few hours (Bluche 1986, pp. 99, 193). In the others the proportion is less than 70 percent and the duration ranges from six to forty-eight hours. The indications that emerge from these figures are confirmed by testimonies and reports (Bluche 1986, p. 62).

Analysis of Similar Events

The conjunction of a vacancy of power, a climate of civil war, and external peril have often led to summary executions of prisoners. We give some examples in this section.

PARIS (1418)

This episode took place at the time of the civil war that for several years opposed the party of the Duke of Orléans and that of the Duke of Burgundy. In the spring of 1418 the Duke of Orléans was master of Paris, but the Parisian population was increasingly unwilling to support his heavy yoke (Coville 1902, p. 374). On the night of May 28–29, a troop of Burgundians succeeded in entering the city and with the assistance of the Parisian militia, gained control of it. Some of the Duke of Orléans's supporters were massacred, others were imprisoned. All this took place in the face of a foreign threat as the English troops of Henry V advanced into Normandy. Alençon (160 kilometers west of Paris) had been taken on October 23, 1417. In Paris a return of the Duke of Orléans was feared. On Sunday, June 12, 1418, the alarm was given at several of the city gates. Bands formed, at the head of which the butchers placed themselves (as in 1413). These bands went to the different prisons of the city and killed the supporters of the Duke of Orléans. The Burgundian leaders let this happen. There were approximately 1,600 victims.

WARSAW (1794 AND 1831)

On May 3, 1791, a new constitution was proclaimed in Poland that abolished the liberum veto, that is, the right of each delegate to call for the dissolution of the diet. The abolition of this clause, which had hitherto paralyzed the Polish state, was very badly received by Russia. In the autumn of 1794 Warsaw was besieged by the Russian army. It is under these conditions that those opponents to the regime of 1791 who were in prison were taken out to be hung after a summary sentence. Among them was Bishop Massalski (Beauvois 1995, p. 182).

A similar episode took place in August 1831. After the division of the country in 1794 the czar took the title of king of Poland, and Russian troops occupied Warsaw. On November 29, 1830, they were driven away by an insurrection that then remained in control of the city for nearly a year. Following the military reverses the Polish generals Jankowski and Bukowski were tried for treason. Although acquitted by the military court they remained in prison. On the night of August 15, 1831, while Russian troops besieged Warsaw, these generals and their co-prisoners were pulled from their prison and killed by the crowd.

CARACAS (FEBRUARY 1814)

In August 1813, during the war for independence in Venezuela, Bolivar took Caracas, but the city was threatened by royalists after their victory at Villa de Cura. Thus one has a situation very similar to the one in Paris in September 1792: (1) a climate of civil war and a vacancy of power; (2) an external peril, the Duke of Brunswick in one case, General Boves in the other. Not surprisingly the effect was similar. Between February 14 and 16, 1814, about 800 royalist prisoners were executed in Valencia, La Guaria, and Caracas. This number represents 0.1 percent of the population of Venezuela, then about 800,000 (Delaunes 1969).

ANTIDRAFT RIOTS IN NEW YORK CITY (JULY 1863)

As the Union became increasingly desperate for manpower during the Civil War, the draft was introduced by the Conscription Act of March 3, 1863. But because it allowed the wealthy to avoid service by paying $300 to the government or by hiring a substitute, it fell on the poorest people. From July 11 to July 14 as many as 50,000 antidraft rioters turned their wrath on the blacks who the rioters felt were responsible for their conscription. Altogether (rioters, blacks, and police) about 1,000 persons are reported to have been killed (Clodfelter 1992; Carruth 1993). Once again, this situation was fairly similar to that of September 1793: (1) a civil war was going on; (2) there was a "clear and present" danger at least for the people called to draft; (3) there was the presence of powerless scapegoats, political opponents in one case, blacks in the other.

To the same category belong the race riots that occurred during the Reconstruction period in the South; for instance in Memphis (1866, forty people, mostly blacks, killed) or in New Orleans (1866, thirty-seven people killed). Here again the mechanism is similar: (1) a climate of post-civil war and a vacancy of power; (2) the presence of scapegoats. Only the danger, alleged black conspiracies, was in this case more self-suggested than real.

PARIS (1871)

Reviving the insurrectional commune of 1792 and 1848, a revolutionary government was formed in Paris in 1871. It refused to accept the authority of the government installed at Versailles. After a long siege, an assault was launched by the Versailles troops in May 1871. Opponents to the Commune found themselves in the Parisian prisons. Faced with the advance of the Versailles troops, some of them were considered as hostages guaranteeing the lives of the prisoners detained by the Versailles forces. Between May 23 and 28 a hundred of them were pulled from their prison and executed, often under popular pressure (Serman 1986).

Paronymic Repetitions of the Revolution of July 1789 in Nineteenth-Century Paris

So far we have showed the roots connecting the Revolution of July 1789 to the past; but one can also invert the perspective and look to the future. In fact the Parisian revolution of 1789 has also served as a model; when one analyzes the revolutionary events that took place in Paris during the nineteenth century, one finds a large number of the mechanisms that were at work in 1789. The repression of the Paris Commune in 1871 marks the end of an era: after 1871 Paris lost its revolutionary capacity. Although there were still some attempts of this type, notably in February 1934 and May 1968, the repertoire (to use Charles Tilly's language) was no longer the same and success was not again achieved.

In this section, we briefly examine the development of the five revolutionary episodes summarized in Table 3.7. As in the rest of this chapter, our attention will be concentrated not on the "causes" of these events or on their political significance, but on the "how"; we will see in particular that from one episode to the other the means employed are very similar.

Invariant Elements

Schematically one can say that in order for a revolution in nineteenth-century France to be successful, the movement first had to take place in Paris and secondly needed the following factors: a troop, arms, and a command center. The troop would be the National Guard. It was a unit recruited

Table 3.7 Nineteenth-century revolutionary episodes in Paris

Year	Month	Result
1830	July	Charles X replaced by Louis-Philippe
1848	February	Establishment of the Republic and universal male suffrage
1848	June	Defeat of the movement; repression
1870	September	Fall of the Second Empire and proclamation of the Republic
1871	May	Defeat of the movement; repression

mainly from the bourgeoisie and one with rather liberal inclinations, since its officers were elected by the troop. Incidentally, note that most European countries had troops of this type. In Britain, for example, it was the "militia" that was reorganized by the Militia Act at the beginning of William Pitt's government in 1757. It had the dual role of being a second line of defense in the case of a foreign attack and of serving to repress popular revolts.

The participation of the National Guard on the side of the rebels was a sine qua non for the success of every insurrection as shown by Table 3.8: putting aside that of 1871, every insurrection supported by the National Guard has been successful. Regarding the only exception, moreover, note that before the May 1871 confrontations there had been a considerable number of defections in the National Guard: of 260 battalion leaders, 60 had left Paris. In some cases, as in February 1848, the National Guard operated practically alone. In most cases, however, the active participation of the population of the worker districts of eastern Paris was indispensable (Figure 3.2). The workers needed arms which could be taken at the Invalides as well as in smaller weaponries. Finally, to coordinate the movement it was necessary to have a center of command and means of communication. In each of the episodes that we analyze the center of command was the Hôtel de Ville, the Paris town hall, also not far from the working-class district of Faubourg St.-Antoine (see Figure 3.2). At the beginning of each movement this building was occupied by a committee that foreshadowed the provisional government. The means of communication and information was the tocsin, the church bells, and the newspapers.

With these elements in place, a revolutionary episode would take place according to the general scheme summarized in the following section.

Table 3.8 Revolutionary episodes in Paris, 1789–1871

	1789 (July)	1830	1848 (Feb.)	1848 (June)	1870 (Sept.)	1871
Outcome	Success	Success	Success	Defeat	Success	Defeat
National Guard on the rebels' side	Yes	Yes	Yes	No	Yes	Yes–No
Occupation of the Hôtel de Ville	July 9, 16, 30	July 30	Feb. 24		Sept. 4	Jan. 22
Mediators between the rebels and the government	Bailly, Lafayette	Lafayette, Lafitte	Lamartine Ledru-Rollin		Trochu	
Construction of barricades	No	July 28	Feb. 23–24	June 23–26	No	Mar. 18 May 21–28
Origin of arms and ammunition	French Guards; Invalides (July 13); Bastille (July 14)	Invalides (July 28)	National Guard		National Guard	National Guard and guns from the siege of Paris
Anticlerical events	Nationalization of Church property	Attack on the archbishop's palace and the Jesuit mission, July 28–29				24 priests executed in reprisals, May 26–27
Deaths:						
Troops	50	200	70	1,600		880
Rebels	100	1,800		4,000		30,000

Source: For the number of deaths, see *Quid* (1997).

Note: There is an almost complete correlation between the success and defeat of the movement and the participation of the National Guard on the side of the rebels. In every movement, furthermore, the first stage was the occupation of the Hôtel de Ville (the town hall).

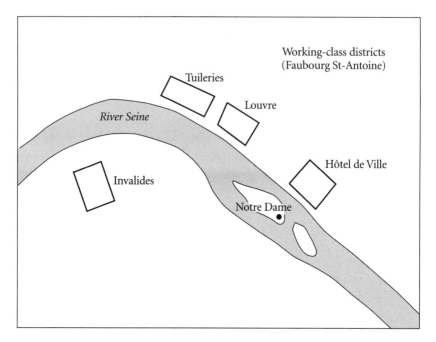

Figure 3.2 Schematic map of Paris in the nineteenth century. The Hôtel de Ville was the center of revolutionary power; the Tuileries were the residence of the king (1815–1848); the Invalides were an important arms depot; the area of the Faubourg St-Antoine was inhabited by artisans and workers. It is particularly important to realize that the Invalides (which was ransacked on July 13, 1789) is on the left bank of the river Seine while the working-class quarters are on the right bank. The fact that the demonstrators were able to cross the bridges (which can be easily blocked by troops) highlights the powerlessness of the monarchy on the day before Bastille Day. By contrast, the Invalides were not ransacked either in 1830 or in 1848. Note that the Hôtel de Ville, the very center of the revolutions, is located in the vicinity of the working-class area (and is of course on the same bank).

Unfolding of a Generic Episode

Insurrections in Paris did not break out like a clap of thunder in a serene sky. They were preceded by smaller movements either in France (such as those of June 3, 1820; March 4, 1823; April 19 and November 20, 1827; June 5–6, 1832; May 12, 1839) or abroad, in particular before 1848.

The first stage of the generic insurrection was often (1789 was an exception) the erection of barricades, in particular through the cutting down of trees along the main boulevards, a practice that would be resumed in 1968. A decisive stage was reached when the first confrontations yielded the first martyrs to the insurgent population. The bodies of these victims were then paraded in carts along the streets of Paris while the alarm bells sounded and the revolutionary chants rang out: the "Choeur des Girondins," the "Parisienne," and the "Marseillaise" (which only became the national anthem in 1879). At the same time, the National Guard occupied the Hôtel de Ville and a provisional committee was formed ready to assume power when the king or emperor abdicated.

In terms of military strength the balance of power was always largely in favor of the government, at least until some regiments crossed over to the side of the insurrection. A determining element in this respect was the geographic origin of the troops; those composed of Parisians would have been subjected to the revolutionary contagion and would rapidly become unreliable; in contrast, provincial troops would be much less receptive to revolutionary ideas.

Confronted with the real or assumed threat that the Tuileries would be invaded by the rebels (as in August 1792, 1830, and 1848), the king left Paris and fled to England. Note that there was a symmetry in this situation since England's Charles II, after the execution of his father, and John II, after he was deposed, had taken refuge in France. After the departure of the king, the insurrection was triumphant and power shifted from the former government to the provisional government. Note that in 1968 a similar result was thought possible for a time when the newspapers announced on May 30 the departure from Paris of General de Gaulle. In this case, however, it was only a trick and after May 31 the popular movement began to ebb.

All the events that we have just mentioned were confined to Paris; the provinces remained generally peaceful. This gave Thiers the idea of a strategy that he proposed in vain in February 1848, but that he applied in 1871, namely a retreat of the government from Paris to St. Cloud or Versailles, then the concentration of troops from the provinces and the reconquest of Paris. The big disadvantage of this method was that it gave a free hand to the insurrection and consequently rendered the reconquest very expensive in terms of human lives.

Summary and Conclusion

A commonly used subdivision in French history is to distinguish the period before 1789, the so-called ancien régime, from the period after 1789. In this chapter we have tried to show that some of the major events that shaped the Revolution have deep roots in the distant past. Stated in a general and fairly philosophical way such an assertion would be almost a tautology. After all, is it not obvious and self-evident that history is a continuum and that each event in some ways depends upon previous ones? But our objective in this chapter was more specific and more ambitious. We showed that the parallel with similar events of the past, far from being restricted to overall meaning and general significance, actually extends to countless practical details. Seen in this way, the analogies that we highlighted cease to be a matter of personal judgment and opinion and become truly testable. Let us recall some of our main conclusions.

1. The meeting of the Estates-General in May 1789 with its 1,139 delegates was a complex event. Yet we have shown that the sheer number of delegates from the Third Estate was in itself an important parameter that announced significant changes. In 1614, when there were only 190 delegates from the Third Estate (representing 41 percent of the Estates-General), the Estates-General submitted to the king's directions without much resistance. In 1560 the delegates of the Third Estate had represented 45 percent of the total (even more, according to some sources); they refused to vote new taxes and offered bold counsels to the king regarding the confiscation of Church property. In 1789 there were 581 delegates from the Third Estate (representing 51 percent of the total). Their number certainly helped to convince them that they truly represented the whole nation, a feeling that strongly shaped subsequent events.

2. Regarding the insurrection in Paris we pointed out that there were two distinct repertoires: the static insurrections, which mainly relied on the building of barricades, and the insurrections with highly mobile groups of insurgents (Table 3.3). From the Invalides to the Tuileries and the Bastille their expeditions extended over the whole center of Paris. It has not been sufficiently emphasized that this behavior was quite exceptional in French history. In order to observe similar behavior one has to go back to the fifteenth century.

If, apart from the question of an insurrection's form, one wants to predict its outcome, then the crucial parameter is the attitude of the National Guard. As shown in Table 3.8, success could only be expected when the National Guard was on the side of the insurgents.

3. For each of the other episodes that we considered, namely, the confiscation of Church property and the summary executions of September 1792, we have been able to show that similar events occurred repeatedly

under comparable circumstances. Thus when there is a vacancy of power, a climate of civil war, and an external peril, then one can expect massacres or summary executions of enemies to occur. That regularity has been illustrated by a number of examples.

4. In the last section we have shown that the insurrections of 1830, 1848 (February and June), 1870, and 1871 follow the same pattern. Between these episodes there is another similarity, which is captured in Figure 3.3. It shows that revolutions are usually preceded and accompanied by an upsurge in social interaction. In Figure 3.3 we estimate the level of social interaction through the creation of newspapers. In sociology the press is currently considered an estimator of social communication; Deutsch (1953, 1979) was one of the first to use it in a systematic way. The increase in social communication seems to accompany many forms of social protest: revolutions, as we have just seen, but also general strikes, as will be seen in Chapter 5. In a sense this is not surprising. These movements are fundamentally collective phenomena that need a great degree of social communication to start and develop. The main difficulty is how to measure these effects.

Many of our observations in this chapter tend to emphasize the role of what can be called the collective historical memory. Studying other building blocks would strengthen our conclusions even further. For instance, rural uprisings against feudal lords (which on August 4, 1789, led to the voluntary surrender by the representatives of the nobles of all feudal rights and privileges) followed patterns often observed in previous centuries. This subject has been thoroughly analyzed by Markoff (1996b). He presents, for example, a fascinating chart (p. 301) that shows the daily number of rural uprisings in July–August 1789; there is a sharp peak on July 27, that is to say just one week (the time it took for news from the provinces to reach Paris) before the historic night of August 4.

The reader may object that we have restricted ourselves to episodes for which there are indeed precursors. Had we examined Louis XVI's trial, there would have been no other example in French history. Nevertheless one can posit (an assumption that of course has to be confirmed by a detailed study) that the judicial procedure followed in the case of Louis XVI was modeled on the procedure used previously in other political trials, such as the trial of the Marquis de Fouquet in 1664.

It is precisely in order to answer this kind of objection that in the next chapter we examine an event for which there are no precursors, namely the

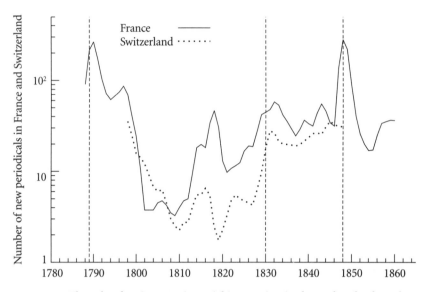

Figure 3.3 The role of an increase in social interaction in the outbreak of revolutions. Social interaction has many facets; many of them, unfortunately, cannot be assessed quantitatively. The diffusion of newspapers certainly reflected the state of ferment that seized a country (here France and Switzerland) prior to a revolution. The graph shows that the number of new periodicals began to increase at least two or three years before the outset of a revolution. This can be observed in 1789, 1830, and 1848. In France there is another peak in 1818 that does not seem to correspond to any large-scale movement. In June 1817, however, there had been several revolutionary disturbances in Sens, Nogent, and Lyon (*Quid* 1997). *Source:* Hatin (1965 [1860]); *Nouvelle histoire de la Suisse et des Suisses* (1983).

American Revolution. It was the first of its kind worldwide; and within the thirteen colonies it is very difficult indeed to find former episodes on which the Revolution could have patterned itself. In other words, for the comparative approach that we champion, the American Revolution presents a real challenge.

4

The American Revolution

The American Revolution seems so unique and unparalleled that it represents a difficult test for comparative history. It is the only colony of the British Empire where colonists demonstrated an unshakable separatist will and that from 1770. This is all the more remarkable when it is put in parallel with other British colonies, such as Canada, Australia, and New Zealand, who are not only currently members of the Commonwealth, but who still recognize the sovereignty of the British crown.

Latin America, of course, presents many examples of countries that have separated from the colonizing nation, Spain or Portugal. But significant contrasts exist between the American Revolution and those that would later take place in Latin America: on the one side, a cohesion and an apparently irresistible march forward; on the other, many faltering revolutions bogged down in civil war and retreats. Such striking opposites in course of the same process of gaining national independence demand an explanation; failing that, they would seem to cast doubt on the basic axioms of our comparative approach.

The challenge is just as serious for longitudinal analysis as it is for cross-national comparative analysis. While in the case of the French Revolution we could identify the movements that foreshadowed what would be the first events of 1789, for the American Revolution it is difficult to find serious precedents underlying what would be the colonies' march to independence. For France, the most convincing precursors arose in the years 1350 and 1413. For the United States the range of past events is obviously smaller, and this limitation may explain the absence of real precedents; perhaps it is necessary to seek them in British history? This route is, however, one that we will leave to a subsequent study. The reader may find interesting parallels between specific regions in Britain and some of the American colonies (for instance East Anglia/New England, South of England/Virginia, North Midlands/Pennsylvania) in a pioneering study by Fischer (1989).

By this brief introduction it will be understood that the American Revolution is not a favorable testing ground for the methods of analytical history. Nevertheless it is important to confront such a difficult case in order to establish the limits as well as the potential of our approach.

In this chapter we concentrate our attention on two specific problems, namely the logistic and military aspects of the War of Independence and the comparison with Latin America. As we have already noted, the latter question can hardly be avoided; as for the first, it is in line with two subsequent chapters devoted to questions of military logistics (Chapters 6 and 7). But before working on these two problems, we will, in the first section, place the start of the American Revolution in the international context of the eighteenth century.

The Triggering of the American Revolution

Where, when, how? These are the three key questions by which all historical events are defined. We first consider why the first War of Independence broke out in North America and not elsewhere; then we examine why the period after 1765 was particularly favorable to this movement. Finally, we explore whether any embryonic building blocks that facilitated the development of the Revolution can be found in earlier American history.

Where?

"This house has all the privileges that the House of Commons has as representative of the people of Great Britain; any instructions of the king or his ministry can neither abridge or annihilate the privileges of the representative body of the people."

In reading this declaration one might believe that it stemmed from an assembly gathered in the thirteen American colonies on the eve of the War of Independence. In reality, this resolution was adopted by the Jamaican assembly in November 1766 (Metcalf 1965, p. 169). Moreover this position was not in the least new; it had been asserted forcefully from the creation of this assembly in 1664. Its first speaker declared in 1680 that "Jamaicans, as Englishmen, ought not to be bound by any laws to which they had not given their consent." Here we find the argument of "no taxation without representation" that would be reiterated by the American patriots in their protest against the Stamp Act. In fact this invocation of the representative principle was common to all assemblies of this type. There was a considerable distance, however, from the rhetoric of principles to the reality of the actual events. To measure this distance, it is interesting to examine the fate of the Jamaican assembly.

Jamaica was a small island that contained less than 13,000 Europeans in 1775; it could hardly be compared to the thirteen colonies, which contained some 2.6 million. Although there were several embryonic revolts against the governor, in particular in 1755 and 1764, it was obvious in London that these movements could not go far. The colonists' desires for greater autonomy were constantly defeated by two unavoidable obstacles: how to ensure the security of the island in the case of either foreign invasion or a slave revolt. In both cases, the Royal Navy and the redcoats of the British army were the only plausible responses. The Jamaican system of assembly was tolerated by the British crown until the middle of the nineteenth century. In 1866, following a state of emergency created by the revolts of former slaves, Jamaica lost its assembly and became a crown colony, in which the governor wielded the only real executive or legislative power. Thus instead of experiencing a gradual evolution to greater autonomy, Jamaica suffered a reverse evolution. It is only in the twentieth century that the representative system was gradually reestablished.

From the point of view of population, Jamaica and the thirteen colonies occupy the two extremes of the range that is summarized in Table 4.1. As can be seen, the most populated countries are also the ones in which the demands for independence were the most advanced. Note that the population figures for the United States and Spanish America cover very different geographic realities: in the first case, a relatively concentrated population; in the second, a population that is disseminated over a whole continent.

Since 1945 we have become accustomed to seeing regions with only a very small population gain independence. The atoll of Nauru in the Pacific, which became independent in 1968 has only 11,000 residents (1996); the archipelago of Saint Kitts and Nevis in the West Indies, which became independent and a member of the United Nations in 1983, has only 50,000 residents (1996). However, this is a relatively recent evolution; in the eighteenth century the rule for "small countries" was to affiliate with larger groupings. Finland, for example, was united with Sweden and Norway

Table 4.1 Populations of European colonists at the end of the eighteenth century

	Independence	Population (thousand)	Year	Reference
Thirteen colonies	1782[a]	2, 600	1775	Howard (1905)
		4, 306	1800	*Hist. Stat. U.S.* (1975)
Spanish America	1816–1826	3, 200	1800	Collier Skidmore, and Blakemore (1992)
Brazil	1822	450	1800	Mitchell (1983), p. 51
Cuba	1899	179	1792	Mitchell (1983), p. 48; *Quid* (1977)
Haiti (Saint Domingue)	1804	100	1784	*Quid* (1997)
Canada (Nouvelle-France)		85	1750	*Quid* (1997)
Puerto Rico		40	1765	Wagenheim (1985)
South Africa		30	1788	Mitchell (1982), p. 41; Ponelis (1993)
Guadeloupe		17	1790	Abenon (1992)
Barbados		16	1790	*Encycl. Brit.*
Jamaica		13	1775	*Encycl. Brit.*
Mauritius (Ile de France)		10	1757	Toussaint (1971)
Réunion Island (Ile Bourbon)		7	1778	Scherer (1980)

Note: Because this chapter focuses on the revolts of colonists, the table gives only the European population. This does not mean that the indigeneous (or half-caste) population did not sometimes play a role. It is true that the main leaders of the liberation struggles in Latin America were of European origin. However in Haiti, the first country in this part of the world to achieve its independence, the revolution was the work of the half-caste population.

a. England accepted the independence of the United States on March 1782.

with Denmark (until 1815). Similarly, the innumerable and often tiny German states were part of the weak Confederation formed by the Holy Roman Empire; after the latter ceased to exist it took only a few decades before the German states formed another federation, the German Empire.

In short, to gain the full independence to which the Americans aspired a country had to have a certain "critical mass." In order to get an estimate of that "critical mass," one can consider the following examples. The Netherlands had a population of about 1.5 million in 1780, Portugal had a population of nearly 2.5 million in 1770, Sweden (with Finland) contained 2.7 million residents in 1780, and Switzerland had 1.5 million in 1780. Moreover, considering that the foreign policy of a "small" country such as the Netherlands or Portugal was in practice subject to British control, one may reasonably assume that the "critical mass" for independence was somewhere between 2.5 and 3 million. Switzerland was under this threshold, but it benefited both from its geographic position and from its long history as an independent entity. With a population of 2.6 million the thirteen colonies, by the standards of the time, were in a good position to form a new state.

Population numbers may have been a necessary condition but they were by no means a sufficient condition. The main question was how a sense of and a desire for unity emerged among the thirteen colonies (for more on this issue, see the interesting discussion by Merrit 1966).

If demographics can explain why the secession movement within the European colonies began in the thirteen colonies, it also brings a first element of response to the question of the date.

When?

STRONG GROWTH OF THE POPULATION

The thirteen colonies experienced swift demographic growth in the second half of the eighteenth century, with their population rising from 1.6 million in 1760 to 2.8 million in 1780 (Kull and Kull 1952). This corresponds to a doubling period of twenty-three years and a growth rate of 3 percent per annum. This very rapid rate was moreover maintained in the following decades, since in 1790 there were 4 million, 7.2 million in 1810, and in 1840, with a population of 17 million, the population of the United States far exceeded that of Britain. Historically an annual growth rate of 3 percent over such a long period is relatively exceptional. For comparison, Egypt, although it experienced steady demographic growth between 1910 and 1995, had an annual growth rate of only 1.9 percent (see Figure 8.2d); in East Africa, one of the regions of the world where the population grows the most rapidly, the rate was 3.1 percent around 1990 (*Quid* 1997). In this way the thirteen colonies could in the space of several decades pass from the stage of a small province, fearing Indian and French encroachments, to that of a large regional power.

It is reported that by learning the terms of the treaty of 1763 that put an end to the Seven Years' War, Vergennes, then French ambassador to Constantinople and future foreign minister of Louis XVI, declared: "I am persuaded England will ere long repent of having removed the only check that could keep her colonies in awe. They stand no longer in need of her protection. She will call on them to contribute toward supporting the burdens they have helped to bring on her, and they will answer by striking off all dependence" (Howard 1905).

This prediction had two parts. One concerned the danger represented by France and Canada, the other related to the consequences of the public debt resulting from the Seven Years' War. The demographic evolution shows that the first danger no longer existed in 1763, even if the war had not detached Canada from France; remember that there were less than 100,000 (French) colonists in Canada, that is, twenty-five times less than in the thirteen colonies. Furthermore, France certainly did not have the means for a significant military intervention on the Mississippi; the best proof is the subsequent failure of the English intervention on the (easier) Atlantic shoreline. Yet the financial side of Vergennes's comment is undoubtedly farsighted, as will be seen later on.

TOWARD NATIONAL COHESION

If the Seven Years' War did not play a large role with regard to the potential danger arising from French Canada, it nevertheless had a crucial influence in the evolution of the thirteen colonies toward unity of action. This war, which lasted in America from 1756 to 1760, in many ways broke down barriers and got people to interact. Legislatures were called upon to discuss similar measures; men from Virginia or Pennsylvania met those of Massachusetts or Connecticut in council, on the march, or by the campfire. The money and troops sent to the North by the southern and less-exposed colonies bred mutual goodwill. The wars against the Indians also played a non-negligible role from this viewpoint. Without going back to King Philip's War (1675–1678), which took place in New England, there was the Cherokee Indian War in the southern colonies in 1759–1761 and especially Pontiac's War in the West in 1763–1764. The latter was the most formidable outbreak of the century. The Indians of the Ohio Valley formed a great confederacy. They captured every western fort, except Detroit and Pittsburgh, and the frontier was ravaged from Niagara to Virginia; hundreds of pioneer families were killed. Although the uprising was crushed by English troops rather than by American militias, a movement of this extent may have contributed to strengthening the sentiment of solidarity between the North and the South.

From demographic expansion to national cohesion, one sees the necessary conditions for a common action gradually put into place. But for history to take the turn that we know it did, there still needed to be triggering

events. This brings us to analyze more closely some of the essential components of the insurrection.

THE OBSTRUCTION OF EXPANSION TO THE WEST

Coming on top of the debt left by the Seven Years' War, the English commitment in Pontiac's War was painful to London. After having conquered
Canada, the English government undertook to extend its limits. This was
done in two stages. By a Royal Proclamation of October 7, 1763, all lands
to the west of the so-called Proclamation Line (Figure 4.1) were closed to
any settlement or purchase. Thus at one stroke the crown swept away every
western land claim of the thirteen colonies. The second stage was the Quebec Act of 1774; this law was promulgated shortly after the Intolerable
Acts, but it had been in preparation for some time before. The act extended
the boundaries of Quebec to embrace the vast country to the west of the
Alleghenies, which constitute the eastern rim of the Appalachians (Figure
4.1). Once again it was a deliberate attempt to discourage expansion of the
colonists beyond the mountains. The Proclamation Line was only an abstract limit that could be modified later; the new frontier with Quebec was
a decision fraught with more consequences, and it is not surprising that
the Americans expressed deep concern.

How? Analyzing Some Building Blocks of the Revolution

As already emphasized, there were no precedents for the large-scale opposition to British rule that characterized the War of Independence. But there
were precedents for some of the events that led to the war. Here we focus
on three of them: the fiscal revolts, the rebellion against governors, and the
American tradition of summoning meetings of delegates from the thirteen
colonies. We first examine how from the Stamp Act of 1765 to the tax on
tea of 1773, via the Townshend Revenue Act of 1767, opposition to fiscal
measures played a primary role in the triggering of the Revolution. Then
we show that revolts against the British governors were a well-established
tradition in the thirteen colonies. Finally, we consider how a nation that
stretched from north to south over nearly 1,400 miles could preserve its
unity during a war that lasted about seven years.

REVOLTS AGAINST STAMP DUTIES

An act to introduce stamp duties in the colonies was passed in May 1765
by the English Parliament by a large majority and almost without debate. It

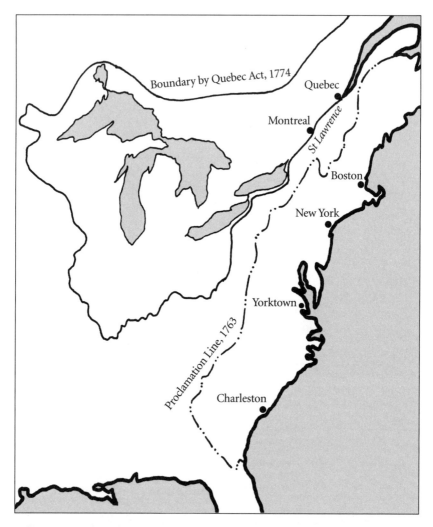

Figure 4.1 Map of northeast America before the American Revolution. All lands to the west of the Proclamation Line were closed to any settlement or purchase. The Quebec Act extended the boundaries of Quebec to embrace a vast country to the northwest of the Alleghenies. *Data source:* Morison (1969 [1930]), p. 126.

seems that the government was very surprised by the outcry that the act provoked in the thirteen colonies: was it not specified that the revenues could only be earmarked for the maintenance of the colonies? Moreover, in other colonies—in Jamaica, for example—there were hardly any protests. Nevertheless a historical examination shows that the revolts against stamp duties were frequent and therefore concerned a sensitive issue.

Stamp duties were a source of fiscal income in both Britain and France. In France, stamp duties date from 1655. At the start the intention was laudable; the duties were intended as a means of standardizing writing styles and avoiding copying errors: this involved making printed forms available to lawyers who would only need to fill in the spaces. In view of the difficulties of applying this edict, in particular because of the varieties of possible clauses, the forms were replaced by blank paper with a printed letterhead consisting of a fleur-de-lis and the name of the province. It is on this type of paper that all official acts had to be written. This reform, which was introduced in 1674, came up against vigorous opposition, mainly in Bordeaux, Nantes, and Rennes. In Bordeaux, the rebellion took control of the city for five days, from March 26 to March 30, 1675. In Rennes, there were disturbances on April 18, April 25, and July 17. The shops that sold stamped paper and tobacco (there had simultaneously been an increase in the taxation on tobacco) were burnt and ten people were killed. On May 3, similar disturbances broke out in Nantes and in the main towns of Brittany. The protests have been called the stamped paper revolt ("Révolte du papier timbré"). As a retaliatory measure for this rebellion, the Parlement of Brittany was exiled from Rennes to Vannes on October 15, 1675; it was not allowed to return until 1689 (Borderie 1975). The decision to exile the Parlement indicates that, as in America, the revolt was supported by the leading citizens.

In 1787 stamp duties only applied to the writing of official acts and yielded only 6 million livres, 1.3 percent of state receipts. An edict of June 1787 aimed to triple this return by applying stamp duties to invoices, posters, newspapers, and so on (Marion 1976 [1929]). Combined with other fiscal reforms, this edict was the starting point of the great parliamentary struggle that would result in the exile of the Parlement of Paris to Troyes in August 1787. It also began an agitation leading two years later to the Revolution of 1789.

A stamp duty extended to newspapers, receipts, and other private deeds was precisely what was introduced in the thirteen colonies in 1765. In Britain, the evolution of this tax was similar to what it had been in France. At the time of its introduction in Britain in 1670, it concerned only certain official documents; then in 1694 a duty was imposed upon paper, vellums, and parchment. The stamp duty on newspapers began in 1711, and every year articles were added to the list upon which stamp duty was made payable. In 1800, stamp duties produced a revenue of £3.1 million in England, 9.8 per cent of total public income (Vincent 1898). Representing nearly one-tenth of the state's income, stamp duties were therefore an important fiscal source and one can understand why Parliament wanted to extend them to the 2 million American subjects.

We have not found any trace of revolts in Britain against stamp duties; nevertheless England had a well-established tradition of fiscal revolt. The revolt against "ship money" and the lawsuit started (and lost) by John Hampden in 1637 may be cited. This rebellion led gradually to the Revolution of 1642. Moreover, after the revolution five of the judges who had delivered judgment in favor of the legality of "ship money" were put in prison (Vincent 1898, p. 994). Another episode of fiscal revolt, less known but just as revealing, took place in 1733. Although this revolt had no longer-term consequences, it shows how concerned the commercial classes can become on such occasions. In 1733 Walpole introduced a plan for an excise tax on wines and tobacco, to be gathered by revenue officers in place of a duty at the ports. The measure was aimed at the extensive smuggling that was affecting this type of revenue. It was vigorously opposed by the commercial classes. Members of Parliament were deluged with letters; popular ballots and pamphlets were thrust under doors; national petitions and meetings were organized throughout the country; doleful images were raised of the tyranny of the excise men. Defeated by such a vehement campaign, Walpole withdrew his reform (*The Sceptred Isle* 1996).

We cite a last example where, as in the United States, a fiscal revolt was the prelude to secession. Portugal had been united with Spain by Philip II in 1580. In the 1630s, supplementary taxes were levied that, added to the other grievances of the Portuguese, resulted in an uprising in 1637. It was suppressed, but a revolution took place three years later that led to the expulsion of the Spaniards and the beginning of a long struggle for Portuguese independence (Ardant 1965, p. 818).

We can retain from the preceding examples that, as a rule, fiscal revolts break out in a sudden manner and spread like wildfire. In two cases (1637 and 1787), they were the prelude to large revolutions. The reaction that this tax aroused in the thirteen colonies is therefore not surprising. It immediately affected a large number of articles, in particular playing cards, pamphlets, and especially newspapers. On October 7, 1765, a month before the law came into effect, the Stamp Act Congress, with delegates from nine colonies, met in New York. A declaration of rights and grievances of the colonists was adopted on October 19. On November 1, the day the Stamp Act was to come into effect, the bells tolled the knell and the flags were at half-mast. In truth, the British government did not have the necessary local personnel in terms of tax officials, police forces, and judges devoted to the crown to enforce this law. Remember that the Navigation Acts, which prohibited direct trade with Europe other than by the intermediary of England, were never really applied. This aroused regular protests of the customs commissioners and English merchants, as for example in 1675 and 1679 (Channing 1908). In the same manner the Stamp Act was hardly applied; indeed, it would be interesting to know what income it yielded in the thirteen colonies during the five months that it was in use. It was abrogated by the British Parliament on March 18, 1766. On February 13, Benjamin Franklin had declared in front of the House of Commons that the Stamp Act could not be enforced. This was only, as we will see, the legacy of decades of laxity. In the absence of local taxes that would pay for them, the crown had not maintained the judicial and administrative personnel in the thirteen colonies that would have been needed, thereby leaving the Americans to become accustomed to de facto autonomy.

REVOLTS AGAINST GOVERNORS

The period 1640–1690 was fertile in revolutions for England. Table 4.2 shows that the American colonies did not tamely follow the regime changes. In 1649, Virginia refused to obey the new power; in 1689, several colonies anticipated events by deposing their governor. There were also several cases where the governors were deposed for reasons of purely local displeasure. What is striking in Table 4.2, however, is the fact that there was little opposition in the period 1690–1750. This period was marked by what has been called the policy of "salutary neglect" in the sense that the British government hardly tried to enforce the English laws. Remember that Walpole, whose government lasted twenty-two years, sought to avoid as much as possible all sources of confrontation and conflict. The clearest result of this policy was a loss of control over the thirteen colonies. As shown by the two following episodes British authority had become purely nominal well before the Revolution.

The first is the *Gaspee* affair in June 1772 in the state of Rhode Island. The *Gaspee* was a British ship that had run aground; attacked by a crowd that overpowered the crew, it was looted and burnt. Lecky (1892) explains why. The mission of the ship was to suppress smuggling, a particularly

Table 4.2 Rebellions against British governors or proprietors before 1750

Year	Colony	Action taken
1635	Virginia	The councillors deposed the governor, Sir John Havey.
1649	Virginia	Assembly condemned execution of Charles I and declared Charles II rightful ruler.
1654	Maryland	Puritans rebelled against Governor William Stone and deposed him.
1676	Virginia	Bacon's rebellion against Governor Berkeley.
1688	Carolina	Assembly refused to accept proprietor's decision.
1689	Maryland	Governor William Joseph overthrown.
1689	Massachusetts	Governor Edmund Andros overthrown by inhabitants of Boston.
1689	New York	Deputy-governor Francis Nicholson overthrown.
1689	North Carolina	The people revolted against a disreputable governor.

Sources: Kull and Kull (1952); Chitwood (1961 [1931]).

flourishing activity in New England; its overzealous captain was detested. A special court was constituted to inquire into the case and turn over to the British Admiralty all persons having participated in the attack. Although these persons were perfectly known in Providence, no evidence could be found against anyone.

A second, more spectacular example is the Boston Tea Party. During this operation, chests of tea to a total value of £10,000 were thrown into the water at the port of Boston (December 16, 1773). One would be wrong to think, however, that this operation was conducted at night by a small group of commandos. In fact, the operation took place in full daylight under the gaze of a crowd that watched the scene. In order to empty the holds of the boats it was necessary to form a chain, and the process took more than an hour. If the participants were disguised as Indians, it was undoubtedly more for derision than disguise; indeed the Tories had nicknamed the Sons of Liberty, the party founded by Samuel Adams, the Mohawks. The fact that it was not possible to bring a single defendant before a court from an affair undertaken in broad daylight made clear that the British authorities did not have the local means to enforce the law. The situation was similar to that experienced by Texas before 1845, when the territory, nominally under Mexican sovereignty, was in fact occupied by an American majority who governed according to their own laws.

DELEGATE ASSEMBLIES

We have already noted how much the conflicts that preceded the Revolution encouraged intermixing and a common awareness. American colonists too deployed great efforts to maintain contact among the thirteen colonies. The organization of meetings and congresses regrouping the delegates of the various colonies was instrumental in that respect. Table 4.3 shows that this method was used on several occasions. But the most judicious debates would have led to nothing without the pressure of circumstances; this is attested by the fact that the "Albany Plan of Union," the work of Benjamin Franklin and Thomas Hutchinson approved by the Albany Congress of 1754, was not ratified by any of the thirteen colonies. At that moment they were simply not ready to give up their autonomy, particularly in the fiscal domain.

In the next section we concentrate our attention on the War of Independence itself. Many of its most dramatic episodes are well known and have become part of world history. We focus on the logistic aspects of the war for two reasons. First, such a vantage point is in line with the subsequent chapters of this book. Second, far from being arid and purely technical, this perspective provides a testimony to the pugnacity of the continental armies, mostly composed of nonprofessional soldiers, to their long marches with guns and equipment, and finally to their victory over a professional (mercenary) army.

Logistic and Military Aspects of the War of Independence

Calhoon (1973) commented about the War of Independence that "patriot leaders in 1775 and 1776 innocently disregarded the practical difficulties of waging war against the greatest military power on earth." Calhoon is in error, for though Britain certainly had the largest fleet in the world, it never had, before the middle of the nineteenth century, a large standing army. All the significant campaigns that Britain led on the European continent were carried out in conjunction with allied troops: Dutch, Austrians, Hanoverians, Hessians, and so on. The English ruling class was firmly opposed to the maintenance of a large permanent army. In this section, we attempt

Table 4.3 Assemblies of delegates before the Revolution

Date	Circumstances
1635, Feb.	Maryland assembly of all freeman convened against the will of Lord Baltimore.
1690, May	Intercolonial congress convened at New York with delegates from the Massachusetts, Plymouth, Connecticut, and New York colonies to plan overland attack upon French at Montreal.
1754, June	Albany Congress, with representatives from New York, Pennsylvania, Maryland, and New England, adopted a plan of union drafted by Benjamin Franklin.
1765, Oct.	Stamp Act Congress with delegates from nine colonies met in New York.
1768, Sept.	Delegates from twenty-six towns in Massachusettes met in Faneuil Hall (Boston).
1774, Sept.	First Continental Congress.

Source: Kull and Kull (1952).

Note: These assemblies played a great role in cementing the unity of the thirteen colonies, a factor that proved essential during the War of Independence.

to throw some light on the military aspect of the War of Independence by comparing it with similar conflicts.

The Opposing Armies

The American colonies were 3,000 miles from England. They had 1,000 miles of seacoast and a territory boundless in extent and resources. From the very beginning British military men thought the enterprise hopeless. In support of this judgment, Van Tyne (1905) cites the assessment made by the British commander in chief. The situation was all the more worrying because the English army had hardly any troops available.

THE ENGLISH FORCES

The English general staff estimated that it needed 30,000 to 50,000 troops to regain New England alone. To see that this is undoubtedly an underestimation, it is sufficient to compare the conquest of Quebec in 1759. For this operation, England committed 12,000 men (Bodart 1908). Yet Quebec had only 80,000 residents, while New England had approximately 1.2 million in 1770, that is, fifteen times more. Although there were some

French troops in Quebec (about 5,000); the main part of the troops was made up by the local militia.

Even if 50,000 men would have been sufficient, how would they be recruited? During the Seven Years' War (1756–1763) Britain had left it to its ally, Prussia, to conduct the operations on the Continent and instead concentrated its efforts on the campaigns in India and Canada. For the American war there were calls upon mercenaries from the Germanic states, in particular the Landgrave of Hesse-Cassel, which had traditionally provided troops to England. In total, the German states provided nearly 30,000 troops (Van Tyne 1905). Once recruited, they needed to be transported to the scene of the war; this was an important logistical problem that we will examine below.

In the second half of the war, Britain increasingly called upon Loyalists, Americans who were opposed to the rupture with the crown. The city of New York, which was the main Loyalist stronghold, alone provided 15,000 men to the British army and navy. (More on British troops in New England can be found in Fischer 1994.)

THE AMERICAN FORCES

On the whole, the battles only brought into play relatively small numbers, five to ten times less than in the principal battles of eighteenth-century European wars (Table 4.4). The size of Washington's army was relatively variable throughout the war. His army reached its first peak of strength with 18,000 men in the summer of 1776, then fell to 5,000 by the end of 1776, rose to 20,000 in mid-1778, and then declined. As can be seen from the dates of the battles, the winter truce was respected. During the winter months, part of Washington's troops returned to their professional occupations. This was a considerable advantage, since it allowed the expense of maintaining the army to be reduced by half; English troops, in contrast, had to be fed and paid even during the winter months.

THE QUESTION OF THE BLOCKADE

Above all, it was by its fleet that Britain dominated the world. Could it not be used to obtain by the blockade what the army could not obtain directly? This means of pressure was in use from March 1774, when the Boston Port Act was passed. It was not, however, a total blockade, since it affected neither food nor heating materials (Lacour-Gayet 1976). In any case, Britain did not have the means to close a coast 1,000 miles long and

Table 4.4 Number of troops involved in the major battles of the War of Independence

Date	Location	Total number of troops
1775, June 17	Bunker Hill	3,200
1776, Aug. 27	Long Island	36,000
1776, Dec. 26	Trenton	3,900
1777, Sept. 11	Brandywine Creek	26,000
1777, Oct. 4	Germantown	25,000
1777, Oct. 16	Saratoga	25,800
1780, Aug. 16	Camden	6,000
1781, Oct. 19	Yorktown	25,000

Sources: Bodart (1908); Clodfelter (1992).

Note: The table gives the number of troops in both camps. In Europe, at about the same time, major battles involved three to five times more troops: for example, for the battle of Torgau (Nov. 3, 1760) between Austrians and Prussians: 110,000; battle of Kunersdorf (Aug. 12, 1759) between Russo-Austrians and Prussians: 118,000. The total number of Americans killed in the major battles of the War of Independence was about 5,000.

containing many important ports. In other conflicts, even selective blockades against the ports of Brest or Alexandria, it proved impossible to prevent the passage of isolated ships.

New York fell practically at the beginning of the conflict and Charleston and Savannah were taken in 1780, but the Americans maintained a sufficient number of other ports. And, by particular irony, the capitulation of Cornwallis at Yorktown that brought the war to an end was precipitated by a blockade imposed by a French squadron.

THE REAL STAKES: AMERICAN COHESION

The Americans were thus in the long term assured of victory, providing that they preserved their cohesion. This cohesion was what was really at stake in the war; to understand this it is sufficient to recall the examples of the wars of independence in Latin America, where rather often a civil war was superimposed on the war against the colonial power. This problem existed in the United States as well, since it has been estimated that between 100,000 and 200,000 Loyalists died, were exiled, or left the country during (or after) the conflict (Howard 1905); this represents about 7 percent of the population. Congress and the local governments knew how to take the necessary measures to preserve unity. What were these measures? Test laws were passed in every state: citizens had to declare before God that the war of the colonies against Great Britain was just and that he would not aid the British forces. During the war, eight of the thirteen colonies formally banished prominent Loyalists. Some who returned were convicted and executed. In January 1776, Congress placed an interdiction upon all speaking and writing against the Patriot cause. In November 1777, Congress approved the confiscation of Loyalist estates. This confiscation was not only a measure of retaliation, but also an important means of financing war. In total, it is estimated that the value of the goods confiscated was at least $36 million (£8 million), which represented ten times the federal budget of 1792 (Calhoon 1973; Kull and Kull 1952; Van Tyne 1905). By its extent this transfer of goods to the state can be compared to the confiscation of the goods of the clergy and noble émigrés during the French Revolution.

Comparison with the Boer War

To estimate what the cost of a victorious war would have been for Britain, we use a real case, the Boer War, for comparison. Of course, as in all comparisons, there are both similarities and differences. We will see, however, that the main parameters are of the same order of magnitude.

COMPARISON OF NUMBERS

During the Boer War, England was opposed not by the whole of South Africa but only by the provinces of Transvaal and the Orange Free State. What was the population of the Boers in these two regions? The question is not easy to answer. The figures for total population are not a great help to us since they also include Africans who were not party to this war, even if they were used by one or the other camp. Even the number of Europeans only gives us incomplete information, because Transvaal contained a large population of English origin, especially in the mining districts. It is not unreasonable to estimate that about half of the population of Transvaal was of English origin, taking as our guide the accounts of contemporary authors who noted that if voting rights had been granted to them (as requested by the English government) they would have had a majority (Hillegas 1899). In 1904 there were 1.12 million Europeans in South Africa (*Quid* 1997); the population of Transvaal and Orange was about 65 percent of the total population of South Africa (Mitchell 1982), which suggests that there were 720,000 Europeans in the two provinces. If we assume (somewhat arbitrarily) that only 70 percent of them sided with the Boers, this results in a population of 500,000 Boers. It is therefore a population five times smaller than that of the thirteen colonies. There was also a notable proportion of Boers among the Europeans of the Cape region and Natal, to be sure, but the English governor hardly let them demonstrate their solidarity with their Transvaal compatriots.

At the start of the conflict on October 11, 1899, the Boers had 30,000 troops. These troops were very similar to those that had been under the orders of George Washington a century earlier. It was more a people in arms than a real army: uniforms were almost nonexistent and between battles, the soldiers returned to their farms; the artillery was in fact the only weapon with a full-time military. At the beginning of the war there were barely 20,000 to 30,000 English troops facing the Boers, and the Boers stole victory after victory. But gradually the English reinforcements arrived, both from England (a distance of 12,000 kilometers) and from India (a distance of 7,000 kilometers). In the spring of 1900 the English army consisted of approximately 150,000 men, and its offensive was unstoppable. At the beginning of June, after a series of victories, it entered Johannesburg and Pretoria. But on the Boer side, with each male citizen being a potential soldier, the armed forces could be built up again and they then had recourse to a guerrilla war that lasted another two years.

Thus to overcome a population of about 500,000 that struggled fiercely for its independence, Britain had to commit 150,000 troops and accept 7,800 deaths on the battlefield; if one includes the losses due to disease, the figure is 22,000 dead (Pakenham 1979). Of course, such a mobilization also had a high financial cost.

COMPARISON OF THE COST OF THE TWO WARS

The war of the Transvaal cost £250 million (Baudhuin 1944), approximately twice the amount of British budget receipts in 1898. This was an easily bearable cost for Britain. The American War of Independence had cost £120 million, but this sum represented eleven times the budget of the period, an effort that was at the limit of being bearable.

What should have been spent in 1780 to put in the field an army of 150,000 men in place of the 30,000 who were committed? A sum on the order of £120 million multiplied by five, or £600 million, would have represented fifty-five times the budget of 1774, an expenditure largely out of reach.

One may wonder about the relationship between the £250 million that the war of the Transvaal cost and the figure of £600 million that we have estimated was needed for the War of Independence. Straightaway one can put to one side the factor of inflation, which was negligible during the nineteenth century. The difference between the two figures comes essentially from the tremendous improvements in maritime transport during the nineteenth century. It concerns not only the shift from sailing boats to steamboats, but also a better knowledge of currents and winds and an increase in the tonnage of boats. This was translated into a reduction in the cost of maritime transportation by a factor between five and ten (Roehner 1995, p. 127). It is therefore hardly surprising that in 1780 it would have cost 2.4 times more to transport an army equivalent to that of 1900.

THE GUERRILLA WAR

As we have already noted, open warfare was followed by a long period of guerrilla warfare in the Transvaal. It is possible that if fortunes had been unfavorable to the American troops, there would have been the same development. This form of struggle was indeed used at certain moments during the conflict. For example in 1780, after the British occupation of South Carolina, there were several episodes involving partisans, with all of the excesses associated with this type of confrontation. For a colonial power partisan warfare presents a big challenge, as demonstrated by the extreme measures the English command had to resort to, to bring the Boer guerrilla war to an end. Inaugurating the tactic of strategic hamlets, often employed thereafter in similar conflicts, Lord Kitchener confined in the camps 116,000 Boers (essentially women and children) and 100,000 Bantus who were in their service. In addition there were 31,000 prisoners of war, of whom 24,000 were in St. Helena or Ceylon (Lacour-Gayet 1970). Transposed to the American War of Independence, this amounts to putting 600,000 Americans in the camps and deporting 124,000 prisoners of war to Jamaica or the Bahamas.

REBELLION IN CANADA

From the figures given above it is clear that Britain was hardly in a position to oppose the American will for independence. What was completely unexpected, however, was that the Americans would show such a will so early and so staunchly. At the beginning of this chapter we stated that their revolution was the only example of its kind in the British colonies. This is not entirely true, however. In 1837–1838 French Canadians rose in armed rebellion against British rule. The revolt was suppressed at the cost of about 250 killed in action and a number of executions. At that time there were about 800,000 French Canadians in Quebec, representing 35 percent of the Canadian population. Although they had greater numbers than the Boer population, their revolt was quelled far more easily. In contrast to French Canadians the Boer had governed themselves for quite a long time before the war and had a standing army.

In the Spanish colonies both the unfolding and the outcome of the struggle for independence were very different from what took place in North America. It is the purpose of the next section to discuss this point in some detail.

Comparison with the March toward Independence in Latin America

In our comparison of the cases of the United States and Latin America we pay particular attention to the following questions: (1) Why did the Spanish colonies disintegrate into a large number of states? While the English colonies of North America produced only two states, Latin America gave rise to nearly twenty: one in North America, half a dozen in Central America and ten in South America. (2) In Latin America the march toward independence was spread over thirty years; why were there so many ups and downs? (3) In many countries civil wars have been superposed on the struggle against the colonial power. Why was the period after independence marked by extreme political instability? Thus in Peru there were no less than forty revolutions between 1815 and 1865 and in Colombia, between 1830 and 1900, there was an average of one revolution per year and a new constitution every ten years (Graham 1994). Before looking for solutions to these paradoxes, let us see in what terms we should pose this problem.

How to Pose the Problem?

THE "EXPLANATIONS"

The structural explanations for postindependence political instability in Latin America that are the most often cited are of two sorts, emphasizing either ethnic diversity or the difficulty of communication.

It is true that ethnic barriers between the populations of colonists, Indians, or former black slaves have been less distinct in Latin America than in

North America. This could in certain phases complicate the solution to social problems. However, the struggle for independence was not primarily a social question. Furthermore, in reviewing the history of liberation struggles in the different countries, one notices that nine times out of ten they were led by the white colonist militia. Where the militia withdrew its support, as for example in Mexico in 1810–1813, the revolution inevitably failed, and where it lent its support, as for example in Argentina, it succeeded rapidly.

Three counterexamples to the thesis of ethnic diversity may be put forward. The first is the example of Brazil. There, ethnic diversity was at least as great, if not greater, than in other regions of Latin America. Yet this country, as Ferguson (1963) summarizes, , "achieved its independence, emancipated its slaves and changed from a monarchy to a republic without resort to arms, a triple record few, if any, nations can compete with." The second example is that of Paraguay. Although this is one of the states in which the proportion of Indians (Guaranís) was the greatest, the country gained definitive independence in 1811 and without a civil war. The third example is that of China. It is in fact a reverse example, in the sense that this almost ethnically homogeneous country has nevertheless experienced many civil wars and rebellions (Taiping rebellion, Muslim rebellion, revolts in Yunnan, in Szechuan, and so on) during the long period of the return to real independence after the period of semicolonization by the large powers.

A variant of the ethnic argument consists in attributing the troubled history of Latin America to tradition and the supposedly fiery character of Hispanics. This thesis may find some support in the fact that the political history of Spain in the nineteenth and the beginning of the twentieth century was equally disrupted by many civil wars. But this type of explanation has several holes. First, while Portugal experienced an unsettled nineteenth century, in Brazil the transition was on the contrary peaceful. Second, the argument that calls on the "character" of peoples is similar to that which "explains" the soporific action of chloroform by its "soporific virtue," in other words it is a largely tautological argument. The character of a people is variable and dependent on history. From 1450 to 1660 the political history of Britain, for example, was disrupted by more civil wars and revolutions than that of Spain or Portugal, but no one points to this period as demonstrative of the fiery character of the English.

The second type of explanation calls on geography and the weakness of the means of communication. It is true that with its vast Amazonian forests and its immense cordillera whose passes are often at more than 4,000 meters, South America has very difficult conditions for communications. It is undeniable that this factor has played a role. When it takes more than three months to get from Buenos Aires to Peru (3,200 kilometers), it comes as no surprise that the governments of these two countries have felt quite distant from each other. However, there are also counterexamples that show that this factor has had only a limited impact. Brazil, a country in which communications have been among the most difficult, has been able to maintain its unity; while on the contrary, Central America, where maritime communications have been relatively easy, has disintegrated into a multitude of small states.

GENERAL FEATURES OF THE STRUGGLE FOR INDEPENDENCE

Before exploring the details of specific events, it may be useful to explain the main characteristics of the struggles for independence in Latin America. We stress first of all that it would be wrong to try to establish a parallel between the American Revolution and what has been called the first Latin American revolution, which lasted from 1808 to 1816. If one wants to seek parallels, they may be found rather between this 1808–1816 revolutionary period and the decade 1640–1650 in the thirteen colonies; we will return to this point later.

Second, we note that often the revolutions in Latin America simultaneously tried to achieve five different transitions: (1) breaking the psychological ties with the monarchy; (2) the gaining of independence; (3) the transformation of a society under the control of the Church to a secular society; (4) the abolition of slavery; (5) the transition from confederate or federal states to a unitary state.

In this broad political program, the American colonies were some way ahead in the sense that stages (3) and (1) were already partially realized by 1770. Stage (3) was semirealized to the extent that, since the secularization of Church goods by Henry VIII and Cromwell's government, the Church of England no longer possessed a sizable fraction of the landed property. Furthermore, regarding point (1), one may reasonably think that in England, as well as in the colonies, the bond between the monarchy and the nation experienced an eclipse during the reign of the first sovereigns of the Hanover dynasty. Could it have been otherwise if one considers that

George I arrived in England at the age of fifty-four and reigned for thirteen years without being able to speak English; he communicated with his ministers in French or Latin. The future George II was thirty-one years old when he arrived in England in 1814. Although he was more at ease with English, to his close associates he confided that he felt only aversion for his English subjects. It was Hanover that retained all his attention, and he made frequent visits there. George III was the first king of this dynasty to be born in England; he had a real interest in the affairs of his kingdom, but this interest was not without friction with Parliament. Similarly one can also stress that many American immigrants belonged to religious minorities (Puritans, Presbyterians, Quakers) who rejected the power of the sovereign in religious matters or the sacred character of the monarchy.

The United States also had the wisdom, or perhaps it would better to say the opportunity, to achieve the other transitions in successive stages. The choice between a confederacy and a federal state was made in 1787, but this problem resurfaced, eighty years after independence, during the crisis surrounding the question of slavery.

THE NEED FOR COMPLEMENTARY STATISTICAL DATA

The analysis that we develop in the following paragraphs remains purely qualitative. To arrive at a more quantitative diagnosis, it would be necessary to use comparative statistical data, which unfortunately are not currently available. For example, if one knew the statistical distribution of the landed property in New England, Virginia, and the main regions of Latin America, one could see whether there was a link between the concentration of property and the frequency of civil wars. Furthermore, if one knew what share of the landed property belonged to the clergy, one could better evaluate what weight the Catholic Church had in Latin America societies. Finally, if one had an idea of the number of English/Spanish/Portuguese troops that were permanently stationed in the respective colonies, one would know to what degree the colonizing power exerted control overseas.

The Two Periods in the Struggle for Independence

FIRST WAVE OF LIBERATION STRUGGLES, 1808–1816

When Spain and Portugal were invaded by the Napoleonic armies in 1808, the umbilical cord between the governments of the Iberian peninsula and its colonies was broken. For the ruling elites of the colonies, however, it was more of a shock than an opportunity to secure independence. The cooking pot of autonomy and secession was still not heated up. For this reason one should rather compare this period with what happened in the American colonies at the time of the English Civil War (1642–1649). In the two examples the periphery gained a de facto autonomy because of the momentary failure of the center.

Certainly there were independence insurrections from 1810 onward and even before (see the overview given in Table 4.5). But, except in Paraguay, they were caused by émigrés, often with the support and logistical aid of England, but without direct contact with the population. One of the most precocious attempts was that of Miranda in Venezuela; it is typical of the interventions that came from outside. Although Miranda was born in Venezuela, he left the country in 1783 at the age of thirty-three and visited the European capitals. On August 3, 1806, he arrived with 400 men in the city of Coro, 300 kilometers to the west of Caracas. This city had been chosen because of the anti-Spanish sentiments it was displaying. Protected by seven British warships, the expedition was organized with English assistance in return for Miranda's promise to open the country to English trade after independence. English landings had taken place in 1806 in Argentina with the same objective. On August 3, Miranda found the city almost deserted and those residents that remained showed very little interest in the proclamation that he posted on the city walls. The clergy turned out to be particularly hostile, and this no doubt largely explains the attitude of the residents. On August 19, after having lost 120 men in skirmishes and short of supplies, the expedition was forced to retreat (Delaunes 1969). In the same manner in Argentina, the events that triggered revolutionary events were the English attempts to take Buenos Aires and Montevideo in 1806 and 1807.

The movements that would take place in Mexico in 1810–1811 did not rely on foreign support, but they were at the same time atypical and marginal. Although led by two priests, Hidalgo and Morelos, these movements were the subject of a unanimous condemnation by the Catholic hierarchy and the Mexican elite. After a number of successes, Hidalgo and his troops were finally defeated by Spanish troops in January 1811. Morelos's campaign would last until 1815. Although the objective of independence was clearly proclaimed, the social color of these movements scared the Mexican aristocracy. In their egalitarian aspirations, they can be compared to the

Table 4.5 Results of the two waves of struggles for independence in Latin America

Country	Leader	War of independence	Independence
First wave of struggles for independence, 1808–1816			
Argentina	San Martín	1812–1816	1816
Bolivia		1809–(see second wave)	
Brazil			
Chile		1810–1814	
Colombia		1810–1815	
Ecuador		1809–(see second wave)	
Mexico	Hidalgo, Morelos	1810–1815	
Paraguay	De Francia	1810	1811
Peru			
Uruguay	Artigas	1810–1814	
Venezuela	Miranda, Bolívar	1811–1814	
Second wave of struggles for independence, 1816–1835			
Bolivia	Sucre	(see first wave)–1824	1825
Brazil	Don Pedro		1822
Chile	O'Higgins	1816–1818	1818
Colombia	Bolívar	1819	1819, 1830
Ecuador		(see first wave)–1822	1822, 1830
Mexico	Iturbide		1821
Peru	San Martín	1821–1824	1824
Venezuela	Bolívar	1820–1821	1821, 1830

Note: To keep the table to a reasonable size we have not listed Central American countries. The first country to gain its independence definitively was Paraguay; along with Brazil, Paraguay was one of the countries where independence was gained without either a war against the colonizer or a civil war.

Taiping Rebellion in China (1850–1864), a movement that took advantage of the void left by the decadence of imperial power.

THE ENGLISH REVOLUTIONS' REPERCUSSIONS IN THE THIRTEEN
COLONIES

First, we should note that in 1640 the total population of the English colonies in America was only 28,000 residents, of whom 22,500 lived in New England. Within such a sparse population one can hardly expect large movements; nevertheless there were sporadic demonstrations of the independence spirit. In 1649, after the execution of Charles I, the Virginia assembly declared its loyalty to Charles II, in open rebellion against Cromwell's government; however it pledged allegiance to Cromwell in 1652 when a fleet was sent there. Maryland was the only colony in which English events triggered a civil war, which was won by Lord Baltimore (Morison 1969 [1930], p. 63).

By 1689, the population of the colonies was more than 200,000. Although the vacuity of power in London was much briefer than in the 1640s, the colonists took action. In Boston, New York, Maryland, and North Carolina the governors were overthrown. The desire for self-determination was already apparent, but independence was not yet on the agenda.

In these movements it was mainly the ruling elites who aspired to greater autonomy; there was not a widespread desire for independence.

SECOND WAVE OF STRUGGLES FOR INDEPENDENCE, 1816–1825

After 1815 a reactionary monarchical wave submerged Europe. In Britain the habeas corpus was suspended (February 24, 1817), the freedom of the press was circumscribed, and public meetings were forbidden as part of the Six Acts of 1819 (Vincent 1898). The repercussions were also felt in Spain and its colonies. Ferdinand VII returned to the throne and, ignoring the constitution of 1812, resumed the authoritative government of the past. He dispatched an army of 10,000 veterans to Venezuela and Colombia. The fragile governments that had proclaimed independence were abolished. In Venezuela, this reaction could count on support from royalist colonists. In Colombia, the restored government executed 500 patriots. Only Argentina, Brazil, and Paraguay could preserve their achievements. In a general way the absolutist reaction aroused sentiments of revolt among the Spanish colonists, which explains the fact that the second wave of liberation struggles was largely supported by the ruling elites; their task was somewhat eased by the anti-autocratic revolt in Spain itself (1820). This time independence triumphed everywhere throughout Latin America.

POLITICAL INSTABILITY

Independence did not put an end to internal rivalries: in 1823, after only a year in power, General Augustín de Iturbide, the liberator of the Mexico, was forced to abdicate; in January 1827 a coup against Bolívar took place in Peru; similarly in April 1828 a *pronunciamiento* (military coup) forced General Antonio José de Sucre, the liberator of Bolivia, to resign.

In the United States there were also rebellions, such as in 1783 in Phila-delphia, where a revolt of unpaid soldiers forced Congress to flee to Prince-ton; revolts (Shays's Rebellion in 1786 and the Whiskey Rebellion in 1794); and even territorial contests between states, but no coup d'état was re-ported, not even an attempted coup d'état. Note that political instability is not common to the whole of Latin America. In Paraguay, the liberator José Rodriguez de Francia remained in power from 1814 until his death in 1840; in Brazil one must wait until 1889 for a military insurrection to oc-cur. On the whole, though, political instability has survived up to the pres-ent time; the reasons for this long-standing turmoil are for the most part not well understood. Coupled with political instability there was also the breakup of the continent into multiple states, the subject of the next sec-tion.

Fragmentation and Failure of Attempts at Federation
THE PROBLEM

To put the problem into perspective, note that Brazil has a surface area of 8.5 million square kilometers, which is only a little smaller than that of the United States (9.4 million square kilometers). If Mexico had not been forced to surrender California, Texas, and New Mexico after the Mexican War (1845–1847), it would have had an area of 3.3 million square kilome-ters, nearly half that of the United States. This shows that the fragmenta-tion process did not affect all parts of the continent in the same way.

On the basis of South America's colonial heritage, one could have ex-pected the creation of five large groups: on the one hand, Brazil, and on the other, three states corresponding to the former Spanish Viceroyalties of New Spain, New Grenada, and Peru and Rio de la Plata. Indeed, after the wars of independence the map of Latin America more or less respected these divisions; but gradually the continent saw the creation of about twenty states, four times the number that one might expect. There are hardly any examples, throughout the nineteenth and twentieth centuries, in which nations having the same language and a common past separated in this way. True, the phenomenon also existed during the breakup of the Ottoman Empire; but the countries involved, before their union with the Ottoman Empire, had often had a prestigious past as independent states. In the case of Latin America, former civilization was represented only by Indians, whose role during the struggles for independence was modest.

The balkanization of Central America and of the northern portion

South America has two facets: the initial separatist trends and the subsequent failure of the attempts at federation. Of these two aspects, the second is easier to analyze because many similar examples can be invoked.

In the twentieth century there have been several failed attempts at federation. Table 4.6 gives various examples. Practically all these cases concern countries having a similar language; nevertheless only one of these federations has survived, the federation of the United Arab Emirates. Note that this federation was set up in 1971 just after its members gained independence and that the countries it gathers together are small (the federation had a total population of 2.2 million residents in 1994).

Thus it is hardly surprising that the (rare) attempts at federation that took place in Latin America came to nothing. For example, the union between Bolivia and Peru lasted from 1835 to 1839, and the "Confederation of Central American States" from 1908 to 1910.

DISINTEGRATION OF GRAN COLOMBIA AND CENTRAL AMERICA

In terms of the increase in the number of states, the two crucial events were undoubtedly the disintegration in 1830 of Gran Colombia, which included Colombia, Ecuador, and Venezuela, and the fragmentation of the Federation of Central American States in 1840. It would be irrelevant, and furthermore contrary to our approach, to examine the "causes" of these

Table 4.6 Attempts at fusion or federation in the second half of the twentieth century

Federation	Countries	Creation	Dissolution
Federation Rhodesia-Nyasaland	N. and S. Rhodesia, Nyasaland	1953	1963
West Indian Federation	Jamaica, Bahamas, Barbados, etc.	1958	1962
United Arab Republic	Egypt, Syria	1958	1971
Arab Federation	Iraq, Jordan	1958 (Feb.)	1958 (Aug.)
Federation of Mali	Ex-French Sudan, Senegal	1959	1960
United Arab Emirates	Seven emirates	1971	
Federation of Arab Republics	Egypt, Libya, Syria	1972	1974
Senegambia	Gambia, Senegal	1982	1989
Yugoslavia	Bosnia, Croatia, Serbia	1919	1990

Note: The only federation still in operation in the early twenty-first century was that of the United Arab Emirates. Note that this federation does not contain Bahrain, Kuwait, or Qatar.

particular events. There have been debates over the role of the large powers in this process. Thus Williams (1916) has maintained that Britain played a role in the fragmentation of the federation, a thesis questioned by other authors, such as Karnes (1961). There are only two cases in which the intervention of the large powers has been without doubt: the creation of Uruguay in 1828 with British support, and the creation of Panama in November 1903 with the blessing of the United States.

Summary and Conclusion

The expression "Manifest Destiny" refers to the inevitable (by Providence or by destiny) territorial expansion of the United States. The term seems to have been introduced into the American political vocabulary during the nomination by the Democratic Convention of May 1844 of a little-known candidate, James K. Polk, in place of the favorite, Martin Van Buren, who was judged to be insufficiently expansionist. Polk was in fact elected, and during his term of office the United States expanded to California, Texas, and New Mexico. One might be tempted to deem the American Revolution an instance of Manifest Destiny as well, since the circumstances and the sequence of events seem to have been particularly favorable.

In the course of this chapter we have stressed the following elements underlying the American War of Independence. (1) In the middle of the eighteenth century several conflicts (Seven Years' War, Cherokee War, Pontiac's War) strengthened the links between the thirteen colonies. (2) In the years 1715–1760, monarchical sentiments were temporarily weakened in the thirteen colonies as well as in England. (3) Faced with the secession of the thirteen colonies, England put up a resistance that was sufficiently forceful to further strengthen American links in the face of the common threat, but was too weak to really challenge the American thrust toward independence. (4) From the very beginning American society was able to keep the power of the clergy under control. While in Europe or Latin America much political energy went into the struggle against the Church, the United States could devote its efforts to the unification of the country. (5) Starting from a limited area on the East Coast, the American Revolution was not immediately confronted by problems on a continental scale as was the case in the Latin American revolutions. (6) Yet these favorable circumstances would have led to nothing without the perceptiveness and the determined action of men such as Samuel Adams or George Washington.

It is clear that there is a strong connection between revolutions and military problems. Without Washington's military skills, the American Revolution would have ended like the Canadian uprising in 1837. Similarly, without the victories of the French revolutionary armies, the Revolution of 1789 would have ended in 1792. Thus in a sense the analysis of military questions that we undertake in subsequent chapters is a follow-up to the chapters about revolutions. Before that, however, we examine a special example of social uprising, the general strike.

5

General Strikes, Mushroom Strikes

At the end of the nineteenth century and the beginning of the twentieth there was a close connection between general strikes and revolutions, not only in socialist ideology but in the minds and reactions of governments. The army was used in an almost systematic manner to protect factories, and confrontations were frequent. It suffices to recall the bloody clashes of May 1, 1886, in Chicago that were the origins of the celebration of the labor movement on that day. Even in Switzerland, a country that is little prone to excesses, the strike of November 1918 was ended by the killing of three strikers by troops. For the labor movement the majority of general strikes launched by unions at the beginning of the century ended in bitter defeat. This resulted in two divergent evolutions. In countries having a strong rate of unionization, such as Germany, England, or the Scandinavian countries, the idea of the general strike was gradually abandoned. The evolution was different in countries where a weaker unionization left open the possibility of spontaneous movements of workers. In these countries, one sees the appearance of what can be called mushroom strikes, that is to say movements that are at the outset confined to a region or a sector, but that gradually spread until transforming themselves into general strikes.

France offers some particularly spectacular examples of such movements in 1936, 1953, 1968, and 1995. The strike of May 1968 was of such a scale that it was believed for some time that it was going to lead to a semirevolution and the ousting of President de Gaulle. It will be seen that these four strikes were paronymic repetitions of the same schema. There are few cases that provide a more spectacular illustration of events in which the starting mechanism is unpredictable, but that, once put in motion, have a relatively foreseeable development. The concept of this type of event was introduced by Tilly (1993) with the help of a very illuminating analogy involving traffic jams. These depend on so many factors (response of drivers to weather conditions, patterns of road maintenance, location of car accidents, and so on) that it is almost impossible to anticipate their appearance. But once a traffic jam has formed, the reactions of the motorists can be predicted fairly well. For mushroom strikes, the pattern similarly repeats itself with such regularity that the outcome can be predicted with some accuracy. In this connection let us mention the following anecdote. The three recurrent strikes of 1936, 1953 and 1968 had been analyzed in a first version of this chapter written in June 1993. When at the end of November 1995 a new strike of that sort began, the parallel with the three previous cases was immediately recognized; on December 3, approximately a week after the beginning of the strike, one of the authors sent to Charles Tilly the following electronic message (here translated from the original French): "We are now in one of these episodes of strikes, of 1936 or 1968 type, that France likes so much. This is the first week, but if we believe these antecedents it could well last a month." In fact, the strike lasted a little less than a month.

We begin by making an inventory of different scenarios of general strikes. As will be seen, even in the fairly well defined category of general strikes, there is room for much diversity. This allows us to better stress the specificity of mushroom strikes within the group of general strikes. Then we undertake a more detailed analysis of five mushroom strikes that have taken place in France and Belgium. Finally, in a concluding section we emphasize that like revolutions, general strikes are characterized by a sudden increase in the number of social contacts between people.

General Strikes: Cross-National Analysis

Strikes can take a wide variety of forms. They differ in their motives, their duration, their extension, the amount to which they are controlled by unions, their degree of violence, and so on. In truth, strikes constitute such a heterogeneous group that they can hardly be the object of a fruitful comparative analysis. If one limits oneself to general strikes, the object of study can be a little better defined. However, we will see in this section that the repertory of general strikes is equally varied and does not correspond in the least to a unique mechanism. It is only in the study of mushroom strikes that we will see the appearance of an underlying mechanism that can be the object of repeated observations and therefore of an analytical study.

General Strikes

It is hardly possible to define the notion of a general strike in a rigorous manner. In fact, no strike is truly general; there are always some districts or sectors that do not participate in it. This is all the more true when the country is large. In a country such as Belgium, the phenomenon of contagion will come into play far more than in a country as vast as the United States. In this latter case one will be more inclined to speak of general strikes when a movement affects a large number of states, even if it covers only a few industries. Such was the case in the strike of 1893, which spread to twenty-six states but concerned only the railroads. Less specifically, we shall speak of general strikes when one is faced with a movement that presents a notable dynamics of contagion, either at the geographical or the sector level.

PREVIOUS STUDIES

The study of strikes has given rise to an abundant literature, but only a small proportion of these studies are made from a comparative perspective. In 1944 Spielmans introduced a graphical means that allowed the association of strikes with a certain profile, in terms of both the numbers of strikers and the duration of the strike. Such strike profiles are very useful for comparative purposes. This method was generalized in 1974 by Shorter and Tilly in their classic study of strikes in France from 1830 to 1968. For a broader comparative perspective we note the volume edited by Haimson and Tilly (1989), and more recently the brilliant study by Silver, Arrighi, and Dubofsky (1995). A very careful and detailed study of the strikes in Italy after World War II is to be found in a recent book by Franzosi (1995).

From the historical point of view an important element is the evolution of the frequency of strikes; annual data on this subject for European countries can be found in Woytinski (1926, vol. 2) for the period 1890–1924; in Flora, Kraus, and Pfenning (1987, chap. 10), where the whole period from 1895 to 1975 is covered; and in Silver, Arrighi, and Dubofsky (1995) for the period 1906–1986. In what follows we will see that the rate of unionization is a crucial variable for the determination of the form of the strike; very complete information in this respect is given in Ebbinghaus and Visser (1997).

Table 5.1 recapitulates certain characteristics of the principal general strikes that have taken place in Western Europe and the United States. The letter P indicates truly political strikes, which form a minority. For example, the strike of 1913 in Belgium had the attainment of universal male suffrage as its goal; that of 1918 in Switzerland demanded proportional representation for National Council elections as well as voting rights for women; that of 1920 in Germany foiled the putsch of Kapp-Löttwitz; that of 1961 in France contributed to defeat the putsch of the French generals who opposed Algeria's independence; that of 1974 in Ulster successfully opposed the installation of the Council of Ireland that united representatives of Northern and Southern Ireland.

The duration of these general strikes is quite variable; they range from one hour to eight weeks. In the discussion that follows it will be seen that these strikes markedly differ in their degree of preparation and their development.

SEASONALITY OF STRIKES

Overall, strikes are more frequent during the six "hot months" (April to September) than during the six cold months (October to March) (see Table 5.2a). This characteristic is relatively robust, since it is borne out over a long period and since it is equally valid in France as in Britain. The overall average for the hot months is 59 percent. It is necessary, however, to stress that this average conceals great disparities from one sector to another. In construction, the winter months are often months of partial unemployment for climatic reasons and it is understandable that they are hardly favorable to the onset of a strike; in fact, construction is one area in which the imbalance of strikes in favor of hot months is the most emphasized: 67 percent of strikes take place in April–September (in Britain for the period 1919–1939, Knowles 1952), which is substantially more than the average. Conversely in the mines one could expect that as a result of the higher demand for coal in winter, these months would be more favorable to the onset of a strike; this is partially confirmed by the data since the dominance of the hot months is no more than 52 percent in the mines, that is to say less than the average.

Table 5.1 Major general strikes in Western Europe and the United States

Date (beginning)	Country	Duration (days)	P?	Number of deaths	Reference
1894, June 26	United States	18		25	Lindsey (1942); Vincent (1898); Gilje (1996)
1903, Feb. 15	Spain (Catalonia)	12		>1	Crook (1931), p. 179
1909, July 23	Spain (Catalonia)	6	P		Crook (1931), p. 182
1909, July 24	Sweden	65		0	*Die Aussperrungen;* Penson (1909)
1913, Apr. 14	Belgium	10	P	0	Vandervelde, Brouckere, and Vandermissen (1914)
1918, Nov. 11	Switzerland	4	P	4	Vuilleumier et al. (1977)
1920, Mar. 16	Germany	2	P	0	Crook (1931)
1920, May 2	France	20		0	Borczuk (1972); *Figaro*
1922, Feb.	South Africa	40		157	Lacour-Gayet (1970)
1926, May 3	Britain	9		0	Symons (1957)
1932, Nov. 10	Switzerland	1	P		*Keesing's Contemp. Archives*
1936, May 28	France	34		0	*Le Temps*
1947, Nov. 15	France	21		3	Courty-Valentin (1981); *Le Monde*
1953, Aug. 6	France	25		0	*Le Monde*
1960, Dec. 20	Belgium	33		4	Féaux (1963); Deprez (1963)
1961, Apr. 24	France	0.04[a]	P	0	*Le Monde*
1968, May 13	France	35		4	*Le Monde*
1974, May 14	Ulster	14	P	2	Fisk (1975)
1980, May 3	Sweden	9		0	*Le Monde*
1985, Mar. 26	Denmark	14		0	*Le Monde*
1995, Nov. 24	France	25		0	*Le Monde*
1996, Dec. 29	South Korea	25		0	*Le Monde*

Note: P denotes political strikes. Sixty percent of the strikes occurred in spring and summer; 50 percent occurred before World War II. We emphasize that the table is by no means intended to be exhaustive.

a. A symbolic one-hour work stoppage to oppose OAS putsch.

EVOLUTION OF THE INTENSITY OF STRIKES DURING THE TWENTIETH CENTURY

Table 5.2b recapitulates the average intensity of strikes in various countries for the periods before and after World War II. For most of the countries one observes a net diminution of strike days. Only Italy is the exception to this rule, which can undoubtedly be explained by the fact that

Table 5.2a Seasonal frequency of strikes

Country	Period	Spring–summer (Apr.–Sep.)	Autumn–winter (Oct.–Mar.)	Reference
France	1871–1890	67%	33%	Perrot (1973)
	1919–1935	56%	44%	Goetz-Girey (1965)
	1949–1962	55%	45%	Goetz-Girey (1965)
United Kingdom	1919–1939	57%	43%	Knowles (1952)
Average		59%	41%	

Note: For France the figures are based on the number of strikers. For the United Kingdom they are based on the number of strikes. On average strikes were more frequent during the April–September period than during the winter period from October to March.

strikes were more difficult from 1922 to 1945 under the fascist regime. In some cases, as for the Nordic countries (Denmark, Norway, Sweden), the reduction was considerable.

RATES OF UNIONIZATION

Table 5.3 compares the rates of unionization in various countries before and after World War II. One can distinguish three types: countries with a very strong rate of unionization, such as the Nordic countries, which all have a rate greater than 50 percent; moderately unionized countries (Argentina, Belgium, Germany, Italy, United Kingdom, United States); and countries having a unionization rate lower than 30 percent (France, Japan, Spain).

In the following section we examine the unfolding of a number of epoch-making general strikes. This discussion parallels the cross-national analysis of Chapter 2.

The Pullman Strike (1894)

The men who worked on the rail carriages of the Pullman Company, whose largest operation was in Chicago, were lodged and supplied with consumer products by their employer, which then charged them rent and for the cost of goods. The strike was motivated as much by the level of the rents and the price of consumer goods as by demands for a salary increase. The strike broke out at the height of a recession, a year after the panic of 1893, when many workers and their families were sick from malnutrition. This could explain both the desperation of the workers and the balance of

Table 5.2b Strikes before and after World War II: Average man-days lost per one
thousand nonagricultural wage-earners

Country	1900–1939	1945–1975	(1900–1939)/ (1945–1975)
Austria	96	14	6.8
Belgium	150	150	1.0
Denmark	150	15	10.0
France	180	180	1.0
Germany	140	10	1.4
Ireland	300	300	1.0
Italy	260	620	0.4
Netherlands	110	9	12.2
Norway	780	23	33.9
Sweden	450	8	56.3
Switzerland	18	1	18.0
United Kingdom	570	150	3.8
Average (geometrical mean)	186	36	5.2

Source: Flora, Krans, and Pfenning (1987), vol. 2, chap. 10.
Note: Except for Italy, the ratio (1900–1939)/(1945–1975) is greater than one, which
means that the number of strikes has decreased since World War II.

power that was very unfavorable to them. Despite this the American Railway Union upheld their struggle by asking all its members across the country to boycott Pullman carriages. This boycott reverberated through most of the railroad companies and spread to twenty-six states and territories. Very quickly, because of the question of mail trains, this strike was transformed into a confrontation with the federal authorities. In effect, the Pullman carriages often belonged to trains that were also equipped with postal carriages, and it was difficult to boycott the first without affecting the second. At the federal level the reaction against the strike was directed by Attorney General Richard Olney, an business attorney who had had close links with railroad companies during his career.

In Chicago, approximately 5,000 deputy marshals were recruited. Any railroad desiring its own corps of deputy marshals would designate one of its officials as a sort of captain, to whom was entrusted the duty of choosing the men and directing their activities. Furthermore, a week after the beginning of the strike federal troops arrived in Chicago. There is no doubt that these demonstrations of force pushed the workers to the limit. The

Table 5.3 Trade union membership

Country	1900–1939 (%)	1945–1990 (%)	Specific years (%)
Argentina		30	
Australia			51 (1979)
Belgium	26	44	51 (1990)
Colombia			6 (1997)
Denmark		73	71 (1990)
France	15	21	10 (1990)
Germany	22	34	33 (1990)
Ireland			68 (1978)
Italy		40	39 (1990)
Japan		26	25 (1990)
Netherlands		25	
Norway		55	
Spain		16	
Sweden	43	72	82 (1990)
Switzerland			34 (1986)
United Kingdom	32	42	39 (1990)
United States	20	32	16 (1990)

Sources: Crouch (1993); *Die Aussperrungen* (1912); Ducatenzeiler (1980); Ebbinghaus and Visser (1997); Knowles (1952); Mitchell (1978); *Tribune de l'Expansion* (Mar. 4, 1992); *Le Monde* (Aug. 25, 1997, Sept. 1, 1999); Lallement (1996); Steinmo, Thelen, and Longstreth (1992).

Note: In the United States there is a notable difference in terms of unionization between the public and private sector; in the latter the percentage is only about 10 percent (1996). The figures show trade union membership as a percentage of nonagricultural employment. Depending upon the source, there may be certain differences with regard to the concept used—for example, with regard to the inclusion or noninclusion of retired workers. But this does not change the figures significantly. We express our gratitude to Dr. B. Ebbinghaus for providing us with some of his data before the publication of his book.

fact remains that fires were lighted on July 5 and 6, 1894. The militia fired, and there were more than a dozen deaths. From July 18 work began to resume at the Pullman workshops; the strike ended in complete failure. The strikers were only reemployed on condition that they give up their union affiliation; no diminution of rent was granted. In August, completely discredited, the Railway Union began to disintegrate.

What can one retain from this episode? It emphasizes the parallel, already noted, between popular revolts and general strikes. It also shows the limits of union action in so sensitive an industry as were the railroads in the late nineteenth century.

Lockout and General Strike in Sweden (1909)

This strike was extremely different from the Pullman strike in its origin, its length of nearly two months, and its nonviolent character. Its origin is to be found in a succession of strikes and lockouts that amplified movements that, at the outset, were of a limited extent. Thus from spring 1908 to spring 1909 there were conflicts in a porcelain factory in Gothenburg and in clothing workshops in Stockholm, as well as in sawmills. At that time the idea of a general strike was on the union's agenda in Sweden as in other industrialized countries. The decision to launch the general strike was taken by the national confederation of unions on July 24, 1909. Almost 97 percent of workers were unionized, and very quickly more than 80 percent participated in the strike. It was anticipated that the strike would be long, and in support collections were organized in America (Figure 5.1). In contrast with the Pullman strike, the recourse to the army remained very limited. It is true that the railroads could not join the strike and that a Public Security Brigade, formed from elements of the bourgeoisie, took charge of some essential services, such as guarding the banks or driving the buses; the army saw to it that supplies were maintained. During the strike the sale of alcoholic drinks was forbidden in Stockholm. It seems that there were fewer crimes during the strike than during similar periods in other years. The return to work took place as shown in Figure 5.2a. The workers that were reemployed in firms that had to give up their union affiliation and promise not to financially help their comrades still on strike. At the end of strike the unionization rate had fallen to 51 percent. The defeat was perhaps less humiliating than in Chicago but for the union it was a defeat nevertheless.

The General Strike of 1918 in Switzerland

Switzerland in the twenty-first century is a country in which the standard of living is very high and where work conflicts are settled by negotiation. But it was not always this way. In the years 1910–1920, workers of the large cities were open to socialist ideas and social conflicts often took a violent

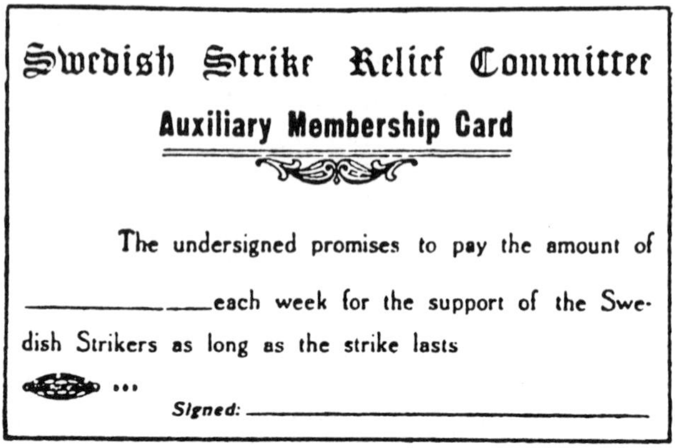

$\mathfrak{Swedish}$ $\mathfrak{Strike}$ $\mathfrak{Relief}$ $\mathfrak{Committee}$

Auxiliary Membership Card

The undersigned promises to pay the amount of

_____each week for the support of the Swe-

dish Strikers as long as the strike lasts

⋯

Signed: _____

Figure 5.1 Form used for collections in the United States for the Swedish strikers in 1909. *Source: Die Aussperrungen* (1912).

turn. The first wave of general strikes occurred at the cantonal level: in 1902 in Geneva, in 1907 in the canton of Vaud, in 1912 in Zurich. On November 17, 1917, a demonstration sparked by the Russian Revolution came up against the police; an exchange of gunfire left four dead, of which one was a policeman. In the wake of this movement the Olten Committee (named after the city midway between Basel and Zurich where its members met) was formed; it regrouped members of the Socialist Party and the unions. The committee also established a plan for the development of the struggle that later, especially during the trial of the members of the committee, became known as the "civil war memo" (Bürgerkriegsmemorial). During the following months the committee went in search of a pretext that would allow it to put its plan into operation. It believed it had found it on April 3, 1918, in the discontent provoked by an increase of the price of milk. But the crisis was defused by a concession from the federal government. In October 1918 a strike was begun by Zurich bank employees. At this point troops were sent to Zurich. The German defeat and the concurrent social agitation in Germany had deep repercussions in the German-speaking cantons of Switzerland, and the subsequent general strike of Novemberwas far more important in this region than in French-speaking Switzerland. On Sunday, November 10, 1918, an anniversary rally of the Russian Revolution ended with four demonstrators hurt and one soldier killed. On Monday the railwaymen and the steelworkers went on strike.

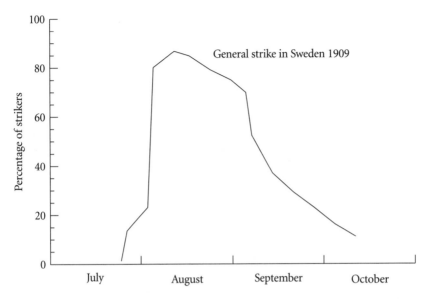

Figure 5.2a General strike in Sweden (1909). *Source: Die Ausperrungen* (1912).

The Olten Committee jumped on the bandwagon and called a general strike for Monday evening at midnight. Its demands were essentially political: (1) immediate reelection of the National Council with proportional representation; (2) voting rights and eligibility for women; (3) a 48-hour work week. The authorities reacted by sending for reliable troops from rural districts. Furthermore bourgeois militias formed in the cities to combat the socialists and start up public services again. These bourgeois militias were in the tradition of those that had ensured order during the wheat riots of preceding centuries. On November 14 the troops fired on a crowd that was preventing the departure of a train, and there were three deaths. The same day under the supervision of a cordon of troops, the Olten Committee gave the order to resume work as of Friday, November 15. In the Zurich region, where the strike had started, the steelworkers resumed work only on Monday, November 18.

What to retain from this episode? In many respects this strike was similar to the Pullman strike. The action started in a spontaneous manner but was thereafter taken in hand and controlled by the unions. The reaction of the cantonal authorities was very severe, especially the plan of military mobilization. Once again the strike ended in a defeat of the labor movement. If the first demand began to be realized in the years that followed, it would be necessary to wait until 1971 for the second, the voting rights of women, to be achieved in Switzerland.

The General Strike of 1974 in Ulster

From the point of view of the study of social dynamics, here is a unique and interesting example. It concerns a political strike begun under pressure at the instigation of minority groups. However, it finally ended in success; we will see some of the reasons for this.

After the partition of Ireland in the 1920s, Ulster enjoyed great political autonomy; it had its own parliament and its own government. But this autonomy resulted in the political and economic domination of the Protestant fraction of the population at the expense of the Catholic minority. At the beginning of the 1970s, following the civil rights movement of the Catholic minority, the British government wanted to find an agreement with the Catholic minority and with the Republic of Ireland: dissolution of certain paramilitary groups, limitation of the powers of the parliament, installation of a Council of Ireland that united the Irish of north and south. It was this evolution that the Protestant Loyalists rose up against. The strike that started on May 14, 1974, was largely imposed by intimidation from commandos of the Ulster Defence Association. Perhaps the most spectacular mass intimidation occurred at Harland and Wolff's shipyards, where it was announced during lunch time that any car still in the employees' car park at two o'clock that afternoon would be burnt. The 8,000 shipyard workers left immediately. Another means of imposing the strike was by reducing the production of the power plants. The British army refused to take control of the plants. In a televised speech Prime Minister Harold Wilson declared that Ulster was sponging on British democracy, an accusation that irritated public opinion in Ulster and ended in tipping it in favor of the strike. On May 28, after two weeks of strikes, the Loyalists could savor their victory over the British government. The Council of Ireland was shelved, as were the attempts at reunification.

What to retain from this episode? Of the four strikes that we have presented, it is the only successful one. In the other cases the troops sided with the government without any question. On the contrary, in Ireland the British army always had an inclination to be on the side of the Protestants. In this respect one can recall the mutiny of a number of British officers in

April 1914 after the vote of the Home Rule Act. If the population sides with the strikers and if the army refuses to commit itself against them, then a general strike can succeed. This almost happened in France in May 1968.

Mushroom Strikes: Longitudinal Analysis

In the preceding section, we described general strikes whose duration, dynamics, and development were strongly variable. Now we will examine a particular variety of the general strike, which we call "mushroom strikes," whose duration, dynamics, and development are very similar: the duration is on the order of one month, the strike starts largely in a spontaneous manner outside of the national union organizations, its phase of extension lasts approximately ten days, then there is a plateau lasting approximately a week; finally the phase of contraction of the strike and the return to work is spread over ten to fifteen days. Note that these strikes also distinguish themselves from those examined previously by the fact that they have generally allowed workers to obtain substantial concessions. After a general overview of these strikes, we will detail their different characteristics.

General Overview

First we examine in what respects mushroom strikes differentiate themselves from other general strikes in France.

THE FRENCH STRIKES OF 1947: STAGGERED VERSUS MUSHROOM STRIKES

In postwar years there were large strikes in most of the industrialized countries. In Britain this began before the end of the war: in 1944 there were 200 man-days lost per 1,000 nonagricultural workers against 77 in 1938 (Flora, Kraus, and Pfennig 1987, p. 751). In the United States there was a considerable strike wave in 1946 (with an index of 270 against 31 for 1938). In France, it was in 1947 that the most important strikes took place, mainly in June and November (Courty-Valentin 1981). These, however, were more a matter of staggered strikes than mushroom strikes. In fact, different sectors struck in relays: from May 10 to May 17, 1947, the Grands Moulins of Paris were on strike; the banks were on strike for several days between May 15 and May 25; there were then work stoppages in the gas and electricity industries between June 9 and June 12; on June 20 the department stores of Paris went on strike for a week; from June 25 to June 28 it was the coal mines that were on strike. The picture is similar in November–December 1947: garbage collection, the railroads, and the Métro were affected by work stoppages. These strikes were coupled with riots in the south of France (Béziers, Marseilles) and with acts of sabotage against the railways; the unbolting of a rail track led to a derailment that left twenty dead near Arras.

In short, the strikes of 1947 in France were rather sporadic movements, led mostly by the instigation of the unions. A headline from the newspaper *Le Monde* (November 28, 1947) is in this respect revealing: "Resistance to the Strike by Provincial Railwaymen." Let us add that at the end of 1947 there was a split within the main union, the Confédération Générale du Travail, its moderate wing separating to form a new union called Force Ouvrière.

The French strike of March 1920 is much nearer to a mushroom strike, but in an embryonic form. In fact the movement was of a long duration only on the railways; the other sectors that joined the movement (dockers, gas workers, metalworkers) did so rather in solidarity and only for a few days, roughly from 10 to 19 May. It is for this reason that we have not included this strike in our sample; however, it was surely a useful "repetition" from which the strike of 1936 profited.

MAIN CHARACTERISTICS

One of the essential characteristics of mushroom strikes is the suddenness of their beginnings. This can be illustrated by the following anecdote. On May 17, 1968, one of the authors of this work went to dinner at a friend's house in an eastern district of Paris. The journey out, at seven o'clock, was made without any problems; all the Métro lines were running and no work stoppage had been announced. But at eleven o'clock, when it came time for the return journey, no more underground trains were run-

Table 5.4 Mushroom strikes

	1936	1953	1960	1968	1995
Country	France	France	Belgium	France	France
Duration (days)	34	25	33	35	25
Sector in which the strike started	Private	Public	Private	Private	Public
Occupation of workplace	Yes	No–Yes	Yes–No	Yes	No
Acts of sabotage	No	Yes	Yes	No	No

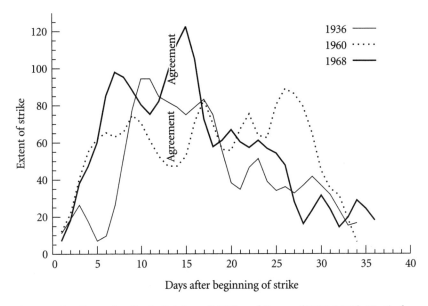

Figure 5.2b General strike in Belgium (1960) and France (1936, 1968). Vertical scale represents amplitude of the strike as defined in the text. *Source:* Belgium–Féaux (1963); France–*Le Temps, Le Monde*.

ning; the evening being beautiful, the journey was transformed into an pleasant walk. The strike of May 1968, which had started some days earlier in the region of Nantes, had reached Paris; the Métros and trains would be idle for approximately three weeks.

Table 5.4 recapitulates the five mushroom strikes that we study in this section. As shown by Figures 5.2b and 5.2c, the total duration of the strike corresponds to a dual movement of growth and decline (further explanation of these graphs is given in the "Quantitative Study" section, pp. 202–203). With the strike being only moderately controlled by the unions, one can truly talk of a spontaneous growth. In this, these strikes are rather different from the strikes that took place under strict union control, such as the strike of 1909 in Sweden or that of 1926 in England.

There are other characteristics that are common to all mushroom strikes. First, even after reaching an agreement, the return to work is not immediate, but progressive. The directives circulated by unions at the national level only materialize at the local level with a certain inertia. Second, strikes are punctuated by immense demonstrations. Third, when they pro-

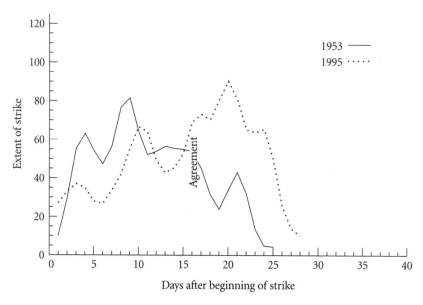

Figure 5.2c General strike in France (1953, 1995). Vertical scale represents amplitude of the strike as defined in the text. *Source: Le Monde.*

duce acts of violence these generally take place at the end of the conflict, when the tension has been intensified in the two camps by weeks of confrontation. Fourth, note that the parallelism between the strikes of 1953 and 1995 includes even the motive of the strike. In the two cases, a law had been passed that raised the retirement age of civil servants, and this provoked the mobilization of the public sector.

Beyond these similarities there are also elements of diversity between these strikes. The most important distinction concerns the respective weights of the public and private sectors at the beginning of the movement. When the strike began in the private sector, as in 1936, 1960 and 1968, it finished by spreading to the public sector; but the reverse is not true. The strikes of 1953 and 1995 only moderately affected the private sector. As a result the strikes of 1936, 1960, and 1968 had a much larger extension than the other two.

AN EMBRYONIC MUSHROOM STRIKE: SOUTH KOREA (JANUARY 1997)

It might appear surprising that our only examples of mushroom strikes are confined to France and Belgium. We are convinced that there are other examples, especially in Latin America; only the absence of adequate sources prevents us from exploring this avenue.

In South Korea at the beginning of 1997 there was a strike that shares several characteristics of mushroom strikes. Thus its launching was not made at the call of the main trade union; its duration was on the order of one month; there were great demonstrations. Let us recall the outlines of this strike. On Thursday, December 26, the South Korean parliament passed a law forbidding the creation of new unions until the year 2000. This meant that the Korean Federation of Trade Unions would remain the only officially recognized trade union, even though there already existed another nonrecognized union claiming 300,000 members. As a reaction to this law the strike spread rapidly, in particular to the naval yards, automobile factories, hospitals, and bus companies. The go-slow strikes continued until January 19, when the government accepted that the law would be discussed further in parliament. The great day of protest organized for January 15 mobilized approximately 500,000 strikers, a figure that nevertheless was inferior to union expectations.

Qualitative Characteristics of Mushroom Strikes
Here we discuss in greater detail certain features of the strikes under consideration; note that they are not necessarily common to all mushroom strikes, in particular because of the public sector–private sector distinction.

PRESENTATION OF THE SYNOPTIC TABLES
Tables 5.5a and 5.5b present a daily chronology of five mushroom strikes in synoptic form. These tables are based on French daily newspapers, *Le Temps* before 1945 and *Le Monde* after 1945. In the discussion below frequent reference will be made to these tables. For the sake of simplicity we mention just the year of the strike and the day; thus "1936–day 16" means the sixteenth day of the 1936 strike, and the corresponding entry begins with "Extension of the strikes to Belgium."

A TEXTBOOK CASE OF PARONYMIC EPISODES
The strikes of 1936 and 1968, on the one hand, and of 1953 and 1995, on the other, provide textbook examples of what we called in Chapter 1 paronymic (that is, similar but not identical) episodes. Consider the start of the strikes in 1936 and 1968. (1) Both began in aviation factories

Table 5.5a Synoptic chronologies of the mushroom strikes of 1936, 1960, and 1968

Strike day	1936	1960	1968
	First Week: Popular Explosion		
1	[11] Occupation by workers of two factories in the Paris region. The day before the workers had begun a sit-in strike. Picturesque scenes took place around the factories as workers received supplies through the gates or over the walls from their wives, their friends, and even the city councils.	[10] The strike starts. There are spontaneous stoppages in the private sector. At Cockerill-Ougrée, workers enter into the struggle against the will of most of the union delegates.	[4] In the style of the student demonstrations, the workers of Sud-Aviation occupy the factory at Nantes. The demonstrators on Tuesday evening imprisoned the director of the factory in his office, blocking all the exits with barricades and soldering shut one of the doors. Two thousand passed the night in the establishment, where a gigantic feast had been prepared and the atmosphere was that of a kind of bazaar. The day before there had been a huge demonstration in Paris.
2	[11] There are a number of demands: 40-hour week, paid holidays, recognition of labor delegations. The strike spreads to Farman and Renault (30, 000 workers).	[16] The strike spreads to the railways.	[8] Renault workers in Cléon (Seine-Maritime) partially stop work and occupy some of the workshops. The director of Sud-Aviation is still "confined" with ten of his colleagues. Students from nearby Nantes demonstrate their solidarity with the workers, joining in by mounting guards in front of the factory gates.

3	[42] Extension of the strike movement. The strike affects 14 factories in the Paris region (42, 000 strikers). The end of the strike is signaled in the Dewoitine aircraft factories at Toulouse. The conflict that broke out in the steel industry spreads to construction, where a strike is envisaged for June 30.	[45] The strike spreads from the Walloon to the Flemish part of the country. Work in the coal mines stops and the trams no longer circulate.	[34] After Renault, Rhodiaceta and Berliet are occupied at Lyons. At Renault the sit-in strike spreads from Cléon to all Renault factories.
4	[11] At Orléans, 500 workers of the Panhard et Levassor factory abruptly cease work and occupy the workshops. Some workers stage walk-outs of their factories.	[55] The strike wins over the public sector: post offices, telegraphs, telephones, ministries, gas, electricity. Cardinal van Roey appeals against the strike.	[34]
5	[6]	[64] Liège magistrates seize an appeal to soldiers for solidarity that had been published by the socialist newspaper *La Wallonie.*	[34]
6	[6] No new walk-outs are signaled.	[64] Christmas Day. A few acts of sabotage in Wallonia.	[70] Several million workers are now on strike. Railways: no traffic. Post offices: strike in sorting offices. The opposition calls for the resignation of the government and new elections.

Table 5.5a (continued)

Second Week: The Unions Join the Movement

Strike day	1936	1960	1968
7	[22] The movement extends to the food and printing industry. The strike affects 66 establishments. The Lido is occupied by its employees.	[69] Military units are brought back from Germany and placed in sensitive areas.	[70] General de Gaulle contemplates consulting the country in June by a referendum on "worker participation." The disturbances worsen in the banks. The gas stations are replenished.
8	[56] A sit-in strike took place the previous day at the important steel factory of Fives-Lille.	[50] The strike spreads again in the Flemish region. There are mass demonstrations in Brussels and several other cities.	[70] The economy is totally paralyzed. Commissariat à l'Energie Atomique (nuclear research centers): all centers are affected by the strike. Coal mines: the strike is total. Department stores: all establishments are on strike. The trade unions develop a program of demands.
9	[78] Extension of the movement to lorry drivers, newspaper distribution, the book industry, and gas distribution. Formation of the Blum government.	[94] Violent clashes in Ghent between the police and strikers. Large demonstrations in several cities.	[63] The labor confederations declare themselves ready for discussions with the employers and the government. Massive purchases during the last few days have provoked a shortage of foodstuffs.

10	[100] Extension of the strike movement and the factory occupations.	[60] Large demonstration in Antwerp: around 20,000 people.	[58] The unions and the employers agree to attend the meeting proposed by the government.
11	[100]	[68] One person is killed at the end of a demonstration by a plain-clothes policeman.	[53] New low for the franc in New York.
12	[78] The delegates of the aircraft factories on strike decide to ask the Minister of Air for his intervention so that the employer federation will accept the workers' demands.	[47] New Year's truce.	[53]
13	[83] A conference at the Hôtel Matignon gathers the delegations of the Confédération de la Production Française (employers) and the Confédération Générale du Travail (union) in the presence of the prime minister. Agreement in principle between the labor and employer delegations.	[47]	[78] The draft agreement between the unions, the employers and the government is put to the strikers. It proposes an increase in the minimum wage, a reduction in work hours, and a lowering of the retirement age. Workers of the large enterprises (Renault, Citröen, Berliet, Rhodiaceta) declare themselves against the return to work.

Table 5.5a (continued)

Strike day	1936	1960	1968
	Third week: In Search of a Second Wind		
14	[83] Work will be resumed on Thursday in the mines. Strike in the restaurants of the Champs-Elysées.	[47] The government makes some concessions. The socialists intensify their pressure.	[73] Negotiations take place, notably at Electricité de France (power utility). Postponement of the Baccalauréate. Coal mines: work would be resumed next Thursday.
15	[67] In the Nord department, increase in the number of establishments closed. Strike in the department stores.	[47] Large demonstration in Liège (12, 000 people).	[100] Huge demonstration in Paris. While the strike movement hardens and politicizes, General de Gaulle leaves Paris. Among the public services the negotiations continue.
16	[83] Extension of the strikes to Belgium. The Belgian police oppose the occupation of the factories. At the coal mines situated to the north of Liège, workers occupy the mines for 24 hours. The government gives the order that the occupations of factories be prevented by any means. The police, supplied with gas masks, begin to evict the strikers.	[69] Teachers who until now had been on vacation, join the strike. Partial stoppage in the department stores of Brussels.	[78] Gaullist demonstration at the Place de la Concorde.

17	[83] The miners' union decide that work will be resumed today in all workplaces. In the Chamber, discussion of the bill instituting the 40-hour work week.	[100] Large demonstration in Antwerp, around 15, 000 people.	[45] The unions speed up negotiations. Return to work in the post offices.
18	[83] The Chamber passes the 40-hour bill by a vote of 408 to 160.	[63] Violent incidents in Liège; one demonstrator is killed by a bullet.	[40] A draft agreement is put to the employees of the Métro and Electricité de France. On the foreign exchange markets there is a strengthening of the franc. Rome: riots outside the French embassy.
19	[50] Cooling of the labor conflict in the steel industry.	[54] New acts of sabotage: dynamiting of roads, trees cut down, derailment of a train.	[40]
20	[39]	[54]	[55] Difficult negotiations continue in the transport and large steel-making establishments. Gasoline: the situation returns to normal.

Table 5.5a (continued)

Fourth Week: The Confrontation Hardens

Strike day	1936	1960	1968
21	[25] End of the strike in the insurance industry. Extension of the strikes in Belgium; the dockers of Antwerp and 115,000 miners join those of the steel industry. Intense agitation in the construction industry.	[60] Nearly 150 arrests (for verification of identity) among the pickets in front of the coal mines. Approximately 3,000 supplementary soldiers are brought back from Germany.	[41] The strike continues in numerous steel-making establishments. Activity from 40 to 60 percent in the coal mines.
22	[50] Agitation in Liège.	[93] New government concessions. The teachers return to work. Demonstration of 20,000 people in Antwerp.	[35] The return to work is complete at Electricité de France and in the coal mines.
23	[61] The strike movement amplifies in Belgium in the coal-mining region; barricades are erected by strikers and in the streets cobblestones are dug up; the police charge and make many arrests; a bridge near Jemmapes is partially burnt.	[54] Demonstration of 15,000 people in Mons (to the south of Brussels). Sabotage on the railways.	[53] The strike ends on the Métro and in the post offices. The conflict continues in the steel industry.
24	[33] Belgium: violent incidents in the coal-mining region.	[54] Incidents between demonstrators and the police in Charleroi.	[35] Incidents at Flins in front of the Renault factory.

25	[28] Lyons has been without trams or buses for one day. The tram workers of Bordeaux are on strike.	[89]	[40]
26	[47] End of the conflict in the department stores. Belgium: the détente becomes more pronounced; the strike ends at the port of Antwerp.	[89]	[40]
27	[22] General strike at the port of Rouen. The city of Bordeaux is still without trams.	[89]	[16]

Fifth Week: The Last Handful of Hard-liners

28	[39] Extension of the strike movement at Lyons. The dockers return to work at Bordeaux.	[78] A third demonstrator is killed by a bullet during the dispersion of a demonstration.	[8] Incidents outside car factories: In Sochaux, a young demonstrator is killed by a bullet. In Flins, a demonstrator drowns.
29	[47] Agreement between the municipal workers and the administration at Lyons. The Chenard et Walker car factory in the Paris region is reoccupied by the workers.	[2] Partial return to work in the post offices.	[15] The government decides to ban all demonstrations and to dissolve all revolutionary groups. New outburst of violence in the capital and in several provincial cities.

Table 5.5a (continued)

Strike day	1936	1960	1968
30	[33] The return to work is refused in the trams at Bordeaux. In Belgium the workers of numerous industries are still on strike.	[37] Partial return to work on the railways.	[30] Talks continue at Renault and Citröen.
31	[33] The Confédération Générale du Travail (CGT) asks workers who have not benefited from the Matignon Agreement to present their demands to their company management and to only go on strike when confronted by employer intransigence.	[33] Partial return to work in the coal mines.	[15] Return to work at Sud-Aviation voted by 55 percent. Discussions continue at Citröen.
32	[28]	[37] In the coal mines only Liège is still on strike.	[9] The employees of all Renault factories will be consulted on Monday morning.
33	[6] Occupations of the steel-making factories in the Moselle department.	[19]	[9]

34	[22] Lock-out of hoteliers on the Côte d'Azur.	[1] Death of a person injured during the incidents of January 6.	[30] At Renault the workers vote 8,701 to 4,327 in favor of a return to work.
35			[14] Partial return to work in the steel industry; the wage increases range from 10 to 14 percent.
36			[13] The last conflicts settle down slowly.

Sources: Le Monde; Féaux (1963).

Note: The numbers in square brackets represent a measure of the extension of the strike as estimated from newspaper accounts (total length of columns expressed in centimeters); for details, see the section "How to Measure the Extent of Strikes," p. 202.

Table 5.5b Synoptic chronologies of the mushroom strikes of 1953 and 1995

Strike day	1953	1995
	First Week: Start and Extension of the Strike in the Public Sector	
1	[4] The strike started the previous evening by the postmen of Bordeaux widens at national level. They are protesting against the decrees raising the retirement age by two years.	[23] A total strike on the trains begins in Tours in protest against the plan to raise the retirement age by two and a half years. The unions are divided, however, over the overall plan for the reform of Social Security.
2	[22] Postal traffic is almost paralyzed. Forty-eight-hour strike in the gas industry and at Electricité de France (power utility).	[36]
3	[70] Two million strikers in the public services. Railway and postal traffic almost null. Stoppage of Paris transport from midday. Refuse collectors in Paris are almost completely on strike. In the mines the situation is still normal.	[37] The strike spreads rapidly to the railways.
4	[61] The strike continues in the post offices and on some railways lines.	[37]
5	[61]	[28] The Métro and Electricité de France join the strike.
6	[35] Railways: Certain categories of employees were required to resume work.	[19]
	Second Week: Continuation of the Confrontation	
7	[59] No trains leave Paris. In the mines the Confédération Générale du Travail (CGT) gives the call for a general strike.	[41]

Table 5.5b (continued)

Strike day	1953	1995
8	[74] The general strike wins over the whole of the public sector. Attempts are made to extend it in the private sector. London suspends transactions on the franc. Mines: general strike in the Nord and Pas-de-Calais departments.	[33] The post offices join the strike.
9	[100] The strike of the public sector seems to extend to the private sector. Banks: between 15 and 50 percent of workers are on strike.	[59]
10	[52]	[69]
11	[52]	[69]
12	[52]	[48]
13	[59]	[32]
	Third Week: An Agreement Is Reached	
14	[57] Deadlock after the breaking off of talks.	[59] The private sector hardly follows the union call. In the car industry, in particular, there are only short stoppages.
15	[50] At Renault certain departments decide to strike.	[32] The teachers join the movement.
16	[63] The strikes threaten to spread to the steel industry. Acts of sabotage on the high-voltage line Quimper-Quimperlé.	[88] Nearly one million people participate in the demonstration of December 7.
17	[39] Agreement between the unions and the government. The return to work in the public services now depends on the local federations.	[68]

Table 5.5b (continued)

Strike day	1953	1995
18	[39] In the Paris Métro 300 stations are open.	[68]
19	[9]	[77]
20	[39] The strike continues in the public sector.	[100] Still large demonstrations throughout France.

Fourth Week: Toward the End of the Strike

Strike day	1953	1995
21	[48] Railway traffic improves on the main lines as well as on the network for the Paris suburbs.	[84]
22	[37] The situation is again normal on the railways, the Paris Métro and in the post offices. New sabotage: the train from Dijon Chalon-sur-Saône hits railroad ties blocking the tracks at 100 km per hour; in the Moselle coal field a cable-car cable is severed, causing considerable damage that takes a week to repair.	[55] The first Métro trains run again.
23	[7] New sabotage on the railways.	[67]
24	[4] Strike since the previous day at the Rouen railway station over the suspension of three railwaymen.	[67]
25	[4] The Rouen railwaymen return to work.	[61]

Table 5.5b (continued)

Strike day 1953	1995
26	[11]
27	[20] Start of social sector summit under the chairmanship of the prime minister.
28	[5] Public transport in Marseilles still paralyzed.

Source: Le Monde.

Note: The figures in square brackets represent a measure of the extension of the strike as estimated from newspaper accounts (total length of columns expressed in centimeters); for details, see the section "How to Measure the Extent of Strikes," p. 202.

(day 1). (2) In both cases Renault, the car manufacturer, joined the strike immediately (day 2); note that in 1968 it was a nationalized company whereas in 1936 it was still a private company, but this seemed to have made little difference. (3) From the very beginning both movements took the form of sit-in strikes.

Similarly consider the strikes of 1953 and 1995. (1) Both started as protests against the raising of the retirement age, by two years in one case and by two and a half years in the other (day 1). (2) Both strikes started (day 1) in the public sector (the postal service in one case, railways in the other) in a provincial city (Bordeaux in one case, Tours in the other). (3) In both cases Electricité de France, the nationalized power utility, joined the strike early on (day 2 and 5).

Not only were the start-up phases the same, but, as will be shown, their dynamics were very similar. Some forty years later the same repertoire was used in almost identical form.

THE INITIAL SPARK

One can truly speak of sparks because these strikes started at very localized points. The strike of 1936 started in the aviation factories of the Paris region; that of 1953 originated from a strike of the postmen of Bordeaux; that of 1960 started in the coal-mines; that of 1968 was initiated in the aviation factories of the Nantes region; that of 1995 began with the railwaymen of Tours. These strikes started at the level of rank-and-file workers outside the control of national unions; often the beginnings of the movement were even against the will of the union; see in this respect 1960–day 1. In December 1960 in Belgium, the unions had planned a day of protest against the vote on the new work regulations, but it was scheduled for April 1961.

PROGRESSION OF THE STRIKE

The extension and contraction phases appear clearly in Figure 5.2a–c. Yet in daily accounts it can be seen that there were also some backward steps. During the extension phase the strike ended in some places, and some factories were evacuated by the workers (see 1936, days 3, 4), and conversely some sectors went on strike during the contraction phase (see 1936, days 24, 27, 28, 33, or 1953, day 24).

OCCUPATION OF THE FACTORIES

The occupation of the factories was a common feature to the four strikes that started in the private sector. If this occupation was only partial during the strike of 1960, it is largely because of the intervention of the troops who prevented access to the factories. This form of struggle had substantial advantages for the workers, as explained by a leader of the movement in 1936 (*Le Temps*, May 28, 1936, p. 8): (1) When strikers left the factory the management could use strikebreakers; furthermore the pickets at the factory gates were often dispersed by the police. Neither action ensued while the strikers stayed inside. (2) The occupation of the factory bound the employees together and gave the strike an attractive and festive character. (3) By means of supplying the strikers, the families and even socialist city councils were associated with the movement. Once introduced in the worker repertoire, the sit-in strike would be a permanent temptation for strikers. The public authorities and employers were well aware of this danger; there were many cases in which strikers were evicted by the police or the army. For example, on August 27, 1953, five postmen were injured by police during an occupation of a telephone exchange in Paris.

INTERNATIONAL REPERCUSSIONS

The international repercussions were of two sorts: (1) in some cases the strikes or disturbances spread to neighboring countries—to Belgium in

1936 (days 16, 21, 23, 24) and to Italy in 1968 (day 18); (2) economic and financial consequences (see 1953, day 8, or 1968, days 11, 18).

PUBLIC DEMONSTRATIONS

All mushroom strikes were marked by mass demonstrations. See in this respect 1960, days 8, 9, 10, 17, 22, 23, 24; 1968, days 1, 15; and 1995, days 16, 20. The greatest of them, in Paris in May 1968, assembled nearly 1 million people. In Belgium, the numbers were more limited, rarely exceeding 40,000, but it is necessary to remember that Belgium's population is a fifth that of France. For the unions the demonstrations have evident advantages. First, they emphasize the participation and the mobilization of the strikers. Second, by the intermediary of the media they exert an influence on public opinion and, through the public, on the government and the employers. If there were no great demonstrations at the time of the general strike in Great Britain, it is because they had been outlawed.

VIOLENCE

During the strike of 1960 the clashes that led to a total of four dead took place on days 11, 18, and 28. During the strike of 1968, the clashes that led to two deaths took place on day 28. In 1953 acts of sabotage took place on days 16, 22, and 23; in 1960 these took place on days 6, 19, and 23. Essentially, therefore, violence took place in the second half of the conflicts. During the strike of 1960 in Belgium, the sabotage and the relatively high number of deaths, especially with respect to the size of the population, is undoubtedly explained in part by the bitterness of the strikers' semidefeat.

The intervention of the troops in the factories seems to be a characteristic of the strikes in Belgium; it occurred in 1936 (days 16, 23) and in 1960 (days 7, 21).

A WELL-ESTABLISHED NEGOTIATION PROCEDURE

During strikes in France, negotiations have taken place according to a relatively immutable procedure. Representatives of the employers and the unions at the national level are called together under the auspices of the government, generally at the Hôtel Matignon, the residence of the prime minister. Because all these strikes brought public enterprises into play, the state itself was an important partner in the negotiations. Often the concessions of the state were then extended in an almost automatic manner to the private sector. The gains of the workers were generally substantial. The success of these strikes partly explains their recurrence. In contrast, after their defeat in 1926, the English miners did not return to the path of the general strike until 1972, when the rise in the price of oil finally gave them a position of strength.

Quantitative Study

Before we analyze the development of strikes in a more quantitative manner, a methodological point deserves discussion. How can the extent of these strikes be estimated?

HOW TO MEASURE THE EXTENT OF STRIKES

The present investigation calls for a daily statement on the scale of the strikes. In France, the Ministry of Labor does not publish such daily statements; it is therefore necessary to find another source. We have used a somewhat indirect means of estimation by measuring the space devoted to strikes in one of the main French daily newspapers, *Le Monde* or, before 1945, *Le Temps*. This is a reliable method of measurement, as *Le Monde* maintains a strict partitioning between the various subject categories (domestic politics, social movements, sports, and so on); thus, important news in another area will only affect the space devoted to social movements in France to a fairly limited degree. This measurement (expressed as the length in centimeters of all columns added together) provides a global estimation of the impact of the strike on public opinion rather than an estimation of the number of strikers. Thus, from this perspective, large demonstrations must be considered as integral to the strikes themselves.

For Belgium there is an official source for the daily statement on the number of strikers (Féaux 1963). This raw data, however, can hardly be used as is; for example, on Monday, January 2, and Tuesday, January 3, 1961, right at the heart of the strike, the figures for the number of strikers are twenty times smaller than on Thursday, January 5. Similarly, on weekends the number of strikers is systematically reduced by half. This undoubtedly corresponds to a legal reality to the extent that a worker on holiday is not, strictly speaking, on strike. But this does not correspond to the sociological reality to the extent that, during an unlimited strike, a worker will consider himself on strike even during public holidays. We have taken this argument into account by smoothing the raw data.

Table 5.6 The dynamics of mushroom strikes

Case	Duration of the build-up phase as percentage of total duration
1. General strike set up by the unions: Sweden (1909)	20
2. Mushroom strikes	
France (1936)	31
France (1953)	32
Belgium (1960)	77
France (1968)	44
France (1995)	71
Average for mushroom strikes	51

Note: In 1909 Sweden had a unionization rate over 90 percent; in France, in contrast, the unionization rate was below 20 percent. As a result the build-up phase is much shorter in the first case.

DYNAMICS OF MUSHROOM STRIKES

If one compares Figures 5.2a and 5.2b,c, one notes a difference in the growth of the strike. In Sweden, the start of the strike took place over the course of several days, while the growth lasted ten to fifteen days in the case of the mushroom strikes. Table 5.6 gives the length of the build-up phase as a percentage of the strike's total duration. For the union-led strike of 1909 the figure is 20 percent, while it is on the order of 50 percent for mushroom strikes.

It is also of interest to see how an agreement achieved at the national level affected the subsequent evolution of the strike. In the strikes involving the private sector an agreement is usually reached around the fifteenth day of the strike; but after that agreement it takes about two weeks for work to resume. In the strikes where only the public sector was involved the agreement was reached later, but subsequently work resumed with less inertia. This makes sense intuitively. Private companies do not necessarily fall in line with an agreement reached at the national level; therefore further pressure has to be applied. The case is different for Sweden, where there was no national agreement and where, even locally, the concessions of the employers were limited; strikers returned to work according to their financial situation.

Summary and Conclusion

In the first part of this chapter we studied several characteristics of strikes and, more specifically, of general strikes. For instance, we showed that the frequency of strikes has become substantially lower since World War II. Concerning the seasonality of strikes, we pointed out that strikes are on average less frequent in the winter time, but that the actual pattern is industry dependent. Furthermore we have seen that the great general strikes that occurred in the three decades between 1885 and 1920 usually ended in crushing defeat for the unions. But we also described a successful general strike, the highly political strike of 1974 in Ulster.

Most strikes described in the first part of the chapter were controlled by the unions. However there are also strikes that develop spontaneously and even (at least initially) against unions' directions; these strikes we have called mushroom strikes. In the twentieth century there have been five major mushroom strikes in Belgium and France. Whereas the duration of the general strikes ranged from one hour to two months, the mushroom strikes have always had approximately the same duration, namely about one month; a little more when the private sector takes part in the strike along with the public sector, a little less when the strike involves only the public sector.

Variations in the strength and frequency of social interaction probably play an important role in the outbreak and spread of mushroom strikes. We already have mentioned this factor in connection with revolutions. The role of social interaction was remarkably analyzed by Tarrow (1995) in a paper about the wave of strikes in Italy in the period 1966–1973; in particular, he shows that the episodes marked by strong interpersonal interaction (occupation of institutional or business premises) brought about numerous new forms of action (in that respect see also Zolberg 1972). Unfortunately social interaction is a factor that is difficult to assess quantitatively; this was true for revolutionary movements, and it is even more difficult here. Qualitatively it is clear, however, that mushroom strikes give people the opportunity to interact more closely. The huge demonstrations bring thousands of people together; the sit-in strikes give the workers the opportunity to talk together or to have meals together; with the Métro and buses idle, people have to cooperate to make their journeys (by hitchhiking, for example), and this again gives them occasion to interact.

Wars

CHAPTER

6

Wars for Territorial Expansion

Lewis Richardson, a pioneer in the quantitative study of war, describes the attitude of the public toward such studies in the following terms: "There is a wide public interest in the subject provided it is expressed in bold rhetoric, but not if it is a quantitative scientific study involving statistics" (1960). Although the main purpose of the present chapter is to make comparisons and find regularities, we do not restrict ourselves to analyzing statistical data.

One might think that territorial expansion is a major reason for wars between nations. In fact the reasons for which nations enter into conflict are innumerable. Practically none of the wars that England waged in continental Europe after the eighteenth century had the objective of territorial expansion. Essentially, England has intervened in European conflicts to prevent the emergence of a hegemonic power or to safeguard its maritime supremacy and lines of communication with its empire. In the same manner, the participation of the United States in world conflicts after 1910 has not resulted in any territorial gain. However, even if territorial disputes constitute only one category within the ensemble of conflicts, this category is still too large and too diversified for comparative analysis to be applied to it in a fruitful manner. In this chapter, we will focus on a more specific category of territorial expansion involving new nation-states.

From the eighteenth century Europe has seen the emergence of a group of nation-states. When society changes from the domination of the aristocracy to a structure that allows large sections of the population to participate in the management of public affairs, the process produces a sort of social mobilization. History has shown that this social mobilization has often been accompanied by increased centralization and efficiency. We use the expression "national activation" to refer to this phenomenon. One of the possible outlets for this new force is territorial expansion. There is no shortage of examples of this phenomenon: Sweden and England in the seventeenth century, France between 1790 and 1815, Prussia and then Germany in the nineteenth and twentieth centuries. Outside Europe, Japan constitutes another spectacular example. Although the expansion of colonial empires in the nineteenth century could equally be considered as an effect related to this mechanism, we will leave this phenomenon outside our consideration here.

In this chapter, we will show that a large number of the conflicts of the nineteenth and twentieth centuries can be regrouped under the common denominator of a national activation. Then, by examining the specific means employed in each conflict, we will see that each country, consciously or not, has used the same tactical or strategic formulas on several occasions, especially when they have proved initially successful. These paronymic recurrences are not only the expression of geographic constraints. Certainly these play a role, and it is obvious that the territorial expansion of a nation established on an island, such as England, would not be the same as that of a more continental nation, such as Germany or Russia. However, one will notice that historical inheritance has essentially determined and modeled the strategic choices of nations. Thus despite their common insularity, England and Japan have had very dissimilar paths of territorial expansion. We shall see that in its ways and means the Japanese expansion of 1937–1942 was largely drawn from the previous experience of 1894–1905.

During the last two centuries, there has been an abundant diversity of conflicts. If at the end of this chapter the reader is able to recognize a framework and some main themes from these conflicts, our objective will be fulfilled. We want to show that there is some kind of order behind the apparent chaos of facts and events. More specifically, we concentrate on three primary questions. (1) In the course of the seventeenth and eighteenth centuries, Sweden was a great conquering nation, yet after 1815 it no longer experienced war. Can this transition be integrated into the proposed general schema? (2) From 1650 to 1830 the French armies fought almost constantly outside their national territory, mainly in the Netherlands, Germany and Italy. Conversely, after 1830 the German armies took the strategic offensive and fought almost permanently away from their own soil, mainly in Austria, France, and Russia. How can we explain this reversal? (3) In 1941 Japan launched itself into the madness of a war against the

United States, a country that had a gross national product nearly ten times superior to its own. Can paronymic analysis explain that strategic choice?

The Study of Wars: Epic Accounts or a Scientific Approach?

If one only takes into account the sequence of facts, each war is certainly a unique event. Nevertheless the degree of recurrence of various kinds of conflicts suggests a certain paronymy at the level of the means of invasion, the places of battle, and the organization of logistics. Let us give some examples of these repetitive conflicts. Between 1710 and 1880, for example, there were eight Russo-Turkish wars: 1710, 1711, 1736–1739, 1769–1774, 1787–1792, 1806–1812, 1827–1829, 1853–1856, and 1877–1878 (Bodart 1908, p. 730). Is it not normal to suppose that in forming their campaign plans the Russian General Staff were as a rule inspired by those of the preceding campaign, especially if they had been crowned in success? In South Africa, between 1779 and 1853, there were eight successive wars between the Cape colonists and the Xhosa tribes. From the Franco-German wars to Anglo-Afghan wars, it would be easy to multiply this type of example. However, there are few fields of history in which the epic account is so dominant over the scientific approach. For instance it is not surprising that in the late twentieth century epic accounts of colonial wars continued to be published in scholarly works (for example, Clammer 1973, Hibbert 1978). Van Creveld (1995 [1977]) stresses with good reason that historians describe in luxurious detail the heroic deeds and defeats while granting only a very superficial attention to the logistics that allowed these battles to take place.

Attempts at a scientific study of conflicts have until now remained very isolated. Let us cite in this respect the pioneering works of Wright (1942), Richardson (1960), Bouthoul (1970), Singer and Small (1972), and Holsti (1991), and Clodfelter (1992). Regarding the impact of technical change (in the broadest sense of the word), the work of Van Creveld (1977, 1989, 1998) opened a new perspective; our comparative approach in this chapter and the next owes much to his careful and well-documented studies. We should also cite the fascinating and remarkable study of the military history of Britain by French (1990). In this work, the author dissects the functioning of the British military institution; seen under this light the recurrent aspects of the military means employed appear clearly.

In recent years there have been a number of comparative studies of war that go in the same direction as the present chapter. These analyses indicate that the topic remains an active field in sociology; see in particular (Lynn 1990, 1993, 1997), Porter (1994), and Black (1998).

Of particular importance for any comparative study of war, whatever its objective, is the availability of systematic statistical data. In that respect the following books are of immense value: Berndt (1897), Bodart (1908), Richardson (1960), and Clodfelter (1992).

Although comparative history offers no exciting accounts of battles and campaigns, it does make connections not otherwise possible. We illustrate the contrast between these two approaches with three examples.

Poltava (1709)

In 1709 the king of Sweden, Charles XII, led his army of 20,000 seasoned veterans across immense Russia. On July 8 (Gregorian calendar) the Russians achieved at Poltava (Ukraine) a victory that had an enormous effect in Europe, because the Swedish had until then been taken to be invincible. Many historians (for example, Svanstrom et al. 1944; Andersson 1973; and Scott 1977) attributed this defeat to the fact that Charles XII, having been injured two days before, could not lead his army. Even if this argument appears reasonable, one can doubt its legitimacy in light of the huge numerical superiority of the Russians. There were 45,000 Russians against only 26,000 Swedes, and above all, they had seventy-two cannons while the Swedes had no more than four (Bodart 1908, p. 159; Andersson 1973). Moreover, the Russians had already achieved a victory several months earlier at the battle of Lesnaya on October 9, 1708 (Sumner 1951, p. 70). In other words, if one calls on more systematic information, the surprise effect of Poltava disappears almost completely. Perhaps the account loses some of its dramatic interest, but there is no doubt that historical analysis gains by it.

Waterloo (1815)

"If it had not rained on the night of 17–18 June 1815 the future of Europe would have changed . . . The battle of Waterloo could not begin until half-past eleven, and that gave Blücher the time to come up. Why? Because the ground was moist and it was necessary for it to become firmer so that the artillery might maneuver . . . Had the earth been dry and the artillery able to move, the action would have begun at 6 A.M. It would have been won and finished by 2 P.M." So writes Victor Hugo about the battle of Waterloo in *Les Miserables* (1997). In his account, he dramatizes the action by multiplying the reversals of the situation. On several occasions, as in the passage cited here, he stresses that the outcome of the battle stemmed from only minor and fortuitous circumstances. Switching rapidly from tactics to strategy, he suggests that the outcome of the campaign, and thus the future of Europe, depended on these circumstances. One is hardly surprised, of course, that a novelist takes such liberties with the historical truth; however, this tendency for dramatization is equally found in most accounts by historians. Moreover, it is interesting to note that another great novelist, Leo Tolstoy, had a more sensible conception of history. The account that he gives in his novel *War and Peace* (1971, p. 890) of the battle of Borodino (September 7, 1812) is an illustration of the concept of "critical distance" introduced by Clausewitz:

> Behind them [the French army] thousands of versts of famine-stricken, hostile country; before them dozens of versts between them and their goal. Every soldier of Napoleon's army feels it, and the expedition advances of itself, by the force of its own impetus. At Borodino the armies meet. Neither army is destroyed . . . The French reach Moscow and there halt. For five weeks after this there is not a single battle. The French do not move . . . And all at once, with nothing to account for it, they flee back.

To return to the battle of Waterloo we call on Clausewitz for a more realistic view of the situation. It is well known that he made a thorough analysis of the Napoleonic campaigns and that his studies had a great influence on the Prussian and Russian military. Clausewitz began by making a precise examination of the opposing forces. For the whole of the campaign the number of allies totaled 645,000: 100,000 Anglo-Hanoverian-Dutch under Wellington, 115,000 Prussians under Blücher, 140,000 Russians, 230,000 Austrians. On the other side there were 195,000 French. For the battle of Waterloo itself the opposing numbers were as follows: 120,000 allies, of which 24,000 were English, 44,000 Hanoverian-Dutch, and 52,000 Prussians (Bodart 1908, p. 487). The French had 72,000 men. From these figures Clausewitz (1972) draws two conclusions. First, in view of the disproportion of the forces (3.3 to 1), it was out of the question that Napoleon could prevail over the whole campaign. Second, the very most that he could achieve was some partial successes by applying his tactic of concentration of forces. The fact that at Waterloo the disproportion of forces could be reduced to a ratio of 1.7 to 1 shows the relative success of his capacities for maneuver. However even if Napoleon had prevailed at Waterloo, the outcome of the campaign would not have been changed.

Hugo's speculations are therefore unfounded. In his defense, it must be said that the military chroniclers of World War II accumulated the same type of speculations. What would have happened if, during the Normandy landing on June 6, 1944, Rommel had not been in Germany? The response again is simple; Allied supremacy in terms of armament production, aerial cover, and balance of power was so overwhelming that the outcome of the war would have remained the same.

By following tactical matters too closely, one loses sight of the strategic situation, that is, the balance of power in the whole theater of operations. The following example provides another illustration of this lack of perspective.

The Pacific War

The Pacific War took place over an immense area. There are approximately 10,000 kilometers between Los Angeles and Tokyo, and quite obviously logistics were going to play a central role in this conflict. Parillo (1993) has made a fascinating contribution to our understanding of this aspect of the war by studying the role of the Japanese merchant navy. As we know, it was decimated by the fleet of American submarines. Parillo details some of the "reasons": lack of reconnaissance planes, not enough torpedo boats to organize convoys, not enough antiaircraft artillery on the tankers, insufficient production of synthetic fuel; this enumeration could be lengthened infinitely. But here also the trees tend to hide the forest. In 1938 the gross domestic product of the United States was ten times greater than that of Japan (Liesner 1989). In view of this disproportion, was it not to be expected that in almost all compartments of the production of armaments, Japan would be outclassed? But this suggests another question: why then did Japan launch itself into such a war? This is one of the issues that we tackle below.

Wars in Europe: Economic and Geographic Constraints

A recurrent theme of this chapter, as indeed in the rest of the book, is the importance of historical constraints. Throughout different conflicts the same strategies will be reused in a recurrent manner. These strategic/tactical choices are furthermore subject to geographic and socioeconomic constraints. To take an extreme example, of all the campaigns that took place between the seventeenth and nineteenth centuries, no major battle (in-

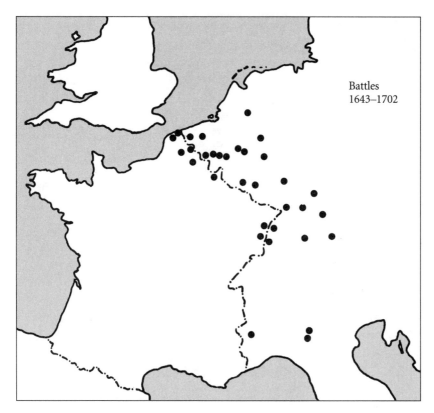

Figure 6.1a Sites of battles and sieges in the period 1643–1702. Not surprisingly, the regions where most battles occurred were fertile plains on which large armies could be deployed and sustained. The wars of the seventeenth and eighteenth centuries consisted in recurring struggles for the control of the same set of fortified cities. *Source:* Bodart (1908).

volving more than 100,000 combatants) took place in a mountainous massif at an altitude over 1,000 meters. Therefore, before further examining the historical constraints in detail, we review the spatial and economic constraints.

Geoeconomic Constraints

As can be seen in Figure 6.1, the favorite campaign terrains of the armies of the seventeenth and eighteenth centuries were large fertile plains: the plains of modern Belgium, the Netherlands, the Rhineland, the Palatinate, and to a smaller extent Bavaria and the plain of the Po. In the seventeenth

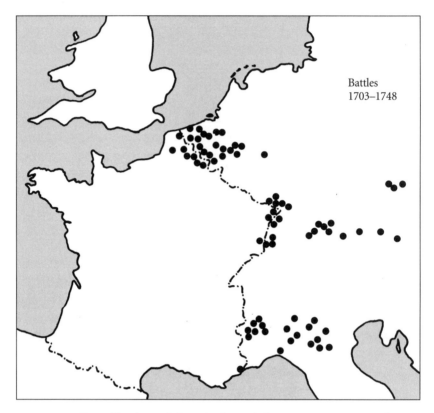

Figure 6.1b Sites of battles and sieges in the period 1703–1758. *Source:* Bodart (1908).

and eighteenth centuries, the food equilibrium was very fragile even in these regions. A bad harvest (reduction in supply) or the passage of an army (increase in demand) could trigger an explosion of grain prices. A multiplication of prices by a factor of two, three, or even four in the space of a year was not rare; the same was also true to some extent throughout the nineteenth century. This is shown clearly in series of wheat prices that cover long periods, as for example the prices at Toulouse that cover the period 1486–1913 (see Drame et al. 1991, pp. 104–105). The armies' supply services were well aware of this problem. One of the essential motivations that pushed the French government to draw up detailed summaries of wheat prices in all the important cities was precisely to ease the stationing of troops and the purchases of the supply services. Typically, troops were

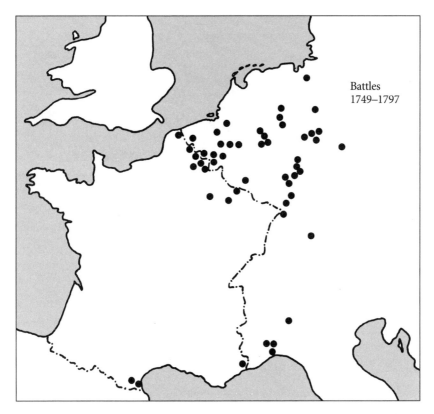

Figure 6.1c Sites of battles and sieges during the wars of the period 1749–1797. Until 1797 the conflicts took place in the same regions as in the hundred years before (see Figure 6.1b); after 1797, during the Napoleonic Wars, there was a major rupture, with wars of movement replacing wars of position and with battle areas shifting to eastern Europe (Austria, Prussia, and Russia). *Source:* Bodart (1908).

directed to regions that were in surplus at the time. This had a double advantage. On the one hand, the supply service could buy wheat at its lowest price, and on the other hand, these purchases allowed the farmers to pay their taxes in cash, which would otherwise have been extremely difficult in view of the small quantity of money in circulation. This preoccupation appears, for example, in the following letter from the intendant of Soissons, dated November 11, 1707, and addressed to the comptroller general of finances: "It does not appear to me to be possible to collect the taxes if you do not have the kindness to mandate the armies' supply service to purchase part of its wheat within Soissons" (Drame et al. 1991, p. 56). Note that

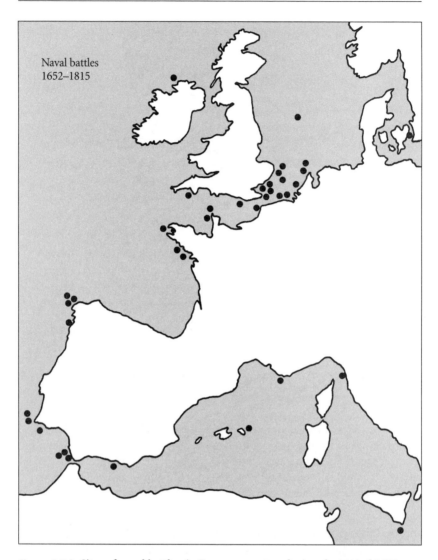

Figure 6.1d Sites of naval battles in European waters during the period 1652–1815. There is a notable permanence of the battle zones during these 164 years. *Source:* Bodart (1908).

Soissons was situated in a rich wheat plain to the northeast of Paris. A confirmation of the importance of supply is brought by the fact that no military campaign of any great extent has taken place in the less fertile regions of Portugal or central Spain. Even the Peninsular War (1807–1814), fought by Britain, Spain, and Portugal against French troops, involved comparably smaller numbers than those of the campaigns that were taking place at the same time in Germany and Austria.

Temporal Constraints

As a corollary of the supply constraint, armies preferred spring and summer campaigns. It was particularly the cavalry that was subject to this seasonal imperative. While an infantryman only needed 1 kilogram of bread per day, a horse needed approximately 10 kilograms of fodder (Van Creveld 1995 [1977]). When this fodder was not available in meadows, the requirement posed almost insurmountable supply problems. However, it must be noted that the size of the cavalry in comparison to the infantry could be quite variable. At the battle of Novi Ligure (August 15, 1799, 40 kilometers to the north of Genoa) the French army counted 33,000 infantrymen and only 2,000 cavalrymen, which is 16 infantrymen per cavalryman. At the battle of Schellenberg (July 2, 1704, 40 kilometers to the north of Augsburg) Marlborough had 4,000 cavalrymen and 20,000 infantrymen, which is 5 infantrymen per cavalryman; but a month later at the battle of Blenheim (August 13, 1704, 35 kilometers to the north of Augsburg), after a strengthening by the army of Prince Eugene of Savoy, the allied troops counted 20,000 cavalrymen for 30,000 infantrymen, which is 1.5 infantrymen per cavalryman (Bodart 1908).

Wright (1942) provides the following figures for the percentage of sieges and battles that took place in spring and summer (April–September):

	Century			
	17th	18th	19th	20th
Spring/summer engagements	75%	67%	56%	57%

In the eighteenth century, there were twice as many sieges and battles in the six hot months as in the six cold months. This figure would be even larger if one considered only the battles involving large numbers and in particular large numbers of cavalry. Of the twenty-five battles between 1643 and 1796 with a number of losses greater than 10,000, only three took place during cold months (Bodart 1908); the excess of the hot months therefore passes from a ratio of 2:1 to 7:1.

In naval battles the question of supply is not an issue, but it is necessary to take account of the fact that in the Atlantic, the cold months are also the months marked by frequent storms. Of the forty-five naval battles counted by Bodart from 1652 to 1815, only sixteen took place during cold months; the excess of the hot months is again double.

Financial Constraints

In the rest of this chapter when we wish to judge the balance of power between two countries, we use three criteria: total population; central government revenue; and gross national (or domestic) product.

The criterion of population is very rudimentary; its main interest consists in the fact that these statistics are available even for ancient times. We know, for example, that the armies of the seventeenth and eighteenth centuries were not very large. It is true that at the battle of Malplaquet (September 11, 1709), the most important in terms of the numbers involved of all those of the seventeenth and eighteenth centuries, there were about 180,000 combatants, but this was an entirely exceptional case. In most cases, the total size of the two armies was around 50,000. Recruiting such numbers did not pose problems from the point of view of demographics, but because they were armies of professionals (and mostly mercenaries), it was essential to be able to pay them. Consequently the level of state income was the essential variable. From this perspective, prosperous and strongly centralized states with an efficient administration became dominant. The citizens' prosperity was the primary condition, because the state could only levy taxes, whether in the form of customs duties or income taxes, if there was strong economic activity. Centralization and the degree of efficiency often went hand in hand. As an example, Holland was the most prosperous country in Europe in the eighteenth century, but the absence of an efficient centralization prevented it from standing up to England; by the end of the eighteenth century it had almost become a British protectorate. In the twentieth century, when the size of armies reached several million people, the demographic argument played a nonnegligible role; however, in this period the imperative of armament production became equally crucial.

Even between two administratively centralized countries such as England and France, there could be notable differences with respect to the productivity of the fiscal systems. For instance, tax farming had been abandoned in England before 1688; taxes were collected relatively efficiently by civil servants. In France, where tax farming was still prevalent, a considerable proportion of the revenues that the state might have collected remained in the hands of private tax collectors. This difference, in addition to the greater commercial prosperity of Britain, explains why the income of the British government was superior to that of France, despite a notably smaller population.

In the case of the wars of the twentieth century, especially when they lasted several years, it was the gross national product that was the significant variable—for two reasons, one industrial and the other financial. First, the national product is an estimator of the industrial capacity that can be redirected to the armament industry for the production of ships, airplanes, tanks, cannons, and so on. Second, as fiscal resources alone could not finance the world wars of the twentieth century, governments were forced to call on both internal and external loans; and the productive capacity of a country is of course an essential criterion for the concession of credits by the international financial community.

Let us note in passing, even though it goes beyond the focus of this chapter, that wars in turn exerted an important influence on the state. First, they contributed to the centralization of the state. Two examples will suffice. (1) In Britain, as a result of the Napoleonic Wars, the government's income doubled between 1799 and 1808 (French 1990, p. 106). (2) In the United States, the ratio of federal receipts to gross national product increased from about 8 percent in 1939 to 18 percent in 1945; after the war, instead of returning to its prewar value, this percentage stabilized at a level between 18 and 20 percent. Second, wars contribute to the improvement of financial institutions. It is certainly not a coincidence that the Bank of England was created in 1694, that is to say during the Nine Years' War; this war cost Britain £49 million, and to generate loans of this size it was necessary to have solid financial institutions (French 1990, pp. 16–17).

Sweden

It may seem paradoxical to begin a study of expansionist wars with Sweden. Is there a more peaceful country than Sweden? It is the only European nation that has succeeded in living continually in peace since 1815. It has not always been this way, however, and one can even say that Sweden was ahead of the other European nations in inaugurating a type of territorial expansion based on the nation-state. In the sixteenth century Sweden was engaged in a modernization of the state and in an expansion based on an army recruited by conscription. Within a few decades, it had established an empire that covered the whole periphery of the Baltic (Figure 6.2). The dimensions of this empire are all the more remarkable if one takes into ac-

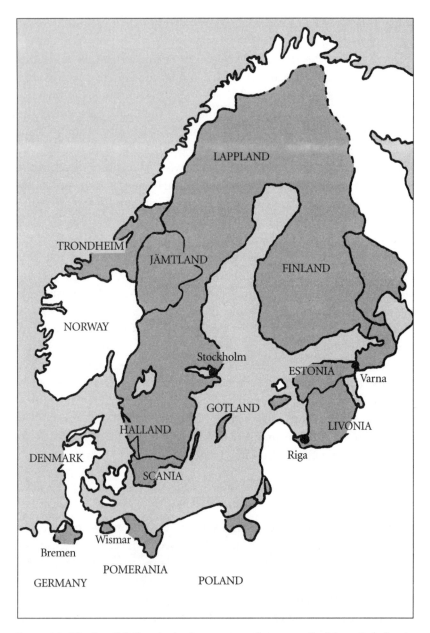

Figure 6.2 The Swedish Empire in the seventeenth century. In this period, despite its limited population, Sweden was a major expansionist power. It occupied many regions on the periphery of the Baltic Sea, particularly in Estonia, Germany, Livonia, Poland, and Russia. Its armies waged major battles in these countries, notably during the Thirty Years' War.

count the small population of the country, on the order of one million residents in the middle of the seventeenth century. This expansion broke sharply with the two types of wars that had until then dominated throughout Europe: dynastic conflicts and struggles between the monarchies and great feudal lords (for example, the wars of the Fronde in France, 1648–1652). In line with the spirit of the time the Swedes presented themselves as crusaders for Protestantism, although this did not rule out a long period of alliance with France.

Sweden presents the first example in Europe of a mechanism that we will find again on several occasions and that can be schematized by the following stages. (1) A coming to power of a ruling class having solid popular support and in which the aristocracy plays a more limited role than in the past. (2) Institution of an army based on conscription. (3) Brilliant military successes and constitution of a vast empire. (4) Maintenance of the army ensured by levies in the conquered territories. At the same time, the militarization of society restores to the nobility a part of its influence that it had lost. (5) Threatened by this expansionist power, Sweden's neighbors unite against it. At the same time, a popular resistance develops in the occupied territories. (6) Confronted with internal discontent and a military threat from outside, the empire finds its days numbered. A military defeat (Poltava in the case of Sweden) formally puts an end to the experience. The empire more or less returns to its former frontiers.

In the case of Sweden, the unfolding of this scenario took place over nearly a century and a half, from 1560 to 1709. The scenario is basically the same for France from 1792 to 1815; for Germany from 1870 to 1918 and 1935 to 1945; for Japan from 1890 to 1945. In the following paragraphs we examine the stages of this process for the case of Sweden.

Dates and Opposing Forces

Sweden's immediate neighbors were Denmark, Poland, Russia, and the states of northern Germany. Let us recall that during the period of the Union of Kalmar (1389–1521), Denmark, Finland, Norway, and Sweden were part of the same kingdom. In 1521 the union was broken under the impetus of Gustav I Vasa, which left on one side a bloc made up of Denmark and Norway and on the other the bloc of Sweden and Finland. For nearly a century and a half, these two blocs of comparable size carried out unceasing struggles. The two other neighbors of Sweden, Poland and Russia, had populations ten to twenty times greater. The fact that this did not constitute an insurmountable obstacle to the expansion of Sweden is in part the result of the weak effect of the total population on military power combined with particular circumstances. Toward the middle of the seventeenth century, Poland was already heading for the political disintegration that would result in its dismemberment at the end of the eighteenth century. As for Russia, it experienced a period of turmoil from 1598 to 1610, and it was only from the reign of Peter the Great (1682–1725) that it played a role consistent with its demographic importance. The states of northern Germany were easier prey for Sweden. At an early stage, it acquired territories in Pomerania and the dukedom of Bremen that would serve as its base for its expeditions to Denmark or toward southern Germany.

Table 6.1a summarizes the wars in which Sweden was involved; Table 6.1b gives population estimates for some of the countries at war.

The Constitution of a Modern State
The realization of internal unity and the setting-up of a centralized state with a large popular base were preliminary conditions to territorial expansion. This was the work of Gustav I Vasa and his first successors.

INTERNAL UNITY
One of the direct causes of the rupture between Sweden and Denmark was what has been called the Stockholm Bloodbath (1520). As a reprisal for previous turmoil and despite a promise of amnesty, eighty-two people were executed; among them were bishops and several members of the

Table 6.1a Sweden: Expansion wars, 1580–1715

Year	Opponents	Total number of battle deaths	Reference
1581	Russia		Andersson (1973)
1595–1648	Denmark		Mousson-Lestang (1995)
1610	Russia		Andersson (1973)
1631–1645	German Empire	10,000	Bodart (1908)
1655–1659	Poland, Russia	800	Bodart (1908)
1658	Denmark		Svanström and Palmstierna (1944).
1674–1680	German Empire	2,000	Bodart (1908)
1676	Denmark		Svanström and Palmstierna (1944)
1700	Denmark		Svanström and Palmstierna (1944)
1700–1710	Poland, Russia	10,000	Bodart (1908)
1713	Denmark		Svanström and Palmstierna (1944)

Table 6.1b Population in northern Europe in the eighteenth century

Country	Population (millions)	Reference
Denmark	1.6 (1769)	Mitchell (1978)
Russia	35.0 (1800)	Mitchell (1978)
Saxony	0.5 (1817)	Flora, Kraus, and Pfenning (1987)
Sweden	1.8 (1750)	Mitchell (1978)

Riksdag. The figure may appear small, but it is necessary to view it in relation to the population of Sweden, which was then on the order of 500,000. In proportion, this figure is of the same order of magnitude as the number of victims of the Saint Bartholomew's Day Massacre in France (1572). Once independence was secured, one of the main tasks of Gustav I Vasa (1521–1560) was to ensure the financial basis of the state and to strengthen national unity. Because of the progress of the Reformation in Northern Europe, these two objectives could be achieved together. In this period in Sweden, the Church possessed 20 percent of the land, against 20 percent for the nobility and 6 percent for the crown. The passage of Sweden to the Reformation resulted in successive expropriations of ecclesiastical goods in 1527, 1530, and 1540. Gustav I Vasa had to suppress two uprisings that put national unity in peril, the first in 1531 in Dalarna to the northwest of Stockholm, the second in 1542–1543 in Smaland to the southwest of Stockholm. Despite some autocratic trends, Gustav I Vasa respected the prerogatives of the assembly of the states, the Riksdag. Uniquely in Europe, this assembly comprised not only the nobility, the clergy, and the bourgeoisie but also the property-owning peasantry. Once these bases were well established, territorial expansion could begin under the reign of Erik XIV, the successor to Gustav I Vasa. In 1561, Sweden got a foothold in Estonia. What rendered the conquests possible was the constitution of an army of a new type.

AN ARMY OF A NEW TYPE IN EUROPE

Erik XIV (1560–1568) created an army based on conscription, which was a radical innovation for the period. In most of the countries of Europe the army was mainly formed of mercenaries. This was true at least until the end of the eighteenth century, when conscription was introduced under the influence of the French Revolution. The army of Gustav II Adolf (1611–1632) equally foreshadowed the armies of the Revolution and the

Empire with regard to tactics. As would be the case with Napoleon, Gustav II Adolf sought mobility both for the infantry and for the artillery. The rapid marches of Gustav required a mobility that could only be obtained by first discarding the pikemen's armor and then the pike itself. In addition to the standard pieces of light field artillery, Gustav introduced light iron guns invented by Alexander Hamilton, one of the many Scots in the Swedish service (Firth 1902). This mobile and light artillery would play a large role in several important battles, of which two may be cited as examples. At the battle of Leipzig, September 17, 1631, the swiftness with which the Swedish light field artillery was charged and fired threw Tilly's infantry into confusion and was the chief cause of their defeat. A second example was the crossing of the Lech in the face of Tilly's infantry that was attributed entirely to the effect of the seventy-two guns that Gustav had concentrated upon the entrenchments of the Imperialists.

A great number of Scottish and English officers had been in the service of Gustav II Adolf. The Cromwellian New Model Army borrowed more from the Swedish army than from any other military system, an indication of the high regard in which the Swedish system was held.

TERRITORIAL EXPANSION

The Swedish army had five primary campaign terrains and routes of penetration.

1. The Baltic countries. Two trouble spots were Varna, situated to the east of Estonia, and Riga, situated to the west of Livonia, currently Latvia. Near Narva, there were two important Swedish victories in 1581 and 1700. The siege of Riga was undertaken in 1621.
2. Russia. There were two Russian campaigns: in 1610, under the command of Jacob Pontusson de la Gardie and in alliance with a dissident Russian party, a Swedish army penetrated as far as Moscow; in 1708–1709, the disastrous Russian campaign of Charles XII took place.
3. Poland. Most notable were the campaigns of Charles X Gustav in 1655 and that of Karl Gustav Wrangel in 1658.
4. Germany. The campaigns of 1631–1645 were part of the Thirty Years' War, and a new campaign took place in 1674–1680. Two important victories took place at Breitenfeld (west of Leipzig) in 1631 and 1642.
5. Denmark. From their possessions in Pomerania, the Swedes had

only 300 kilometers to cover (approximately two to three weeks of marching) to reach the Danish Jutland. Such campaigns took place in 1644, 1658 and 1713.

The Treaty of Westphalia (1648) that marked the end of the Thirty Years' War gave the status of Great Power to Sweden, a remarkable fact given its small population.

LOSING GROUND

From the second half of the seventeenth century, the rise to power of Brandenburg (in 1701, Frederick III took the title of king of Prussia) and of the Russia of Peter the Great rendered things more difficult for Sweden. In 1699 a coalition was formed consisting of Saxony, Poland, Denmark, and Russia. Furthermore, in several of the occupied territories a popular resistance developed, especially in Poland (Svanström and Palmstierna 1944). Even in Scania (the southern province of Sweden), acquired in 1658 from Denmark, there was in 1678 the uprising of the Snapphanar, supported secretly by Denmark.

During the period of intense military activity, one witnessed a renewal of the nobility's influence. The numerous aristocratic residences constructed in the years 1630–1660 provide eloquent testimony to their owners' power. During the second half of the reign of Charles XI (1680–1697), the struggle against the nobility led the state to an increasingly autocratic form. The period 1680–1718 was in fact the only period in Sweden when the Riksdag was deprived of its traditional prerogatives. This was a source of deep internal discontent. The Russian campaign of Charles XII in 1708–1709 marked the beginning of the disintegration of the Swedish Empire. Nevertheless, it was only ten years later, after the death of Charles XII in 1719, that the Riksdag resumed its traditional role. A constitution put into place a constitutional monarchy.

From this period of territorial expansion, Sweden nevertheless preserved a certain numbers of possessions, especially Scania, Halland with Gothenburg, Jaemtland, and the island of Gotland.

England

The case of England is paradoxical. Here is a country that fairly early established a centralized and efficient government system, along with a dynamic economy. These are the ingredients for what we have called a national activation. However, this country did not experience a spectacular period of territorial expansion, or more precisely the British expansion was of a different type; it was confined to Ireland and Scotland. From the seventeenth century on there was also an important colonial expansion in North America and the Caribbean. The general schema therefore seems to apply, but in a slightly modified form. To what must we attribute this singularity? Unquestionably to the fact that England was essentially a maritime power. This predominance of the colonial phenomenon is found for other maritime nations, such as the Netherlands or, in an earlier period, Spain, Portugal, and Venice. Even so, it remains remarkable that England, in spite of its dominant position from the end of the eighteenth century, avoided any direct territorial expansion. After 1750 the Netherlands were practically a British protectorate, as already noted, and the British armies made frequent incursions there in the course of their European wars. However the stage of a disguised annexation was never reached, in contrast to Japan in Korea and Manchuria.

The rest of this section will be devoted to England's expansion of 1649–1652 in Ireland and the expansion of 1650–1654 in Scotland. What renders these two expansions unspectacular is the fact that they were preceded by a long series of incursions. However, the expansions of 1649–1654 were by their extent truly the prelude to a de facto annexation, even if this would only arise some time later. Thus in Ireland the share of landed property held by Catholics fell between 1641 and 1688 from 60 percent to 20 percent (Edwards 1981).

Dates and Opposing Forces

In the enumeration of conflicts (Table 6.2a) we restrict ourselves to the period 1649–1680. After this date, there were several more limited Jacobite uprisings in Scotland; as for the history of Ireland, it was, as we know, filled with a long series of insurrections. The ratio of populations in Table 6.2b reflects only imperfectly the balance of power. Because of its centralization, the efficiency of its system of fiscal collection, and its commercial development, the English government disposed of an income largely superior to that of its neighbors.

The New Model Army

Conquests were rendered possible by the numerical importance of the army and by its new efficiency. We have already pointed out that Crom-

Table 6.2a England: Expansion wars, 1640–1680

Year	Opponents	Total number of battle deaths	Reference
1649–1651	Ireland	7,000	Guizot (1854); Lingard (1829)
1650–1652	Scotland	>3,700	Bodart (1908), pp. 77–78; Donaldson (1971)
1653–1654	Highlanders		Reid (1971), p. 208
1655	Spain		Guizot (1854)
1679	Scotland	700	Bodart (1908), p. 103

well's New Model Army was largely based on that of Gustav II Adolf, which was at the time the most innovative in Europe. From a numerical point of view, important numbers were maintained even after the conquest of Ireland and Scotland. In 1645, the Parliament's army consisted of 65,000 men without counting the Scots. In 1652, there were 70,000 soldiers (34,000 in Ireland). In 1657, there were still 43,500 soldiers, for which Firth (1902) gives the following geographic distribution:

England	10,000
Ireland	15,000
Scotland	10,400
Flanders	6,600
Jamaica	1,500

In the history of England it was quite uncommon to have a standing army of that importance. With regard to finance, the expenses for the army were equally considerable. In March 1649, after having voted for the abolition of the royalty, the House of Commons voted an amount of £1.4 million per year for the maintenance of an army of 44,000 men (Guizot 1854). This was a huge sum if one remembers that in 1692 government income reached only £4.1 million (Mitchell 1971).

In 1645 the so-called New Model Army was one of several armies, but in 1649 it had absorbed and incorporated into itself all the other armies of the Parliament. Two distinctive features of this army are well known. First, it followed a rule of promotion by merit, which meant that the officer corps was to a certain extent open to men not coming from the aristocracy. Second, this army was animated by a religious zeal that served as a spur. Just as the political commissioners propagated the revolutionary fervor in

Table 6.2b Population and public revenue of England, Ireland, and Scotland

Country	Population (millions)		Government revenue (million pounds)		Reference
England	6.4	(1750)	4.3	(1700)	Mitchell (1971), p. 386
Ireland	3.2	(1754)	0.3	(1680)	Mitchell (1971); Macaulay (1989 [1861])
Scotland	1.2	(1755)	0.003	(1700)	Mitchell (1971); Coupland (1954)
			0.06	(1700)	Macaulay (1989[1861]), vol. 2, p. 1011

Note: The Scottish revenue reported by Coupland may seem excessively small, and we only cite it with reservation. However, it must be remembered that even before 1707 Scotland did not maintain a fleet or a permanent army. The figure cited by Macaulay corresponds to an annual fiscal levy voted by the Scottish parliament after the accession to power of William III. It is not known if this tax was fully collected. In any case it is clear that government revenue was at least twenty times smaller for Scotland than for England.

the French armies of the 1790s, the puritanical chaplains similarly maintained the religious zeal of the officers and the troops.

Ireland

English incursions into Ireland began at the end of the twelfth century. Until the seventeenth century, however, the Irish were often in a position to defeat the English armies. This took place in particular during the insurrection of Hugh O'Neill (1597) with the victory of Blackwater in 1598 (Vincent 1898). After the invasion of Cromwell in late 1649 there were still insurrections, but the Irish were unable to challenge English forces successfully.

At the beginning of June 1649 only Londonderry and Dublin were in English hands. In the first days of July the Cromwellian vanguard entered the port of Dublin. The garrison was supplied and a sortie enabled the city siege to be broken. On August 31, 1649, Cromwell left Dublin with an army of approximately 10,000 men. On September 12, he captured Drogheda to the north of Dublin. To set an example, Cromwell gave the order not to take prisoners; the 2,500 men of the garrison were put to the sword. Cromwell wrote in his letter to Parliament concerning the battle: "It will tend to prevent the effusion of blood for the future" (Firth 1953, p. 255). Whether or not this calculation proved correct in this case, it must be emphasized that such a tactic was commonly used at the time. For instance, the French used the same tactic during their wars in northern Italy in the sixteenth century, and the troops of the Holy Roman Emperor Charles V did the same in northern France (Lemonnier 1926 [1911]).

A number of fortified towns held out for a long time. For example, Limerick was still besieged in 1651 and Waterford resisted with such obstinacy that Cromwell was forced to lift the siege.

Scotland

On several occasions England has had to repel Scottish invasion attempts, especially in 1513 and 1547. In view of the disproportion of forces (Table 6.2b), however, these invasions never went very far. It was not the same for the English invasions of Scotland. Edinburgh had been taken in 1544, and in 1547 there was even an early attempt at union. Then in 1650–1651 the Scots suffered a series of crushing defeats at the hands of Cromwell's troops at Dunbar (July 29, 1650), Inverkeithing (July 20, 1651), and Worcester (September 3, 1651). Militarily the victory of Dunbar was achieved under difficult conditions; Cromwell's army was cornered by the sea, and the opposing forces were twice as large (23,000 against 11,000). Despite this, the English forces achieved a dazzling victory. Continued in a systematic manner, the conquest of Scotland was completed in May 1652.

Even before this date, in October 1651, it was announced that England and Scotland were henceforth to be one Commonwealth. At the same time all public meetings were forbidden. The army of occupation initially had 36,000 men, but from 1652 on this number was reduced to approximately 15,000 (remember that Scotland had to support the maintenance of the army of occupation). At least 500 opponents were transported to the Barbados (Donaldson 1971, p. 350). Those persons who declined to take an oath to the Lord Protector were excluded from office. Many peers who had supported the Worcester campaign had their estates forfeited, and fines were imposed on many others. In summary, these actions constituted a real takeover of Scottish society by the occupying power. This gave rise to several revolts, even before the dynastic change of 1689 and subsequent Jacobite risings. One of these revolts, an insurrection provoked by religious persecution, took place in November 1666 (Lingard 1829). About 2,000 rebels advanced on Edinburgh but were defeated by the royal army: 50 were left dead on the field and 40 prisoners were executed on December 17.

War against Spain

A plan was conceived to wrest from Spain the island of Saint-Domingue (Haiti), which was one of its more important possessions in the Caribbean.

An expeditionary force of 9,000 men, under the command of Admiral Penn and General Venables, disembarked on the island of Saint-Domingue in April 1655, but was repelled by the Spaniards. In order not to return empty-handed the expedition seized Jamaica, which was four times smaller than Haiti. The disappointment of Cromwell and the extent of his initial plans are certified by the fact that on their return the two commanders were sent to the Tower of London for several months (Guizot 1854).

France

Between 1814 and 1945 France was invaded five times by Germany (1814, 1815, 1870, 1914, and 1940). But between 1643 and 1814, the French armies had penetrated into Germany on thirteen occasions (1643, 1675, 1689, 1702, 1713, 1734, 1757, 1792, 1799, 1806, and 1809). It will be one of the objectives of this and the next section to explain such a spectacular reversal. The general argument is certainly well known and lies in the gap of more than a century between the two polities' establishment of themselves as nation-states. The discussion here will allow us to fill out and illustrate this argument.

All conflicts, but perhaps still more those of the eighteenth and nineteenth centuries, appear chaotic. Series of battles with uncertain and changing conclusions, ebbs and flows of the armies, alliances and reversals of alliances, precarious peace and repetitious wars; all these aspects combine to render military history difficult to understand. Behind the apparent chaos, however, it is possible to find some permanent structures, some simple mechanisms. If it is difficult or even perhaps impossible to anticipate wars, once they have broken out their progress follows relatively well structured patterns and scenarios.

Dates and Opposing Forces

Table 6.3a recapitulates the principal wars of the Revolution and the Empire. Over the course of these twenty-three years, the conflicts became increasingly bloody. During the War of the First Coalition (1792–1797), the average annual number of deaths was approximately 10,700 (59,000 divided by 5); at the time of the Third Coalition (April–December 1805), it was 20,500 per year; during the Fifth Coalition (1809) this number climbed to 65,000 per year, a figure that would not be surpassed during the last campaigns of 1813–1815. This multiplication by six of the intensity of the wars corresponds to deep strategic and tactical upheavals. By listing the

Table 6.3a France: Expansion wars, 1792–1815

	Year	Opponents	Total number of battle deaths
1st Coalition	1792–1797	Austria (1792–1797), Baden-Hessen-Hanover (1793), Britain (1793–1797), Netherlands (1793), Portugal (1793), Russia, Prussia (1792–1794), Spain (1793)	59,000
Campaign in Egypt	1798–1801	Britain, Egypt, Turkey	12,900
Campaign in Ireland	1798	Britain	1,300
2nd Coalition	1799–1802	Austria, Britain, Portugal, Prussia, Russia, Saxony, Turkey	52,500
3rd Coalition	1805 (Apr.–Dec.)	Austria, Britain, Russia, Sweden	15,400
4th Coalition	1806–1807	Britain, Prussia, Russia, Saxony	46,000
Peninsular War	1807–1814	Britain, Portugal, Spain	79,000
5th Coalition	1809 (Apr.–Oct.)	Austria, Britain, Spain	41,700
Campaign in Russia	1812	Russia	55,250
6th Coalition	1813–1815	Austria, Britain, German Kingdoms, Prussia, Russia, Spain, Sweden	136,500

Sources: Atlas Historique (1968); Bodart (1908); *Grand Larousse Encyclopédique* (1963); Vincent (1898); Wright (1942).

Note: The total general of the number of battle deaths is of the order of 500,000.

members of the various coalitions one can see that Britain was the essential pillar; that is why in the following we concentrate our attention on the role played by Britain. The balance of power for the Napoleonic Wars is illustrated in Tables 6.3b and 6.3c (whose exchange rates are needed to make the relevant comparisons) and Figure 6.3, which summarizes the data given in the tables.

A Parallel between the Napoleonic Wars and the Second World War
The established practice of reserving the term "world war" to the two great conflicts of the twentieth century is unfortunate from a historical viewpoint. A number of earlier wars were truly global, especially those of the

Table 6.3b Population and central government revenue of European countries at the beginning of the nineteenth century

Country	Population (millions)		Central government revenue (millions)			Reference
Austria	13.4	(1818)	136	Gu	(1810)	Mitchell (1978)
Bavaria	3.7	(1817)	21	Fl	(1837)	Flora, Kraus, and Pfenning (1987); *Zeitschrift* (1896)
Britain	18.0	(1811)	73	£	(1810)	Mitchell (1971, 1978)
France	29.1	(1806)	879	F	(1816)	Mitchell (1978)
Netherlands	2.0	(1816)	56	Gi	(1846)	Mitchell (1978)
Prussia	10.3	(1816)	57	Th	(1849)	Flora, Kraus, and Pfenning (1987), p. 34, 309
Russia	40.7	(1810)	323	Ru	(1816)	Mitchell (1978)
Spain	10.5	(1797)	318	Pa	(1850)	Mitchell (1978)

Note: F = French franc; Fl = florin; Gi = guilder; Gu = Gulder; Pa = peseta; Ru = ruble; Th = Thaler.

Table 6.3c Exchange rates in the nineteenth century

Country	Currency	1830 (pounds Sterling)	1857 (pounds Sterling)	1875 (pounds Sterling)
Austria	Gulden	0.12	0.11	
Bavaria	Gulden	0.14	0.09	
France	Granc	0.041	0.041	0.040
Germany	Mark			0.050
Japan	Yen			0.204
Netherlands	Gulden	0.087	0.085	
Sweden	Riksdaler		0.058	
Sweden	Kronor			0.056
United States	Dollar			0.204

Sources: 1830–Heinig (1962); 1857–Seuffert (1857), p. 351; 1875–Bank of Japan (1966), p. 121, and Roehner (1995), p. 158.

Note: Some currencies, such as the yen, have fluctuated over the course of time. For the purpose of our comparisons, however, approximate estimates are sufficient.

Balance of power, 1795–1815

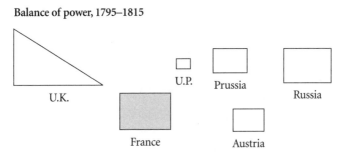

Figure 6.3 Balance of power in Europe during the wars of the Revolution and during the Napoleonic Wars, expressed in terms of state revenue. Each rectangle/triangle's area is proportional to the public revenue of the corresponding state. *Source:* Table 6.3b.

Revolution and the Empire. These struggles extended to practically all the continents; in addition to the European powers (Austria, Britain, Denmark, France, Netherlands, Portugal, Prussia, Russia, Spain, Sweden), there were wars in Turkey (Russo-Turkish war of 1806–1812), the United States (war against England of 1812–1815 with the capture of Washington, D.C., in August 1814), Argentina (British invasion attempts at Buenos Aires in 1806 and 1807), India (occupation of the eastern coast of India in 1803–1805), and the West Indies, where some particularly fierce battles took place.

Indeed, the strategic problem was essentially the same during the Napoleonic Wars and during World War II. How can a maritime power, with only a small army, put an end to the hegemony in Europe of an essentially continental power? The responses to this problem were in the two cases very similar. By stressing this parallel, our objective is twofold. First, it is pedagogical, as the events of 1939–1945 that are relatively familiar to us can serve as guide for those of 1795–1815. Second, this parallel will bring to the fore the underlying logic behind events of seemingly different appearance.

The parallels to be discussed below are summarized in Table 6.3d.

ANALOGIES IN THE STRATEGY OF THE CONTINENTAL POWER

After having established its hegemony in western Europe, how can the continental power threaten the maritime power? The first and most direct approach is to mount an amphibious operation to invade the maritime

Table 6.3d Confrontation between a continental power and a maritime power: Similarities between the Napoleonic Wars and World War II

	Napoleonic Wars	World War II
1. Economic blockade	Continental blockade	Unrestricted submarine warfare
2. Attempt to dominate the Mediterranean	Campaign in Egypt and Palestine (1798–1801)	Afrika Korps in Libya (1941–1942)
3. Attempted invasion of Britain (abandoned)	Spring 1805	Autumn 1940
4. After this attempt, war in the East	Campaign in Austria (spring 1805)	Invasion of Russia (June 1941)
5. British attempt to ease pressure on the eastern front	British landing at Walcheren Island (July 1809)	Landing at Dieppe (August 1942)
6. Failure of the campaign in Russia is turning point of the war	Retreat from Russia (winter 1813), Battle of Leipzig (Oct. 1813)	Battle of Stalingrad (Feb. 1943)
7. Encroachment of the European bloc by the maritime power(s).	Peninsular War in Portugal and Spain (1807–1814)	Campaign in Italy (1943–1945)

power. This was attempted by France in spring 1805 from the camp at Boulogne. Note that similar preparations had already taken place during the Seven Years' War (1756–1763). This was also attempted by Germany in spring 1940. In the first case, the invasion was canceled because it was impossible to ward off the British fleet in the English Channel and because an Austrian attack against the Bavarian allies rendered the plan impracticable. We note in passing that, contrary to an idea that can be found in certain works, the naval defeat of Trafalgar did not lead to the cancellation of the plan. The battle of Trafalgar took place on October 21, 1805, when the Austrian campaign had already begun: the capitulation of Ulm took place on October 17. In 1940, it was the impossibility of ensuring aerial supremacy that led to the abandonment of the plan.

The second means available to a continental power is the economic blockade. This idea led Napoleon to implement the continental blockade.

In retaliation, the British fleet seized even neutral merchant ships, thus taking possession of about 2,000 ships per year (*Atlas historique* 1968, p. 305). This same idea was behind the submarine warfare and economic blockade against England during the two world wars.

The third means is to carry the war into the regions that are vital to the economic interests of the maritime power. With the intention of ensuring the mastery of the Mediterranean, a French expeditionary corps occupied Malta, Egypt, and Palestine (1798–1799). The expedition eventually was a failure because of the impossibility of taking Acre (currently Akko in Israel) and the constant presence off Egypt of the British fleet, which rendered the provision of supplies for the expeditionary corps difficult. With the same intention of ensuring the mastery of the Mediterranean, Rommel's Afrika Korps disembarked in Libya in February 1941; Crete was taken by an airborne operation (May 1941); Malta was fiercely attacked but remained in British hands. As in 1798–1799, the supply question was essential for Rommel's army.

The West Indies constituted another crucial region for British interests. The murderous battles that took place there between 1793 and 1801 accounted for the lives of nearly 85,000 British soldiers and sailors (French 1990, p. 97).

Geographically, Russia, like Britain, occupies a special position in Europe. For Britain, the barrier to invasion is its insularity; for Russia, it is the immensity of the distances. There are 1,600 kilometers between Berlin and Moscow, while there are only 900 kilometers from Berlin to Paris. Every invasion of Russia during the last three centuries has ended disastrously for the invader. King Charles XII of Sweden was defeated at Poltava in 1709 and, after having lost his army, had to flee to Turkey. Napoleon was the only one of the three invaders to reach Moscow (1812), but during the course of the retreat, he lost the majority of his army. Hitler's armies got bogged down in Russia literally and figuratively and the defeat at Stalingrad (February 1943) marked the turning point of World War II.

Up to this point we have considered the strategy of the continental power. Interesting regularities are also to be found, however, in the strategy of the maritime power.

ANALOGIES IN THE STRATEGY OF THE MARITIME POWER

By virtue of its world trade the maritime power is a rich country, and as such can play the role of financial backer for its allies. Britain held this role in 1795–1815 (French 1990). In 1799, for example, in return for a British subsidy of £44,000 per month, the Russians supplied 11,000 men; in June 1800, the Austrians obtained a subsidy of £2 million on the condition that Austria would not make a separate peace before February 1801; in 1808, money and weapons were granted to Portugal and Spain; in 1813–1815, more than £11 million was distributed among Austria, Prussia, Russia, and Sweden. The United States played the same role during World Wars I and II (Figure 6.4).

From the point of view of offensive strategy, two methods were successively attempted: small-scale landings and a strategy of encroachment starting from an allied territory. After 1805, the first method had the specific objective of easing the military pressure on the Allies. For instance in December 1808, the Austrians asked the British to launch a diversionary attack on the north German coast. The Cabinet preferred to mount a diversion in the Low Countries, and in July 1809, 40,000 troops were sent to seize Antwerp. However, the expedition sailed too late to help the Austrians, who were defeated at Wagram (July 5, 1809). The British troops got no further than the island of Walcheren (situated in the estuary of the Schelde), where a mixture of dysentery and malaria killed 4,000 and left 11,000 sick. Previously there had been landings undertaken in support of the French royalists, notably at Toulon (autumn 1793), Cherbourg, and Quiberon (July 1795). In a somewhat similar manner, the landing in Dieppe on August 19, 1942, was launched in response to an urgent demand from the Soviets to ease the eastern front. The extent and objectives of this landing were limited; the 6,000 men and supporting tank regiment had to hold their position for a day before withdrawing. The objective was partly reached, but at the cost of heavy losses.

The strategy of encroachment was used successfully from 1808. British forces were landed near Lisbon, and thanks to subsidies were augmented by Portuguese troops. Between 1808 and 1813 this army forced its way north toward the French frontier through Portugal and Spain. The Spanish city of San Sebastian (on the French border) was reached on September 8, 1813, and Toulouse (in southern France) on April 10, 1814. On that date the allies (Austrians, Prussians, and Russians) were already in Paris. There is no doubt, however, that the Peninsular War tied up a substantial number of troops in Spain, estimated at 250,000, who were thus lacking in other theaters. During World War II, the British advocated a similar strategy of encroachment and encirclement. After initial reservations, the Americans finally accepted this plan. The result was the landings in North Africa (No-

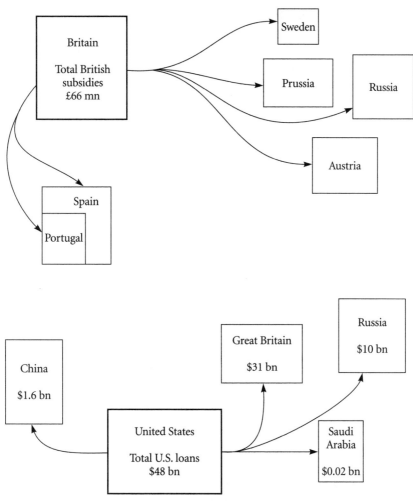

Figure 6.4 Parallel between the role of financial backer played by Britain *(top)* during the Napoleonic Wars and that played by the United States *(bottom)* during World War II. *Sources:* French (1990); Gilbert (1966).

vember 1942), followed on July 10, 1943, by the landing in Sicily. Here also the progression to the north was very slow. Rome was reached only on June 4, 1944; in April 1945, a month before the armistice of June 8, the front still stretched from Genoa to Ravenna. Although the battles of the Italian campaign were of limited extent in comparison to those in other arenas, they tied up several German divisions.

One can note another similarity between the war led by the British in

1795–1815 and that led by the Americans during World War II. Britain, like the United States, only committed its forces in situations where there was a favorable balance of power. The losses of the Anglo-Spanish or Anglo-Portuguese armies during the Peninsular War represented only 10 percent of the total losses of the period 1799–1815. Similarly, the American losses in the European arena only represented approximately 5 percent of the global losses of armed forces in Europe.

PATRIOTIC REACTIONS IN THE OCCUPIED TERRITORIES

The patriotic resistance in the occupied countries was more belated during the Napoleonic Wars than during World War II. In the first case, it took on average six years before the formation of national resistance movements, while this period was reduced to two years in World War II. In 1809 the Tyrolese rebellion led by Andreas Hofer fought against the Bavarians and the French before being defeated in 1810. In Prussia, it was mainly after the disastrous retreat from Russia that national sentiment became inflamed. It was in Spain and Portugal that guerrilla warfare was the most active (1808–1813); these efforts were supported by the presence of British forces and by the delivery of arms and subsidies. The same phenomenon took place in Italy during World War II.

Recurrent Patterns

In the first section of this chapter, we described geographic and economic constraints. No less important are the constraints imposed by national military traditions. From this viewpoint, the wars of the Revolution and the Empire are a particularly interesting example, because they show both a continuity and a rupture. Continuity, because as we shall see the wars of the Revolution followed very similar schemas to previous "world" conflicts, particularly the Nine Years' War (1688–1697) and the Seven Years' War (1756–1763). Rupture, because by their extent and their intensity, the Napoleonic Wars foreshadowed modern conflicts. Before looking at greater length into the aspect of continuity, let us remind ourselves of the strategic and technical innovations of the Napoleonic Wars.

INNOVATIONS OF THE NAPOLEONIC WARS

This question of the innovations of the Napoleonic Wars has been the subject of detailed studies by military historians, in particular by Karl von Clausewitz (1976) and Antoine Henri de Jomini (1838), who both took an active part in the campaigns against Napoleon. Here we will be content to recall some remarkable points.

From 1798 it was apparent that an evolution in military strategy was taking place. The static war, consisting of many sieges of fortified towns and limited losses, gave way to a war of movement whose objective became the capture by pincer movement and destruction of the enemy forces. Between 1500 and 1700 there were 200 sieges and only 60 battles. Napoleon, however, conducted fewer than 10 sieges during his entire career. There are many reasons for this evolution. The eighteenth-century tacticians considered that in order to besiege a city including a garrison of 1,000 men, it was necessary to have an army numbering at least 7,000, so as to prevent a possible sortie at all points of the surrounding perimeter. During the eighteenth century the towns became large, and surrounding them would have required exorbitant numbers; it was then preferred to "mask" the fortified towns by leaving beside them a number approximately double that of the garrison. This allowed the main army to continue its path. This evolution was of course also made possible by the increase in the size of the armies. The passage to the war of movement was also furthered by many technical improvements. Thus as guns and cannons became lighter, there was a considerable increase in the artillery. At the battle of Malplaquet (September 11, 1709) between the allies (English, Dutch, and Austrian) and the French there was approximately 1 cannon per 1,000 soldiers. A century later, at the battle of Leipzig (October 19, 1813) between the Allies (Austrian, Prussian, Russian, and Swedish) and the French, there were 4.2 cannons per 1,000 soldiers (Bodart 1908, pp. 160, 461).

EIGHTEENTH-CENTURY WORLD CONFLICTS

The Nine Years' War (1688–1657), the War of Spanish Succession (1702–1712), and the Seven Years' War (1756–1763) were essentially conflicts between Britain and its allies, notably Holland, and France and its allies. These conflicts involved nearly all the European nations and spread to other continents (America, India) by means of colonial possessions. This is particularly true for the Seven Years' War, of which a very important part took place in Canada. Basically these were conflicts between maritime powers (Britain and Holland) and continental powers; therefore it is not surprising that one finds several of the features that we highlighted earlier. However the parallel with World War II is less clear-cut here, for three reasons. First, in the eighteenth century, France was far from occupying the whole of Europe. Second, there were also some continental powers among the allies of Britain, for instance Prussia in the Seven Years' War. Third, before the Seven Years' War, France was itself an important colonial and maritime power by virtue of its possessions in North America and India. In 1763 it lost Canada and the eastern coast of India except for some trading posts; Louisiana was sold to the United States in 1803.

BRITISH RECURRENT STRATEGIES

Three examples will illustrate England's recurrent strategies and tactics. (1) England's subsidy policy had already been used during the Nine Years' War. Note that in a similar manner France under Louis XIV distributed subsidies to its allies. (2) The tactic of limited landings that would be found later at Toulon, Cherbourg, and Quiberon was used on many earlier occasions: Brest (1694), Toulon (1705), Rochefort (September 1757), Saint Malo (June 1758), and Cherbourg (7 August 1758). (3) In this period, the dispatch of forces to Portugal became a tradition. In 1705, there were 5,000 Anglo-Dutch troops in Portugal under the Earl of Galway to support the Portuguese against Spain. In January 1762, 6,000 British troops were sent to Lisbon to protect Portugal from the Spanish.

FRENCH RECURRENT STRATEGIES

On the French side, there is also continuity in the strategies and tactics used.

There is a long tradition of French landings in Britain. In 1798 an invasion force of approximately 1,000 men disembarked in Ireland to support the Irish rebels. One finds antecedents of these invasion plans in previous conflicts. (1) In 1545, in order to support the Scots, a fleet of 175 vessels tried to take the Isle of Wight; but on July 18 it turned back (Lemonnier 1926 [1911]). (2) In March 1689, French troops accompanied James II at the time of his endeavor in Ireland. (3) In 1692, Louis XIV made preparations to land a Franco-Irish army of 24,000 men in England. He hoped that their landing would be the signal for an uprising by the English Jacobites. The naval defeat of Barfleur (May 28–June 1, 1692), however, marked the end of any immediate hope of an invasion of England. (4) In 1759, preparations took place to send an invasion force to Scotland; however, the convoy was intercepted and partly destroyed in November in the Quiberon Bay by Admiral Hawke.

The search for a dominant position in the Mediterranean that took shape with the expedition of Bonaparte to Egypt led in 1756 to a French landing in Minorca, where the British garrison was forced to surrender in May 1756.

The submarine warfare of the two world wars had as its precedent in the eighteenth century the privateering led by French privateers (French 1990). During the Nine Years' War, French privateers captured about 4,000 vessels; during the War of Spanish Succession, with the aid of royal vessels, the French privateers took more than 3,000 prizes. As would be the case during the conflicts of the twentieth century, the English response was the organization of convoys. In 1708, Parliament passed a "Cruisers and Convoy Act," reserving forty-three warships for commerce protection.

Until 1800–1802 the military means implemented were essentially the same as those used during earlier conflicts. After this date, the Napoleonic rupture took place. For example, in previous French campaigns there are hardly any precedents to the campaigns in Prussia (1806–1807) or Russia (1812).

After 1815 there is no longer any notable French expansion in Europe; and after 1848 begins the period of German national activation. Innumerable kingdoms that had constituted the Holy Roman Empire merged to form the German Empire. By its population and economic power this country could claim a dominant role. Its national activation would shake Europe. This is the subject of the following section.

Germany

The phenomenon of national activation in Germany comprised two parts: a reduction in the domination of the aristocracy, with a concomitant increase in participation of the population in the management of the country; and greater centralization, which resulted in an increase in the income of the state and an equalization of regional idiosyncrasies. Note that both aspects also existed during the French Revolution.

During the first half of the nineteenth century there was intense social unrest in Germany, but by 1870, when Germany constituted itself as a state, the struggle against the aristocracy was almost over. This is confirmed, for example, by the extension of voting rights. In 1848 Germany was one of the first European countries to adopt the principle of the secret ballot, and in 1871 the franchise was extended to include all men twenty-five years and older. At the same time, the fusion of sovereign kingdoms

Table 6.4a Germany: Expansion wars, 1845–1945

Year	Opponents	Total number of battle deaths	Reference
1848–1850	Denmark	2,000	Bodart (1908)
1864	Denmark	4,000	Richardson (1960), p. 60
1866	Austria, Bavaria	40,000	Richardson (1960), p. 45
1870–1871	France	250,000	Richardson (1960), p. 45
1914–1918	Britain, France, Italy (1915), Russia, United States (1917)	8,000,000	*Dict. Larousse* (1973)
1938	Bohemia-Moravia		
1939–1945	Britain, France, Poland, Russia (1941), United States (1941)	15,000,000	Richardson (1960)

Note: For the two world wars we have indicated only the main belligerents.

into a new national entity was a long-term process. Thus Bavaria preserved its king as well as a great deal of autonomy at least until the beginning of the twentieth century. The constitution of the Weimar Republic accelerated the centralization, and this evolution would again be intensified after the coming to power of the National Socialists in 1933.

In this section we are essentially interested in observable paronymies at the strategic as well as at the tactical level. We give special attention to the beginnings of the campaigns because these put the ideas of the military staff into action. Thereafter, with the passing of the war, unforeseen events took place that necessitated improvisation.

Dates and Opposing Forces

Table 6.4a provides an overview of Germany's wars of expansion in the period 1845–1945. We make two observations. First, in a European context, the two Schleswig-Holstein wars against Denmark may appear relatively minor. For Denmark, however, the result of these conflicts was dramatic; by losing Schleswig-Holstein and Lauenburg it lost approximately half of its territory and 30 to 40 percent of its population. If one recalls that Denmark had incorporated Sweden and Finland until 1523 and Norway until 1814, one sees that before stabilizing within its current frontiers, this country experienced a long phase of territorial contraction. Second, in considering Table 6.4b, we note that for Germany, because of its federal structure,

Table 6.4b Population and central government revenue of belligerents, 1865–1870

Country	Population (millions)		Central government revenue (millions)			Reference
Denmark	1.6	(1865)	3.2	£	(1889)	Vincent (1898), p. 316
Baden	1.5	(1871)	5.0	£		Flora, Kraus, and Pfenning (1987), p. 34
Bavaria	4.8	(1867)	36	Fl	(1868)	Flora, Kraus, and Pfenning (1987), p. 34, 310
France	37.0	(1861)	126	£	(1890)	Vincent (1898), p. 431
Germany	41.0	(1871)	169	M	(1872)	Flora, Kraus, and Pfenning (1987), p. 42, 307
Prussia	24.0	(1867)	79	£	(1891)	Flora, Kraus, and Pfenning (1987), p. 34, 309
Saxony	2.5	(1871)	7	£		Flora, Kraus, and Pfenning (1987), p. 34
Wurtemberg	1.8	(1871)	6	£		Flora, Kraus, and Pfenning (1987), p. 34

Note: Fl = florin; M = Mark.

the level of income of the central government on the eve of World War I was not very significant; it was half that of France while in terms of population or gross national product, Germany's figures approached the level of twice those of France. If in 1870 and 1914, the balance of the two camps was almost equal, in 1940 it was clearly unfavorable to the Franco-British Allies; this imbalance was made worse by the delay with which these two countries proceeded to rearmament in the 1930s. After the evacuation of English forces from Dunkirk (end of May 1940), the situation became even more unequal. It was only by Russia's entry into the war that the balance of forces would be reestablished. The entry into the war of the United States in December 1941 tipped the scale very clearly in favor of the Allies. The balance of power for World Wars I and II is illustrated in Tables 6.4c,d and Figure 6.5.

Paronymy at the Strategic Level: The Paradigm of Cannae
If the Sarajevo assassination attempt (June 28, 1914) against the Archduke Francis Ferdinand had taken place in winter, it would certainly not have led to the outbreak of World War I. The reason for this is very simple. For the German offensive in 1914 a considerable number of horses were

Table 6.4c Population and central government revenue of belligerent countries, 1914

Country	Population (millions)		Central government revenue (millions)		Reference
Austria	28.5	(1910)	3,486 Kr	(1913)	Mitchell (1978)
Britain (U.K.)	46.0	(1914)	198 £	(1913)	Mitchell (1978)
France	39.1	(1911)	5,092 F	(1913)	Mitchell (1978)
Germany	65	(1910)	2,095 M	(1913)	Mitchell (1978)
Russia	160	(1910)	3,417 Ru	(1913)	Mitchell (1978)
United States	100	(1915)	726 $	(1914)	Mitchell (1983)

Note: As a result of the federal structure of Germany, the revenue of the central government is too low and cannot validly be compared with the revenue of other countries. Kr = kronen; F = French franc; M = Mark; Ru = ruble.

Table 6.4d Population and central government revenue of belligerent countries, 1940

Country	Population (millions)		Central government revenue (millions)		Reference
Britain (U.K.)	47.3	(1937)	1,132 £	(1939)	Liesner (1989), p. 38; Mitchell (1978)
Bohemia-Moravia	7.0	(1937)	10,014 Ko	(1937)	Mitchell (1978)
France	41.1	(1936)	63,005 F	(1939)	Mitchell (1978)
Germany	76.2	(1936)	23,575 M	(1939)	Mitchell (1978)
Poland	32.1	(1931)	2,049 Z	(1937)	Mitchell (1978)

Note: Ko = koruna; F = French franc; M = Mark; Z = złoty.

used. The army of von Kluck alone had 84,000 (Van Creveld 1995 [1977], p. 124); the total number of horses can be estimated at a minimum of 300,000. With each horse consuming 10 kilograms of fodder each day, it was imperative that this fodder be available locally, given the impossibility of forwarding such quantities from the rear even by rail. Fodder would not be available locally for this number of horses in winter. This example shows that some facts have become so familiar to us that we no longer question them. The same is true for German strategy. We are so used to recurrent German invasions that we tend to forget that they were a distinc-

Balance of power, 1914–1918

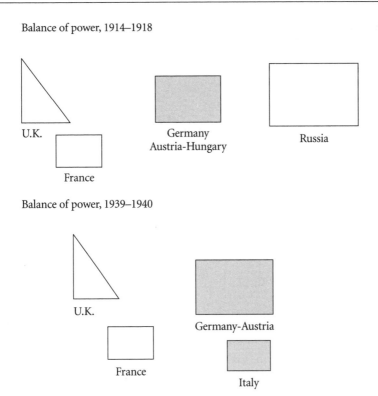

Balance of power, 1939–1940

Figure 6.5 Balance of power in Europe at the outbreak of war in 1914 *(top)* and 1940 *(bottom)* expressed in terms of population. Each rectangle/triangle's area is proportional to the population of the corresponding state. *Source:* Table 6.4b,c.

tive feature of German military doctrine. Let us first examine the origins of this doctrine.

CLAUSEWITZ, MOLTKE, AND SCHLIEFFEN

Clausewitz had studied 130 military campaigns, in particular the Napoleonic campaigns; on the basis of these observations he advocated a strategy, the so-called pincer movement strategy, consisting in two stages. First, draw the enemy forward. Second, turn the advancing enemy and strike it at the flank and the rear. German strategists called this maneuver of encirclement the paradigm of Cannae in remembrance of the victory achieved in 216 B.C. by Hannibal with a maneuver of this type (Figure 6.6a). This doc-

Cannae (216 B.C.)

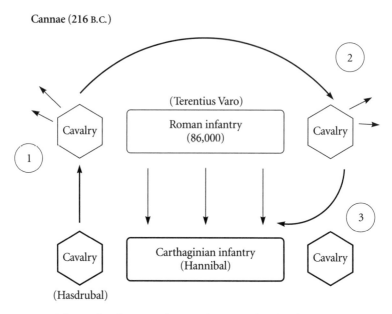

Figure 6.6a The Battle of Cannae (216 B.C.) is considered a classic example of the pincer-movement strategy. Its principle is to lure the enemy forward and then, by a sweeping movement of the (left) flank, to strike them at the flank and rear. At Cannae the Roman infantry thrust forward while Hasdrubal led his cavalry around it.

trine of encirclement and destruction of the enemy forces was used in the battles of 1870, 1914, 1940, and 1941, as well as in 1944 at the time of the Ardennes offensive against the Allies. Figure 6.6, panels b–e, summarizes four of these scenarios.

Passing from the principle to its application demanded a great deal of organization. In the period before 1914 this practical implementation was assured by two men. Field Marshal Helmuth von Moltke (1800–1891) remained the chief of staff for thirty-one years (1857–1888) and had a deep influence. His successor, Field Marshal Alfred von Schlieffen (1833–1933), a devotee of military history, was head of the historical service of the army before he was appointed in 1891 as the chief of the General Staff. He developed the plan that was to be used in August 1914.

In applying his theories to France, Schlieffen observed that the fortified line Verdun-Toul-Epinal would not allow him to achieve a swift result with a head-on assault. He therefore resolved in 1898 to outflank the French army by pushing the main body of his forces through Belgium. In later years he spread the outflanking maneuver even more to the west to include the entrenched camp of Paris. The broad outlines of this campaign plan, called the Schlieffen Plan, were followed by the German armies in August 1914 under the direction of General Helmuth von Moltke, nephew of the field marshal, who had died in 1913.

In 1940, with a vast circular movement from Sedan to Dunkirk, the German armies would succeed in turning the English and French armies in Belgium and the north of France.

Here is the comparative chronology of these conflicts:

Declaration of war	End of the concentration of German troops	End of the encircling movement	Duration of encircling
July 17, 1870	July 29, 1870	September 1, 1870 (Sedan)	32 days
August 3, 1914	August 5, 1914	September 7, 1914 (Marne)	29 days
September 3, 1939	May 10, 1940	May 28, 1940 (Dunkirk)	18 days

Channeling the troops from barracks to battlefield is a process known as "concentration."

With the time necessary for the concentration of German troops being on the order of fifteen days in 1914, one can discern that this was started on approximately July 21, that is, at a time when the chanceries were still striving to save the peace.

COMPARISON OF THE RETREATS OF 1914 AND 1940

The outcomes of the battles of 1914 and 1940 were very different. In 1914, the retreat could be considered a deliberate strategy aiming to lengthen the lines of communication of the enemy before the decisive battle. In 1940, the retreat took the appearance of a rout. Detailed explanations were given by historians researching the causes of these two outcomes, in particular the actions of the respective generals. Here we stress the similarities between these two retreats and the crucial role played in 1914 by logistic factors.

The British Expeditionary Force only arrived in France quite late. Its

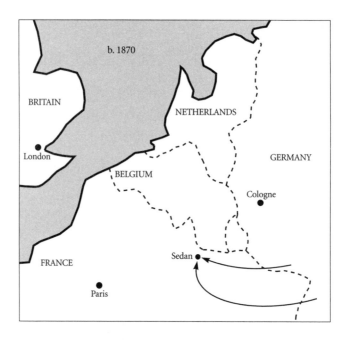

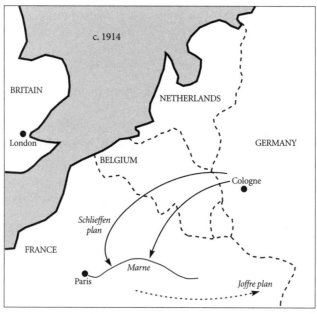

Figure 6.6b–e Envelopment maneuvers effected by the German armies at the start of the wars of 1870, 1914, and 1940 and during the Ardennes offensive of 1944. In the battles of 1914 and 1940, the Joffre and Dyle plans repeated Terentius Varo's error. In the Ardennes offensive (the Battle of the Bulge) in 1944, General

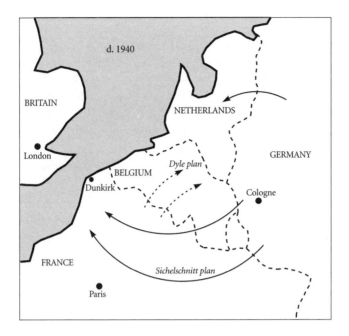

von Rundstedt was able to drive the vanguard of the Allied forces back to the Meuse; there they rallied and counterattacked strongly on both sides of the bulge. *Sources:* Van Creveld (1995 [1977]); *Entwicklung* (1989).

transportation to France began on August 9, 1914, and its concentration around Maubeuge ended only on August 20. On August 24 its commander in chief, Sir John French, sent to Lord Kitchener, chief of the War Office, the following telegram (Churchill 1925), p. 268): "I have just received a message from G.O.C. [General Office Commander] 5th French army that his troops have been driven back, that Namur has fallen, and that he is taking up a line from Maubeuge to Rocroi. I have therefore ordered a retirement to the line Valenciennes-Longueville-Maubeuge, which is being carried out now. It will prove a difficult operation, if the enemy remains in contact. I remember your precise instructions as to method and direction of retirement if necessity arises. I think that immediate attention should be directed to the defense of Havre."

Namur was, it must be noted, an essential position in the defense system; its very rapid loss was an important reversal. Following this message, on August 24 the British admiralty sent the French admiralty the following telegram: "Admiralty thinks it most important to naval interests to defend Dunkirk, Calais and Boulogne as long as possible. We release Admiral Rouyer's armoured cruiser squadron to co-operate in the land defences of these three places . . . We wish also to receive without delay French views about land defences of Dunkirk, Boulogne, Calais and Havre and what the military prospects are of holding on to all of them. We will, of course, assist in any way in our power. Lastly, we are considering shifting all military stores of [the] British Expeditionary Force now at Boulogne to Cherbourg" (Churchill 1925, pp. 269–270).

Thus from August 24, French and the admiralty looked for a solution for the possible withdrawal of the Expeditionary Force, a situation that was not too dissimilar to that of May 1940. Between August 18 and September 4, 1914, the retreat rather resembled a collapse. On August 23, the headquarters of the Fifth Army (General Lanrezac) were to be found in Philippeville near the Franco-Belgian frontier, where thousands of refugees could be seen passing in large wooden wagons (Conte 1991, p. 192). On September 3, this same headquarters was installed at Sézanne to the south of the Marne; in ten days it had been forced to retreat 170 kilometers.

However, in 1914 the mobility of the German army was largely restrained by logistics. Between 1870 and 1914 the mass of artillery, and therefore of ammunitions, had notably increased without a parallel increase in transport capacities; in 1870 there were only 1,600 pieces of artillery while in 1914 there were 8,000 of them. This factor, combined with the great increase (multiplication by a factor of ten) in the quantities of supplies consumed, was responsible for the fact that the so-called critical distance, the maximum distance at which a force could operate away from its railhead, fell between 1870 and 1914 from about 100 miles to about half that number (Van Creveld 1995 [1977], p. 113). Thus when on the fortieth day of the battle the French armies made a U-turn and blocked the German advance on the Marne, this counterattack was greatly helped by the exhaustion of the German troops. It is also necessary to note that at this time, as the rest of the war would amply show, defense enjoyed an indisputable superiority over attack thanks to the progress of the artillery.

In 1940, a similar maneuver was attempted. At the beginning of June 1940, after the first phase of the battle the French General Staff threw all its reserves into the establishment of a ultimate line of resistance on the lower Seine and the Aisne. The district of Rethel on the Aisne was the scene of violent battles led by the Fourteenth Infantry Division of General de Lattre de Tassigny; elsewhere, however, the front was rapidly pierced. During this war, thanks to the introduction of tank divisions acting together with the air force, attack had been able to regain precedence over defense.

Some historians have attributed the German failure of 1914 on the Marne (at a moment when the war was thought to be won) to the abrupt deviation to the east of von Kluck's army, a move that was in conflict with orders received. It is certainly possible that this maneuver played a role, but other elements may have contributed; for example, the fact that two army corps and a cavalry division were sent from the western front to the Russian front may have played a part. Furthermore in the next section we show that far from constituting an exceptional and isolated fact, von Kluck's "disobedience" (or what should rather be called his initiative) was in fact common practice in the German command.

Paronymy at the Tactical Level

FLEXIBILITY IN THE EXECUTION OF ORDERS

The "Moltke system" had the important characteristic of leaving a substantial degree of freedom of action to army commanders. There is an obvious justification in terms of efficiency: is not the army commander best able to appreciate the specifics of the local situation and to profit from them if need be? But it is doubtful that this flexibility had been a conscious objective; more probably it was a historical legacy from the period when, as

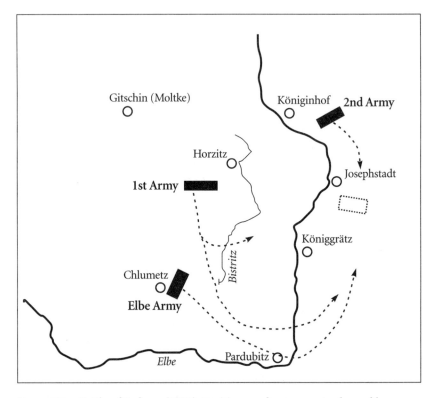

Figure 6.7a Battle of Sadowa (1866): Positions and movements planned by von Moltke. Sadowa is a small town located 10 kilometers to the northwest of Königgrätz. The black rectangles give the positions of the German armies. The dotted-line rectangle refers to the position of the Austrian army as presumed by von Moltke. The dashed lines indicate the marching directives for the German armies.

was still the case in 1870, the army commanders were princes or kings for whom it was necessary to leave plenty of elbow room. Thus in 1870, the Second Army was under the orders of Prince Frederick Charles, nephew of the king of Prussia, and the Third Army was commanded by Prince Frederick William, son of the king of Prussia. Let us show with three examples from the campaigns of 1866, 1870, and 1914 that this flexibility of command was an ingrained characteristic of German tactics.

The campaigns of 1866 and 1870 had been prepared by Moltke, but at the time of execution, he withdrew. The reconnaissance cavalry was left to the army commanders, the general in chief keeping only few means of information to himself. As will be seen by the two examples below borrowed from de Gaulle (1972 [1924], pp. 24–30), it often resulted in large distortions between the orders given and the tactics effectively followed.

1. *Campaign of 1866: Königgrätz-Sadowa (July 3)*   On July 1, 1866, the situation of the different armies was as follows (Figure 6.7a):

- The Austro-Hungarians concentrated their troops between the Elbe and the Bistritz to the southwest of Josefstadt
- The Prussian Army of the Elbe was at Chlumetz. The First Prussian Army was to the south of Horzitz. These two armies were under the command of Prince Frederick Charles.
- The Second Prussian Army (royal prince of Prussia) was at Königinhof.

Moltke, the general in chief, had just arrived the day before from Berlin and had set himself up at Gitschin. His armies had temporarily lost contact with the enemy, but he presumed that they were to be found between Königgrätz and Josefstadt to the east of the Elbe. This led him to order for 2 July the following movements: "The army of the Elbe will head towards Pardubitz to cross the Elbe there and outflank the left of the Austrian army at Benedek. The 1st army will follow the movement of the army from the Elbe but would send a detachment of reconnaissance cavalry between the Bistritz and the Elbe. If they meet unimportant Austrian forces, they should attack them. The 2nd army will remain on the spot and prepare to make a movement to the south."

Yet, on the morning of July 2, the cavalry of the First Army spotted a considerable number of Austrians on the east bank of the Bistritz. Immediately, Prince Frederick Charles took it upon himself not to execute the movement prescribed by Moltke. Instead he advanced all his forces against the enemy army to deliver battle; furthermore, he decided to ask the royal prince for the help of the Second Army (Figure 6.7b). Thus, Frederick Charles took his decisions, dictated his orders, and began to put them into operation even before warning the general in chief, who would have entirely approved of them anyway. The result of this improvisation was the victory of Sadowa; needless to say the Moltke system was showered with praises.

2. *Campaign of 1870: Gravelotte (August 16–18)*   On August 15, 1870, the situation of the different armies was as follows (Figure 6.7c):

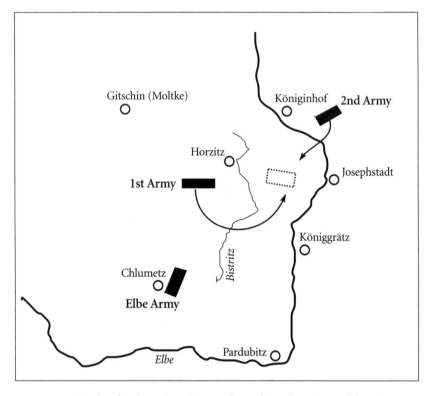

Figure 6.7b Battle of Sadowa (1866): Actual marching directions of the German armies. The dotted-line rectangle refers to the actual position of the Austrian army. The black rectangles give the positions of the German armies. *Source:* de Gaulle (1972 [1924]).

- After the defeat at Borny (August 14), the French army at Metz planned to fall back to Verdun, but it had been considerably slowed in its advance and used the day to regroup near Gravelotte.
- The First German Army that had been engaged at Borny was concentrated to the southeast of Metz in the corner formed by the Seille and the road from Metz to Saint-Avold.
- The Second Army under the command of Prince Frederick Charles was dispersed along the Moselle, from Novéant up to Marbache.

Moltke had established his headquarters at Herny. For the day of August 16, he dictated the following orders: "The circumstances under which the

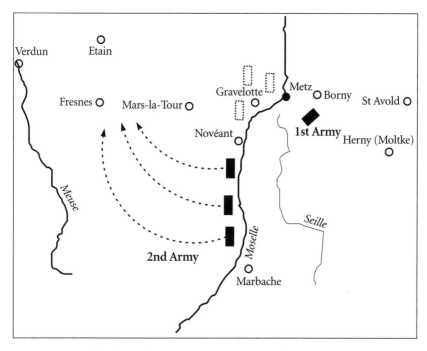

Figure 6.7c Battle of Gravelotte (1870): Positions and movements planned by von Moltke. The black rectangles give the positions of the German armies. The dotted-line rectangles refer to the actual positions of the French armies; von Moltke believed them to be more to the west on the march toward Verdun. The dashed lines indicate the marching directives for the German armies.

1st and 7th Army Corps, as well as portions of the 18th Division, gained a victory last evening at Borny precluded all pursuit. The fruits thereof can only be reaped by a vigorous offensive on the part of the 2nd Army toward the Metz-Verdun roads, by Fresnes and by Etain."

Thus the main body of the army was boldly oriented to the west; only the 3rd army corps (which belonged to the Second Army), located to the south of Novéant, was ordered toward the northwest (Figure 6.7d). It was this army corps that discovered the whole French army located around Gravelotte the following day. Instead of moving to the northwest, the German corps turned northeast and attacked the French. Only the inertia of Marshal Bazaine allowed the Germans to transform this disastrous tactic into victory. As after Sadowa, the Moltke system and the independence of Frederick Charles would be held up as examples throughout Germany and

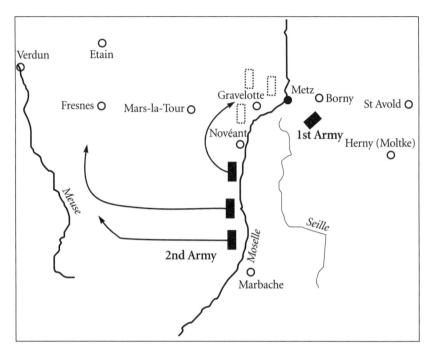

Figure 6.7d Battle of Gravelotte (1870): Actual marching directions of the German armies. The black rectangles give the positions of the German armies. The dotted-line rectangles refer to the actual positions of the French armies. *Source:* de Gaulle (1972 [1924]).

it would be forgotten that they had come within a hairsbreadth of catastrophe.

3. Campaign of 1914: The battle of Alsace (August)   In 1914, the right wing had to do most of the work. The left wing, under the command of the prince of Bavaria, von Rupprecht, had to lure the French armies to the east and to assume a defensive role in Alsace-Lorraine. However, faced with the success achieved by the other armies, von Rupprecht fidgeted with impatience. Without orders from Moltke, he went on the attack without allowing the French troops to fall completely into the Alsatian trap. He thus created a front which, at the critical moment, took up a larger share of the German troops than anticipated.

4. Campaign of 1914: The Marne (September 6)   The decisive action took place on the right wing; thus let us come back to von Kluck's case. Here are Moltke's directives on August 27, concerning the marching direction of the armies (Conte 1991, p. 204): "It is essential for the German armies to march on Paris, to not leave any breathing space to the French armies, to prevent all new organization of force and to deprive the country the largest part of its means of struggle. His Majesty orders the forward march of the German armies in the direction of Paris. All armies will have to operate in flawless agreement and help one another for the conquest of different segments of territory."

These directives were relatively confusing. Certainly, the march on Paris was ordered, but it was also ordered to deprive the enemy of its means of struggle, in other words, to crush its armies. This is precisely what von Kluck wanted to achieve by bypassing Paris, a city that would have necessitated a long and inglorious siege, and heading toward the French armies massed to the south of the Marne.

Here is the telegram that von Kluck sent to Moltke on September 4: "Following continuous battles and exhausting marches, the 1st army has arrived at the limit of its endurance. It is only at this price that it has succeeded in opening the Marne crossing to other armies and forced the enemy to prolong its retreat. Instruction 2.220 of the Supreme Command (night of 2–3 September) which ordered the 1st army to space itself out behind the 2nd cannot be followed in this case. The planned driving back of the enemy to the south-east can only succeed if the 1st army advances" (Conte 1991).

On perusal of this message, one discovers, hardly concealed, the personal ambition of von Kluck, who, estimating that his army had done most of the work, did not want to hand over the fruits of victory to the Second Army. But his initiative appears completely contradictory with the judgment that he makes of the state of his troops, who had "arrived at the limit of their endurance."

In short, what numerous historians have called "von Kluck's disobedience" was well in the German tradition of freedom of action left to army commanders. This is also indicated by the fact that, after the failure of the Marne, it was Moltke who was dismissed and not von Kluck.

THE FRENCH TACTIC OF THE OFFENSIVE AT ALL COSTS

In 1914 the doctrine of staying on the offensive at all costs prevailed in the French army. It would cost thousands of lives in the first weeks of the war. It is interesting to analyze the origin of this doctrine. It can again be explained by paronymic repetition, in this case the paronymic continuation of the colonial wars.

It must be stressed that this tactic was instead the official doctrine of the

French army. The Directive of 28 October 1913 on the conduct of large units states (Engerand 1918, p. 228; Conte 1991, p. 160): "The first duty of the leader is to desire the battle; a leader that is tempted to wait on the arrival of more precise information courts the risk of seeing his adversary piercing the mist with decisive acts. To conquer, it is necessary to destroy the enemy's battle plan by force; this rupture can only be obtained at the price of bloody sacrifice. Only the advance pushed until the hand-to-hand fight is decisive and irresistible. It is with the bayonet that the infantry breaks the last resistance of the enemy."

These instructions constitute a reaction against the lack of fighting spirit (largely of political origin, in any case) that led to the defeat of 1870. The directive first offers several sententious sentences ("The first duty of the leader is to desire the battle . . .") that are pure truisms. It is only in the last few sentences that a more precise concept appears, that of the bayonet charge. This concept is presented as a logical consequence of the choice of the offensive, but this is not the case. The German armies, while extolling the offensive, did not lead heroic charges that would be immediately scythed by machine-gun fire. How did this concept emerge?

We may ask what provoked the emergence of this concept. Without a doubt, it was a consequence of the colonial wars. The period 1880–1914 was the great period of colonial expansion. The main campaigns in sub-Saharan Africa include:

1888–1893	General Archinard conquers the empire of Ahmadu in Sudan
1893	General Dodds seizes Dahomey
1894	Joffre enters Timbuktu
1895	Expedition occupies Tananarive
1896	Upper Volta is conquered
1912	General Mangin drives out from Marrakech in Morocco the army of the pretender to the throne al-Hiba

Generals Franchet d'Esperey, Gallieni, Gouraud, Joffre, and Mangin, who would become famous during the war of 1914–1918, all made careers of varying length in the Empire. Joffre, for example, served in Taiwan under Admiral Courbet, at Hanoi (siege of Ba Dinh), and in the Sahara, where he would become known for the march from Ségou on the Niger to Timbuktu, which he seized on February 12, 1894.

Against the slow-loading guns at the disposal of France's adversaries in sub-Saharan Africa, Morocco, or Tonkin, the concept of the bayonet charge could have an operational value. Against German machine guns this was no longer the case.

Paronymy at the Level of the Armistice Treaty

It is well known that the Franco-German armistice of 1940 was signed in the same railway carriage as the armistice of 1918. However, this is only an anecdotal detail. A more significant case of paronymy consists in the layout of the armistice line between the north of the country, which was occupied by the German army, and the so-called free zone, in the south. This is the subject of Figure 6.8. Until Tours the two lines, for 1870 and 1940, almost correspond. In 1940 Germany wanted to occupy the whole of the Atlantic coast, for two main reasons. First, during World War I, the passage of submarines from the North Sea to the English Channel by the Straits of Dover had caused the loss of a large number of units. The occupation of the coast provided the German navy several bases for its submarines. Second, the occupation of the coast permitted the construction of the Atlantic Wall against attempted landings.

The Two Battles of the Atlantic

The history of submarine warfare during World War I offers an interesting illustration of the resistance to innovations and of the delay required until they eventually gain acceptance. In 1914 submarine warfare was completely new. It compelled the German General Staff to a succession of innovations that aroused much controversy. However, a consensus was eventually reached. This is best shown in the fact that during World War II unrestricted submarine warfare would be started in 1939. The same observation applies to the Pacific War. The United States knew how to profit from the lessons of World War I in a remarkable manner: unrestricted submarine warfare was launched and proved successful practically from the day after the attack on Pearl Harbor.

RESISTANCE TO INNOVATION

Privateering was long engaged in by privateers on behalf of their monarchs. The English admiral Sir Francis Drake (1540–1596) distinguished himself in this type of war against the Spaniards. French (1990) reports that between 1693 and 1708, nearly 7,000 vessels were seized by French privateers. Furthermore, the economic blockade had for a long time been a major weapon in conflicts of long duration. This was the case in particular

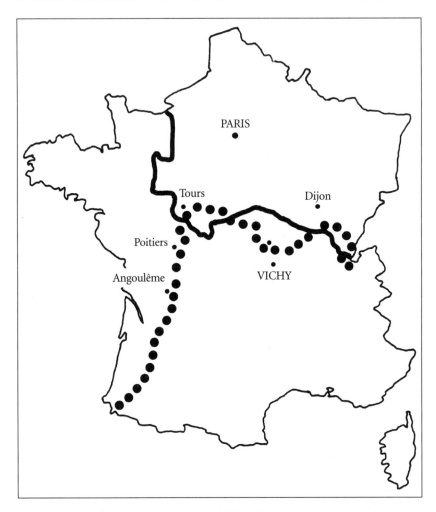

Figure 6.8 Comparison of the demarcation line during the armistices of 1870 (solid line) and 1940 (dotted line).

during the Napoleonic Wars. In 1914, from the beginning of the conflict, Germany encountered a naval blockade as a result of Britain's mastery of the seas. To be able to retaliate and so challenge Britain's mastery was an objective of paramount importance to Germany. This objective, which was out of reach for the High Seas Fleet, was entrusted to the submarines.

At this point it is necessary to recall the procedure in force against the ships of neutral countries at the beginning of World War I. It comprised the following stages: (1) A warning shot was fired across the bow to ask the ship to stop. (2) A rowing boat brought on board an inspection team to examine the papers and the cargo. (3) If the ship was transporting goods prohibited by the treaties in force, the crew had to abandon its boat, after which the valves were opened and it was sunk. This procedure constituted a highly inefficient use of a submarine. Submarine warfare could only be efficient if it was engaged in without restrictions. Sparing the neutrals could not be envisaged because, very quickly, the British navy had its freighters sail under neutral flags. To warn and evacuate the crews rapidly became impossible, especially after the British navy introduced trap-boats, the "Q-ships," which were freighters that concealed antisubmarine weapons. However, unrestricted submarine warfare went against tradition and aroused strong objections from the neutral countries and above all the United States.

The arguments were simple in essence, but various questions and personal antagonism meant that the debate between the German government and the admiralty would last for more than two years. On the side supporting submarine warfare, one found Admiral von Tirpitz, the father of the High Seas Fleet, as well as Pohl the general chief of staff of the navy and Admiral Bachmann who would replace von Pohl in 1915. At the polemical level, their main argument consisted in promising that six months after the beginning of unrestricted submarine warfare, England would be forced to surrender. On the opposing side, one found Chancellor Bethmann Hollweg and the members of his cabinet. As for Emperor William II, he sometimes sided with one side, sometimes with the other.

Consider five episodes from this fluctuating struggle for influence (de Gaulle 1924; Michelsen 1928; Churchill 1928, 1930).

- On February 2, 1915, submarine warfare was launched by Germany.
- On April 18, 1915, the submarines received the order to no longer sink neutral ships.
- On May 7, 1915, the *Lusitania*, an English liner with thousands of ammunition cases on board (Gibson and Prendergast 1932) as well as a large number of Americans, was sunk. On May 31, William II signed the order to henceforth spare all neutral ships and, some days later, to no longer sink the liners, even those of enemy powers.
- On August 26, 1915, Bachmann was dismissed and replaced by an opponent to submarine warfare, Admiral von Holtzendorff, who would nevertheless soon change camp.
- On January 29, 1917, thanks to the support of Hindenburg, the new

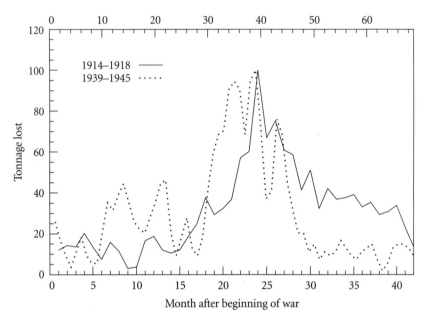

Figure 6.9a Comparison of the monthly tonnage sunk by the German submarines during World War I (solid line, lower horizontal axis) and World War II (dashed line, upper horizontal axis). The horizontal axes are graduated in months from the beginning of each conflict. The vertical scale has been normalized so that the maxima are set at 100. *Sources:* Churchill (1930); *Grand Larousse Encyclopédique.*

general chief of staff, unrestricted submarine warfare was decided on, and the United States was notified. For a few months, the tonnage sunk made a tremendous progression (Figure 6.9a). But soon the Allies' countermeasures proved effective.

SIMILARITY OF THE TWO BATTLES OF THE ATLANTIC

Figure 6.9a summarizes the progress of tonnage sunk during the two wars. There is a striking parallelism between both curves. Incidentally one should note that the decrease during the second half of the conflicts was not due to a relaxation of German efforts. On the contrary, the number of submarines constructed was on the increase: in 1918 at the time of the Armistice, no fewer than 226 submarines were under construction. The decline of tonnage sunk was due to antisubmarine warfare.

How can this similarity of evolution be interpreted? It suggests that, beyond technical progress, the logic of the confrontation between the submarine and its predators remained fundamentally the same from one war to the other. Would it be the same again in a future conflict even though nuclear propulsion has considerably altered the problem? We are convinced that the response to this question must be sought not in an evaluation of the technology of submersibles, but in a comparison of the economic and naval potential of the belligerents. The argument can be summarized as follows.

If, during World War I, the Allied losses in number of ships had been sustained on a long-term basis at their level of April 1917, the existence of the Allied fleets would have been called question within a short period. Submarines could therefore make the difference in the outcome of the war, and the English and American Allies used all their industrial and naval potential to tip the scales. Submarine warfare is often thought of in terms of technological improvement, such as, for example, the improvement in the means of detection or the means of propulsion. However, in the battle against submarines the quantitative is at least as important as the qualitative. Thus during World War I the Royal Navy barred the Straits of Dover using immense nets that were connected to buoys and supervised by patrols of destroyers. The Americans and the English also laid tens of thousands of mines: 15,000 mines were laid in 1917 in the Bay of Heligoland; in the 300 kilometers that separate Norway from the Orkney Islands the Americans laid 57,000 mines and the British 13,000 in 1918. Plans of such an extent require a huge industrial and naval capacity, but their efficiency is largely independent of the mode of propulsion of the submarine. Thus, the curves of Figures 6.9a and 6.9b illustrate the superiority of the economic potential of the Allies after the entry of the United States into the war.

A CONFIRMATION: THE PACIFIC WAR

A confirmation of our previous argument can be found in the Pacific War (see Figure 6.9c). We have seen how the hesitations of the German government between 1915 and 1917 led to a succession of orders and counter orders. At the time of the Pacific War the United States took advantage of this lesson of history with remarkable efficiency. On December 7, 1941, the American forces received the following order: "Execute unrestricted air and submarine warfare against Japan" (Peillard 1970). This innovative directive contrasted with the previous positions of the American government. On February 12, 1915, during the first few days of the submarine war, the American government wrote in a note to the German govern-

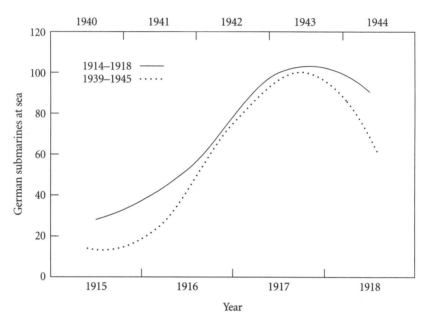

Figure 6.9b Comparison of the number of operational German submarines during World War I (solid line, lower horizontal axis) and World War II (dashed line, upper horizontal axis). The horizontal axes are graduated in months from the beginning of each conflict. The vertical scale has been normalized so that the maxima are set at 100. *Sources:* Churchill (1930); *Grand Larousse Encyclopédique.*

ment: "To destroy every ship in a delimited zone without first verifying that it belongs to a belligerent nation or that it carries prohibited goods would be a way of doing things that are so opposite to all the customs of naval war that the American government can hardly believe that the German imperial government would consider it possible" (Spindler 1933). In 1941, the "Instructions for the Navy of the United States governing maritime and aerial warfare" again prohibited the attack on merchant ships. The order of December 7 was thus a rapid adaptation to a new situation. Note that throughout the war the names and tonnage of the sunken boats were not published; in a general manner, the submarine war remained relatively confidential.

As the Allies found an efficient reply to the submarine threat, the Japanese maritime connections with Indonesia and Malaysia were gradually interrupted. One can summarize this evolution with some figures. In the Atlantic, the gross tonnage lost per submarine sunk was 140,000 tons in 1940, but in 1943–1945, this relationship fell to 3,000 tons. In the Pacific, in con-

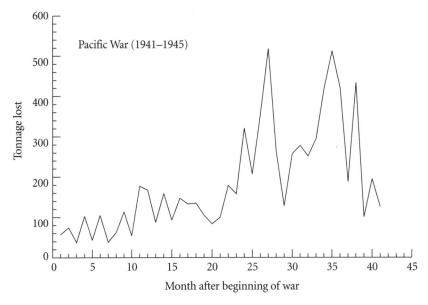

Figure 6.9c Tonnage sunk by American submarines during the Pacific War (1941–1945). The horizontal axis is graduated in months from the beginning of the conflict. In contrast to Figure 6.9a, the tonnage sunk increased throughout the conflict and remained at a high level (albeit with temporary fluctuations) until the end of the conflict. *Source:* Ellis (1993).

trast, this relationship remained in the region of 150,000 tons throughout the whole conflict. At the same time, the gross tonnage of the Japanese merchant navy dropped from 6 millions tons in 1941 to 1.5 millions tons in 1945 (Parillo 1993).

The reply to the threat of privateers or submarines is simple in its principle: it is the organization of convoys flanked by warships. At the height of the Atlantic campaign in May 1943, 96 percent of merchantmen in convoys arrived safely, as opposed to only 21 percent of ships sailing independently (Parillo 1993). However, the implementation of this response required important means. First it required a merchant navy sufficiently homogeneous to be able to sail in convoys; this excluded in particular ships that were too slow and would have imperiled the whole convoy. Then it was necessary to be able to divert from the navy the ships needed for the organization of the convoys. Furthermore it was necessary to be able to produce the ships and airplanes equipped with the most efficient means of antisubmarine warfare, without which the convoy itself would be of little use. All this required a powerful navy, a challenge the United States knew how to meet.

Japan

Despite his extraordinary sense of history, Winston Churchill confessed to not understanding how Japan had allowed itself to be led into the madness of a war against the United States: "It had seemed impossible that Japan would court destruction in war with Britain and the United States, and probably Russia in the end. A declaration of war by Japan could not be reconciled with reason. I felt sure she would be ruined for a generation by such a plunge, and this proved true. But Governments and peoples do not always take rational decisions" (1950, p. 536). In view of the disproportion of forces (see Tables 6.5a,b and Figure 6.10), one may tend to accept Churchill's judgment. We shall see, however, that there was a rationale to this decision in terms of paronymic behavior, that is, as a consequence of Japan's previous wars. Table 6.5a summarizes Japan's wars and Tables 6.5b and 6.5c estimate the balance of power; Figure 6.10 provides a corresponding graphical representation.

Dates and Opposing Forces

CONFLICTS

During World War I, Japanese participation consisted in occupying the German trading posts in China and their archipelagos in the Pacific. With regard to territorial expansion, the outcome was a League of Nations mandate to administer some of these islands. The period 1914–1918 also saw the continuation of Japan's policy of encroachment in China. An important claim was the Twenty-one Demands addressed to China in September 1914. Japan was able to take advantage of the fact that the great powers were engaged in a conflict in Europe so as to continue its program of expansion.

Japan's conflicts of 1918–1925 and 1938 are interesting because they show that at first Japan envisaged the pursuit of its westward expansion at the expense of Russia, who had been so heavily defeated in 1904–1905. In 1918 the operations in Siberia were led together with the Allies, that is, the United States, France, and Britain. However, while the western Allies withdrew their troops in 1920, Japan maintained its own for two further years; the north of Sakhalin Island was evacuated only in 1925 (Morley 1957). In

Table 6.5a Japan: Expansion wars. 1874–1945

Year	Opponents	Total number of battle deaths	Reference
1874	China		Bujac (1896)
1894–1895	China	10,000	Richardson (1960), p. 64
1904–1905	Russia	126,000	Richardson (1960), p. 47
1914	Germany		Benoist-Méchin (1984)
1918–1925	Russia	>700	Benoist-Méchin (1984); Morley (1957)
1931–1933	China	63,000	Richardson (1960)
1938, 1939	Russia	17,000	*Kodansha* (1983)
1937–1945	China		
1941–1945	Britain, Netherlands, United States	2,200,000	Ellis (1993)

Table 6.5b Population and central government revenue for China, Japan, and Russia (1890)

Country	Population (millions)	Central government revenue (millions)	Reference
China	430 (1850)		Mitchell (1982)
Japan	40 (1890)	507 Y (1904)	Mitchell (1982)
Russia	126 (1904)	5,887 F (1904)	Mitchell (1978); Helfferich (1989)

Note: Y = yen; F = French franc.

Table 6.5c Population and gross national product for China, Japan, and the United States (1940)

Country	Population (millions)	Gross national product (billions)	Reference
China	452 (1937)		Mitchell (1982)
Japan	72 (1940)	33.1 Y (1939)	Liesner (1989), pp. 260, 252
United States	130 (1938)	91.3 $ (1939)	Liesner (1989), pp. 92, 74

Note: Y = Yen.

Balance of power, 1904–1905

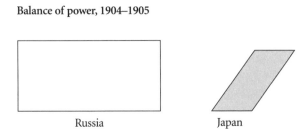

Figure 6.10a Balance of power during the war of 1904–1905 between Russia and Japan, expressed in terms of state revenue. Each rectangle/triangle's area is proportional to the public revenue of the corresponding state. *Source:* Table 6.5b.

Balance of power, 1941–1945
(Netherlands and United Kingdom omitted)

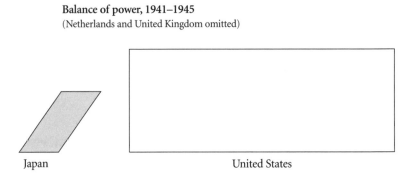

Figure 6.10b Balance of power during the Pacific War of 1941–1945 between the United States and Japan, expressed in terms of gross national product. Each rectangle/triangle's area is proportional to the gross national product of the corresponding state. *Source:* Table 6.5c.

the summers of 1938 and 1939, a series of clashes between Japanese and Soviet forces took place on the border between Manchuria and Outer Mongolia. The superiority of the Soviet mechanized units resulted in repeated reversals for the Japanese, culminating in a complete rout in late August 1939 (*Kodansha* 1983). This military humiliation resulted in a setback for those in the army who advocated military confrontation with the Soviet Union rather than with the United States.

THE BALANCE OF POWER

In 1940, as we have already noted, the balance of power was very unfavorable to Japan. Nevertheless, preceding conflicts had accustomed it to the idea of a confrontation with countries whose population or economic power was largely superior to its own. In 1904, after all, there had been an enormous imbalance in terms of economic resources between Russia and Japan. Nevertheless, Japan had known how to impose an advantageous peace treaty on this strongly centralized country possessing a powerful army. Similarly, there was a considerable disparity in terms of population between China and Japan. Nevertheless at the time of the war of 1894–1895, Japan made short work of this country whose population was ten times that of its own. With the success of these conflicts, the General Staff came to the conclusion that it did not have to listen to the prophets of doom.

Here we will distinguish between two periods: the first from 1894 to 1905 and the second from 1935 to 1945. A recurrent theme of this section is the analogies between these two conflicts. Of course the limiting dates are only indicative; thus it would not be unreasonable to bring the second period of conflict back to 1931 (to the dynamiting of the Manchurian railway line) or even before.

The Planning of Wars

Although we employ the term "planning" in the title of this section, we do not want to suggest that the march to war took place according to a concerted and systematic political plan. The fact that there had been a large number of disagreements between civilians and the military, on the one hand, and between the army and the navy, on the other, is certified by the political instability and by the rebellions that marked the years 1932–1936. It is at the level of armament production and naval construction that planning played the largest role. This is clear from the time required for the construction of large naval units: five years for the construction of a Yamato-class battleship; at least two years for a carrier; and one year for a 430-ton submarine.

THE FUNCTIONING OF GOVERNMENT

Even in the most democratic countries, the decisions regarding the initiation of a conflict are only rarely the subject of public debate. Karp (1979) shows this in a very convincing manner with respect to two wars led by the United States: the war of 1898 against Spain and the entry in 1917 into the war against Germany. In the case of Japan, the policy of secrecy was so strongly pronounced that even members of the government did not have full access to strategic and military data, a paradoxical situation. When the prime minister, who was appointed by the emperor, formed his government, he needed in practice the approval of the high command for the nomination of ministers of the army and the navy; these had inevitably to be active generals and admirals. By this means, the General Staff had the right to approve the formation of the government. This was not purely a theoretical possibility; an illustration of this took place in 1937. Ugaki tried to form a cabinet, but because of the army's opposition to him, no one would serve as army minister and finally he had to give up (Ienaga 1968). After the increased intervention in China that same year, the military were unwilling to discuss certain matters at cabinet meetings because civilians were present. Thus when the minister of the colonies asked in what area of China the military action would stop, he was only given a vague response. The crucial decision to go to war against America, England, and the Netherlands followed the same pattern (Ienaga, 1968).

MILITARY PREPARATIONS

1. The 1894–1905 conflict   The war of 1894 against China does not seem to have demanded a notable war effort from Japan. From 1890 to 1895, military expenses remained practically constant at 22 million yen (*Hundred-Year Statistics* 1966, p. 131). After 1895, in contrast, these expenses increased rapidly (see Figure 6.11). In 1894 Japan did not possess a navy capable of confronting that of Russia. The whole indemnity paid by China after its defeat, 100 million dollars (200 million yen at the 1900 exchange rate), was devoted to the creation of a modern fleet. The program was spread over seven years and yielded six battleships, seven cruisers, and several torpedo boats. Most of these ships were not constructed in Japan, which still did not have the necessary industrial infrastructure, but were ordered from German and English naval yards. Just before the war, however, Japan was able to manufacture its own guns of up to 320 caliber.

The new ships, as a result of their recent construction, reflected the latest technology, both in their high speed (around 17 knots) and in the maneuverability of their artillery. Furthermore, fifteen large dry docks were created for the maintenance and repair of these units. Two new naval bases were created at Maïdzourou and Moïdzi, and the old ones were fortified (Térestchenko 1931, p. 52). Education and training maneuvers were also the object of great attention. Education took place not on school ships, but on powerful cruisers such as the *Matsushima*. Large-scale maneuvers involving the whole fleet took place in the presence of the Mikado in 1900 and in 1903.

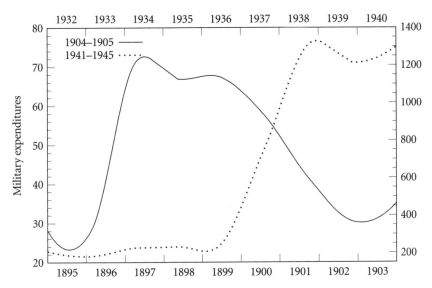

Figure 6.11 Comparison of the growth of Japanese military expenditures in the nine years preceding the conflicts of 1904–1905 (solid line, left vertical axis) and 1941–1945 (dashed line, right vertical axis). The two vertical axes are graduated in millions of yen (1900 prices). The "size" of the war effort during the Pacific War is underlined by the fact that the amounts spent are seventeen times higher than those during the previous conflict. The preparation for the 1904 war was completed at least three years before its outbreak, which suggests that it was delayed for diplomatic reasons. *Source: Hundred-Year Statistics of the Japanese Economy* (1966, p. 35).

2. The 1935–1945 conflict   An important armaments program was developed between 1924 and 1941. From the point of view of the budget, expenditures reached a record level in 1934–1937 (Figure 6.11). From the point of view of the tonnage of the war fleet, the acceleration took place in particular after 1938, as shown by the following figures (Military Yearbook of the League of Nations):

	Navy tonnage (thousand tons)
1924	568
1928	714
1938	874
1941	1, 270

(At the same time, the tonnage of the American navy fell from 1,528 to 1,099 thousand tons.) Dive-bombing and aerial torpedoing were relatively new techniques in 1940 for air forces generally; in Japan they were systematically developed. Training for Japan's operation of December 1941 took place in Kagoshima Bay, chosen for its topographic similarity with the Bay of Pearl Harbor.

DIPLOMATIC PREPARATIONS

A permanent concern of the Japanese General Staff was to avoid war on two fronts. To this end, treaties of alliance were signed in anticipation of the conflicts to come.

1. The 1894–1905 conflict   A treaty of alliance with England was signed on January 31, 1902. It said that in case of military operations in the Far East, each party had to assist the other if it had to face more than one adversary. But in case of a war involving one of the parties against a single adversary, the other remained neutral. Japan thus protected itself against the possibility of having to make war with both Russia and France, its ally. In addition, through the signature of the Sino-American-Japanese treaty of January 11, 1904, the United States showed that it was increasingly siding with Japan.

2. The 1935–1945 conflict   The Tripartite Pact signed on September 27, 1940, between Germany, Italy, and Japan had no immediate military significance. But the Japanese-Soviet Pact signed on April 13, 1941, two months before the German offensive against the Soviet Union, had the explicit objective of avoiding war on two fronts. In fact, this objective was largely reached, since the Soviet Union, though an ally of the United States, only declared war on Japan on August 8, 1945.

Figure 6.12 recalls the geographical extension of the Japanese empire in 1914, 1933, and 1942.

The Strategic Situation

THE 1894–1905 CONFLICT: THE COLLISION OF TWO EXPANSIONISMS

In 1904, at the time of the outbreak of the conflict between Russia and Japan, each nation had been engaged for more than a decade in an expansionist phase that made a collision almost unavoidable. Russia's secular goal was to have access to a port on an open sea (as opposed to the closed seas of the Baltic and the Black Sea) and at a sufficiently low latitude to not be blocked by ice in winter. It had once believed that it could take advantage of the decomposition of the Ottoman Empire to extend its zone of influence up to Constantinople, but this hope had been ruined by the Treaty of Berlin (1878). Then it had realized that perhaps the solution resided in

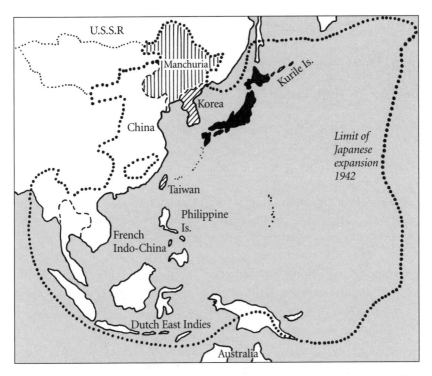

Figure 6.12 Successive extensions of the Japanese Empire from 1870 to 1942. The diagonally hatched areas correspond to territories conquered in the period 1870–1914: Taiwan in 1895 and Korea in 1910. The vertically hatched area corresponds to territories conquered in the period 1918–1933: Manchuria (1931–1932) and Jehol (a northern province of China) in 1933. It should be noted that Manchuria (now the Chinese province of Heilongkiang), which in the 1930s constituted the Japanese puppet state of Manchukuo, is vastly larger than Korea and in fact is 30 percent larger than Japan itself. Its huge mineral resources played a key role in Japan's war effort. The dotted line indicates the maximum extension of the empire in August 1942. *Source:* Adapted from Gravereau (1988).

those distant oriental lands of Siberia, to which it had until then given little attention. A first port had been created during the period of Peter the Great to the north of the Kamchatka Peninsula; this was Petropavlovsk, but it hardly satisfied the second criteria stated above. Then in 1850 the port of Nikolayev was established at the outlet of the Amur River. But because of the shallow waters, ice blocked it six months out of twelve and frequent storms made it hardly more usable than Petropavlovsk. In 1860 the port of Vladivostok (which means "Rule the East") was created; but it was seized by ice until March and to make matters worse, it opened onto a closed sea, the Sea of Japan, which was only connected to the Pacific Ocean by a series of straits. Attempts to settle on the island of Tsushima in the middle of the Korea Strait or at Pusan on the eastern shore of Korea came up against an English veto. The construction of the Trans-Siberian Railroad (9,700 kilometers from St. Petersburg) constituted an important stage in Russian settlement; inevitably Japan saw a threat in this expansion.

At the time Japan was also trying to increase its vital space. This country, which was sometimes called the England of Asia, had a population of 44 million in 1900, which was 27 percent more than Britain, for a territory of 370,000 square kilometers, which was 38 percent larger than Britain. The latter had partly solved its population problem by spreading overseas. Japan tried to do the same in Korea, Manchuria, Taiwan, and Hawaii, the difference being that the first three countries already had strong indigenous populations and belonged traditionally to the sphere of influence of the Chinese empire. In this process of expansion that would reach its peak in 1942, a confrontation with China was therefore unavoidable. It was equally so with Russia to the extent that it had similar aims. We may also note the extraordinary growth in the Japanese population after 1870. After having been practically stationary from 1720 to 1870 with approximately 26 million residents, this population rose to 49 million in 1908 and to 72 million in 1938. Thus in the space of seventy years the population had tripled (Requien 1934).

THE 1935–1945 CONFLICT: THE JAPAN–U.S. COLLISION IN CHINA

In its territorial expansion in China, Japan found itself increasingly confronted by the United States; the latter was installed in the Philippines, and it must be remembered that the island of Luzon is less than 600 kilometers from the Chinese coast. Furthermore, the United States had commercial interests and a zone of influence in China. In 1931, relations between Japan and the United States reached a critical phase. The United States supported a League of Nations resolution (even though it was not a member) that called on Japan to withdraw its troops from Manchuria. With Japan's refusal, the tension between the two countries rose to such a point that their respective fleets were put on a state of alert. During the next few years, other crises occurred that would bring the two countries almost to war. For example, three people were killed in 1937 during the bombing of the *Panay,* an American gunboat on the Yangtze, by the Japanese air force. Japan was still not ready for war and preferred to end the incident with a compensation payment (Costello 1981). In Japan war was nevertheless considered unavoidable. In 1932 and 1933, for example, two books were published with revealing titles: *The Necessary War between Japan and the United States*, by Ikezaki, and *The Inevitable War between Britain and Japan, by* Ishimaru; the latter work was translated in 1936 into English under the title *Japan Must Fight Britain*. On April 30, 1934, General Araki declared, "The war against the United States has become a national duty" (Zischka 1935).

THE JAPANESE WAR OBJECTIVES

Japan's objective in the 1894 war with China was to have a free hand in Korea; it was achieved. The objective of the 1904–1905 war against Russia was to stop Russian expansion toward Korea and Manchuria and make quasi-protectorates of these two regions. It too was achieved. The objective of the war against the United States, Britain, and the Netherlands was to accelerate the breakup of the colonial empires and spread Japan's zone of influence toward the south in a manner analogous to what had been done in Korea and Manchuria. Just as Japan had not envisaged a total war against Russia, it similarly did not envisage a total war against the United States. It hoped that the prospect of the excessive cost of a protracted war would bring the United States to the negotiating table. This is shown by the following excerpt from the background materials to the Imperial Conference (September 6, 1941): "Although America's total defeat is judged utterly impossible, it is not inconceivable that a shift in American public opinion due to our victories in South-East Asia or to England's surrender might bring the war to an end. At any rate, our occupation of vital areas to the South will ensure a superior strategic position" (Ienaga 1968). But none of these eventualities materialized. Furthermore, the submarine warfare led by the U.S. Navy against the Japanese freighters deprived Japan of its sources of supply from the conquered territories.

The Development of Conflicts

Our objective here is not to retrace these conflicts but rather to stress the similarities in the strategies and the tactics that were implemented.

WHY A SURPRISE ATTACK?

The surprise attack against the enemy fleet before or at the same time as the declaration of war appears consistently in the Japanese war strategies of 1894, 1904, and 1941. On July 25, 1894, five days before the declaration of war, the Japanese navy defeated the Chinese fleet in the Kanghwa Bay. On the night of February 8–9, 1904, two days before the declaration of war, Japan moved against the Russian Pacific fleet at Port Arthur. Finally on December 7, 1941, at the same time that it declared war, war, Japan attacked the American fleet at Pearl Harbor. From the first to the last of these events, there is a sort of crescendo both in the extent of the operation and in its success. Before exploring the similarities among these events, we first examine the military relevance of a surprise attack.

A surprise attack is intended to give the attacker an advantage to compensate for numerical inferiority. Such a situation occurred, for example, in 1914 between Germany and England. Both countries were naval powers of primary importance; however despite the important program of naval construction implemented by Germany in the years that preceded the conflict, it remained the challenger as its fleet was much smaller than the English fleet. In a global confrontation Germany's chances were weak. Thus a surprise attack on the English fleet in its ports and at the beginning of the conflict would have been the only reasonable option for Germany. This risk was indeed taken very seriously by the British Admiralty, as Winston Churchill relates in his memoirs: "We decided that the Fleet should leave at such an hour on the morning of the 29th [July 1914, six days before the declaration of war] as to pass the Straits of Dover during the hours of darkness, that it should traverse these waters at high speed and without lights, and with the utmost precaution proceed to Scapa Flow . . . A surprise torpedo attack before or simultaneous with the declaration of war was at any rate one nightmare gone for ever" (1923, pp. 211–213).

In short, a Japanese-type strategy was almost the only chance for the German navy to escape either destruction or, as took place in 1918, disarmament, as demanded by the conditions of the Armistice. If this choice was not made, it was because it would have necessitated the invention of a whole new set of operational concepts. There was no leader to advocate this with sufficient persuasion. We have seen with the example of submarine warfare that the introduction of new strategic concepts is, by the reservations and inertia that need to be overcome, a long-term operation.

Further, it can be noted that the Japanese strategy of crushing the enemy fleet in port has never been employed in a systematic manner by Britain. The attacks of Basque Roads in April 1809 (Vincent 1898, p. 104) against France, of Navarino (1827) against the Turks, and of Mers-el-Kebir (Algeria) against the French fleet in 1940 constitute rare exceptions.

In the case of Japan and China, the Japanese fleet was not in the least inferior to the Chinese fleet in 1894. Similarly in 1904 the Japanese fleet largely outclassed the Russian Pacific Fleet, as shown by its subsequent overwhelming victory against the Russian Baltic Fleet, which was much more important than the Pacific. In 1941, the American and Japanese fleets were of quite comparable force; for 1938 the figures are 874,000 tons for Japan and 1,099,000 tons for the United States, but by 1941 this gap had undoubtedly been further reduced. The surprise attack was thus not in the least a tactical necessity. Certainly, the surprise effect facilitated the achievement of a more complete victory than would have been possible in a classic naval battle, but it was at a high political price. In effect, the attack gave the United States a considerable moral advantage. Let us imagine for an instant that Japan had limited itself to an attack against the Philippines; it is more than probable that the American public would have reacted with much less fervor. In truth, the 2,433 American deaths at Pearl Harbor would greatly stimulate the American war effort.

In summary, one can say that although the surprise attack was not required militarily from either a tactical or a strategic viewpoint, the Imperial Navy was anxious to revive the glorious tradition of February 1904. This is confirmed by an analysis of the military operations.

SIMILARITIES AMONG THE SURPRISE ATTACKS OF 1894, 1904, AND 1941

1. *Leaders*   Admirals Togo and Kamimura, who would lead the campaigns of 1904, had already participated in the campaigns against China. Furthermore, Admiral Yamamoto, who directed the operation on Pearl Harbor, had taken part as a cadet at the age of twenty-one in the overwhelming naval victory of Tsushima against Russia in 1905, losing two fingers on his left hand. Later, he would give the name Operation Z, which had been on the flag of Admiral Togo at Tsushima, to Pearl Harbor, thus establishing a direct relationship between the two battles.

2. *The beginning of the conflict and the declaration of war*   In each of the two conflicts, there was no real declaration of war, but a diplomatic rupture that, from the Japanese perspective, took its place. When on the night of February 5–6, February, Admiral Togo received the order to set sail, the Japanese ambassador to St. Petersburg, Kurino, had still not returned his credentials to the Russian government. He would do it on the day of February 6, after which, accompanied by all the embassy officials as well as all

the other Japanese who lived in St. Petersburg, he left the capital of the Russian Empire. Military operations began on February 8 with an attack on the Korean port of Chemulpo. The actual attack on Port Arthur would take place on the night of February 8–9. However, because the Japanese had taken control of the telegraph service, no one in Port Arthur was aware of the attack on Chemulpo; indeed it seems that neither Port Arthur nor the Russian ships were provided with radiotelegraphy (Térestchenko 1931, p. 89).

The period between the departure of the ambassador (which was, to the Japanese, equivalent to a declaration of war) and the beginning of hostilities was therefore two days in 1904. This period would be considerably reduced in 1941, but the method would be the same. On the morning of December 7, 1941, the Japanese ambassador, Nomura, had to transmit a message to Secretary of State Cordell Hull; it notified the United States "that it was not possible to arrive at an agreement by new negotiations." This message had to be delivered at 1 P.M., which was 7:30 A.M. in Hawaii. Given that the Japanese fighter-bombers had to arrive at their target by 8 A.M., the period between the declaration of war and the attack was reduced to 30 minutes. In fact, because of various delays, Nomura would not be received by Hull until 2:05 P.M., and the latter was by then already aware of the attack.

3. Proclamations to the sailors   Here is Admiral Togo's proclamation at the time of setting off in 1904: "I plan to attack the enemy ships that are at Port Arthur and Chemulpo. This war is linked to the very existence of our homeland and I ask from the bottom of my heart for everyone whatever his rank to put all his strength into performing his duty" (Térestchenko 1931, p. 86).

Echoing him thirty-six years later, Admiral Yamamoto gave the following proclamation to his crews off Hawaii: "The rise or the fall of the Empire depends upon this battle. Everyone will do his duty with utmost effort" (Costello 1981, p. 124).

One might be tempted to attribute the similarities between the two to the nature of this type of message. A comparison with the proclamation that Lord Kitchener addressed in August 1914 to the Expeditionary Force departing for France, however, shows a great difference in the form: "Soldiers of the King, you are being sent abroad to come to the help of your French comrades whose home has been invaded by a common enemy. At every opportunity be courteous, kind and good. You will only be able to do your duty if your health is good so always guard yourselves against all excess. In the new life that is ahead of you, you will no doubt meet with temptations, wine and women; of these two temptations, you must resist them without fail and, while treating women with perfect courtesy, you will have to avoid all intimacy. Do your duty in bravery. Fear God. And Honour your King" (Conte 1991, p. 182).

4. A combined naval and terrestrial operation   In 1904 as well as in 1941, the planned operation combined the attack of a port with the landing of troops. In 1904, the first landing of troops took place on the night of February 8–9 in the Bay of Chemulpo near Seoul. It involved two battalions of infantry (2,500 men) who had to occupy Seoul immediately. The attack on Port Arthur only took place on the following night.

In 1941, the landing operations were of a much larger scale; at the same time as the attack on Pearl Harbor, troop landings were anticipated in Malaysia, the Philippines, and Thailand. Here also the landing of troops slightly preceded the attack on Pearl Harbor; it was in at 5:45 A.M., Hawaii time, that the invasion force (5,000 men) of General Yamashita disembarked on the beach of Kota Bharu on the coast of Malaysia to the north of Singapore.

5. Russian and American myopia   It is of interest to stress the similarity between the lack of Russian initiative at Port Arthur and the American myopia at Pearl Harbor. Of course, at Port Arthur as at Pearl Harbor something was expected, but what? Would the attack be on Port Arthur or on Vladivostok, on Pearl Harbor or on the Philippines? At Port Arthur, the fleet was on alert and measures had been taken to counter a torpedo boat attack. The artillery guns were loaded and the searchlights lighted. The fleet was not in the port itself but in the outer harbor. This was a result of the port's shallow waters: had the fleet remained inside, it would only have been able to leave at high tide. The dangers of this choice had nevertheless been stressed in a letter dated February 7, 1904, from Admiral Makarov to the Ministry of the Navy: "The presence of the ships on an open roadstead gives the enemy the possibility of executing a torpedo attack. Reason demands holding the fleet in the internal basin of Port Arthur while it is not engaged in operations. If we do not do it now we will have to do it after the first night attack and we will pay dearly for this fault" (Térestchenko 1931). Despite its risky position, the Russian fleet did not send out patrol boats on lookout, and Japan's torpedo boats were able to approach within several hundred meters without being noticed.

In 1941 an attack on the Philippines was considered a strong possibility, but no one seriously believed that Pearl Harbor was under direct threat.

The leader of the American army, General Marshall, wrote after a visit to Pearl Harbor: "With adequate air defense enemy carriers will begin to come under our attack at a distance of 750 miles . . . A major attack against Oahu is considered impractical" (Costello 1981, p. 99). The logic of this official position explains why a set of indices were not exploited in a optimal manner. In addition, no aerial reconnaissance was undertaken in a systematic manner.

6. *The lessons of Port Arthur for the Japanese*   In fact the attack on Port Arthur was a semi-defeat for Japan. The attack took place as anticipated: ten torpedo boats succeeded in approaching within approximately 300 meters of the fleet and sixteen torpedoes were launched (Térestchenko 1931, p. 105), but only three hit their target, damaging two battleships and a cruiser. On the following day, however, it was discovered that one of the battleships and the cruiser could be refloated and returned to the port. In fact, it is difficult to understand why Admiral Togo assigned only ten torpedo boats when there were sixty-two of them in the Japanese fleet (Térestchenko 1931, app. I). But the lesson was learned; at Pearl Harbor, instead of a raid, the Japanese led a massive attack.

THE CAPTURE OF PORT ARTHUR

In 1894 the citadel of Port Arthur was armed with Krupp cannons, and its garrison contained 12,000 men. But because of a lack of pugnacity on the part of the Chinese troops, Japan took the citadel without great difficulty in a night attack. In October 1895, however, six months after the conclusion of the Peace Treaty of Shimonoseki (April 17, 1895), Japan was forced to give up Port Arthur under Russian pressure. In compensation, it received a supplementary war allowance. Thus in 1905 the Japanese once again found themselves faced with the citadel of Port Arthur, and this time it would surrender only after a dogged resistance of more than four months. The carnage of this battle, the result of the new power of the artillery, anticipated the devastation that was to come in the trench warfare of 1914–1918. The obstinate Japanese assaults also foreshadowed the bitterness of the terrestrial battles of the Pacific War. General Niox described the 1905 struggle: "One must admire the dedication, the heroism, the contempt of death, the patriotic enthusiasm of the Japanese. Each of the assaults is followed by a frightful slaughter. These assaults are renewed unceasingly, day after day, night after night without obtaining results in proportion to the efforts and losses. And the gaps created in the ranks are fulfilled by reinforcements brought continually by the transportation fleet. They have lost approximately 15,000 men. On two occasions, during the nights of 20 and 23 November, they got to scaling the parapets: each time they were repelled with knives, losing nearly 2,000 men" (1906, p. 59).

THE PURSUIT OF THE "ONE BIG BATTLE"

On September 17, 1884, the Imperial Navy's victory over the main Chinese battle squadron at the battle of the Yalu River set the stage for Japan's resounding triumph in the war. This success had not been anticipated, since the northern Chinese squadron contained two battleships (constructed in Germany) and seven cruisers (constructed in England). Furthermore, the determination of the Chinese command was such that after the defeat of the fleet, Admiral Ting and his principal officers committed suicide.

On May 17, 1905, the Japanese victory over the Russian fleet in the Tsushima Strait was dazzling. The whole Russian Baltic Fleet was sunk (4,000 killed) or forced to surrender (7,000 taken prisoner); on the Japanese side there were 116 deaths (Benoist-Méchin 1984).

It is therefore not surprising that, with the memory of similar victories still relatively recent, the Japanese constantly sought a decisive naval battle throughout the whole war of 1941–1945. They would seek it at Midway (June 5–6, 1942), where they experienced defeat, and finally at the battle of Leyte Gulf (October 24–26, 1944), which ended in disaster for them. This pursuit of the decisive battle would force them to make choices that are difficult to explain otherwise. Instead of assigning their sixty submarines to attack American communication lines, they allocated them to the accompaniment of the war fleet, a task for which the subs had only very limited usefulness.

THE PURSUIT OF AN HONORABLE PEACE

In 1905 Theodore Roosevelt had offered to mediate the conflict between Japan and Russia, and this was accepted with eagerness by both sides. During the Pacific War, however, the United States was the master of the game, and no country would offer its mediation services. Nevertheless, Japan did make efforts in this direction, as revealed by the declaration of Prime Minister Koiso, the successor to Tojo, in July 1944. He called for throwing all remaining military resources into one all-out effort to win a battle before seeking an end to the war. Japan thus hoped to reiterate the scenario of

1905. But the tactical victory so hoped for never came, and the dropping of the atomic bomb took away all hopes of a negotiated peace.

DEMONSTRATIONS AFTER THE SIGNING OF PEACE TREATIES

The signing of peace treaties has given rise to recurrent demonstrations of anger in Japan. (1) In September 1905 there were citywide riots in Tokyo to protest against the Treaty of Portsmouth, which concluded the Russo-Japanese War. Nine police stations, 350 buildings, and 13 Christian churches were either smashed or burned down; there were 17 deaths. (2) Similarly, a number of riots occurred soon after the Treaty of San Francisco became effective (April 28, 1952). On May 1 in Tokyo, demonstrators set fire to parked cars belonging to American military personnel, causing 2 deaths. On July 7 in Nagoya, the rioters threw Molotov cocktails and stones at the police; 1 police officer was killed. (3) In June 1971 there were other riots in Tokyo after a new agreement had been signed regarding the American bases on Okinawa; 700 people were arrested (*Times,* June 18, 1971).

United States

In contrast to the countries considered so far, the United States is a young nation, and this has allowed it to free itself of the secular traditions that weigh on European nations. It constitutes a separate and remarkable example of territorial expansion; we begin by stressing its main characteristics.

The success of American expansion can be characterized in one sentence: for all the countries that we have examined so far, their phase of expansion was followed by a phase of contraction, but there was nothing of the sort for the United States despite the extent of its expansion. From an initial nucleus consisting of the thirteen colonies, this nation has been able to expand in a substantial manner both to the west and to the south. The expansion to the west can be compared to the colonization of Siberia by Russia at the time of Peter the Great (1682–1725) and Catherine the Great (1762–1796). It is essentially the expansion to the south and in the Pacific that will concern us in this section. In the course of this process, the United States was confronted with the interests of Britain, Spain, and Mexico. Yet expansion was achieved at the price of conflicts that were of short duration and cost few American lives.

The United States' immense military dominance would have allowed it to annex much larger territories, both toward Canada and beyond the Rio Grande, had it so desired. This is not a matter of speculation; voices were raised at the time in favor of a country that would extend from the Hudson Bay to Panama. Successive American presidents had the wisdom to resist these Sirens. Furthermore, unlike European tradition, the annexations were always accompanied with the payment of financial compensation. In a certain manner one could therefore say that it was more a matter of acquisition than of annexation.

To fully measure the success of American expansion we should compare it with the examples that we analyzed earlier. (1) Sweden's expansion toward Germany was of short duration; even Finland, which was more a traditional possession than an annexed region, separated itself from Sweden. (2) The English expansion to the west came up against the resistance and resentment of the Irish, who eventually gained their independence. (3) The territorial expansion of France under the Revolution and the Empire was so excessive that it could not last. (4) The German expansion during the nineteenth century aroused the resentment of its neighbors to the east (Silesia, Poland) and to the west (Alsace-Lorraine); following World War II Germany lost large sections of territory, including regions that had belonged to the historical nucleus of Prussia. (5) The Japanese policy of annexation and encroachment in Korea, Manchuria, and China aroused strong resistance. But its long phase of territorial expansion, which had begun in 1874, was canceled in one go by the defeat of 1945; Japan lost all its "exterior" possessions, including Taiwan and the Kuril Islands. (6) Although Russia has certainly been able to preserve its immense territory of Siberia, it has lost most of the gains of its expansion toward the south, efforts that were marked by so many conflicts with the Ottoman Empire in the eighteenth and nineteenth centuries.

Dates and Opposing Forces
Table 6.6a outlines the main stages of the American expansion. These conflicts were few and of short duration. Although the conflict of 1812–1815 has often been presented as a naval and commercial confrontation with Britain, it was not only that. Pratt (1925) shows convincingly that the conflict of 1812 resulted from a deliberate desire for expansion toward Canada and Florida. In 1813, there were many battles on the Canadian frontier. In August 1814, the British seized Washington; the Capitol and the White House were burnt and the incursion was only stopped at Baltimore.

Finally, in 1815, a British attempt to seize New Orleans was repelled. The number of American troops committed to this conflict was far superior to that of all the other conflicts mentioned in Table 6.6a: 576,000 against only 112,000 at the time of the war with Mexico and 312,000 for the war with Spain (*Statistical Abstract of the United States*, 1984). Of the efforts at territorial expansion cited in Table 6.6a, that of 1812 was the only failure. Nevertheless the moment had been well chosen, since the attention and the forces of Britain were being taken up with the struggle against Napoleon. However, America's 1812 conflict is also the only one to have been led as a classic war of conquest, and this largely explains its failure.

In what way do the other conflicts differ from a "classic" war of conquest? There were generally four phases: (1) infiltration and colonization; (2) incidents directed against American citizens and providing a pretext for intervention; (3) open war, with a rapid military victory; (4) a peace treaty, with financial compensation for the territories annexed. These phases are detailed in the following paragraphs.

Note that Table 6.6a mentions only in a very partial manner the wars and battles against the Indians. These were numerous and covered the whole period from the proclamation of independence to the end of the nineteenth century. An enumeration of these conflicts can be found in Wright (1932), in the *Times Atlas of World History* (1989, p. 217), or in Clodfelter (1992).

The balance of power for the expansion wars waged by the United States is summarized in Table 6.6b–d.

Table 6.6a United States: Expansion wars, 1812–1905

Year	Opponent	Location	Total number of battle deaths or [number of troops]	Reference
1812–1815	Britain	Canadian border	[576,000]	*Stat. Abs. U.S.* (1984)
1813	Creeks	Alabama	[14,000]	*Stat. Abs. U.S.* (1984)
1833–1839	Cherokees	Georgia	[9,500]	*Stat. Abs. U.S.* (1984)
1835–1842	Seminoles	Florida	[41,000]	*Stat. Abs. U.S.* (1984)
1846–1848	Mexico	Mexico	16,000	Richardson (1960), p. 57
1898–1899	Spain	Philippines, Cuba	200,000	Richardson (1960), p. 46

Note: When the total number of deaths is unknown, we have indicated in brackets the number of troops engaged. The list of wars against the Indians is restricted to three major disputes, but there were many others.

Table 6.6b Population and central government revenue for Britain and the
United States (1812)

Country	Population (millions)	Central government revenue (millions)	Reference
Britain (U.K.)	18	71 £	Mitchell (1971)
United States	7.7	14 $	*Hist. Stat. U.S.* (1975)

Note: During the nineteenth century £1 was approximately $4.80.

Table 6.6c Population and central government revenue for Mexico and the
United States (1846)

Country	Population (millions)	Central government revenue (millions)	Reference
Mexico	7.8	24 Po	Mitchell (1983)
United States	21.0	30 $	*Hist. Stat. U.S.* (1975)

Note: Po = peso.

Table 6.6d Population and central government revenue for Spain and the United
States (1898)

Country	Population (millions)	Central government revenue (millions)	Reference
Spain	18	868 Pa	Mitchell (1983)
United States	73	405 $	*Hist. Stat. U.S.* (1975)

Note: Pa = peseta; in 1913, 1 Pa = $0.18 (*Quid* 1997, p. 2183), and thus the revenue of the
Spanish government was approximately $158 million.

Supporters and Opponents of the Policy of Expansion
The United States was more successful than most countries in controlling
and moderating its expansionist policy. This moderation was a product of
the political debate within the country.

THE SUPPORTERS OF EXPANSION

The United States demonstrated its expansionist desires well before the
Mexican-American War of 1846–1848. Pratt (1925) and Barnet (1990) cite

many arguments supporting this thesis; we note some elements here. (1) In a letter to Thaddeus Kosciusko (June 1812) written ten days after the declaration of war, Thomas Jefferson wrote: "The infamous intrigues of Great Britain to destroy our government, and with the Indians to tomahawk our women and children prove that the cession of Canada must be a sine qua non at a treaty of peace" (Pratt 1925). (2) The invasion of East Florida by General Mathews and his patriots in March and April 1812 was effected with the full knowledge of the administration; the territory Mathews took from the Spanish was held for over a year. (3) For more than twenty-five years, the United States tried to purchase Texas from Mexico. In 1819, Secretary of State John Quincy Adams offered $1 million, and President Andrew Jackson (1829–1837) raised the offer to $5 million. (4) The South was almost unanimous in its demand for the annexation of Florida.

RESISTANCE TO THE POLICY OF EXPANSION

The main resistance to an extension to the south came from the northern states, who knew that every annexation to the south would strengthen the pro-slavery party. Expansion only achieved unanimous approval when it could be done in a balanced manner, to the north as well as to the south. But this condition was never fulfilled. From the moment that the northern states realized that expansion to the north was blocked by British power, they only consented to successive expansions to the south with large reservations. These fears were well founded; even if slavery was not officially recognized in Texas, its practice was nevertheless accepted. In particular, new immigrants could settle with the slaves that they had possessed before moving to Texas. In 1860 there were among the eleven future Confederate states four states (Alabama, Florida, Louisiana, and Texas) that had been added to the Union during the course of its expansion to the south. These four states represented 33 percent of the population of the Confederacy. In this way, one can understand how General Grant was able to write in his memoirs that the Civil War was largely an outgrowth of the Mexican War (Barnet 1990). The war against Mexico, however, was only the final stage of a process that had started at the beginning of the century.

We now examine the different phases of the process of annexation.

The Preparatory Phase

IMMIGRATION AND COLONIZATION

The progressive encroachment on territories occupied by Indian nations is a well-known illustration of the mechanism of immigration and colonization. The same process was used in the case of the territories held by Spain or Mexico.

We have already highlighted the immigration to Florida that received the armed support of General Mathews's patriots in 1812 and 1817, that is, before the transfer of this territory from Spain in 1819. In California and Texas, immigration from the eastern United States brought these two territories to declare themselves independent of the Mexican central government. Texas proclaimed its independence in 1836 (the Lone Star Republic) and California in 1846 (the Bear Flag Revolt). We examine this process a little more closely for the case of Texas.

In 1823, a law authorized the Mexican governor of Texas to apportion land either directly among immigrant families or indirectly through middlemen, who would agree to bring in no less than 200 families. Each farming family was to have 70 hectares (177 acres) of land, and each cattle farm would receive 1,770 hectares (4,420 acres). A colonist who married a Mexican was allowed more land than one who did not. In principle, all the immigrants had to prove that they were Roman Catholics. The intention of the Mexican government was to facilitate the economic development of the region while taking certain steps to assimilate the immigrants into the Mexican population. But the situation rapidly went out of control through a lack of officials, priests, and troops. In 1836, there were 30,000 Americans in Texas, approximately 12,000 Indians, and only 3,500 Mexicans. Even well before 1836, Mexican laws had ceased to apply in Texas. Thus a law of September 15, 1829, abolishing slavery throughout Mexico, was never applied in Texas. A good part of the customs services had slipped from Mexican hands to those of the Texans. Even the official postal services between the governor and the Mexican government were often intercepted by Texans (see Stephenson 1921 on the events of this period). In other words, the separation of Texas from Mexico only confirmed the actual situation.

Another example of this process of infiltration is that of Hawaii. Christian missionaries arrived on the islands in 1820 and exerted a strong influence upon religious and secular life. Soon the "missionary party," an alliance of missionary descendants and plantation owners, became a powerful force. As in the case of Texas, these groups were the ones that argued that Hawaii should have closer links with the United States. The Hawaiian monarch opposed these plans but in 1887, under force of arms, he signed what became known as the "Bayonet constitution." Note that until this stage, whether in California, Hawaii, or Texas, there had still not been an official intervention of the American government.

KNOWING NOT TO BE HASTY

After the intervention of U.S. settlers and calls on the federal government to act, it would have been tempting for the American government to jump at the opportunity and decree the annexation of the territory in question. Militarily this would not have posed any problem; but with regard to future relationships with the annexed territory, this would have had unfortunate consequences. The American government had the wisdom not to be hasty. At several opportunities, it even refused the U.S. settlers' demands, as can be seen from the following examples. (1) While General Mathews and his patriots were occupying the east of Florida for over a year, a declaration from James Monroe, then secretary of state, crushed the patriots' hopes for assistance from Washington. He declared (April 19, 1814): "The United States being at peace with Spain, no countenance can be given by their government to the proceedings of the revolutionary party in East Florida, if it is composed of Spanish subjects, and still less can it be given to them if it consists of American citizens" (Pratt 1925, p. 246). (2) President Jackson's Indian Removal Act became law in 1830. Nevertheless, the transfer of the Georgian Indians to the territories situated to the west of the Mississippi was only undertaken in 1836 for the Creeks and in 1838 for the Cherokees (Zinn 1990). (3) The intervention of Santa Anna's army in Texas and the sacrifice of the 150 defenders of Fort Alamo (February 24, 1836) provoked a great fury throughout the United States. Nevertheless, it was nearly ten years before the decision to annex Texas was made, an annexation that would lead to war against Mexico. (4) In 1844–1845 a crisis arose with Britain over Oregon country in the Pacific Northwest; American settlers fomented the unrest, established a provisional government, and sought U.S. intervention, even though the territory had been placed under joint American-British administration in 1827. President James Polk ran for office on the slogan "Fifty-four [degrees] forty [minutes] or fight" which implied the annexation of large parts of western Canada. But once elected he accepted the extension of the 49 degree frontier to the Pacific. (5) In 1893, the provisional government of Hawaii sent a delegation to Washington to request annexation, but in January 1894 the United States declined to take action (Vincent 1898, p. 970). It was necessary to wait until July 1898 for Hawaii to be annexed. In the meantime, warships and American soldiers were present on the islands, but officially only to protect the goods of American citizens. (6) The Cuban liberation movement against Spain began in 1868. In February 1895, the landing of a group of Cuban Americans in Cuba renewed interest in the United States in this guerrilla war. An intense press campaign, led in particular by the Hearst Group, demanded American intervention on the side of the Cubans. Nevertheless, President William McKinley did not declare war on Spain until April 25, 1899. It is useful to compare the delays between the request for intervention and the actual intervention in the cases we just examined.

	Request for intervention	Annexation or declaration of war	Delay (years)
Florida	1812	1819	7
Texas	1836	1845	9
California	1846	1848	2
Hawaii	1893	1898	5
Cuba	1895	1899	4

How can one explain this procrastination, which contrasts with the more expeditious methods used in Europe? Undoubtedly many reasons can be cited, including (1) the well-established English tradition of using caution and temporization in affairs of state; (2) the opposition of certain U.S. states; (3) the president's need for congressional endorsement; and (4) the U.S. dominance in this part of the world, which allowed it to treat such problems without haste.

Open War

SEARCHING FOR AN INCIDENT

From the point of view of public opinion, it is better to be taken for the victim than for the assailant. The United States was probably the first country in the world in which public opinion played a substantial role, and its importance explains why the American government has yielded to this rule since the middle of the nineteenth century. Two examples are pertinent here.

First, when the war with Mexico appeared imminent, President Polk secretly ordered a contingent of regulars under the command of General Zachary Taylor to cross into a strip of Texas territory that he knew Mexico considered its own. Colonel Hitchcock, who commanded one of the regiments, wrote in his diary: "It looks as if the government sent a small force on purpose to bring on a war, so as to have a pretext to take California and as much of this country as it chooses" (Barnet 1990). On May 9, 1846, the not unexpected news arrived that two of the companies had been ambushed and three Americans killed.

A second example is provided by the war against Spain. When the situation between the two countries was already very tense, on January 24, 1898, after warning the Spanish ambassador that an anti-American outburst would compel him to send troops, President McKinley ordered the warship *Maine* to Havana. It remained there for nearly a month without provoking any incident that could provide a pretext for intervention. But on the evening of February 15, the *Maine* exploded, killing 252 of the 350 men aboard. Perhaps this was not the type of incident that was expected, but it was sufficient to justify a declaration of war. Again, however, there was no haste; time was taken to appoint a commission of inquiry, and the declaration of war (April 24, 1898) arrived two months after the explosion.

A SWIFT WAR

In 1812 the United States had launched into war without being truly prepared. In the forests of the border regions of Canada, the offensive had became bogged down because of a lack of means of transportation. In 1846 and 1898, on the contrary, the campaigns proceeded briskly. The 1898 war resulted in a particularly small number of battle deaths; they did not exceed 0.1 percent of the number engaged.

MAGNANIMITY IN VICTORY

The United States' peace treaties with Mexico and Spain must be evaluated in the light of other treaties that were signed at the time. France, after its defeat in 1870 by Germany, lost Alsace-Lorraine and furthermore had to pay an indemnity of 5 billion francs (or about $1 billion), which represented twice the annual income of the state. China, after its defeat of 1894 by Japan, lost Taiwan and the Pescadores Islands and had to pay an indemnity of $20 million. Germany, after its defeat in the war of 1914–1918, lost all of its colonies and had to pay an indemnity of 132 billion gold marks, which represented more than fifty times the state receipts in 1914. After their defeat by the United States, Spain and especially Mexico certainly lost a notable part of their territory, but in contrast with practices elsewhere they received compensation. These indemnities, which rose to $20 million for Spain and $10 million for Mexico, were certainly modest; that of 1898 represented only 5 percent of the U.S. federal budget, while that of 1848 represented 14 percent. The psychological impact of not having to undergo a double humiliation, however, was significant. The indemnities could even create the false impression that the annexed territory had been bought. In truth, as Table 6.6e shows, the level of the indemnity was almost independent of the surface area of the territory; it was a uniform amount rather than a purchase price.

Expansionist Wars in the Second Half of the Twentieth Century

In this chapter we have mainly examined the experiences of the great powers. But there have also been a notable number of wars of conquest on the part of regional powers. This type of conflict has become even more important since 1945 because of the absence of conflicts between the great powers. One will see in this section that the objective of territorial conquest remained relevant until the end of the twentieth century and beyond.

The Case of Chile (1879–1929)

Although the case of Chile does not belong to the post-1945 period, it is representative of what might be called conquests under international control, a class of conflict that has become standard in the postwar world. In the western region of South America, Chile is indisputably the dominant power. At the time of the War of the Pacific in 1879–1884, which left 12,000 dead according to Richardson (1960), Chile conquered a vast zone on its northern frontier and enlarged its territory by approximately 20 percent. It was not until nearly fifty years later, however, that these conquests were ratified by the United States and the international community. More precisely, these territories were formed, from the south to the north, of four regions: Atacama, Tarapaca, Arica, and Tacna. The first two were acquired by Chile in 1883, despite the fact that they deprived Bolivia of an outlet onto the Pacific. The other two regions were inhabited by a population whose Peruvian element was twice as numerous as the Chilean element. A plebiscite in these regions had been anticipated by the agreements of 1884 but, because of Chile's hostility, it was never organized. Finally, following a long process of negotiations under the auspices of the United States, an agreement was signed on June 3, 1929; Chile received Arica and Peru kept Tacna.

Table 6.6e Financial compensations for annexed or purchased territories

Year	Area	Territory formerly belonging to	Amount (million dollars)	Reference
1803	Louisiana	France	15	*Grand Larousse Encyclopédique*
1819	Florida	Spain	5	*Quid* (1997), p. 1205
1848	Arizona, California, New Mexico, Utah	Mexico	15	Langer (1968), p. 815
1853	Southern Arizona	Mexico	10	*Atlas of Amer. History* (1987)
1867	Danish West Indies (St. Thomas, St. John)	Denmark	7.5	Vincent (1898), p. 1159
1867	Alaska	Russia	7.2	Vincent (1898), p. 29
1889	Part of Sioux reservation	Sioux		Vincent (1898), p. 1164
1891	36, 000 sq. km in Oklahoma	Sauk, Fox, Potawatomie		Kull and Kull (1952), p. 178
1892	12, 000 sq. km in Oklahoma	Cheyenne, Arapaho		Kull and Kull (1952), p. 179
1898	Guam, Philippines, Puerto Rico	Spain	20	Richardson (1960), p. 46
1903	Philippines (friars' land)	Papacy	7.2	Kull and Kull (1952), p. 198
1903	Panama Canal Zone	Panama	10	*Grand Larousse Encyclopédique*
1912	Projected canal zone in Nicaragua	Nicaragua	3	Karnes (1961)
1916	Virgin Islands (Caribbean)	Denmark	25	Langer (1968), p. 1074

Territorial Expansion in the Postwar Period

When one reads the minutes of the discussions within the American government that preceded the interventions in Korea, Vietnam (see Khong 1992), or Kuwait in 1990, one is struck by the number of references made to the Munich crisis of 1938. The argument is always the same: to not react to a first annexation only encourages the assailant; in other words, a capitulation such as that of Munich can extract a high price in the future. Whether this analogy is or is not applicable is only of minor importance here. What renders it operative, especially in public opinion in Europe and the United States, is the fact that it concerns an episode with which everyone is familiar. By virtue of the paradigm of Munich, rather few territorial conquests after 1945 have been endorsed by the United States and the international community. This is shown in Table 6.7; of seven conquests only one was endorsed, and this in a more tacit than explicit manner. Let us review some of these episodes. The entry of Chinese troops into Tibet in October 1950 was more a reconquest than a conquest. Tibet has effectively been part of the Chinese sphere of influence since approximately 1640. But it is also true that the Chinese presence was marked by many revolts, in 1905–1906, 1911, and 1959. In contrast, the 1961 episode in Kuwait constituted an endeavor rather than a real invasion. Six days after Kuwait received its independence from Britain in June 1961, Iraq claimed Kuwait as Iraqi territory. About 6,000 British troops were sent to Kuwait (French 1990), and the show of force deterred Iraq from acting. Israel's annexation of the Sinai and the West Bank was a consequence of the Six Days' War. This region, East Timor, and Kashmir constitute three cases of annexation that have aroused violent opposition by the population and for which there has still not been a return to the previous status quo. The Falklands War and Gulf War were two cases in which only armed force was able to reestablish the preinvasion situation.

If one compares the half century 1945–1995 to the two or three previous half centuries, one notices that the number of wars of territorial expansion have been much smaller than previously. This is all the more remarkable as nearly 130 new states have come into existence since 1945. Among these a certain number, situated mainly in Southeast Asia, have experienced a rapid economic development. Several of the conditions for what we have called in this chapter a process of national activation have thus apparently been brought together: a strong increase in the resources of the state, rapid

Table 6.7 Annexation (or attempted annexation) in the second half of the twentieth century

Year	Country	Annexed territory	Current situation
1949	India	Jammu-Kashmir	P
1950	China	Tibet	A
1961	Iraq	[Kuwait]	R
1967	Israel	Sinai	R
		Golan Heights	P
		West Bank, Gaza	P
1974	Turkey	Northern part of Cyprus	P
1975	Morocco	Ex-Spanish Sahara	P
1976	Indonesia	East Timor	P
1982	Argentina	Falkland Islands	R
1988	China	Spratly Islands	P
1990	Iraq	Kuwait	R

Note: A = "Accepted by international community"; P = "Provisional annexation"; R = "Territory returned to pre-annexation status." The source for the Spratly Islands is Clodfelter (1995).

demographic growth, and democratization allowing large layers of the population to participate in public affairs. But this has not, for the moment, been translated into the type of phenomena observed in Europe in the eighteenth and nineteenth century.

Nevertheless it would be wrong to jump to the conclusion that territorial issues have lost their importance. They are still important, but in a subdued form. Latent conflicts between two states because of a territorial dispute include Morocco/Algeria, over the Spanish Sahara; India/Pakistan, over Kashmir; China/Vietnam/Philippines, over the Spratly Islands; Japan/Russia, over the Kuril Islands; and Peru/Ecuador, over a contested border line. China's extreme sensitivity regarding the question of Taiwan should also be mentioned.

In a long-term perspective the importance of wars of territorial expansion has been assessed by Holsti (1991). Since the seventeenth century the percentage of wars motivated by territorial disputes has fluctuated as follows:

1648–1714: 35%
1715–1814: 35%

1815–1914: 19%
1918–1941: 24%
1945–1989: 19%

There seems to be a slow downward trend.

Summary and Conclusion

Why have we devoted a chapter to the study of wars of territorial expansion? The reason is very simple. Wars constitute an ideal "laboratory" for studying repertoires and paronymic repetitions. Systematic statistical data pertaining to wars exist for all countries, and most are readily available. Perhaps we are too used to this situation to fully appreciate it; yet this is quite an exceptional situation in the social sciences. As a comparison, consider the study of trade rivalry between two nations (in this respect see, for example, Hoffman 1933); in this case many of the relevant data, especially at the level of private companies, are unavailable. Similarly the statistical data for the study of social disturbances are for the most part available only from local sources such as city archives or newspapers. A number of scholars, such as Tilly and his group, have collected such data systematically, but only for a few countries. For wars, by contrast, the relevant data are available on a worldwide basis (for example, in Clodfelter 1992).

In this chapter we have not considered all types of wars for territorial expansion. The latter (which represent about 25 percent of all wars) comprise several categories that were not appropriate to include in our sample. In the sixteenth and seventeenth centuries, for example, a number of conquest wars were motivated by dynastic disputes; thus for more than sixty years (between 1494 and 1559) France was at war with Austria in northern Italy because of Charles VIII's claims to the region of Milan. For the sake of simplicity we restricted our attention to a number of great expansionist waves.

Throughout this chapter we have pursued three levels of explanation: macrohistorical, strategic, and tactical. These different facets were not presented separately; to do so would have been artificial and would have made the reader's task even more difficult. Instead, we followed the events in roughly chronological order. Now, however, it will be useful to distinguish between these different levels of explanation.

The Macrohistorical Perspective

We understand the term "macrohistorical" (as in the word "macroeconomics") to refer to issues that concern the whole society. At the beginning
of the section on Sweden we tried to define a social mechanism that could
account for the development of expansionist waves in a given society. At
least qualitatively the schema seemed to work fairly well. We did not try to
test it in a systematic way, however; since the investigation would involve
the whole society this would be a problem of great complexity.

In this respect one must of course mention the work of Snooks. In a
number of books, but especially in *The Ephemeral Civilization* (1997),
Snooks investigated the relationship between the structure of a society and
its long-term strategic objectives. He distinguished three main categories:
the conquest society, the commerce society, and the technological society.
Let us consider more closely the conquest societies. With the help of two
specific case studies, Snooks analyzed the complex links between the organization of the society and its ability to wage conquest wars. Rome, the first
of the case studies he considered, was an extremely successful conquest society. Between 367 and 264 B.C., that is to say just after the establishment of
the Roman Republic, no less than sixty-seven triumphs were celebrated.
Subsequently, during the period of the Empire, the state income per inhab-
itant reached a level of about one dollar (in 1850 dollars; Tainter 1988).
Such a level was not reached again by Western societies until the beginning
of the eighteenth century. Similarly, and both facts are of course closely related, the size of the Roman army, about 300,000, remained unparalleled
for about 1,500 years. Snooks shows how the conquest strategy has shaped
the institutions and organization of those societies. There were complex
links between the conquest economy, on the one hand, and the public, private, and household economies, on the other (see in this respect Snooks
1997, p. 32, fig. III). It would certainly be of great interest to see if other
conquest societies were structured in the same way.

From the perspective of macrohistory there is another point that deserves to be mentioned. Ant societies seem to have developed a kind of
conquest warfare which, seen from outside, appears to have strong similarities with the conquest wars studied in this chapter. We do not speak here
of wars between different species of ants, but wars among different groups
(usually different nests) within the same species. Mabelis (1979) gives a
fascinating account of such wars. They last several months, with as many as

8,000 ants killed on a given (sunny) day. At the end the territory of one of the groups has expanded while that of others may have become smaller; some groups may be completely wiped out (Figure 6.13). We take such an account as an interesting and intriguing observation. Nothing more. We do not want to take sides in the current debate about sociobiology; a useful discussion can be found in Snooks (1997).

Strategic Regularities
Let us recall some of the results obtained in this chapter.

1. For each of the wars studied in this chapter we have estimated the strength of the opposing forces in terms of either public revenue, national income, or population. Usually the outcome of the war can be predicted on the basis of respective strength. The few exceptions are explained away easily: thus Japan was able to defeat Russia in 1905 because the theater of war was much closer to Japan than to Moscow; similarly Japan was able to invade China because the latter was weakened by an ongoing civil war.

2. We emphasized that there have been other world wars preceding World War I, notably the Seven Years' War (1756–1763) and the Napoleonic Wars. This led us in the section on France to establish a parallel between different episodes in which a continental power opposed a maritime power. Several regularities emerged regarding invasion attempts, encroachment strategy (through Spain in one case and through Italy in World War II), the crucial role played by the war against Russia, economic warfare, and submarine warfare (see section on Germany).

3. In the same line of thought we pointed out the parallels between German offensives in the West in 1870, 1914, 1940, or 1944. The similarities extend to the German pincer-movement strategy as well as to British and French retreats (section on Germany).

4. Regarding the Pacific War, we showed that the Japanese decision to wage war against the United States can only be understood in the light of previous similar episodes, namely, the war against China and against Russia.

Tactical Regularities
It is at the tactical level that the similarities between different episodes are the most striking.

1. The Japanese attacks of 1894, 1904 (Port Arthur), and 1941 (Pearl

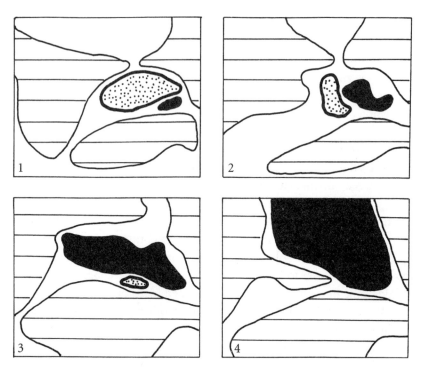

Figure 6.13 Territorial expansion of a colony of ants. The observations concern the species *Formica polyctena först* (red wood ants) and were made in the Netherlands in the early 1970s. The population of a nest is on the order of 150,000. The four panels show the expansion of the colony represented in black, which is accompanied by the contraction (and eventually the disappearance) of the territory of another colony (dots). The territories with horizontal hatching belong to three other groups. Panel 1 corresponds to the situation on April 17; panel 4 corresponds to the situation on August 26. On a warm sunny day the number of ants killed is several thousand. From left to right the distance represented on each panel is about 55 meters. *Source:* Adapted from Mabelis (1979).

Harbor) followed the same tactical patterns (see section on Japan). Needless to say these operations were on very different scales; the attack on Port Arthur was conducted by ten torpedo boats while the one on Pearl Harbor comprised thirty-one ships among which were six aircraft carriers and two battleships.

2. One of the characteristics of the German army was to give its generals great tactical freedom of action. That kind of improvisation was often suc-

cessful, as in 1866 or 1870; sometimes, however, it failed, as in 1914 (see section on Germany).

3. With the exception of the War of 1812, which was a failure, the American attempts at territorial expansion followed a common pattern and turned out to be remarkably successful (see section on United States).

4. Since 1945, thanks to the "Pax Americana," there have been fewer wars for territorial expansion than in the period before World War II. Moreover most of these conquests have not been recognized or accepted by the international community.

CHAPTER

7

The Constraints of Logistics

The name of General Helmuth von Moltke, chief of the German General Staff at the time of the offensive of August 1914, plays a large part in the historical accounts of World War I. In contrast, the role of General Wilhelm Groener, head of the Field Railways Section of the General Staff, has received much less attention. Responsible for the organization of logistics for the campaign, Groener played a role just as crucial as that of the generals who led the armies. Since his appointment in 1912, he had established and executed a plan which, within fifteen days, permitted the transport of nearly 3 million men to the east and west borders of Germany. More than 29,000 trains ran day and night to carry out this task.

When two armies face each other, it is easy to forget the enormous amount of preparatory work that has been undertaken upstream. The troops must have been brought to the place with their equipment, supplies, and means of transportation; prior to this, the equipment has had to be tested and the men trained. Again, even farther upstream, all this equipment has to have been produced or bought from abroad, which in turn supposes that political decisions have been made to finance these productions or purchases. Throughout the war, this immense chain passing from the Parliament and the ministries to the battlefields via the planning departments and factories must function at the peak of its capabilities. If any one of the elements—resources, finances, raw materials, or labor—is lacking, the war effort will be compromised.

Despite its importance, logistics has been the focus of only a limited number of studies. It is clearly an immense subject, and in this chapter, we limit ourselves to three themes: the financing of wars, the means of trans-

300

porting armies, and landing operations. Our objective is to see whether it is possible to identify relevant regularities and orders of magnitude.

The Cost of Wars and Their Financing

Before 1914 a war chest of 205 million gold Marks, from the French indemnity of 5 billion francs received in 1871, was stacked in the Julius Tower at Spandau near Berlin and guarded by Prussian grenadiers. Nevertheless, the size of this reserve was tiny in relation to the expenses of World War I. They reached 20 billion Marks for the first year of war alone (Wagemann 1941), and the Spandau Treasury could therefore only finance three days of war. In fact, the greatest part of the German war effort was financed by loans. The method of financing a war by drawing from the royal treasury had become inadequate much earlier. By the time of the War of the Spanish Succession (1701–1714), which brought a large part of northern Europe (Austria, German states, Britain, the Netherlands) into conflict with France and Spain, each camp largely had to resort to loans.

In the analysis of these phenomena, we distinguish between two very different aspects: on the one hand, the financial and economic effects of the wars, and on the other, the financing techniques. The former display conspicuous regularities from one conflict to the other. The latter, on the contrary, have evolved over the centuries; most are very complex in their implementation. To illustrate these two facets of the problem let us return to the case of Germany during the war of 1914–1918. The servicing of debt, that is, the share of government revenue allocated to the payment of interest, rose from 25 percent in 1913 to 79 percent in 1919 before falling to 2 percent in 1924 (Liesner 1989; Wagemann 1941); these three figures indicate clearly and simply both the burden of the war effort and the spectacular effect of the hyperinflation of 1923. In contrast, one may wonder why the Helfferich plan of creating the "Rentenmark" (which replaced the devalued Mark) allowed the spiral of hyperinflation to be stopped in November 1923; this question remains as controversial today as it was at the time. Wagemann (1941) reports that when this plan was proposed it was greeted by university economists with derisive comments: "It is the height of delirium and insanity"; "It is nothing other than a repetition of the fraudulent enterprise of John Law [in France, 1716–1720]." Maybe, but it worked. This example explains why in this chapter we leave aside controversial questions about financial techniques.

Table 7.1 The cost of war

Began	Duration (years)	Country	Cost (millions)	War cost as equivalent to number of years of prewar annual revenue	Reference
1701	13	Britain	37 £	8.6	Baudhuin (1944)
1740	8	Britain	31 £	5.4	Baudhuin (1944)
1755	7	Britain	73 £	11	Baudhuin (1944)
1775	8	Britain	120 £	11	Baudhuin (1944)
1775	8	United States	100 $	28	Hist. Stat. U.S. (1975)
1793	22	Britain	830 £	43	Baudhuin (1944)
1812	2	United States	93 $	6.5	Hist. Stat. U.S. (1975)
1846	2	United States	73 $	2.4	Hist. Stat. U.S. (1975)
1854	1	Britain	75 £	1.3	Baudhuin (1944)
1854	1	France	1,500 F	0.98	Baudhuin (1944)
1859	0.5	France	500 F	0.27	Baudhuin (1944)
1861	4	United States (North)	3,200 $	71	Hist. Stat. U.S. (1975)
1870	1	France	9,250 F	4.7	Baudhuin (1944)
1898	1	United States	400 $	28	Hist. Stat. U.S. (1975)
1899	3	Britain	250 £	2.1	Baudhuin (1944)
1904	2	Japan	1,750 Y	4.4	Baudhuin (1944)
1914	4	Britain	8,000 £	40	Langer (1968), p. 980
1914	4	France	156,000 F	31	Quid (1997), p. 786
1914	4	Germany	92,000 M	44	Wagemann (1941)
1917	0.5	United States	26,000 $	24	Hist. Stat. U.S. (1975)
1939	6	Germany	716,000 M	16	Boelcke (1985), p. 8
1941	5	United States	288,000 $	42	Hist. Stat. U.S. (1975)
1950	3	United States	54,000 $	1.3	Hist. Stat. U.S. (1975)
1965	6	United States	110,000 $	0.98	Hist. Stat. U.S. (1975)

Note: Until 1945 the federal budget of the United States represented only a small fraction of the national income; this explains the high cost/annual revenue ratio for American wars before 1945. F = French franc; M = Mark; Y = yen.

In this section we first consider the cost of war and its evolution over the years. Next we examine the economic consequences of war. Finally, we compare different methods of financing wars.

The Cost of War

Table 7.1 provides data on the cost of war over a period of nearly three centuries. Expressed in terms of years of central government revenue, the price of war hardly ever exceeds 50. The highest figures are found for Germany during the 1914–1918 war (44) and for Britain during the Napoleonic Wars (43) and during 1914–1918 (40). Note that the figures for the United States before 1945 are not directly comparable to the others. The U.S. federal budget at that time represented a far smaller share of national income than in more centralized countries; in 1938 this share was only 7 percent as against 13 percent for France or Japan. It is only after 1945 that the American federal budget would reach approximately one-fifth of national income, a proportion comparable to that observed in most other industrialized countries (with the notable exception of Switzerland, where this proportion has remained stable at approximately 7 percent).

Note also that during the three centuries covered by Table 7.1 there has been no tendency for the costs of the largest conflicts to increase. In other words, the intensification of war over the course of time and the escalation of destruction have merely reflected the rising productive capacities of nations.

One of the crucial factors in this matter is the degree of centralization of the state. The Roman Republic and Empire, thanks to their centralization, were able to set up armies of 100,000 soldiers. At Cannae (215 B.C.), for example, as mentioned in Chapter 6, Varro's army comprised an infantry of 86,000 plus the cavalry. The contrast with the wars of the sixteenth century is striking. The armies of Charles V, in spite of his extended empire which comprised Spain along with the Holy Roman Empire, hardly ever exceeded 20,000. Moreover, many campaigns had to be suspended simply because the troops could not be paid any longer. One major example was the suspension of the siege of Metz in 1552. Such deficiencies can be traced back to the lack of financial centralization of the state and to the fact that the armies of that time were largely composed of mercenaries.

The Economic Effects of the Wars

During a major war, state expenses are much higher than receipts. This has several consequences. First, the state is obliged to borrow and therefore

Table 7.2 Ratio of cumulated expenditures *(E)* to cumulated receipts *(R)* during major wars

War	Country	E/R	Debt charges increase (postwar/prewar)
1775–1781	Britain	1.53	1.6
1793–1815	Britain	1.37	3.5
World War I	Britain	3.51	7.2
	France	4.78	11
	Germany	7.91	18
World War II	Britain	1.91	2.5
	France	1.89	
	Germany	2.72	16
	United States	2.15	2.7

Sources: Davin (1949); *Hist. Stat. U.S.* (1975); Liesner (1989) Mitchell (1971, 1978); Table 7.3.

Note: Not surprisingly, the larger the expenditure-receipt ratio, the larger the burden of debt after the war; this is confirmed by the fact that there is a correlation of 0.80 between the ratio *E/R* and the debt charges increase in the last column.

sees its debt inflate. Second, a certain amount of inflation generally occurs. Third, to face up to its increased expenses, the state is tempted to increase taxes. During a prolonged war the requirements of armament production tend to provoke planning action by the state, in particular at the level of the allocation of raw materials, labor, or means of transport. The outcome can be an increase in the importance of the state within national activity, an aspect that we have already seen with regard to the United States. We shall consider each of these consequences in turn.

THE INCREASE IN NATIONAL DEBT

By how much do expenses exceed receipts during a conflict? Table 7.2 offers a response to this question for four major conflicts of the past several centuries. One can see that the ratio of expenses to receipts fluctuated widely. The lowest value corresponds to the war of 1793–1815, but this is of course offset by the exceptional length of this conflict, which was spread over twenty-two years with only brief interruptions. The highest value is reached by Germany during the war of 1914–1918. Note also that although most of the nations had a balanced budget in the years preceding the con-

Table 7.3 Increase in debt charges during major wars

War	Country	Prewar debt interest as percentage of prewar receipts	Postwar debt interest as percentage of prewar receipts
1701–1714	Britain	28	76
1775–1781	Britain	43	69
1793–1815	Britain	49	173
World War I	Britain	11	143
	France	18	196
	Germany	20	359
World War II	Britain	21	53
	Germany	6	106
	Japan	3	21

Sources: Britain: Liesner (1989), Mitchell (1971); France: *Annuaire Statistique* (1986); Germany: Davin (1949), Liesner (1989), Mitchell (1978), Wagemann (1941); Japan: *Hundred-Year Statistics* (1966).

flict, Germany did not: for the years 1910–1913, expenses represented nearly twice the level of receipts. In 1914–1918 France too found itself in a very unfavorable situation from a budgetary point of view, since it had to meet the costs of the war while its most industrialized regions—the north and northeast—were being occupied by Germany and could not contribute to receipts.

For countries faced with this acceleration of expenses, there is hardly any other recourse than loans. Table 7.3 describes the increase in debt servicing in the budget of the belligerents. One expects a notable correlation between budgetary deficits (the E/R ratio in Table 7.2) and the increase of the debt in Tables 7.2 and 7.3, and such is indeed the case, the correlation being equal to 0.80 for the different belligerents. But the link between the budgetary deficit and the rate of inflation is much less direct, as will be seen in the next section.

INFLATION

Table 7.4 shows that there is no simple relationship between budgetary imbalance and inflation. What concerns us here is inflation of monetary origin, in other words, due to the creation of money; this type of inflation

Table 7.4 Price increases during major wars

War	Country		Price increase (%)	2. Countries at Peace		Price increase (%)
	1. Countries at War					
1775–1781	United States	(beef-wheat, Phila.)	16,300			
1793–1815	Britain	(wheat-barley-oats)	−12.0			
		(Rousseau index)	−6.7			
	France	(wheat)	−1.7			
World War I	Britain		121	Argentina	73	
	France		162	Spain	110	
	Germany		315	Sweden	169	
	United States		59	Switzerland	96	
	Geometric average		*138*		*102*	
World War II	Britain		56	Argentina	124	
	France		514	Spain	184	
	Germany		32	Sweden	71	
	United States		39	Switzerland	100	
	Japan		111			
	Geometric average		*81*		*112*	

Sources: United States (1775–1781): Bezanson (1951); Britain (1793–1815): Mitchell (1971); France (1793–1815): Drame et al. (1991); for subsequent wars: *Hundred-Year Statistics* (1966), Liesner (1989), Mitchell (1971, 1983).

Note: For the war of 1793–1815 in Britain the first index covers the period 1794–1815 whereas the second is for the period 1800–1815; for France the index is for the period 1797–1815; the results show that there has been no general price increase.

has a very recognizable signature in that it is translated into a progressive rise in prices (that can possibly accelerate) and is spread over several years. Price increases due to situations of shortage, on the contrary, are generally brief and highly variable. Thus the price variations during the period of the Napoleonic Wars were only fleeting fluctuations; it seems that strictly monetary inflation was close to zero during these twenty years, which were nevertheless characterized by strong budgetary imbalances.

Inflation was on average not significantly higher in countries at war than in countries not involved in the conflict. During World War II, inflation was even higher in nonbelligerent countries than in belligerent countries. This shows that there is a strong element of contagion from one country to another in the phenomenon of inflation.

HYPERINFLATIONS

One can mention several examples of wars that led to hyperinflations (Chou 1963; Morison 1969; *Le Monde,* December 30, 1993).

1. During the American Civil War, Confederate tax receipts did not exceed $27 million, while expenditure amounted to several billion dollars; the Confederacy floated bonds to a value of $700 million and issued a total of $1.5 billion in Treasury notes. Inevitably these depreciated; by January 1864 (that is, more than a year before Lee's surrender), they were worth five cents on the dollar and later became virtually worthless. While the Confederacy had derived nearly 50 percent of its revenue from paper money, the Union relied on it money for only 13 percent.

2. In China from July 1937 to April 1949, prices multiplied by a factor on the order of 10^{14}. This period was marked by the Japanese invasion and by a civil war between the Kuomintang of Chiang Kai-shek and the Communists of Mao Tse-tung.

3. In Greece, from 1939 to November 1944, prices multiplied by a factor on the order of 10^{11}. During this period, the country was confronted with the Italian and German invasion, on which was superimposed a civil war between different resistance movements.

4. In Hungary, between July 1945 and July 1946, prices multiplied by a factor on the order of 10^{29}. This inflation, like that of 1923 in Germany, followed a war, but took place when peace had returned after the Red Army's occupation of the country in April 1945.

5. In Yugoslavia (Serbia and Montenegro), between the start of 1992 and the end of 1993, prices multiplied by a factor on the order of 10^{10}. This in-

flation was an indirect consequence of the international blockade imposed on the country following its support for the war led by the Serbs of Bosnia-Herzegovina.

THE INCREASING IMPORTANCE OF THE STATE

The Bank of England was created in July 1694 at a time when the country had been at war with France for five years. One of the first actions of the bank was to lend £1.2 million to the government (Langer 1968, p. 466). In France the central bank was created in January 1800, while the country faced the Second Coalition (1799–1802). These two episodes illustrate the tendency for increased centralization that has often accompanied a country's war efforts. Figure 7.1 gives a more quantitative description of this phenomenon. The case of the United States is particularly eloquent: the ratio R of federal budget receipts to gross national product, which was on the order of 2 percent before 1915, rose to 5 percent between the two world wars and then to 18 percent after World War II. France presents a similar phenomenon: the ratio R rose from 10 percent before 1914 to 16 percent on average between the wars and to 22 percent after World War II. For Japan, the same effect is present but it is markedly smaller: the ratio R, which was on the order of 10 percent before the Russo-Japanese War of 1904–1905, rose to an average of 14 percent in the interwar years. After the huge increase in R in the period 1940–1945, however, this ratio returned to its 1939 level in the years 1960–1970. Nevertheless one may wonder if this was not a secondary effect of the extremely rapid growth (with an annual rate of 9 percent in constant yen) of the Japanese economy from 1948 to 1974. After this date, when growth slowed down, the ratio R had a tendency to move closer to the level reached in other industrialized countries.

The case of Switzerland brings a supplementary confirmation insofar as, among the countries analyzed, it is both the only one in which the ratio R remains inferior to 9 percent and the only one to have had no external wars since 1815. Nevertheless, there may be a large degree of state control even in the absence of war, as shown by the cases of countries such as Denmark, Norway, or Sweden; although these countries have not been actively involved in a major war since 1870, their ratio R was on the order of 25 percent in 1980.

TECHNIQUES OF FINANCING WARS

It is on financing methods that most war historians have focused their attention. But, as we have already observed, this is a highly techni-

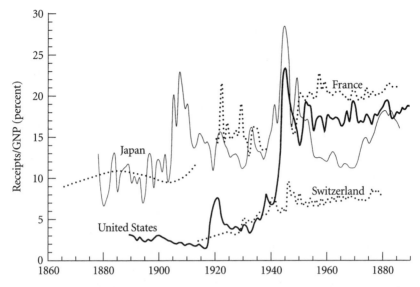

Figure 7.1 Evolution of the ratio of government receipts to gross national product. The centralizing influence of war is clearly distinguishable, especially for the United States. For France and Japan, the ratio has risen from 10 percent to about 20 percent in the past century. Surprisingly, even for Switzerland, which has not been at war for the whole period covered by this graph, the ratio has a upward trend of about 9 percent per century. *Sources:* Flora (1983); *Japan Statistical Yearbook; Historical Statistics of the United States* (1975); *Statistical Abstract of the United States.*

cal question; in the following we make only a brief incursion into this subject.

Schematically one can distinguish five financing methods: states may (1) increase taxes; (2) seek long-term loans; (3) obtain short-term loans by Treasury bonds (usually this short-term debt is subsequently merged into longer-term loans); (4) resort to the printing press; or (5) "plunder" occupied countries (this can, for example, take the form of imposing on the conquered countries an unfair exchange rate).

There is a definite difference between the cases (2) and (3), on the one hand, and case (4), on the other. The former involve a monetary transfer from citizens to the state; in the latter, on the contrary, there is pure monetary creation. Expected inflationary effects are very different in the two cases.

In both the third and the fourth cases the government asks for an advance from the central bank; but while in the fourth case there is pure monetary creation, in the third the central bank keeps this advance in the form of a short-term debt that must be, as soon as possible, merged into longer-term loans.

Historically all these processes have been utilized, but to varying degrees. A rich and relatively under-taxed country would turn to methods (1) and (2), while a poorer and already over-taxed country would have to make do with the two last ones. Thus during World War I, taxes were hardly increased in Germany or France, while in Britain the yield from the income tax rose from £69 million to £261 million (Baudhuin 1944). The United States fared even better, since it could cover 32 percent of its war expenses by taxation against only 19 percent for England.

After the war, governments may attempt to reduce the national debt by more or less honest means. For example, they may (1) leave the borrowed capital to be eroded by inflation; (2) lower the nominal interest rate on the loans; (3) suspend, at least for a certain amount of time, the payment of interest; or (4) repudiate the whole of the debt. All these means have been used at one time or another. After the War of the Spanish Succession (1701–1714), both France and Britain, knowingly or not, turned to inflation to reduce the debt. In England this was the "South Sea Company bubble"; in France it was the speculative bubble linked to John Law's Mississippi Scheme. For many speculators these bubbles were a disaster, but at the level of the state the debt was greatly reduced.

In Germany the hyperinflation of 1923 reduced, in a matter of months, the service of debt to 91 million Marks from 7.5 billion in 1919. The mechanism was simple. Suppose in 1917 a German citizen had bought war bonds worth 10,000 Marks; in April 1924, when the new Reichsmark was introduced at a rate of 10^{18} old Marks for one new Mark, the value of the 10,000(old)-Mark bonds was reduced to almost nothing.

This example, incidentally, permits an understanding of why in the case of hyperinflation the stoppage of the spiral can be extremely rapid and not accompanied by an increase in unemployment. In effect, if one selects the working hypothesis that in order to stop inflation it is necessary to curtail the means of payment, this is indeed what happened in Germany in 1923; within several months a large part of the public lost most of their savings. On the contrary, when a country is consumed by chronic inflation for several years, the owners of loans, whether individuals or institutions, have the time to put mechanisms into place that allow them to protect their assets. The curtailment of the means of payment then becomes more difficult. Note, moreover, that deflation and the accompanying rise of unemployment is a slow and inefficient method for stopping inflation, because it particularly affects those with low incomes and, at least under modern welfare systems, is partially countered by the payment of unemployment benefits.

The manipulation of the rate of interest was used regularly in France under the monarchy. One can find many examples of this in Marion (1976 [1929], p. 481). Thus Louis XIV, prompted by Colbert, did not hesitate to declare: "The excessive profits offered by government stocks encourage idleness and prevent our subjects from being devoted to trade, manufactures or agriculture . . . we have resolved to reduce the profit on them."

The repudiation of the whole debt is an extreme measure that is only taken in the event of a radical change of regime. Thus the Bolshevik government repudiated the external debt of the tsarist regime; with respect to France this debt had risen to 7 billion gold francs, approximately 50 percent of the 1919 budget, and with respect to Britain it had risen to £900 million, 67 percent of the 1919 budget (*Quid* 1997, p. 1373).

Means of Transportation

On May 4, 1899, in a dispatch to his government, the British high commissioner in South Africa described "the thousands of British subjects [of the Transvaal] enduring unquestionable injustices with a growing impatience, permanently reduced to the position of Helots and calling in vain for help from Her Majesty's government." Following this call and others of similar content, the secretary of state for the colonies, Joseph Chamberlain, declared on June 26, 1899: "We can wait no longer. We have reached a critical point and a turning point in the history of the Empire" (Lacour-Gayet 1970). The war in South Africa therefore appeared unavoidable; nevertheless it would only begin four months later, on October 11, 1899, and the major British offensive only occurred in January 1900. Why such a delay? Essentially because of the constraints of logistics. In June the British had only 20,000 troops in South Africa; it took about nine months to transport 120,000 more from England and India to the theater of war.

During the first months of the war the balance of power was in favor of the Boers. Why then did they not begin the war before October? Again logistics were key. They needed to wait for the southern spring rains to fertilize the pasture lands and thereby obtain the necessary fodder for their horses. It must be remembered that the cavalry formed the main part of the Boer forces (30,000 men). While a man required a daily ration of 1 kilo, a horse needed 10 kilos of fodder per day. In Chapter 6 we noted that in Europe most of the battles involving a large cavalry took place in summer. The peak in the utilization of horses was reached in 1914, when the German offensive used 850,000 horses. It was impossible to provide them with fodder if it was not found in the fields; below we give a detailed calculation showing the impossibility of transporting this fodder by rail.

As dramatic as these examples are, they still suggest only imperfectly the immense role of logistics in the march of armies. All the great military leaders were brilliant logistical tacticians, including Eisenhower, Marlborough, Napoleon, and Rommel. If financing a war is certainly a necessity, it is generally not on this factor that victory or defeat is decided. Logistics, on the contrary, directly condition the outcome of the struggle. The Russo-Japanese War provides an illustration of this argument. From the point of view of financial resources, Russia had a distinct advantage. The movement of the price of Russian loans shows that in August 1904 the financial circles were still betting on Russia's victory despite some initial Japanese successes (Helfferich 1989). Nevertheless logistics were clearly in favor of Japan. The shipment of its troops to the battlefields of Korea could be made by boat (1,000 kilometers) while the Russians were forced to convey everything by land across the entire 8,000 kilometers of the Trans-Siberian railroad line.

According to a formulation attributed to Napoleon, war is a barbaric business in which victory goes to the side that knows how to concentrate the largest number of troops at the decisive spot. As Van Creveld (1995) comments, identifying the "spot" may be a matter of either genius or good luck, but once it is identified the feeding into it of men and material becomes a sheer question of logistics. The problems of logistics that the military face are complex because of the great variety of equipment necessary, the multiplicity of suppliers, and the importance of deadlines for delivery and shipment. To get an idea of the diversity of the problems facing a modern army, one can consult the works of Dunnigan (1993), Huston (1989), or Pagonis and Cruikshank (1992); for a historical treatment, seethe innovative study of Van Creveld (1995). Our goals in this section are quite different. Rather than account for the multiplicity of problems, we want to establish some basic orders of magnitude that can provide landmarks. One of our essential objectives is to establish a line of demarcation between what is possible and what is not. If, for example, one reads that before the

Table 7.5a Approximate size of military units

Unit	Strength (men)
Platoon	20–60
Company	120
Battalion	500–1,000 (4 or more companies)
Regiment	2,000–4,000 (several battalions)
Brigade	5,000
Division	8,000–15,000
Corps	16,000–30,000 (2 divisions)
Army	100,000–200,000

Sources: Van Creveld (1995); *Quid* (1997).

Note: A platoon is commanded by a lieutenant, a regiment by a colonel. In 1864 a Prussian infantry division comprised 15,500 men, 4,600 horses, and 377 vehicles. Some modern-day American infantry divisions have as many as 18,000 men. In 1914 the five German armies engaged in the West comprised 77 divisions.

Table 7.5b Increase in the consumption of ammunition and fuel

	18th century	1800–1875	1914	1941	1950
(Rounds/gun)/day	1	2	25		40
Foodstuffs (% of total supplies)	95	90		33	10

Sources: Van Creveld (1995), p. 35 (eighteenth century), 57 and 102 (1800–1875), 110 (1914), 152 (1941), 233 (1950), Huston (1989), p. 164; Dunnigan (1993), p. 548.

Note: While in 1870 foodstuffs still represented the majority of supplies, they only represented a small fraction in 1950. Fuel and ammunition then formed the majority of consumption. In 1990, during the Gulf War, fuel constituted 52 percent of supplies. For World War I, the figure of 25 rounds per gun concerns the first two months of the war, not an average for the entire war.

era of the railway, an army of 20,000 men covered a distance of 1,200 kilometers in a month, one will be prone to skepticism; that represents an advance of 40 kilometers per day, a speed that is approximately three times greater than the average speed of armies at the time.

Some Orders of Magnitude

Table 7.5 summarizes some key figures. Often military historians speak in terms of regiments, divisions, army corps; the role of Table 7.5a is to allow a translation in terms of numbers. Table 7.5b shows that within the space of a century a radical transformation has occurred in the nature of sup-

Table 7.5c Some orders of magnitude relating to the consumption and the means of transport of armies

Consumption	Reference	Transport		
		Means	Capacity	Reference
Before 1870				
(1.5 kg/man)/day (10 kg/horse)/day	VC, pp. 34, 50, 106	Wagon (4 horses)	1 ton	VC, p. 50
1870–1918				
(4 kg/man)/day	VC, pp. 100, 105	Train (20 cars)	500 tons 500 men	H, p. 14
1939–1950				
(10–30 kg/man)/day	VC	Plane	5 tons	VC, p. 112; H, p. 77
		Truck	2.5–10 tons	
		Double-track railroad	12,000 tons/day	
		Ship	10,000 tons	
		Pipeline	500 cubic meters/day	
1990				
(15–130 kg/man)/day	P, p. 7; D, p. 460	Plane	20–85 tons	D, p. 562

Sources: D = Dunnigan (1993); H = Huston (1989); P = Pagonis and Cruikshank (1992); VC = Van Creveld (1995).

Note: For the period after 1939, there is an enormous difference in consumption between the mechanized and nonmechanized units. Thus in 1990 the former needed 130 kg per day and per man; the latter needed only 15 kg per day and per man. During World War II the figure of 350 tons per day was commonly assumed for German semi-mechanized divisions.

plies; whereas even as late as 1870 ammunition formed no more than two percent of all supplies, by the end of World War II subsistence accounted for only 10 per cent of all supplies. This evolution, plus the fact that the quantity of ammunitions consumed can vary in huge proportions according to the intensity of battle, has rendered the task of permanently ensuring an adequate supply far more difficult.

Table 7.5c describes the supply needs and the transportation possibilities available in each period. In addition to the capacities of these various means of transportation, another important element is their cost. Schematically one can say that for freight a plane is approximately one hundred times more expensive than a boat, while for the transfer of persons the ratio of costs is on the order of three or four or even less, when the points of departure and arrival are a long way from the coast. This is explained by the fact that passengers need a cubic capacity that is much greater than their own volume to travel comfortably; furthermore they have to be fed during the whole duration of the journey. Since the Korean War, aerial transportation has largely been called upon for the shipment of personnel. In the shipment of American troops to Vietnam in 1964, approximately 50 percent of troops were sent by plane even though there was no real emergency as there had been during the Korean crisis in July–August 1950. By 1990, during the Gulf War, 99 percent of troops were conveyed by air. On the other hand, for freight it is the maritime route that is the most used. During the Gulf War only 3 percent of the tonnage conveyed during the first ninety days was shipped by air (Pagonis and Cruikshank 1992, p. 7), despite the increased capacity of cargo planes; for example, a Lockheed AC-5 can carry 32 tons and a KC-10 up to 85 tons (Dunnigan 1993), while at the time of the Korean war the capacity of planes was around 5 to 10 tons.

In general, from the arms depots or factories to the theater of war several means of transportation have to be used. For example, during the Korean War freight had to be carried from the production sites in the United States to the Pacific Coast either by train or by road; then by boat to Korea or possibly to Japan; once unloaded in the port of Pusan or Inchon the rail or the road took over until the front line (Figure 7.2). It is generally in the transitions between the different means of transportation that bottlenecks and stoppages arise. Thus during the German campaign of 1941 against Russia, because the gauge of the rail line was not the same on the Russian track as on the German track, the content of the rail wagons had to be

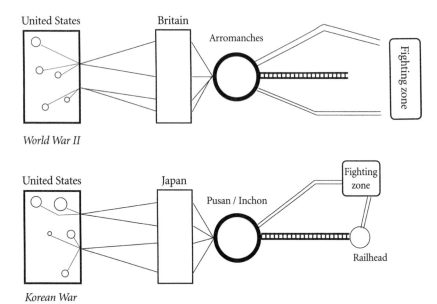

World War II

Korean War

Figure 7.2 Schematic representation of logistics for the war in Western Europe (1944) and the Korean War (1950). The capacity of the whole chain is determined by that of the weakest link. In Normandy, the critical point of the chain was the unloading capacity of the port of Arromanches, at least until the taking of Cherbourg. In Korea the weakest link was the rail or road connection between the ports and the combat zones.

transferred from one train to the other. Although the planners had anticipated that this operation would only take a few hours, it often took much longer, with the result that immense bottlenecks would take place at the transfer points (Van Creveld 1995, p. 160).

In Table 7.5c we have omitted the supply needs (spare parts, ammunition, fuel) of the air force. These are highly variable according to the type of plane. For a number of aircraft the figures for 100 missions are as follows: F-111, 2,500 tons; F-16, 1,000 tons; Harrier, 710 tons; Mirage 3, 420 tons. In fact, the determining element for planes is less this tonnage than the maintenance time and the multiplicity of spare parts. The cost of spare parts to keep an F-15 in battle is on average $300,000 a day. In these conditions one will hardly be surprised that a single sortie of a fighter-bomber can cost $500,000 (Dunnigan 1993, p. 459).

To show how the orders of magnitude given in Table 7.5c can be used to render the figures provided by military historians more legible, we now apply them to several examples.

1. During the battle of Stalingrad (November 1942–February 1943), the German General Staff promised Paulus's army 300 tons of supplies per day by airlift. This represented nearly one hundred plane journeys. In fact hardly 100 tons arrived per day. The figures from Table 7.5c show that in these conditions capitulation was unavoidable. Indeed at the heart of the battle the German army (17 divisions) consisted of approximately 300,000 men; the supply of 100 tons per day therefore only represented 0.3 kilograms per day, which is 30 times less than what would have been necessary. An army cannot fight without ammunition; thus, after the failure of Manstein's army to rescue Paulus, there was no other solution than the surrender of the 80,000 survivors.

2. Next we consider what effort would have been necessary to supply fodder for the 850,000 horses of the German army during the campaign of August 1914 if it had taken place in winter. On the basis of 10 kilos per horse per day, 8,500 tons of fodder would have been needed per day. This represents 71 percent of the transportation capacities of a dual-track rail line; since only one dual-track line was available, it would have been necessary to use it largely for the transportation of fodder alone.

3. Concerning the war led by General Rommel in Libya, Van Creveld writes: "From February to May [1942] Rommel and his Italian allies [in total seven divisions] received 325,000 tons of supplies" (1995, p. 186). Is this figure compatible with the data above? For simplification let us reason on the basis of 10,000 men per division; for a period of 4 months one therefore arrives at a total of: $30 \times 10,000 \times 7 \times 4 \times 30 = 252,000$ tons. Although somewhat smaller, this figure is of the same order of magnitude than the one given by Van Creveld; he notes, moreover, that the 325,000 tons received exceeded actual consumption by 45,000 tons, which makes the agreement even better.

4. Pagonis and Cruikshank (1992, p. 7) note that during the first ninety days of the Korean conflict, 979,000 tons of equipment were conveyed. This represents a little more than 10,000 tons per day. Is this figure compatible with the capacity of the transportation chain in Figure 7.2? The capacities of transportation inside the United States were of course more than sufficient; furthermore, with a large part of the maritime tonnage used during World War II still available, shipment across the Pacific did not pose any more problems. The only possible bottlenecks could arise

from the capacities of the ports of Pusan or Inchon and the transportation routes in Korea itself. Yet the port of Pusan, for example, had an unloading capacity of 40,000 tons per day. The most serious limitations therefore came from the capacities of transportation in the hinterland. These consisted of a railway with a capacity of 12,500 tons per day and a large road with a capacity of 8,000 tons per day (Huston 1989). In other words, the transportation capacities were sufficient provided that the whole of the chain operated smoothly and without major disruptions.

5. During most of the three years of the Korean War, the American task force consisted of 300,000 men. What was the resultant total figure for consumption? Huston informs us that "the total of all tonnage shipped from the United States to Korea from the beginning of the conflict until the armistice (30 June 1953) was roughly equivalent to 18 million tons" (1989, p. 118). With the figures from Table 7.5c we arrive at an estimate of $3 \times 360 \times 40 \times 300,000 = 13$ million tons, a figure that although appreciably smaller is nevertheless of a good order of magnitude (we have used the upper limit of 40 kilograms/day because the supply also included that of the air force).

Speed of Advance of Armies

What is the average traveling speed of an army? In stating this question two details are important, on the one hand the expression "average," and on the other the word "army." The latter implies that we are interested in the movement of large units consisting of at least an army corps (16,000 to 30,000 men). As for the expression "average," it means that we restrict ourselves to long-distance movements of at least 500 kilometers. For shorter distances, the speeds reached are not representative of the total advance of an army. An illustration is provided by the Russian campaign in 1941. German armored divisions advanced by "flea jumps," their fuel reserves allowing them to cover 400 kilometers independently; but on reaching this point of the advance, they were forced to wait for the arrival of the supply tankers. Thus Manstein's army corps covered 320 kilometers in five days (64 kilometers per day), but was then forced to remain stationary for eight days (from June 26 to July 4).

It is clear that the speeds given in Table 7.6 are comparable only for similar resistance offered by the enemy. For the sake of comparability, we have not included in this table cases in which the resistance was strong to the

Table 7.6 Average speed of advance of armies

Year	Campaign	Average speed (km/day)
1707–1708	Charles XII's campaign in Russia	7
1812	Napoleon's campaign in Russia	
	Invasion	11
	Retreat	19
1914	German invasion of Belgium and France (right wing)	11
1940	German invasion of Holland, Belgium, and France (left wing)	25
1941	German invasion of Russia	
	Army group North	14
	Army group Center	9
	Army group South	13
	Average	12
	Campaign in North Africa (Libya)	
1940	First British offensive	12
1941	Rommel's first offensive	26
1941	Second British offensive	12
1942	Rommel's second offensive	6
1950	North Korean invasion	6

Source: Appendix, p. 329 below.

Note: The average velocity does not show any upward trend. Although there has been substantial progress in transportation means, there is also more equipment to be transported; one factor cancels out the other.

point of making the very notion of mobile warfare inapplicable. Such was the case, for example, during the German retreat on the Russian front; the latter advanced at an average speed of only 2.5 kilometers per day. The reconquest of Western Europe from the Normandy beaches to Berlin took place at an appreciably more rapid speed of 4.0 kilometers per day.

What is most striking in Table 7.6 is the absence of a consistent increase in speed over time. The immense development in the means of transportation has been counterbalanced by the parallel increase in the tonnage to be transported. The result is that the top speed of an eighteenth-century light infantry (25 kilometers per day) has hardly been exceeded. As Van Creveld (1995) demonstrates very convincingly, the lowest point was reached in 1914: between 1870 and 1914 transport tonnage increased a great deal, particularly because of the more rapid fire of the artillery, while in the same time period the means of transportation hardly evolved, motor transport only beginning to play a substantial role in 1940.

Landings and Task Forces

Landing operations are a specialty of the great maritime powers such as Britain, the United States, and Japan. From the perspective of logistics they constitute both an ideal drill and a particularly demanding challenge. By definition they involve the most difficult operation, which is the transfer from one means of transportation to another. Furthermore, as the duration of shipment by the maritime route is generally on the order of several weeks, planners have to make very precise forecasts so that each element is present at the right time and in sufficient quantities. The United States has pushed this organizational activity to a remarkable degree of perfection.

Before 1940, landings were fairly hazardous (Table 7.7). Thereafter the conditions of the operation were completely transformed with the possibility of aerial cover. Previously the cover for the landing troops had been provided by the navy artillery, but very imperfectly, even in the vicinity of the shore. This is illustrated by the successive defeats of the landings in the Gallipoli peninsula. In contrast, since 1940 all major landings that have enjoyed aerial supremacy have invariably succeeded.

Tactics

Before aerial cover was possible, military commanders relied on tactics to compensate. There were essentially two possibilities, either to take advantage of the protection of the navy artillery or to launch a surprise landing.

THE PROTECTION OF THE NAVY ARTILLERY

As already noted, reliance on the navy artillery was fairly unsatisfactory. This is obvious for the eighteenth century, when the range of navy guns was insufficient to reach targets not directly situated on the shore. At the end of the nineteenth century, the navy artillery became capable of neutralizing artillery installed on forts guarding the ports, especially if they were of older construction. Thus a major bombing of the fort and the city preceded the English landing at Alexandria (1882). In 1915, however, the navy artillery was largely inefficient against the buried and fortified cannons of the Gallipoli peninsula. The massive bombing of March 18, 1915, ended with the loss of three battleships sunk by mines without successfully reducing the Turkish artillery.

THE SURPRISE EFFECT

To undertake a surprise landing, commanders have found it necessary to give up all artillery preparation. Often diversionary actions have been launched to deceive the enemy. Thus the landing of April 24, 1915, on the north bank of the Dardanelles strait was combined with a diversionary landing on the south bank; after having been landed, these troops were reembarked shortly afterward and rejoined the site of the main landing. Similarly, the landing of August 6, 1915, at Suvla Bay (20 kilometers to the north of the entry to the strait) was combined with a diversionary landing at Kaba Tepe a little to the south.

The use of the surprise landing was undoubtedly an inheritance from a period when these undertakings involved small numbers. For the massive landings of World War II, it was no longer a tactical surprise effect that was sought but a strategic surprise effect. For the Normandy landing the parachuting in the night preceding the operation of 20,000 airborne troops gave a clear indication to the enemy. However much more than one day was needed to assemble divisions that were hundreds of kilometers from the landing place.

Landing Tests

Before engaging in operations involving thousands of boats and hundreds of thousands of soldiers, it was imperative to test landing techniques on a smaller scale or in easier conditions. Certainly maneuvers could be organized; thus in the weeks preceding the Allied landing in North Africa exercises were organized on the western coasts of Scotland (Robichon 1965). In the absence of the enemy, however, such exercises lacked realism. The three major landing operations led by the Allies in 1943 and 1944 show an obvious progression. The first, in North Africa, was met with only a symbolic resistance by French troops loyal to the Vichy government; the second, in Sicily, was met with only a moderate opposition from the Italian troops; only the Normandy landing clashed head-on with the German armies.

Small-scale landings in enemy territory were equally organized to serve as testing grounds. The Dieppe operation took place on August 19, 1942, three months before the Allied landings in North Africa. It had to serve as a testing ground for various technical aspects; thus the operation comprised

Table 7.7 Landings in hostile territory

Year	Country	Location	Number of troops landed	Number of deaths	Air supp.	S/F	Reference
1596	Britain	Cadiz (Spain)				S	Vincent (1898)
1625	Britain	Cadiz (Spain)	90 vessels			F	Macaulay (1989 [1861])
1694	Britain	Brest (France)	30,000	1,100		F	Bodart (1908)
1702	Britain	Cadiz (Spain)				F	Vincent (1898)
1707	Britain, allies	Toulon (France)	38,000			F	Bodart (1908)
1758, June	Britain	St. Malo (France)				S	Vincent (1898)
1758, Sept.	Britain	St. Malo (France)	8,000			F	Bodart (1908)
1759	Britain	Quebec	12,000			S	Bodart(1908)
1780	Britain	Charlestown				S	Langer (1968)
1793	Britain, Spain	Toulon (France)	18,000			S–F	Bodart(1908)
1807	Britain	Alexandria		450		F	Langer (1968)
1809	Britain	Walcheren (Hol.)	40,000	4,000		F	French (1990)
1830	France	Algiers	30,000	600		S	Quid (1997)
1882	Britain	Alexandria	6,000			S	Vincent (1898)

			Troops	Air supp.	S/F	Source
1915, Apr.	Britain, France	Gallipoli	9,000		F	Churchill (1928)
1915, Aug.	Britain, France	Gallipoli	25,000		F	Deygas (1932)
1940	Britain, France	Norway	13,000	N	F	Montagnon (1992)
1941	Germany	Cretea	17,000	Y	S	Montagnon (1992)
1942	Britain	Dieppe (France)	6,000	N	F	Michel (1968)
1942	Britain, U.S.	Morocco	35,000	Y	S	Sainsbury (1976)
1943	Britain, U.S.	Sicily	150,000	Y	S	Blumenson (1968)
1944	Britain, U.S.	Anzio (Italy)	36,000	Y	S–F	Churchill (1965)
1944	Britain, U.S.	Normandy	250,000	Y	S	Thomson (1968)
1944	Britain, U.S.	Provence	250,000	Y	S	Robichon (1965)
1950	U.S.	Inchon (Korea)	18,000	Y	S	*Le Monde*
1982	Britain	Falkland Is.	5,000	Y–N	S	Quid (1997)

Note: S/F = Success or failure. This list seeks not to be exhaustive but to give representative examples for each period. The "Air supp." column indicates whether (Y) or not the task force enjoyed air supremacy. The possibility of aerial cover since 1940 has greatly reduced the risks inherent in landing operations; this is shown by the frequency of successes after that time. In the case of large-scale landings such as those of 1943 and 1944, it is the number of troops landed during the first two days that is given.

the landing of thirty tanks. However in its general concept this operation was more the inheritor of an outmoded tradition than the prototype of future landings. On June 11, 1943, a month before the Sicily landing, the operation on Pantelleria Island between Tunisia and Sicily took place. Because they are representative of two completely different concepts, we will examine these two episodes more closely.

DIEPPE

Members of the Second Canadian Infantry Division were the primary leaders of the Dieppe landing. Approximately 6,000 men were committed and there were nearly 1,500 deaths, or 25 percent. The motivations that caused Winston Churchill to launch this operation have been the subject of many discussions. Some historians have maintained that the Dieppe operation had the principal objective of giving a pledge to Stalin, who was asking insistently for an action on the Western Front to ease German pressure in the East. One can note, however, that Churchill's interview with Stalin had taken place on August 12–13, 1942, while the Dieppe operation was only put into effect one week later.

The military objective of the operation was to occupy the port, destroy its installations and reembark the troops at the end of the day before the arrival of reinforcements. In this, it was the inheritor of a long British tradition of "raids" against French or Spanish ports. These include Brest (June 6, 1694), Toulon (July–August 1707), Saint-Malo (June 1758), Cherbourg (August 6–7, 1758), and Toulon (September–December 1793); see Table 7.7. In all these actions the objective was to occupy the port, destroy its installations, and burn the vessels found there. In the case of Dieppe, one of the objectives was to force the Germans to deploy forces to guard against similar operations, thereby diverting forces from the Russian front.

But it is by its organization rather than its objectives that the Dieppe raid is connected to the British landings of the previous centuries; this is shown by the following characteristics (Robertson 1962). First, to bring about the surprise effect there was no artillery preparation: the first naval salvo was fired at 5:12, 8 minutes before the landing. Second, there was practically no aerial cover; certainly an aerial battle took place during the same day, but far away from Dieppe. At Dieppe itself, as shown by photographs taken during the operation, the landing crafts as well as the accompanying flotilla were the target of German bombers; one destroyer as well as less important ships were sunk. (3) The operation was a continuation of earlier commando raids on the French coast, in particular that of Hardelot (April 21–22, 1942) in the vicinity of Boulogne/Mer.

THE PANTELLERIA OPERATION

Very different was the operation led on Pantelleria Island. This island is situated 60 kilometers from the Tunisian coast and 110 kilometers away from Sicily. It was fortified and defended by 12,000 Italian troops. Between June 1 and 10, 1943, it was submitted to an intensive aerial bombing, totaling 5,000 tons of bombs. On June 11 the landing flotilla appeared at the island. The element of surprise played no role, but the aerial supremacy of the Allies was total. On June 12, the garrison surrendered. This success foreshadowed that of the Sicily landing, where there were only 5,500 deaths on the Anglo-American side, which is less than 2 percent of the troops committed.

Logistics

How many tons of equipment must be provided for each soldier taking part in a landing? This is the first question for the planner. From this figure he will be able to estimate the tonnage of transport ships needed and forecast, as a function of the capacities of the port installations, the necessary time required for the loading of the landing fleet. Of course, in the organization of a landing and in particular in the choice of the place and the hour, there are many other important parameters. The necessary beach length is one of them; for World War II it has been estimated at approximately 4 kilometers of beach for 10,000 men per day (Thomson 1968). There was also the question of the tides, the moon, and so on. The question of total tonnage takes on a particular importance, however, because it is the foundation for all the upstream operations.

In truth this question of tonnage may be divided into two. It is first necessary to bring soldiers to the site with their different equipment; this is what we call "equipment tonnage." Thereafter it is necessary to provide for their needs in food, ammunition, fuel, spare parts, and so on; this we refer to as "consumption." The second question is fairly similar for a land army, but the equipment problem is one we have not considered yet.

EQUIPMENT VERSUS CONSUMPTION

The data only rarely make the distinction between equipment and consumption. In order to separate these two components we consider two extreme cases. We first posit that the tonnage arriving with the first wave of landing troops, that is to say in the first few days, almost exclusively involves equipment. Second, we assume that for an operation that lasts several years the largest part of the tonnage conveyed corresponds to consumption. Are these assumptions realistic?

Let us assume for equipment a figure on the order of one ton per man, which corresponds to the case of an American infantry division in 1950 (Huston 1989); let us assume for consumption a figure on the order of 20 kilos per man per day. If one assumes that the first wave of landing ships, in addition to equipment, bring consumption items for about ten days, one arrives at the following orders of magnitude: equipment, 1,000 kilos; consumption, 200 kilos. That is, the tonnage of consumption is small in the face of that of equipment. In contrast, over a duration of three years (the case of the Korean War), one has: equipment, 1,000 kilos; consumption, 20,000 kilos. This time it is the tonnage of equipment that is negligible in the face of that of consumption.

In an intermediate manner, for a duration of 50 days one will have approximate equality between the two components: equipment = consumption = 1,000 kilos; in other words, the total tonnage will be distributed almost equally between equipment and consumption.

Of course, the figures of 1 ton and 20 kilos per man may have notably increased since 1950. It is not unreasonable to assume, however, that they have increased in an almost parallel manner and by this hypothesis our reasoning remains valid. The evolution in the tonnage needed by a task force is summarized in Table 7.8.

EXAMPLES

Let us apply the interpretative framework provided by the above figures to some historical examples. It is for the recent period that the most reliable data exist.

1. The Gulf War (1990–1991). The Gulf War is a particularly interesting example from the point of view of logistics because, with the exception of oil, very few goods were available locally. The figures given by Pagonis, the general in charge of the logistics of the operation, inform us that during the first thirty days 38,000 men and 163,500 tons were conveyed, which represents 4.2 tons per man. If one assumes that consumption had been forecast for one month in advance, corresponding to a total period of sixty

Table 7.8 Tonnage needed for a task force

Year	Equipment (kg/man)
1800	15 + horses
1944	1200
1950	1000
1990	2100

Sources: Campbell (1990); Huston (1989); Pagonis and Cruikshank (1992).

Note: The figure for 1950 refers to major equipment and vehicles for an American infantry division.

days, one is nearly in the above situation where there is approximate equality between the tonnage of equipment and consumption. One thus obtains: equipment per man = 2.1 ton; consumption = 2.1 ton/man, that is, 2100/60 = 35 kilos/man/day. The figure of 35 kilos/man/day is indeed consistent with our previous estimates.

2. The Korean War (1950–1953). As an application, we show that the figures given by Pagonis and Cruikshank (1992, p. 7) for the Korean War cannot be correct. For the first ninety days of this campaign these two authors give: passengers airlifted to theater: 32,357; passengers shipped to theater: none; tons of supplies and equipment shipped or airlifted: 979,833 tons. This represents 30 tons per man, a figure that is (at least) three times larger than the above figure for the Gulf War. The error comes from the figure of 32,357; in fact after ninety days there were in Korea six American divisions and eleven allied divisions, representing about 300,000 troops (*Le Monde,* August 23, September 22, 1950). With that correction the order of magnitude of the tonnage becomes consistent with our previous estimates.

3. 1914. The 1914 German offensive to the west was a land operation; however, because most of the troops were transported to their bases by train, it is somewhat similar to the situation for a landing. Van Creveld (1995, p. 136) informs us that to transport an army corps, 240 trains of 25 carriages were necessary, which is 120 trains per division. An infantry division consisted of 15,500 men, 4,600 horses, and 44 cannons. Are these figures compatible with the total figures of Conte (1991), who informs us that 29,000 trains were necessary to transport the 190 divisions committed in total? This leads to 152 trains per division, or 304 trains for an army corps (that is, two divisions), a figure that is indeed consistent with that of Van Creveld.

Summary and Perspectives

In this chapter we have systematized some of the observations already made in Chapter 6. In contrast to previous studies, such as the pioneering work of Van Creveld, we were less interested in the description of historical evolution than in specifying a number of *permanent* constraints and regularities. Five findings should be highlighted.

1. The size of armies and the length of wars is conditioned by the degree of centralization of the states. While the Roman Empire has been able to field armies numbering 100,000, one has to wait until the middle of the eighteenth century to again see armies of that size. Similarly, prosperous but loosely centralized states were unable to finance large armies or large fleets, an assertion that can be illustrated by the case of the Netherlands.

2. Because centralization improved the capacities of states to wage war, there has been a trend toward greater centralization, especially in federal states. A case in point is the United States, where the revenue of the federal budget increased from 3 percent of national income before 1914 to about 20 percent after World War II.

3. Hyperinflations (that is, inflation episodes with a price increase over 10^{10}) have occurred almost exclusively in the wake of wars. One of the main effects of hyperinflation episodes has been to reduce the war indebtedness of the state to almost nothing.

4. An army with a large cavalry can only operate in the summertime, when fodder is available in the fields. Attila the Hun was defeated at the battle of the Campi Catalauni (near Troyes) in June (451). Such a battle, involving a large cavalry, could only take place in summer. As another example, Charles Martel arrested the advance of the Muslims at Tours in June (732). Similarly the fact that World War I broke out in August (1914) can largely be explained by the fact that the German army comprised no less than 850,000 horses.

5. Airpower radically changed the conditions of military landings. Since 1942 all major landings that have enjoyed aerial supremacy have been successful. The landing at Anzio-Salermo (September 9, 1943) in southern Italy, which was only a semi-success, provides a confirmation of that rule. Allied aerial supremacy was far from complete in that case: the Allies lost

about 90 aircraft while the German air losses totaled 220 (Clodfelter 1992, p. 845).

These are only some of the regularities discussed in this chapter. Thanks to the existence of extensive comparative sources, the logistics of war constitute a fascinating topic for analytical history. Unfortunately the comparative historian is in a less favorable position for many other fields. It is the purpose of the next chapter to confront the ambitions and the objectives of analytical history with its means of investigation and to explain how the latter can be improved.

Appendix: Speed of Advance of Armies

For the Russian campaigns of Charles XII (1707–1708) and Napoleon (1812), the advance of the armies is easier to follow than in the campaigns of the twentieth century, when the front was spread over a large area and did not advance everywhere at the same speed. It is for this reason that we have made a detailed analysis of these two cases (Tables A7.1 and A7.2). This allows the fluctuations in speed during the campaign to be followed. In particular, in 1812 the speed was greater during the retreat from Russia than during the invasion. This is explained by two obvious reasons: (1) the army had been notably reduced in size during the campaign; and (2) faced with the cold and the lack of supplies, surviving troops depended on speed as a condition for survival.

Table A7.3 provides the data on which we based the estimates for army velocities in Table 7.6.

Table A7.1 Charles XII's campaign in Russia, 1707–1708

Date	Location	Distance (km)	Speed (km/day)
Sept. 7	Oder		
Dec. 30	Vistula	3	2
Jan. 23	Grodno	13	1
Feb. 8	Smorgon	13	5
June 30	Holovzin	1	4
Aug. 31	Malatitze	3	1
Oct. 30	Mezin	5	8
Apr. 20	Kasnokutsk	1	8
June 22	Poltava	2	6
July 7	Perevolutny	5.8	
Average speed		6	7

Sources: Bain (1895); Bengtsson (1960).

Table A7.2 Napoleon's campaign in Russia (1812)

Date	Location	Distance (km)	Speed (km/day)
A. Invasion			
June 24	Kaunas (Kovno)		
June 30	Vilna	99	16.5
July 24	Kamen	222	9.3
July 28	Vitebsk	105	21.0
Aug. 18	Smolensk	142	6.8
Aug. 29	Viasma	154	14.0
Sept. 7	Borodino	111	11.1
Sept. 15	Moscow	117	14.6
	Average speed		11.4
B. Retreat			
Oct. 19	Moscow		
Oct. 24	Maloyaroslavets	117	19.5
Oct. 30	Gzatsk	123	20.5
Nov. 9	Smolensk	216	19.6
Nov. 27	Borisov	247	13.7
Dec. 8	Vilna	210	17.5
Dec. 12	Kaunas (Kovno)	99	24.7
Dec. 20	Königsberg	225	18.7
	Average speed		18.7

Sources: Clausewitz (1900); Fezenzac (1970); Palmer (1967); Segur (1910).

Table A7.3 Average velocities

Year	Campaign	Route	Distance (km)	Dates	Average speed (km/day)
1914	German invasion of Belgium and France	Border, Brussels, Mons, Le Cateau, Soissons, Clay	370	Aug 4–Sept. 5	11.2
1940	German invasion of Holland, Belgium, and France	Border, Sedan, Cambrai, Boulogne	250	May 10–25	25.0
1941	*German invasion of Russia*				
	Army group North	Tilsitt–Tallinin	572	June 22–27	16.3
		Tilsitt–Lake Ilmen	659	June 22–July 31	16.9
		Ostrov–Leningrad	313	July 2–Sept. 4	9.5
		Average			14.4
1941	Army group Center	Border–Vyazma	756	June 22–Oct. 10	10.8
		Border–Bryansk	886	June 22–Oct. 14	7.8
		Average			8.9
1941	Army group South	Border–Odessa	757	June 22–Aug. 17	13.3
		Average			13.3
	North African campaign				
1940	First British offensive	Mersa Matruh–Beda Fomm	674	Dec. 9–Feb. 5	12.0
1941	Rommel's first offensive	El Agheila–Sollum	673	Mar. 31–Apr. 23	25.9
1941	Second British offensive	Sidi Omar–Mersa Brega	582	Nov. 18–Jan. 6	11.6
1942	Rommel's second offensive	Mersa Brega–Mersa Matruh	933	Jan. 21–June 27	6.0
1950	North Korean invasion	Chunchon–Taegu	320	Jun25–Sept. 15	6.3

Sources: 1914–Gray (1990); WWII–Messenger (1989); 1950–Cook and Stevenson (1978).

Prospects

8

Historical Forecasting

The plan Marc Bloch initially drew up for his book *Apologie pour l'histoire* (Eulogy for history) included a chapter devoted to the question of historical forecasting. Destiny, with Bloch's tragic disappearance in 1944, did not leave him the time to write this section. Recalling Bloch's plan emphasizes that the question of historical forecasting is an integral part of the comparative perspective. Once comparative analysis has drawn attention to regularities, is it not natural to test them by making projections for the future? Even if at present such an objective still appears relatively distant, it is useful to look at the problems associated with historical forecasting.

In the first section we review a range of forecasts made by statesmen, historians, or economists and discuss the relevance of various methods of forecasting. In the second section we examine the potential role of forecasting as well as its necessary limitations, both for the actors of history and for historians. Finally, we explain why in our opinion it would be sterile and counterproductive to make forecasting a central objective of analytical history.

Examples of Historical Forecasting

The examples of historical forecasting presented in this section could be ordered and classified according to different criteria: the forecasting method used, their degree of accuracy, or the distinction between short-, medium- and long-term forecasts. We adopt here the first criterion.

Brilliant Intuitions
With the field of history having so far been unable to develop reliable forecasting methods, political and military leaders have had to rely on their in-

tuition and "sense of history." The following examples mainly concern military logistics, an area in which chance and the unexpected have relatively little place.

On August 13, 1911, Winston Churchill, then the home secretary in the Asquith Cabinet, published a memorandum on the military aspects of a future conflict with Germany. His forecasts turned out to be astonishingly accurate:

> It is assumed that an alliance exists between Great Britain, France and Russia, and that these powers are attacked by Germany and Austria. The decisive military operations will be those between France and Germany. The German army is at least equal in quality to the French army and mobilizes approximately 2,200,000 against 1,700,000. The French must therefore seek for a situation of more equality.
>
> The balance of probability is that by the twentieth day the French armies will have been driven from the line of the Meuse and will be falling back on Paris and the South. If the French army has not been squandered by precipitate or desperate action, the balance of forces should be rather favorable after the fortieth day, and will improve steadily as time passes. For the German armies will be confronted with a situation which combines an evergrowing need for a successful offensive with a battle front which tends continually towards numerical equality. Opportunities for the decisive trial of strength may then occur. (Churchill 1923, pp. 60–63)

Churchill's convictions relied not only on his "sense of history" but also on attentive observation. Since 1911 the Germans had prepared all the necessary infrastructure for launching an invasion: large military camps near the frontier, huge deposits of equipment, railway stations with immense platforms.

The French General Staff scarcely took advantage of Churchill's perceptiveness. The hypotheses upon which General Joffre's famous Plan XVII were based were very distant from those of the memorandum. Plan XVII planned a French penetration into Alsace-Lorraine and hardly took into account the risk of the French left wing's being turned by the German armies.

Most remarkable in Churchill's memorandum is the forecast that after a first phase of retreat, the stretching of the German armies could allow a counteroffensive by the French armies on the fortieth day of the battle. This is indeed what happened, almost to the day. In the first week of September 1914 the French armies counterattacked on the Marne and checked the German advance. Churchill had his memorandum reprinted on September 2, 1914, a month after the declaration of war, to encourage his colleagues, as he says, "with the hope that if the unfavourable prediction about the twentieth day had been borne out, so also would be the favourable prediction for the fortieth day" (Churchill 1925). Churchill's own confidence in his forecasts is also astonishing. When he republished his memorandum the Battle of the Marne had not yet begun; it would essentially take place from September 5 to 13. Not only was his forecast correct, but it was purposely published in an attempt to change the course of events.

DE GAULLE AND THE OUTCOME OF WORLD WAR II

From the early 1930s, de Gaulle had been an advocate of a mechanized and professional army, as his 1934 book and 1935 article make clear. He was largely ignored, however. Nevertheless, the manner in which the Polish army was crushed in 1939 brought confirmation of his views. This led de Gaulle to make one last attempt, and in November 1939 he wrote a memorandum to the high command. He had a clear view of what would be the German invasion in May 1940: "The engine bestows to the means of modern destruction a power, a speed such that the present conflict will, sooner or later, be marked by surprise movements and invasions whose extent and rapidity will infinitely exceed those of the most dazzling events of the past. One has already seen how the rush of tanks and the assault of airplanes annihilated in two weeks a good army of 1,200,000 soldiers" (de Gaulle 1945).

After the evacuation of the British at Dunkirk and the defeat of the French army, a request for an armistice was sent to the Germans by General Pétain on June 17, 1940. The following day General de Gaulle issued a radio appeal from London for the struggle to continue: "Whatever happens, the flame of French resistance must not and shall not die" (for the whole text, see de Gaulle 1954). De Gaulle based his argument on the conviction that sooner or later the conflict would become worldwide: "This war has not been settled by the battle of France. This war is a world war." For him the final victory was only a question of time. Four years in advance he could see Germany being crushed by planes and tanks produced in American factories. Although evident a posteriori, in June 1940 the idea was audacious. Again, what is striking is de Gaulle's confidence. Many listeners may have seen more of a pious vow in his message than a historical forecast. For him, on the contrary, it expressed a deep conviction, which in the years ahead inspired his actions as the leader of "France libre."

AN ANTICIPATION OF WORLD WAR I

A book by Colomb, Maurice, and Maude, published in 1893, more than twenty years before the outbreak of World War I, proposed a prospective calendar of events; several phases were anticipated with striking accuracy. (1) The Great War, as the authors termed it, was thought to be much more likely to break out in the region of the Danube than on the banks of the Rhine. They suggested that an attempted assassination of Prince Ferdinand of Bulgaria near Sofia could provide the pretext for an invasion of Serbia by Austrian forces. (2) Three weeks later, the authors believed, the Russian troops would move toward the Austrian frontier, while at the same time German troops would penetrate into Russia. (3) A month after the start of the crisis, France was expected to declare war on Germany. Shortly afterward the German First Army would penetrate into Belgium while the Second Army passed through Luxembourg. (4) Two months after the beginning of the French campaign, the German armies would be found on the outskirts of Paris, but a sharp French counterattack would force them to retreat. (5) In the following weeks the conflict in France would get bogged down, and six months later a cessation of the hostilities would be negotiated, by the terms of which Alsace and Lorraine remain German.

Although this forecast is quite close to the actual scenario, there are also some important differences. First of all the war is placed, by the book's own title, in the last decade of the nineteenth century, at least fifteen years before the real conflict. Britain remains outside the conflict. The timing of the invasion is less precise than that of Churchill, since the decisive battle on the outskirts of Paris arises only two months after the beginning of the campaign. Finally, the war only lasts nine months, as did the Franco-Prussian war of 1870, instead of four years.

To emphasize the realism of this forecast, it is interesting to contrast it with another prevision of the Great War that appeared ten years later (Fitzpatrick 1909). In this extravagant scenario, the Austrian and German armies occupy the whole of central Europe and the Middle East as far as Jerusalem. A German army lands in Brazil while Japan invades Mexico. Almost certainly such an invasion would have been countered by the United

States, and under that assumption the orders of magnitude given in Chapter 7 show that the logistics for the massive landings required would by far exceed the capabilities of Germany and Japan.

THE NATIONALISTS' CHANCES IN 1920S GERMANY

In an article in the *Berliner Tageblatt* of April 23, 1926, General Berthold von Deimling refers to a plan by members of right-wing circles, according to which Poland would be invaded from the west by German troops and simultaneously from the east by the Soviet Union. He stressed that such an invasion would result in a European war. He noted that the plan had no chance of success at the time, because it would need a leader with political as well as military capacities, and who would be able to inflame the masses. Finally he indicated that this type of perspective would find a favorable welcome among a certain section of the German youth.

Thirteen years before the events, we have here the essential ingredients of the outbreak of World War II: the invasion of Poland, the agreement with a Soviet Union anxious to reestablish its frontiers of 1914, the role of the German youth, and finally the outbreak of a European conflict under the impetus of a charismatic leader.

The Future That One Prefers to Ignore

Often the future can be guessed without ambiguity, but government and public opinion prefer to ignore it. Here we provide two illustrations of this attitude.

IGNORING THE WARNINGS BEFORE THE GERMAN AGGRESSION IN 1939

After the National Socialist party came to power in Germany, its program could not have been more explicit; few people, however, wanted to believe it. A notable exception was the publication, in 1934, of a book written by an English financier, Paul Einzig. In it he put forth his view of what the major events of the following ten years would be. He wrote: "The trend of evolution in Europe points inexorably towards another world war in the lifetime of our generation. Before the advent of the National Socialist regime there was every reason to hope that a recurrence of the disaster of 1914 could be avoided. The victory of Hitler, its circumstances and its consequences, have made another war most likely, if not inevitable."

As for the mechanisms that would lead to the war, they were analyzed with great lucidity. "The only means by which Germany can increase her agricultural production is by the annexation of adjacent agricultural territories, such as Denmark, Holland, the Polish Corridor, and so on. The annexation of Austria which is the immediate aim of German imperialism, is a mixed blessing from the point of view of Germany's economic self-sufficiency. One of the objects of the 'Drang nach Osten' tendency of Germany's foreign policy is to establish a direct frontier with Russia, so as to be able to rely upon the vast raw-material resources of that country. In order to attain that end, Poland as well as one or several Baltic states would have to be defeated first."

From where did the author draw his conclusions? First, from the official program of the National Socialist party, which he published as an appendix; second, from the orientation of the German economy toward the objective of self-sufficiency even at the expense of economic profitability; and finally, from the German rearmament program.

Why did this and similar warnings have so little consequence for British and French public opinion and government? Certainly there were all sorts of circumstantial reasons, but their common denominator was the unconscious desire to ignore the disturbing evidence. An intensive rearmament program would have been expensive and unpopular, especially during the recession of the 1930s; thus it was better to make a pretense of believing that these warnings did not have to be taken seriously. Even rearmament, however, would probably not have prevented the outbreak of the conflict. The example of 1914 shows that despite the intensive English and French rearmament after the Tangier crisis of March 1905, the march to war continued inexorably.

IGNORING THE WARNINGS BEFORE THE PACIFIC WAR

A second illustration is provided by the example of the Pacific War. From 1925 on, several books appeared in Japan and the United States with rather revealing titles: *The Great Pacific War* (1925) by H. Bywater; *The Necessary War between America and Japan* (1932) by I. Choko; *The Inevitable War between Britain and Japan* (1933) by T. Ishimaru; *Japan over Asia* (1936) by W. H. Chamberlin; *When Japan Goes to War* (1936) by O. Tanin and E. Yohan; and *War in the Pacific* by S. Denlinger and C. B. Gary. Thus in the 1930s the idea of a Japanese attack on the Philippines and Guam had become a banality. As an example, consider the predictions of Bywater (1925), the earliest of the studies that we have cited. He anticipated the at-

tack on the Philippines in very precise terms: "As the garrison of Luzon including native troops did not exceed 17,000 men, they could not hope to
fight more than a delaying action against an army of 80,000 Japanese." In
fact, these figures were very close to those of December 1942 when 80,000
to 100,000 Japanese troops landed in Lingayen Gulf (Kull and Kull 1952).
The author equally anticipated a pro-Japanese uprising in Hawaii, which
did not take place but was undoubtedly feared by the American authorities, since Hawaii remained under martial law from December 1941 to
June 1945, that is, long after all danger of invasion had disappeared (Daws
1968).

In his State of the Union address of January 6, 1942, President Franklin
D. Roosevelt called for the production of 60,000 planes, 45,000 tanks, and
6 million deadweight tons of merchant ships in 1942. Why, if the war appeared so inescapable, was this war effort not made earlier? Could it not
have stopped the Japanese slide to war? The response to these questions is
simple. From the point of view of public opinion, there is a huge difference
between a conflict that is expected by strategists and a war that has broken
out and is being reported in vivid detail by the media. In any case in 1941
the United States, thanks to its geographic position and to the immensity
of the Pacific, did not suffer as a result of its relative unpreparedness to the
extent that France had in 1940.

Extrapolating from the Past

Believing that a recently observed evolution will continue in the future is
a natural tendency of the human mind; it is at the root of one of the
most commonly used forecasting methods, extrapolation from past trends.
When continuity prevails over innovation, this method generates acceptable results; on the contrary, if there is a shift in the trend, it becomes inappropriate. In this section, through several examples, we highlight the pit-
falls that the application of this method can present.

ECONOMIC FORECASTING

Economic forecasting is based on dynamic models that can at first sight
appear more sophisticated than a simple extrapolation from the past. Nevertheless in the case of a rapid change in the trend, most of the models become inadequate. Figure 8.1 presents forecasts of the unemployment rate
in the United States made at different times between 1981 and 1983. The
predicted unemployment rate is the median of about twenty forecasters

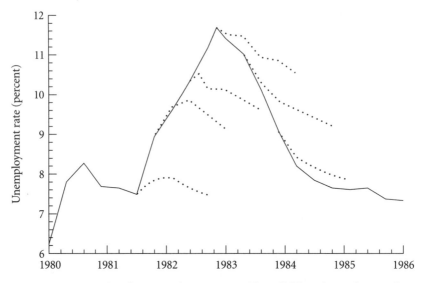

Figure 8.1 Forecasting the unemployment rate. The solid line shows the actual unemployment rate. The broken line shows the predicted unemployment rate at six points in time. The forecasters missed both the rapid rise and the subsequent rapid decline. *Source:* Adapted from Mankiw (1992).

surveyed by the American Statistical Association and the National Bureau of Economic Research. Of six predictions only the last, made at the end of the recession, is relatively close to the observed reality. In the other five predictions the forecasters missed both the rapid rise and the subsequent rapid decline.

THESES ON THE FUTURE OF THE JAPANESE ECONOMY

When one reviews the forecasts for the Japanese economy published in the last thirty years, one notices that, with few exceptions, they were strongly influenced by the current state of the economy. Schematically one can say that the Japanese economy has experienced four distinct periods since 1945. First, we find a period of reconstruction and strong growth lasting from 1946 until the oil shock of 1974–1975. The latter resulted in a doubling of the price of oil imports, on which Japan is so strongly dependent. Second, there ensued a period of readjustment from 1975 to approximately 1980, during which Japan's economy was restructured toward industries that consumed less energy and raw materials. Third, a triumphant and conquering phase ended in 1990 with the burst of the speculative bubble that had resulted in a doubling of the Nikkei index within three years. This phase was marked by a policy of commercial and financial expansion, with spectacular purchases of companies and assets abroad. Fourth, a phase of recession followed the financial crisis of the early 1990s, with a gradual increase in the public debt and the rate of unemployment.

Table 8.1 gives a sample of book titles that appeared in each of these phases. A strong correlation between the orientation of the title and the current economic situation is apparent. We certainly do not claim that the content of a book is always faithfully represented by its title. Nevertheless the role of the current economic situation remains impressive.

THE NEXT AMERICAN REVOLUTION

In 1927, in a memorable little book entitled *The Natural History of Revolution*, L. P. Edwards examined past revolutions from the eye of a naturalist. He did not look into their "causes," but rather considered the characteristics of their development. In the last chapter the author ventures to make some forecasts, which are of two types: those that are the result of rules inferred from observation and those that result from an extrapolation of past trends.

One of the rules drawn from observation is that revolutions are preceded by many portents: rebellion of intellectuals, aborted or successful attempts in neighboring countries, and so on. On this basis the author concluded that the next American Revolution would not occur in the twentieth century.

In the second type of forecast the author presented the following argument: "We already have religious and political democracy and it is most unlikely that the democratic trend will cease until we have industrial democracy also. Industry is the last stronghold of autocracy . . . If the public will not assume the ownership and control of the machines, then the labor unions probably will." One could be tempted to attribute this opinion to the influence of the October Revolution, which had occurred ten years earlier in Russia. In the rest of the book, however, the author shows such a detachment from the fashions of the time that this judgment seems unwarranted. In fact his prediction has been partially realized insofar as, in the half century that followed the appearance of his book, the influence of the state and the unions upon American economic life expanded. This trend materialized first in the New Deal, then in the postwar years with the vigorous action of the unions. Remember, for example, the immense strikes that hit the large firms (including General Electric, Westinghouse, General Motors, coal mines, and railways) in 1946, resulting in the loss of 116 mil-

Table 8.1 The effects of the state of the Japanese economy on judgments about its future (1960–1997)

Period	Economic status	Book titles
1960–1974	Very rapid economic growth	1. *The Emerging Japanese Superstate* (1970) 2. *Japan: The Risen Sun* (1970) 3. *Japan: The New Superstate* (1974)
1974–1980	Following the rise in the price of oil, the Japanese industry undergoes a period of difficulty and adjustment	1. *Japan: The Fragile Superpower* (1975) 2. "The Reconsolidation of U.S. Economy" (1976, article) 3. *The Japanese Challenge* (1979)
1980–1990	Spurred by the speculative bubble, the Japanese economy is booming	1. *The New Samurais* (1982, in French) 2. *The Decline and Fall of the American Automobile Industry* (1983) 3. *Japan as Number One: Lessons for America* (1983) 4. *Can America Compete?* (1984) 5. *After Hegemony* (1984) 6. *Les Dents du Géant: Le Japon à la Conquête du Monde* (1987) [Japan sets out to conquer the world] 7. *The Enigma of Japan's Power: People and Politics in a Stateless Nation* (1989) 8. *Japan's New Imperialism* (1990)
1990–1997	The burst of the speculative bubble brings about financial difficulties (bank failures) and weak economic growth	1. *Japan as Anything but Number One* (1990) 2. *Japan, the Coming Collapse* (1992) 3. *Beating Japan: How Hundreds of American Companies Are Beating Japan Now and What Your Company Can Learn from Their Strategies and Successes* (1993) 4. *Successful Gaijin in Japan: How Foreign Companies Are Making it in Japan* (1996) 5. *The High Japanese Saving Ratio: Will It Really Decline Rapidly?* (1996)

Note: If the economic situation influenced many forecasters, there were also a few perceptive analysts who detected the underlying trend and went against the prevailing mood of the moment. One of the most remarkable examples is the work *Comeback, Case by Case: Building the Resurgence of American Business*, by Ezra Vogel, which appeared in 1985, nearly seven years before the new dynamism of the American economy became evident.

lion working days (Kull and Kull 1952, p. 284). However, Edwards undoubtedly underestimated the resistance of the system. The Taft-Hartley Act of June 1947 was a response to the strike wave of 1946. More recently, since the beginning of the 1980s, the trend anticipated by Edwards seems to have been reversed.

FORBIDDEN LONG-TERM TRENDS

Often it is in a negative way that the extrapolative method can be most relevantly used. If one knows that a certain type of growth cannot continue forever, for example, one can anticipate with certainty a shift in the current trend.

This is particularly the case with exponential growth; relatively unspectacular in its first phase, it becomes explosive over time. One of the simplest criteria allowing the identification of exponential growth is the fact that the phenomenon doubles in size within a fixed time period. Thus, during the period 1945–1975, electricity production doubled every ten years in most industrialized countries. It was evident that this growth could not last for a long time, because a simple projection showed that after several decades the turnover of the electricity companies would have been larger than the gross national product. Similarly in the postwar period, the share of scientific research in the national product of the United States grew so rapidly that, had the trend continued, the percentage would have exceeded 100 after a few decades.

In this type of situation, even if we are sure the trend cannot continue indefinitely, we do not necessarily know what will happen next. Different possible scenarios are illustrated by Figure 8.2. First, the rapid growth can be followed by a contraction. Thus the sailing ship reached its pinnacle in the middle of the nineteenth century, and then sharply declined (Figure 8.2a). Second, the exponential growth can tend toward a plateau in an oscillating and more or less disorderly manner. Such was the case for zinc production (Figure 8.2b). Third, the exponential growth can be followed by a plateau, followed after a certain amount of time by a new period of growth. Such is the case for the human body, which experiences rapid growth after conception, then a second period of rapid growth at the time of adolescence. The evolution of the number of universities, shown in Figure 8.2c, constitutes another example of growth by successive plateaus. A first period of growth took place between the years 900 and 1200, mainly in the Arabic countries; a second at the time of the Renaissance; a third

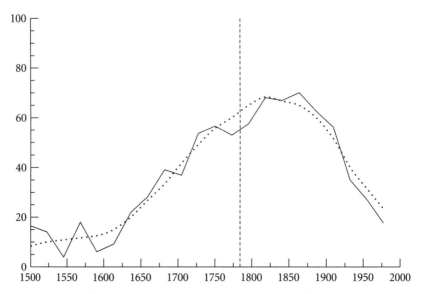

Figure 8.2a Predicting the future after a period of exponential growth: (1) after the growth there is a decline. To the left of the vertical line, the growth is exponential. An example of such a reversal of trend is given by the number of sailing ships, which reached their peak in the nineteenth century just shortly before their replacement by steamships.

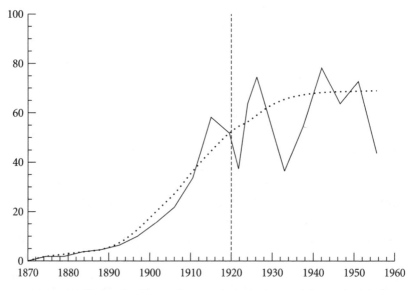

Figure 8.2b Predicting the future after a period of exponential growth: (2) after the growth there is a leveling off. To the left of the vertical line the growth is exponential. An example of such an evolution may be seen in the growth of a tree, •
or in economics in the growth of copper or zinc production from 1870 to 1960.

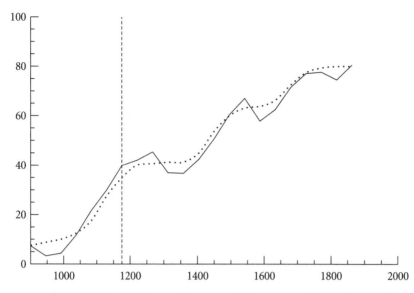

Figure 8.2c Predicting the future after a period of exponential growth: (3) after the growth there is a leveling off followed by later periods of growth. To the left of the vertical line the growth is exponential. An example of such an evolution is found in the growth of the human body, which is rapid in the first two years after conception, experiences a leveling off and becomes rapid again during adolescence. Similarly, between 900 and 1970, the number of universities in the world has risen, albeit with several successive plateaus.

during the nineteenth century at the time of the industrial revolution; and a fourth after 1945. In each of these periods the quantitative growth was accompanied by a qualitative transformation, so that the university of the twenty-first century has no more than a distant relationship with that of the eleventh century.

Another interesting example in the field of scientific research is the change in publication patterns. From 1910 to 1970, the proportion of scientific articles written by a single author fell from 80 to 10 percent (Price 1963). At the same time the proportion of articles having three or more authors rose from 3 percent to more than 30 percent. The continuation of this trend was unlikely, however, because it would have implied that by 1980 the percentage of articles written by a single author would be next to zero.

Figures 8.2d and 8.2e provide a fourth and fifth example of exponential

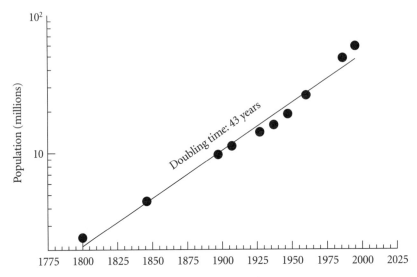

Figure 8.2d Growth of the population of Egypt, 1800–1995. Egypt is one of the few developing countries for which there exist relatively reliable demographic statistics since the start of the nineteenth century. Over the past two centuries the growth has been exponential; since the vertical scale on the graph is logarithmic an exponential growth would result in a straight line; the doubling time of 43 years has been calculated using a least-square fit. If this type of growth continues, Egypt will have about 75 million people in 2025. One can note that in the last two decades the growth has tended to outstrip the secular trend rather than to slow down. *Sources: Statesman's Year-Book;* Mitchell (1982).

growth over a long period. The fourth concerns the population of Egypt. Although one can certainly predict that such growth will not last forever, it is more difficult to say whether the change in the trend will take place in twenty, fifty, or seventy-five years. The final example concerns the growth of health expenditures in the United States. Because the growth in per capita national product is far less rapid, the share of health expenditures in the GNP has increased steadily since 1960, rising from 5 percent in 1960 to 14 percent in 1994. A similar evolution of health care expenses is observable in other industrialized countries. Again, this trend cannot hold indefinitely.

Forecasting using the extrapolative method in a negative form gained considerable importance in the 1970s, when it was realized that the growth that had prevailed since the end of World War II could not continue

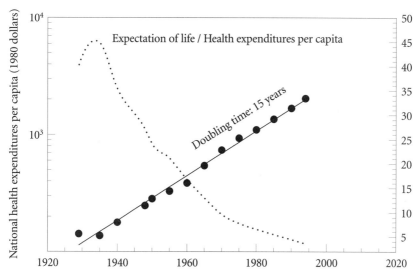

Figure 8.2e Growth of health expenditures in the United States, 1929–1994. Over a period of more than sixty years, health expenditures per capita (in 1980 dollars) have grown exponentially (the left-hand axis is logarithmic). The dashed curve (corresponding to the right-hand scale) represents a productivity index of health expenditures; after 1940 it shows a steady decrease. Expressed as a fraction of GNP, the share of health expenditures remained stable at about 5 percent from 1930 to 1960, before climbing strongly and reaching a level of 14 percent in 1994. Note that the same pattern is observed in other industrialized countries. *Sources:* Kurian (1994); *Statistical Abstract of the United States.*

indefinitely in the same form and at the same rate. This prediction proved correct in many respects.

THE COLLAPSE OF THE SOVIET ECONOMIC SYSTEM

Another example of an inescapable evolution is the collapse of the economic system put into place by the Soviet regime after the October Revolution. This system's lack of efficiency had long been highlighted by perceptive economists (see, for example, Allais 1950). In 1982, one of us published an article that showed that a rigid hierarchical bureaucratic system can only function under an iron discipline, as was the case in Nazi Germany or in Russia under Stalin. When this discipline was relaxed, as was inevitable in a period of peace, the system would drift inexorably to inefficiency and impotence (Roehner 1982).

But for how long would this drift last? Ten, twenty, or fifty years? What form would the transition to a different system take? That of gradual reforms, as Czar Alexander II attempted to impose between 1855 and his assassination in 1881? Or that of a collapse, as in 1917 and 1991? A response to these questions is much more difficult than identifying the inevitability of the collapse, because these phenomena depend on a great number of parameters.

Haphazard Forecasts

Certain forecasting methods appear to us to be inappropriate or insufficient. Historical forecasting is far from being a science, but some stumbling blocks can and should be avoided. Here we call attention to three of them: "acrobatic stacks," premature analogies, and gaps in empirical evidence.

"ACROBATIC STACKS"

By "acrobatic stacks," illustrated by Figure 8.3a, we mean reasoning that leads to a scenario in which each element is built upon the result of the preceding stage. In such a construction, if only one element in the chain of reasoning is defective, the whole structure will crumble. We illustrate this point by examining a predictive study of the relations between the United States and Japan.

In 1991 a book appeared in the United States with the provocative title *The Coming War with Japan*. Behind this somewhat commercial cover there was, however, a detailed analysis of the economic, political, and military relations between Japan and the United States. Yet the scenario that the authors proposed in their concluding chapter is typical of an acrobatic stacking. Their scheme has five main elements (Friedman and Lebard 1991). (1) For Japan the existence of an important trade surplus and continuous growth is of vital importance, for otherwise its financial stability would be threatened. (2) In response to Japan's refusal to open its domestic market to American imports, the United States would reply with restrictions on Japanese exports. (3) This would encourage Japan to withdraw into Southeast Asia, thus reproducing the scenario of the 1930s. (4) The United States, seeing its influence in the Pacific gradually wane, would be tempted to put pressure on Japan by using as a weapon its dependence on the outside world for various resources, including oil and raw materials. (5) This economic warfare would open the road for a military conflict.

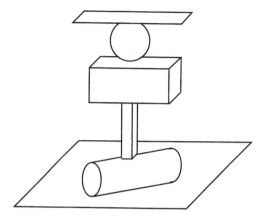

Figure 8.3a Schematic illustration of a forecasting method consisting in piling up successive arguments. By this method one creates a scenario in which the final outcome is dependent on the validity of all previous stages. If the scenario has five stages, as is the case in the figure, and if each stage has a probability of 0.5, the probability of the whole scenario will be $0.5^5 = 0.03$.

One could raise objections to several of these arguments, but the crucial point is less their individual validity than the fact that each objection makes the whole construction highly unlikely. If the probability of each stage falls to 0.5, the five-phase scenario has a probability of $0.5^5 = 0.03$, which means that the whole scenario becomes highly improbable.

Indeed, it is easy to imagine alternative scenarios. For example, one might think that the opening of the Japanese market that occurred in the 1980s would continue into the 1990s. It is not unreasonable to imagine that given the size of the Asian market (nearly 3 billion people), there is room for both Japan and the United States, which together total less than 400 million residents. Furthermore, the United States' control over world oil resources is currently less complete than it was in 1940. In 1950 the Western (mostly English and American) oil companies known as the Seven Sisters controlled about 90 percent of crude oil trade; by 1980 this percentage had fallen to 24 percent (Vernon 1983).

From a methodological viewpoint this approach has another fundamental defect: the proposed scenario responds only very partially to the actual question of whether or not there might be a war between Japan and the United States. In effect, there are many possible scenarios that could lead to such a conflict, the one sketched by Friedman and Lebard being only one of them, albeit perhaps the most obvious since it more or less reproduces the stages that led to Pearl Harbor. To truly answer the question posed in the book's title, it would be necessary to take into account all possible paths that history might suggest. Then the probability of each of these paths has to be estimated, and finally, by summing these various probabilities, one would get the probability of a war. The procedure is summarized in Figure 8.3b. This method, sometimes called path summation procedure, is identical to that used for complex industrial systems (nuclear plants, satellite launchers) in order to estimate the probability of a major breakdown. For industrial systems, the functions and breakdown probabilities of each component can be clearly identified and estimated; this is much more difficult for a political system. Even for industrial systems, moreover, the best calculations are very often thwarted and invalidated by human errors that cannot be anticipated.

PREMATURE ANALOGIES

Reasoning by analogy is a useful approach in the exact sciences (see Hesse 1966 in this respect) and in the social sciences. In the latter case, however, its handling and control are more delicate because of the multiplicity of variables and mechanisms. An illustration is provided in a book written in 1934, in which the author estimates the odds of a fascist revolution in the United States (Soule 1934). A large number of the ingredients that habitually feed fascist movements were present in the United States at that time: the suffering ranks of the unemployed; a dwindling number of small businessmen fighting a losing battle against monopoly; racial and religious prejudice; lawless suppression of strikes and radicals by violence, either through the organization of vigilantes or the hiring of gunmen; the Ku Klux Klan, an incipient fascist movement if there ever was one; and Senator Huey Long, an almost perfect American counterpart of Hitler in his early stages.

But analogies are never complete. Between the United States and Italy or Germany there are also major differences: a powerful democratic tradition; the absence of all feeling of humiliation following a lost war; no will for territorial extension at the expense of neighboring peoples; and finally the fact that Huey Long was assassinated on September 8, 1935, at Baton Rouge and could therefore no longer contribute to this scenario. Very justly the author remarks that it was perhaps Roosevelt's New Deal that was the best vaccination against a rise of fascism. In short, analogies can

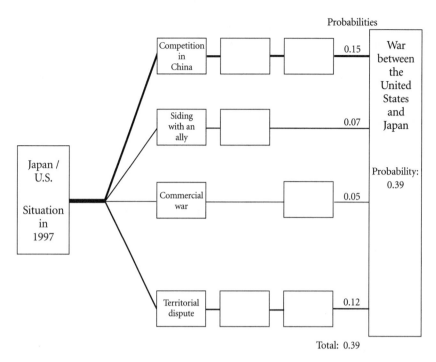

Figure 8.3b Illustration of the path summation prediction method. Each path corresponds to a possible scenario that could lead to war. Thus the path labeled "Commercial war" corresponds to the scenario proposed by Friedman and Lebard (1991). The thickness of the lines is proportional to the path's probability, which is also indicated numerically in the right-hand column. The values of these probabilities are only illustrative; to get more realistic estimates would require a satisfactory "theory" for each path, an objective that is currently out of reach.

provide interesting insight into actual mechanisms, but should always be viewed with a critical eye.

INFORMATION GAPS

Limited by time and his own competence, the historian cannot study all the aspects of a question in detail. This can result in obvious errors. We refer here to *The Coming War with Japan*, discussed earlier. Asking themselves how Japan could rapidly develop its military capacity, the authors suggest that a strategic force could be built around the H-2 rocket. If the authors had had the time to consult specialized publications, they would have seen that the H-2 launcher has an oxygen/hydrogen engine that excludes its use for military means. The time required to fill the tanks is several hours, and they can only be kept full for a very short time because of rapid evaporation of the liquid oxygen and hydrogen; for this reason all strategic missiles are solid-rocket boosters. This point, which can seem minor at first sight, has important implications. The development of a new launcher takes at least ten years. If the H-2 cannot be used for military purposes and if no secret program is under way, this means that Japan if it started now, would have no strategic missiles before 2012. It is therefore out of the question that it could consider a major war before this date.

Role of Historical Forecasting

If, as the saying goes, "to govern is to anticipate," it is clear that the development of efficient tools for historical forecasting should be a central concern for statesmen. Next we examine the performance of governments with respect to forecasting in two historical examples, namely, the French policy at the time of the war of independence in Algeria and the Vietnam policy of the Johnson administration. Then, in the following section, we address the question of the actual impact of forecasts on the course of events.

"To Govern Is to Anticipate"
Our first example is taken from France's Algerian policy after the insurrection of November 1954.

ALGERIA
On November 1, 1954, just before the United Nations began to examine the Algerian question, insurrectional activities took place in a coordinated manner in thirty Algerian localities. The toll was a dozen dead. On August 20, 1955, on the Collo Peninsula to the north of Constantine, thousands of Algerians, prompted by the National Liberation Front, attacked Europeans; 171 people were killed. More than the 1954 insurrection, this massacre provoked a psychological rupture between the two communities.

As we explained in Chapter 1, to understand an event one should consider it not in isolation but rather in conjunction with similar events. In the case of Algeria, at least four observations can be made. (1) In the past, the Algerians had proved on many occasions (1870, 1916, 1945) that they were ready to fight French domination. (2) Among French colonies, Vietnam had recently shown the way by obtaining its independence (1954). Similarly, internal autonomy had been granted to Tunisia in 1954. As for Morocco, it was in complete turmoil following the 1953 toppling of the sultan Muhammad V. (3) At the international level, Egypt had obtained at least formal independence in 1936, the Philippines in 1946, Indonesia in 1949, and Libya in 1951. (4) What was the situation in the British Empire? In 1947 Britain had withdrawn from India, since 1952 it had been faced with the Mau Mau revolt in Kenya, in Cyprus there has been a latent revolt since the 1930s, and in Malaysia Britain had to fight a long struggle against Communists. In 1953 political agitation in Uganda led to the removal of the king (Kabaka) of the province of Buganda.

Thus the decolonization movement was clearly under way by the end of 1954. With the United States being favorable to this evolution, it was obvious that liberation movements could count upon substantial support from international public opinion.

If these arguments pleaded in favor of a policy of concessions in Algeria, there were, however, some considerations that pointed in the opposite direction. In effect none of the territories that had obtained their independence had a large European population, as was the case in Algeria with about one million Europeans. The example of Kenya, where there existed an European community of 30,000 people, shows that the great powers were not yet ready to sacrifice their interests for the sake of decolonization. In November 1952, returning from an inspection tour of Kenya, the minister of the British colonies, Lord Lyttelton, reaffirmed to the House of Commons Britain's resolution to remain in Kenya and not to be diverted from its task by a "band of terrorists." As a matter of fact all the colonies comprising a substantial European population (that is, Angola, Kenya, Namibia, Rhodesia, South Africa) were to gain their independence only in the 1970s or even later. The only exception was perhaps the Dutch East Indies (Indonesia), but the European population was about seven times smaller there than in Algeria.

What was the reaction of French public opinion to the insurrection of November 1954? To answer this question, we will examine the reactions of the press. From 1954 and during the whole of the Algerian conflict, the reactions of the press were very diverse. As a whole, the left-wing press sensed a deep problem that repression would not solve. The newspaper *Combat* commented: "Brutal repression cannot be a complete solution." *L'Humanité*, the newspaper of the Communist Party, went along the same lines: "Terror would not be a solution." The newspaper *Le Monde* implicitly put forward the same argument by devoting a detailed article to the insurrection of May 1945 and by showing that repression had not solved anything. But none of these newspapers used the taboo words "autonomy" or "independence." The right-wing press only wanted to see Communists behind the rebels. Throughout the period of the cold war, the thesis of the Communist plot would, in Algeria as elsewhere, rule out all serious reflection. It is hardly surprising that the newspapers of the Algerian colonists reacted the most sharply. *L'Écho d'Alger* wrote: "It is necessary to strike this handful of agitators and strike them at the top, it is necessary to behead the organization."

What was the reaction of French politicians? The declarations of political leaders, even those on the left such as Pierre Mendès-France, almost modeled themselves on the position of the colonists; thus on November 12, 1954, Mendès-France, then prime minister, declared before the National Assembly: "One does not compromise when it comes to defending the internal peace of the nation, the unity and the integrity of the Republic. The Algerian departments are part of the French Republic. They have been French for a long time and they are irrevocably French. Between them and metropolitan France there can be no secession. That must be clear once and for all in Algeria and in metropolitan France as much as in the outside world. Never will France or any French government, or parliament, whatever may be their particular tendencies, yield on this fundamental principle" (*Le Monde*, November 13, 1954).

The bluntness of this declaration is all the more surprising if one considers that the same Mendès-France had several months earlier negotiated the French withdrawal from Indochina and had been involved in discussions on the autonomy of Tunisia.

François Mitterrand, then minister of the interior, declared on the day after November 1, 1954: "By attacking our Algerian compatriots, the murderers and rioters have drawn up against them the French force. If the leaders had wanted to alert international opinion just before a session of the United Nations, they have been wrong. Algeria is France and France will not recognize any other authority than its own."

The position of Prime Minister Edgar Faure on the day after the events of August 1955 is just as abrupt. "Honor as well as France's humane mission requires absolutely, unequivocally and without reservation to keep Algeria with France and in France. It must be understood at home and abroad that we are faced with a vital imperative."

If "to govern is to anticipate," then truly the definitive words that were pronounced in 1954 and 1955 filled this role quite poorly. In defense of the political leaders of the period, one can say that the liberation war of the Algerian people was the first of its type to be led in Africa, well before Angola, Mozambique, Rhodesia, or South Africa. In South Africa, moreover, the political leaders made no less peremptory declarations. Thus the South African prime minister P. W. Botha, who was at the time considered a reformist, declared to American television in 1976 (*Rand Daily Mail*, Johannesburg, August 30, 1976): "We openly say that we do not want to share power with the Blacks. We do not want to share it with anyone. When Britain wanted to share power with us, we had a war."

VIETNAM

In 1965 the Johnson administration made a crucial decision by sending 100,000 supplementary troops to South Vietnam and introducing bombing against North Vietnam. The manner in which this decision was taken has been analyzed in detail by Khong in a remarkable study that appeared in 1992. The discussion of this case is particularly interesting because the United States did not have any vital interests in Vietnam; there were neither American citizens nor investments to defend. The discussion could therefore be more open and less passionate than in the case of Algeria. Reasoning by analogy played a crucial role in this debate. Among the arguments used, one of the poorest was the invocation of the Munich crisis in 1938. Those who held this position believed that a retreat from Vietnam would lead to a war against the Soviet Union in the same way that the Munich retreat had led to World War II. This argument had already been used during the Korean War; it would be used again in order to justify the Gulf War in 1990.

The analogy invoked the most frequently was that of the Korean War. One of the main questions of the Vietnam debate was whether this analogy was valid or not. George Ball, who was one of the opponents to the dispatch of troops, made a very lucid analysis by drawing attention to several differences between the two cases. First, the United States had intervened in Korea under a mandate of the United Nations and in symbolic collaboration with fifty-three other nations. In contrast, in Vietnam the U.S. intervention relied only upon a request for intervention from the government of South Vietnam. Second, the Korean War had started with a massive land invasion by 100,000 troops, a classic invasion across an established border. In South Vietnam there had been no invasion, only slow infiltration. Many other differences between the Vietnamese and Korean cases could be cited, in particular from a historical viewpoint.

It emerges from Khong's study (1992) that eventually the 1965 decision was not taken on the basis of arguments or counterarguments of this type. It was taken because no other honorable way out could be seen. The following dialogue between President Johnson and George Ball is revealing. "George, can you offer another course of action?" asked the president. In response, Ball suggested that it could be arranged for the Southern Vietnamese themselves to request the departure of American troops. To which the president made this revealing response: "But George, wouldn't all these countries say that Uncle Sam was a paper tiger, wouldn't we lose credibility breaking the word of three Presidents, if we did as you proposed? It would seem an irreparable blow." In fact, to follow the path recommended by Ball would have demanded a deep rupture with the steady line up to that point. It is always easier to repeat than to innovate.

Can the perspective of analytical history allow us to illuminate this question? In the case of Algeria, the problem was relatively well defined: it concerned the liberation struggle of a colonized people; since 1945 several examples had shown the strength of this movement. In the case of Vietnam, the problem was less clear: did it concern a liberation struggle or a struggle against Communist subversion? In the latter case the postwar years had shown that victory was possible. In Greece the Communist movement had been overcome; in Malaysia, after six years of struggle, Britain had succeeded in eliminating the Communist guerrilla; finally in Korea, the growth of Communism had been contained. In truth the situation was undoubtedly mixed, but as the American commitment became more massive, it seems that in the minds of the South Vietnamese the liberation struggle aspect took over. From then on, the American position became ideologically untenable. But, one could wonder, why was there no similar drift in Korea or Malaysia? The response is simple. In Korea it was a classic war, not a guerrilla war, while in Malaysia, there were only a few insurgents: at its maximum their number was estimated at 8,000 (Clutterbuck 1973).

One can conclude that President Johnson and his team had to solve a difficult problem. It is possible, as Khong suggests, that they did not use very elaborate arguments; but in the current state of the historical science it is not certain whether a more subtle discussion would have allowed them to see the matter more clearly.

Does the Forecast Neutralize the Forecast?

It remains to discuss the impact of forecasts on the actual course of events. The argument by which forecasts may neutralize forecasts is standard in the area of stock market speculation, and we begin by considering this case. We will see that, depending on the viewpoint adopted, the forecast can either neutralize the forecast or, on the contrary, amplify it.

FORECASTING IN STOCK MARKETS

Schematically one can say that traders belong to two different schools. Some, who could be called fundamentalists, maintain that the value of a share is determined by a certain number of variables, called the fundamentals, indicating the economic health of the company and its perspectives for development. Others, who could be called chartists, think that the observation of past prices may allow their future behavior to be anticipated. Depending on the theory to which they adhere, traders will not have the same reaction in the face of forecasts.

In a market composed of fundamentalists, let us assume that an astute trader has been able to notice that a share was quoted at a price p_1, superior to the price p_0 that follows normally from the values of the fundamentals. Anticipating that this anomaly is going to correct itself in the future, and that the price will decrease from p_1 to p_0, he will sell until the share has returned to the level p_0. He will thus gain relative to the other traders. However, if there are a large number of astute traders in the market, they will all want to sell at the same time, so that each of them will have a great deal of difficulty in selling shares at the price p_1. In this case the spread of the forecast has killed the possibility of any gain (Fama 1965).

In a market formed of chartists, if an astute operator expects a price increase from level p_1 to level p_2, he will become a buyer, and if the increase occurs, he will have gained. If there are a large number of astute chartists in the market, they will all become buyers and the market will climb over a fairly long time interval, regardless of the accuracy of the initial forecast. One will have simply created a speculative bubble. In this case the forecast has amplified (or even created) the possibility of gain.

In practice, each of these schools harbors a number of different currents,

---

WHY DID THEY DIE?

BRIAN BORU	1014	NOT	to give a colourable sanction to the
EARL OF DESMOND	1467		slavery of Ireland
SHANE O'NEIL	1567		
HUGH ROE O'DONNEL	1605		
OWEN ROE	1649	NOT	to secure the partition of Ireland
BISHOP McMAHON	1650		
FATHER SHEEHY	1766		
ARCHBISHOP O'HURLEY	1798	NOT	to pledge to a foreign government
FR. JOHN MURPHY	1798		the treasure and the manhood of
LORD FITZGERALD	1798		Ireland
WOLFE TONE	1798		
EMMET	1803	NOT	to enable out-of-date political hacks
O'NEILL CROWLEY	1867		to bargain over Ireland
PEARSE	1916		
CONNOLLY	1916		
ASHE	1917		
COLEMAN	1918		

THEY DIED TO SECURE THE LIBERATION OF THE OLDEST
POLITICAL PRISONER IN THE WORLD
IRELAND!
RELEASE IRELAND!

Figure 8.4 Electoral posters used in Ireland during the elections of December 14, 1918, by Sinn Féin. The left-hand poster is a longitudinal analysis; it puts the emphasis on the long tradition of struggle. The right-hand poster is a cross-national analysis; it stresses that the international situation is favorable to people's struggles for their independence. *Source:* Kee (1972, p. 625).

so that one can never be sure what the next person will do in a given situation (for more detail, see Roehner 2001, p. 177).

AMPLIFICATION OF AN EVENT BY A CREDIBLE FORECAST

The forecasting of prices is the raison d'être and the essential occupation of stock market traders. One might think that for historical events the only professional forecasters are statesmen, political leaders, and maybe some historians. But we will see that in some cases, at certain privileged times, it

CZECHO-SLOVAKS

INDEPENDENCE   X

Foreign (German) domination

THE VOTE OF THE CZECHO-SLOVAK PEOPLE IN 1918 WON THEM THEIR FREEDOM.

JUGOSLAVS

INDEPENDENCE   X

Foreign (Austrian) domination

THE JUGOSLAVS DEMANDED NOT HOME RULE WITHIN THE AUSTRIAN EMPIRE, BUT
ABSOLUTE INDEPENDENCE. THEY ARE NOW ACKNOWLEDGED A NATION.

THE IRISH

INDEPENDENCE

Foreign (English) domination

IRELAND'S MARK IS NOT YET MADE. YOU CAN MAKE IT. WILL YOU HAVE
THECOURAGE TO DEMAND WHAT RACES INFINITELY LESS HISTORIC HAVE
DEMANDED? THE YUGOSLAVS ARE YOUNGER THAN THIS ANCIENT COUNTRY BY A
THOUSAND YEARS. THEY HAVE VOTED FOR INDEPENDENCE, AND ARE NOW FREE.

is the whole population that may change into a group of proven chartists. This point is illustrated by Figure 8.4. It presents two posters used for the elections of December 14, 1918, in Ireland. These elections resulted in a crushing victory for Sinn Féin, the party of independence. Almost overnight Home Rule, which had aroused so many debates for so many years, was displaced by the demand for independence. The underlying "theory" in these posters is close to the one sustained throughout this book. The poster on the left presents the longitudinal analysis, with a list of recurrent episodes personified by victims. The poster on the right presents a cross-national analysis of the recent past. The underlying argument was the following. By an evocation of previous uprisings the first poster asks the Irish to be faithful to the memory of their ancestors. However, some could be tempted to conclude that since the preceding insurrections failed, the next had a strong probability of meeting the same fate. To this, the second poster brings the assurance that, since other people have already obtained their independence, the world has indeed changed.

To prolong our stock market parallel, one can list a number of "fundamentals," for example, the wish of the Irish to be the masters of their own destiny, their resentment toward England, their attachment to their country, and devotion to the memory of their fathers. Just as a stock market may shift abruptly, similarly Ireland swung from its demand for Home Rule to a demand for its independence. In the formation of this patriotic bubble, the Sinn Féin historians certainly played a large part.

Summary and Perspectives

Apparently there is a strong desire among humans to be able to read the future. Alexander the Great consulted the Pythia, almost all Renaissance statesmen had a private astrologer (Kepler was one of them, in the service of the German emperor), and even today the business of astrologers and fortune tellers is flourishing; furthermore all governments have an economic forecasting division. Although, quite intentionally, no forecasts are made in the present book, it was essential to discuss the question of historical forecasting.

Our discussion leads us to the following main conclusions.

1. Some historical forecasts have turned out to be surprisingly accurate and farsighted. We mentioned several examples of forecasts by statesmen (Churchill, de Gaulle) or by historians about World War I and II. These brilliant forecasts, however, were more the result of intuition than of a well-defined methodology.

2. It appears that most standard forecasting techniques are fairly crude and unreliable. Nevertheless, they provide useful guidelines provided one remains aware of their limits. We have seen that most ad hoc methods, such as the construction of (unlikely) scenarios or the use of inappropriate analogies, lead to even poorer forecasts than standard techniques.

3. By examining the performance of statesmen with regard to historical forecasting we noted that most often the main obstacle is not the lack of knowledge but rather the (unconscious) refusal to take into account un-

pleasant information or conclusions. It is only in this way that one can understand how in the 1930s the clear signals pointing to an impeding war were ignored by the British and French governments. The same effect helps to explain the myopia of French officials during the independence war in Algeria between 1954 and 1958.

Before we close this chapter a last point has to be made, which is of cardinal importance. Certainly humans want to know the future, and certainly governments would take great interest in historical forecasts (provided they were reliable). But from a scientific point of view, forecasting should not become an objective in itself. Once one understands the basic mechanisms of a phenomenon, one can contemplate making forecasts, but not before. Without knowing the basics about barometric pressure and temperature, without knowing the Navier-Stokes equations or the effect of the Coriolis force, it would be illusory to make meteorological forecasts. This difficulty can be illustrated by economics. Because from its origin this discipline was associated with state management, it has always been confronted with difficult forecasting problems; not only was it most often unable to solve them satisfactorily, but they most likely proved distracting from the necessary study of basic underlying mechanisms. Schumpeter made that point very clearly in his editorial for the first issue of the journal *Econometrica* (1933): "No science thrives in the atmosphere of direct practical aim, and even practical results are but by-products of disinterested work at the problem for the problem's sake. We should still be without most of the conveniences of modern life if physicists had been as eager for immediate applications as most economists are and always have been." Analytical history should refrain from becoming "as eager for immediate applications" as economics.

Perspectives

We now examine to what extent the objectives set in the introductory chapter have been achieved. If, as will be seen, they have been only partially carried out, we should ask ourselves how further progress can be achieved in the future. What instruments of observation do we need? How can comparative history fruitfully develop? Is the time ripe for a real breakthrough?

In the first section we examine to what extent our objectives have been achieved. One of our conclusions will be that only additional empirical work can substantially improve the situation. Then we discuss some of the challenges this book presents. In the second section we describe the Very Large Chronicle (VLC) project, which is aimed at improving observation in the field of comparative history. We emphasize that the worldwide computer network and the fact that English is quickly becoming a universal means of communication greatly favor the realization of such a project. Finally, in the last section we look back twenty years to examine the status of historical sociology at that time, considering how it has fared since then and what its prospects for the future may be. In spite of many obstacles, we note, historical sociology has established itself as an active, spirited, and fruitful discipline. Moreover, similar ideas have led a number of physicists to develop a comparative approach in economics, which is known under the name of econophysics.

About This Book

Charles Tilly's Agenda Revisited
In his book *As Sociology Meets History*, Tilly (1981) defined an agenda for the study of historical repertoires, a concept that has played a central role

here. The first task, he noted, was "to determine whether repertoires in some strong sense of the word actually exist." The second objective was to examine "how and why the particular forms of collective action vary and change." Although the goals were clearly and concisely set, the undertaking was immense. To show that repertoires actually exist one has to examine similar episodes in the history of various countries and at different times, a fairly unusual task from the point of view of standard historiography. This is precisely what we have tried to do in the present book, seeking to provide a body of convincing evidence for a variety of topics ranging from revolution to wars and general strikes.

The second objective is more ambitious; in the language of economics one would say that it belongs to the difficult class of time-dependent, nonequilibrium problems. Nevertheless, in some cases we have been able to show the impact on repertoires of major social transformations. In Chapter 2, for example, we examined the consequences of a shift from religion to language as the defining principle of a nation.

In 1976 the French historian Paul Veyne set up an agenda for comparative history that had strong connections with Tilly's ideas on the subject. Within a little more than twenty years, what was at the time a set of bold but isolated attempts and assumptions has become an active field of research. We come back to this topic in the final section.

The Challenges of This Book

Sympathy with our approach, we have discovered, does not necessarily make for ease of reading. Our methodology may be challenging at times. It also, however, leads to rewards difficult to obtain by other means.

Reading a novel from the first to the last page is usually a pleasant exercise; but reading ten novels from page 100 to page 120 will certainly be frustrating even (or especially) when each novel is quite enthralling in itself. Yet this is precisely what is done in the preceding chapters. Because our objective is to compare different repertoires, we must constantly shift from one story to another, from one country to another, or from one time to an earlier or later one. At the very moment when the narrative becomes interesting, it is broken up! This is the price we pay for a comparative perspective, and what we lose in storytelling we gain in awareness of new connections and relationships.

Nobody would expect a book about geodynamics, chemistry, or astrophysics to make "pleasant reading." Such a book may prove fascinating because of the new understanding it permits, but all readers accept that a good amount of work is needed to acquire that understanding. The present book is certainly easier to read than one with many mathematical formulas, yet it presupposes some acquaintance with a great variety of historical backgrounds, a requirement that may make reading it demanding at times. There seems to be no obvious solution to this difficulty, since it is inherent to the field of comparative history, but any suggestions would be greatly appreciated.

One solution may lie in the choice of cases to be examined. In 1916 Pareto published his treatise on general sociology. Translated into English in 1935 and republished in many subsequent editions in various other languages, it was undoubtedly a work of major importance. Today, however, few sociologists have read Pareto's book even partially. Why? One of the main obstacles is the fact that Pareto drew all his historical examples from Greek and Roman history. In the nineteenth and early twentieth centuries many scholars had a good knowledge of ancient history. Nowadays this is no longer the case. As a result Pareto's examples appear unfamiliar and exotic, and this makes reading his treatise almost impossible. We have tried to avoid this pitfall by selecting our historical examples from different historical eras and locales, though we are well aware that East European and Asian history are quite underrepresented.

We have for the most part let our results speak for themselves, leaving them to provide a new perspective. But they are rarely as shattering as some scientific findings. We already have an intuitive knowledge of the phenomena that we investigate, and therefore what we uncover is usually not as stunning or amazing as, say, the discovery of quantum mechanics. Historical sociology is less like physics, which in the last two centuries has been able to unravel so many facets of the universe, and more like meteorology, a field in which there has been steady progress and less dramatic achievement.

We have, moreover, concentrated on patterns, on the question of "how." Such an approach is not uncommon in sociology, from Durkheim and Pareto to Lieberson and Tilly, but it is quite uncommon in history. The work of the historians Veyne and Snooks are the only exceptions we know of. For historically minded readers, it may be frustrating to leave the "why" question untouched, despite the insight the "how" answers may provide.

Finally, although some may believe there are too many statistical tables in this book, we are more inclined to apologize for having too few. To be convincing, analytical history has to be quantitative. While we tried to provide figures as often as possible, our case studies are at best semi-quantitative. They are a first step. With the help of the VLC project, described below, the situation should markedly improve.

Perspectives: The VLC (Very Large Chronicle) Project

Until now data processing has contributed very little to the development of the historical sciences. Nevertheless it opens up extraordinary possibilities. One of these is the possibility of constructing what we call a Very Large Chronicle (VLC) that could play the same role for historians as observatories do for astronomers.

Europeans are often proud of their long tradition in historical research. Yet tradition can be a liability rather than an asset. What is needed here is systematic and possibly quantitative coverage. In that respect the United States has a long tradition of excellence; one only needs to mention the many outstanding American historical dictionaries and encyclopedias. The development of computerized databases for comparative history would be an essential tool for further research in historical sociology.

The Current Situation Regarding Historical Information

THE QUESTION OF DATA COLLECTION

For comparative history, the question of data collection is essential, as essential as the availability of telescopes for astronomers or microscopes for biologists. We can illustrate this by an example already mentioned in Chapter 1 from a different perspective.

In 1997–1998 there were riots in Indonesia between the Javanese and the ethnic Chinese. The clashes were by no means the first of that sort; there had been several similar riots since 1945 and even earlier, before independence. Suppose one would like to make a precise count of such recurrent riots. On which source can one rely? On the indexes of the *Times* or the *New York Times?* Although these sources are of considerable usefulness for microsociological studies, in this case they are of little help, because these newspapers had no reason to report small-scale riots in Indonesia. Since Indonesia was formerly a Dutch colony, the researcher has a better chance of finding such information in Dutch newspapers. But even assuming one is able to read Dutch, without the help of an index of major Dutch news-

Table 9.1 Evaluation of selected historical dictionaries and encyclopedias

Title	Author and publication year	Countries covered	Type[a]	Period covered	Coverage density ([pages]/country]/year)	Index (pages)
Haydn's Dictionary of Dates	Vincent (1898)	World	M	1000–1898	0.01	40
A Short Chronology of American History	Kull and Kull (1952)	U.S.	P	1492–1950	0.64	90
The Encyclopedia of American Facts and Dates	Carruth (1956)	U.S.	M	1600–1955	1.67	105
An Encyclopedia of World History	Langer (1968)	World	P	500 B.C.–A.D. 1964	0.005	183
Dictionnaire Encyclopédique d'Histoire	Mourre (1978)	World	P	1000–1960	0.05	
The Chronology of British History	Palmer and Palmer (1992)	Britain	M	1000–1990	0.57	

Note: Coverage density is a concept analogous to the magnification of a telescope; it indicates the number of pages devoted to each country per year. As a matter of comparison, the coverage density of a work as detailed as Macaulay's *History of England* is 133 pages/country-year. Note that the starting date is necessarily rather arbitrary, because the earliest sections are often sketched in a few pages. Moreover, for the calculation of the coverage density we have (somewhat arbitrarily) assumed that the world consists of 100 countries. The geographical coverage is of course far from being uniform; Africa and Asia are underrepresented with respect to Europe and America.

a. M = multisubject; P = principally political.

papers it would require a considerable amount of work to extract reports on such riots from the daily press.

In short, what is needed is a computerized index of major newspapers. Such an index would serve as a historical microscope. We come back to this question below when we discuss the question of the VLC.

Historical dictionaries and encyclopedias to some extent have the same objective as such an index. In Table 9.1 we list a number of them. Unfortunately world history encyclopedias are not detailed enough for our purpose. For instance, in Langer (1968), which is one of the most comprehensive, there are 66 entries for the Dutch East Indies (that is, Indonesia) in the period 1914–1964, and there is only one mention of a riot between the Chinese and Javanese. To be useful for microhistorical analysis, a historical encyclopedia should have at least twenty entries on ethnic riots in Indonesia; in other words, it should be at least ten times more detailed than Langer's. Such an encyclopedia of about $1,400 \times 10 = 14,000$ pages would be cumbersome to use in book form, but a computerized encyclopedia would present no such problem. An electronic encyclopedia, moreover, can solve the question of the control and reliability of the information, a point of great importance. Indeed because in this case there is no limitation in size, primary sources can be appended to the database; in the next section we consider this point more closely.

RELIABILITY OF HISTORICAL INFORMATION

The question of the reliability of historical information is a difficult one. To pose the problem we again set up a preliminary test. Let us assume that we want to know the number of victims of the Gordon Riots that took place in London between June 2 and June 9, 1780. To this end we call on several sources. Vincent (1898, p. 205) gives 210 killed and 248 wounded, of whom 75 later died in hospital. Rudé (1964), who in the 1960s was one of the great specialists on such questions, gives 285 killed and 25 hanged. At this stage we might be satisfied, since the figures given by these two authors are consistent. However, according to Palmer and Palmer (1992), there were about 850 people killed, and according to Carruth (1993), "more than 800 people" died; yet other post-1990 sources (for instance, Clodfelter 1992) continue to give 285 deaths. There is therefore an uncertainty of (at least) 270 percent, and the situation is all the more uncomfortable since none of these authors indicate any sources. This is only one example among many others; in Chapter 3 we saw a case where the uncertainty was on the order of 1,000 percent. Obviously this question is one of fundamental importance, and a solution has to be found. This brings us to the VLC project.

The VLC Project

To guarantee quantitative history a certain reliability, it is necessary to make it possible to verify the information. The solution that we recommend is illustrated in Figure 9.1, which shows the way one would look up the Monmouth Rebellion in a Very Large Chronicle. A first stratum in this large computer database will give the facts in the same form as, for example, in a historical encyclopedia. After all, for most studies it is irrelevant whether there were 310 or 850 victims during the Gordon Riots. When greater precision is necessary, a second stratum will provide access to discussions of the event or figure found in secondary sources. Finally, but this is a more ambitious objective, a third stratum might give access to the primary sources themselves.

DEVELOPMENT OF THE VLC PROJECT

The VLC project could be developed by stages. In its first stage, for example, it would be based on the following sources.

1. A first-rate encyclopedia of world history, such as Langer (1968).
2. The computerized indexes of the *Times* (1788–) and of the *New York Times* (1857–).
3. A version of all available indexes of major newspapers that would be both computerized and translated into English. For instance, in France there is an index of the newspaper *Le Monde* for the time intervals 1860–1900 (under the name *Le Temps*) and 1955–; translating that index into English would provide detailed coverage of one century of French history.
4. The VLC could also incorporate existing newspaper databases such as the one developed for the period after 1945 by the National Foundation for Political Science in Paris.

This first stage of the VLC could be developed, given adequate resources, within three or four years. It would permit us to know the microhistory of Argentina, France, Germany, Japan, Spain, Sweden, or Turkey as well as we know that of the United States or Britain, and would open the possibility to do comparative history in a truly systematic way. Initially the first stage might comprise the equivalent of about 100,000 pages. This could be ex-

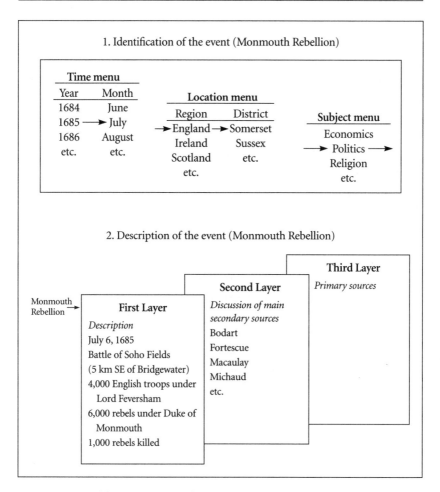

Figure 9.1 Possible organization of a Very Large Chronicle (VLC), illustrated with a search for information on the Monmouth Rebellion. The reliability of the information would be ensured and controlled in the second layer by examining and comparing various sources and discussing their levels of accuracy. Finally, the primary sources could be given in the third layer in the form of connections to computerized books and manuscripts.

tended by steps. Ultimately the VLC could include an unlimited number of pages. The reliability of the information in the first layer would be controlled by the discussion of sources in the second layer.

In a second stage the project could be extended to the countries for which there is presently no index for any newspaper. The task of creating a newspaper index for a period covering several decades represents a significant undertaking, because in this case one has to read all the articles. The VLC could be extended progressively at the rate of two or three more countries every decade.

Finally, the primary sources could be given in the third layer in the form of links to electronic books and manuscripts.

WHY THE VLC HAS TO BE A MULTIPURPOSE DATABASE

Throughout this book we have advocated and illustrated the idea that analytical history has to concentrate on the study of specific and sharply defined mechanisms. Is it not curious then that at the same time we propose the creation of a VLC intended to ensure extensive coverage? The paradox is more apparent than real. If the analysis must focus on precise mechanisms, the observational instrument must on the contrary be as universal as possible. The analogy with astronomy is again helpful. While each astronomer pursues his or her particular research, the observatories must be adapted to a wide range of researches. Obviously one would not consider constructing such expensive instruments to serve only a few astronomers. Of course this does not exclude the development of specialized instruments (spectrographs, coronographs) for particular tasks, but the telescopes themselves are as multipurpose as possible. Similarly the VLC should be as universal and flexible as possible.

DIFFICULTIES LINKED WITH THE EVOLUTION OF HARDWARE AND SOFTWARE

The difficulties linked with data processing relate essentially to the rapid evolution of the hardware and the software. Just as we still use chronologies and historical encyclopedias written in the eighteenth or nineteenth century, similarly a computerized chronicle designed in the year 2000 should still be readable in 2100 or 2200. This will not be the case if the institution that has produced it, whether it is a university or a commercial publisher, does not make an effort to maintain its compatibility with the development of computer systems. A computerized database abandoned on a library shelf in 1963 would be illegible in 1998; both equipment and software have completely changed.

THE CONSORTIUM FOR POLITICAL AND SOCIAL RESEARCH

Databases already exist that foreshadow the VLC. One of the most important has been developed by the Inter-University Consortium for Political and Social Research (ICPSR), based at the University of Michigan in Ann Arbor. By examining the functioning of such an institution one can gauge the progress already made as well as the difficulties of such an undertaking.

Since its foundation in 1962, the ICPSR has collected a large number of files of social, political, economic, and historical data provided by many teams of researchers. Documentation is available for each of these files that summarizes its content. Furthermore, as technology has progressed, the medium on which these files are recorded has been constantly updated. To measure the extent of this problem, recall that until the early 1980s computer data was stored on punch cards or magnetic tapes.

By enabling a large number of users to access files that represented years of work, the ICPSR prevented the loss and dispersion of information that is otherwise so frequent in historical research. However, this type of information also has its limitations, chief of which is a lack of uniformity and homogeneity. Because the files were designed for a particular research project, they do not provide systematic coverage. As an illustration, consider the file "Data Bank of Assassinations" (ICPSR no. 5208). It summarizes data on 409 assassinations in 84 countries between 1948 and 1967. Because the source was the *New York Times* index, the coverage will certainly be more complete for Western countries than for other countries; moreover the file's usefulness is limited by the fact that it stops abruptly in 1967.

FAVORABLE CIRCUMSTANCES

In Chapter 1 we noted that there are many academic obstacles to the development of comparative history. But there are also several circumstances that are eminently favorable: (1) English has become a lingua franca for scholarly communication; (2) computer networks make it possible to send data from one country to another quickly, easily, and cheaply; and (3) we have seen the development of transnational organizations such as the United Nations, UNESCO (United Nations Educational, Scientific and Cultural Organization), and the European Union.

The first two factors provide the technical means that are essential for the development of comparative history. An example of the possibilities opened by computer networks is the Internet site "quanhist.recurrent" (Table 9.2), set up by one of us in collaboration with Francesco Galassi of the University of Warwick. The object of this site is to permit the exchange

Table 9.2 The Internet site quanhist.recurrent

Creation	October 1994
Number of subscribers (2001)	185
Editors	Francesco Galassi, Bertrand Roehner
Editorial board	Deirdre McCloskey, Charles Tilly
Subscribers belong to the following countries	Australia, Brazil, Canada, Denmark, Finland, France, Germany, Greece, Italy, Netherlands, Russia, Spain, Sweden, U.K., U.S.
Organization supporting the site	Cliometric Society

Note: Quanhist.recurrent is an abbreviation for "quantitative study of recurrent historical events." The purpose of the site is to enable historians around the world to exchange their data sets. The necessary information for connecting to quanhist.recurrent can be obtained from the site www.eh.net under "Lists" ("eh" is the abbreviation for "economic history"); at this site one can also find other useful tools and services relating to economic history. Samuel Williamson played a key role in setting up eh.net; many thanks to him.

of information between scholars in different countries on specific topics such as general strikes or hyperinflations.

EXAMPLES OF "DOABLE" QUESTIONS

In sociological history (and even more in analytical history), the crucial step is to find a "good" subject and to ask the "right" questions. Here are some obvious requirements for the selection of a phenomenon. (1) One should be able to observe it repeatedly in different historical episodes. (2) Detailed and possibly quantitative sources should be available in a language that the researcher is able to read. (3) Once the documentation has been collected, the "right" questions, those that lead to the discovery of well-defined regularities and conclusions, must be posed.

The case studies treated in this book have been selected on the basis of the above criteria. Needless to say, many others could be profitably investigated; Table 9.3 provides examples.

Glimmers of Hope

Is it wishful thinking to find reason to hope in recent scholarly developments? Perhaps, but the fact remains that the comparative and observational approach that we have advocated in this book has in recent times

Table 9.3 Selected "doable" questions in analytical history

Topic	Period	Approximate number of episodes	Availability of sources
1. Separatist struggles	Antiquity to the present	>200	B
2. Manifestations of hostility against immigrants	Antiquity to the present	>100	C
3. Expulsion of colonists	17th–20th century	>20	C
4. Scapegoating reactions	Antiquity to the present	>100	C
5. Expulsion of Jesuits	17th–20th century	30	A
6. Suppression of monarchy by a revolution	18th–20th century	30	A
7. Transition from republic to monarchy or empire	Antiquity to the present	10	A
8. Hyperinflation episodes	17th–20th century	15	B
9. Speculative bubbles	17th–20th century	100	B

Note: A = "good"; B = "medium"; C = "difficult." In separate publications (Roehner 1997a,b; 1998; 1999a,b) we have begun at least a preliminary investigation of topics 1, 5, and 9. This list presents only a few examples of "doable" (in Lieberson's sense) questions.

benefited from growing support. More and more researchers are questioning what may be called the "econometric" approach that has exercised so great a fascination during the past forty years both in economics and in (causal) sociology. This opens the way for historical sociology and observational economics. In this section we examine this evolution in some detail.

The Fortunes of Historical Sociology

The debate about historical sociology is an old one. In 1983, in a book review of Tilly's *As Sociology Meets History* and Abram's *Historical Sociology*, Chirot (1983) wrote : "History continues to interest a small number of sociologists, enough so that a trickle of books are published each year explaining the meaning and practice of historical sociology . . . That is not to say that mixing sociology and history is necessarily silly . . . but how much sociology as a distinct discipline may have to contribute to good history is open to doubt."

Seventeen years later, not only has the "trickle" not stopped, but the interest in historical sociology has expanded. In addition to its pioneers and long-sighted advocates like Hechter, Lieberson, Tilly, and Wallerstein, the field has received the backing of several other prominent sociologists and historians such as Abbott, Goldstone, Hall, Laitin, and Snooks. In order to better understand that evolution it is necessary to briefly explain why the so-called "econometric approach" has proved disappointing. This is the purpose of the next paragraph.

Inadequacy of the "Econometric Approach"

In past decades some historians and sociologists have been tempted to adopt the approach used in econometrics. Yet in both economics and sociology there is a growing awareness of the fact that taken alone, statistical techniques cannot solve any problem. It is now commonly recognized that the achievements of this approach have been far from impressive; see in this respect the papers by Summers (1991), Granger (1991) or Roehner (1997a). The following analogies can help explain that point.

Different substances can be characterized by various parameters, such as color, density, stiffness, coefficient of reflection, and viscosity. Can one understand anything about these physical properties simply by plotting one parameter as a function of one or several others and by estimating multivariate correlation and regression? Probably not. Yet this is the analog of the procedure used in sociology that consists in plotting different characteristics of (for instance) wars, such as duration, number of deaths, size of the countries, and whether the country is a democracy or not, and performing multivariate regression analysis. In order to get a better understanding one has to concentrate on a specific property, say, viscosity, and consider a whole range of carefully defined situations where viscosity plays a role.

The second example is an analogy with meteorology; it has been shown elsewhere (Roehner 1997a) that meteorology often provides useful insights into the structure and problems of social sciences. Like sociology and economics, meteorology concerns highly complex systems but, in contrast to sociology and economics, it has the advantage of being well understood at the level of basic concepts and equations. The state of the atmosphere can be characterized by parameters such as temperature, pressure, humidity, and wind velocity. Can one understand anything about the laws of meteorology simply by applying multivariate time series analysis to data records of these parameters? Probably not. Yet this is the analog of the procedure used in econometrics that consists in applying time series analysis to records of different macroeconomic variables such as interest rates, GNP growth, unemployment rates, and so on. In order to get a better understanding, one alternative approach is first to empirically identify similar *patterns* and *regularities* corresponding to a specific phenomenon; for instance, the arrival of a cold front will always be characterized by the same succession of events (first wind, then rain and a drop in temperature). Once such patterns have been identified, they can be studied in detail.

The Promise of Econophysics

Among the sociologists who favored the econometric approach, many had received robust training in mathematical statistics. The prestige attached to such technical skills probably played a non-negligible role in the acceptance and popularity of that approach. Yet, by a strange irony, the econometric approach was challenged in the late 1990s by a movement that originated in a field having a well-established tradition of mathematical sophistication, namely, theoretical physics. This new approach is now known as "econophysics," a term coined in 1996 by Eugen Stanley, a renowned expert in statistical physics at Boston University. Between 1995 and 2000 at least two hundred papers and several books were published in the field of econophysics. In many respects the difference between econometrics and econophysics is the same as between "causal" sociology and observational (that is, historical) sociology. It is too early to say if the promise of econophysics will be realized. There are many dangers along the path; one of them is the fact that modern physics has a marked tendency to favor theoretical investigation and computer simulation at the expense of experimental and observational work.

Qualitative, Quantitative, Comparative, and Analytical History

It is a long way from qualitative history to historical sociology or, as we have often called it in this book, analytical history. Qualitative history is concerned with the narrative of isolated events; analytical history implies quantitative analysis of a set of similar episodes. The transition from one to the other was discussed in Chapter 1; it is summarized in Table 9.4.

Table 9.4 From qualitative history to analytical history

Qualitative history	Quantitative history	Comparative history	Analytical history/ Historical sociology
Narrative of iso- lated events	Quantitative description of isolated events (cliometrics)	Comparison of a given phenome- non in different countries	Quantitative compari- son of several modules and building blocks ("simple" mechanisms)

Even if social phenomena are too complex for us to predict, it is possible, in Abbott's (1998) terms, to sketch the "rules of the game," to portray the limits and possibilities of action in such systems. This is what we have tried to do in this book.

From Modules to Global Events

The objective of analytical history is to define and analyze building blocks, modules, and simple patterns. In a sense, this work is similar to that currently in progress in genetics, where researchers attempt the constitution of a dictionary of genes. But in the same way that most diseases depend upon several genes, it will take several building blocks in order to reconstitute a revolution, and that recombination is by no means straightforward. In order to illustrate that point, suppose an American professor wants to relate his most recent vacation to a Chinese friend who does not know English. The professor can of course buy an English-Chinese dictionary, but that will not enable him to write even the simplest sentence in Chinese. Only a knowledge of all its grammatical rules would tell him how to combine words into sentences. Similarly, there is a wide gap between defining the modules of the French Revolution and understanding how they should be combined in order to form a real revolution. We must first search out the building blocks, while finding the "grammatical rules" for historical events is undoubtedly our ultimate objective.

REFERENCES

INDEX

References

Abautret, R. 1969. *Le sacrifice des Canadiens: 19 août 1942*. Paris: Robert Laffont.

Abbott, A. 1998. The causal devolution. *Sociological Methods and Research* 27, 2, 148–181.

Abenon, L.-R. 1992. *Petite histoire de la Guadeloupe*. Paris: L'Harmattan.

Abrams, P. 1982. *Historical sociology*. Ithaca, N.Y.: Cornell University Press.

Ageron, C.-R. 1980. *L'Algérie algérienne de Napoléon III à de Gaulle*. Paris: Sindbad. English translation: *Modern Algeria: A history from 1830 to the present*. Trenton, N.J.: Africa World Press, 1991.

Akenson, D. H. 1973. *The United States and Ireland*. Cambridge: Harvard University Press.

Albin, C. 1898. *L'île de Crète: histoire et souvenirs*. Paris: Sanard et Dérangeon.

Allais, M. 1950. L'économie soviétique est-elle efficiente? *Nouvelle Revue de l'Economie contemporaine*, 4–12.

Alleg, H., ed. 1981. *La guerre d'Algérie*. 3 vols. Vol. 1: *De l'Algérie des origines à l'insurrection*. Paris: Temps Actuels.

Anderson, M. L. 1993. Voter, junker, landrat, priest: the old authorities and the new franchise in Imperial Germany. *American Historical Review* 98, 5, 1448–1474.

Andersson, I. 1973. *Histoire de la Suède des origines à nos jours*. Paris: Editions Horvath.

Annuaire Statistique de la France 1986: résumé rétrospectif. Institut National de la Statistique et des Etudes Economiques. Paris.

Archer, D., and R. Gartner. 1984. *Violence and crime in cross-national perspective*. New Haven: Yale University Press.

Ardant, G. 1965. *Théorie sociologique de l'impôt*. Vol. 2. Paris: S.E.V.P.E.N.

Ardouin-Dumazet, V. E. 1910–1912. *Voyages en France*. 58 vols. Paris: Berger-Levrault.

Atlas historique. 1968. Paris: Stock.

Atlas of American history. 1987. New York: Facts on File.

Der Aufbau des Vereignigten Staaten von Amerika. 1945. Quellen zur Neueren Geschichte 6. Bern: Verlag Herbert Lang.

Die Aussperrungen und der Grosstreik in Sweden 1909. 1912. Stockholm: Labor Division of the Royal Commerce Department.

Avenel, G. D'. 1909. *Les riches depuis sept cent ans: revenus et bénéfices, appointements et honoraires.* Paris: Armand Colin.

Bain, R. N. 1895. *Charles XII and the collapse of the Swedish Empire, 1682–1719.* New York: Putnam's Sons.

Baloff, N. 1971. Extension of the learning curve: some empirical results. *Operational Research Quarterly* 22, 4, 329–340.

Bank of Japan. 1966. *Hundred-year statistics of the Japanese economy.* Tokyo.

Barnet, R. J. 1990. *The rockets' red glare: when America goes to war—the presidents and the people.* New York: Simon and Schuster.

Barruel, Abbé. 1793. *Histoire du clergé pendant la Révolution française.* Paris.

Barton, H. A. 1986. *Scandinavia in the revolutionary era, 1760–1815.* Minneapolis: University of Minnesota Press.

Baudhuin, F. 1944. *Le financement des guerres.* Louvain: Institut de Recherches Economiques et Sociales.

Baynes, N. H., ed. 1942. *The speeches of Adolf Hitler.* Vol. 1: April 1922–August 1939. Oxford: Oxford University Press.

Bazaz, P. N. 1954. *The history of struggle for freedom in Kashmir, cultural and political: from the earliest times to the present age.* New Delhi: Kashmir Publishing.

Beaudet, P. 1991. *Les grandes mutations de l'apartheid.* Paris: Editions de l'Harmattan.

Beauvois, D. 1995. *Histoire de la Pologne.* Paris: Hatier.

Bendix, R. 1978. Kings or people: power and the mandate to rule. Berkeley: University of California Press.

Bengtsson, F. G. 1960. *The life of Charles XII, King of Sweden 1697–1718.* London: Macmillan.

Bennoune, M. 1988. *The making of contemporary Algeria, 1830–1987: colonial upheavals and post-independence development.* Cambridge: Cambridge University Press.

Benoist-Méchin, J. 1984. *Histoire de l'armée allemande, 1918–1937.* Paris: Robert Laffont. English translation: *History of the German army since the Armistice.* New York: H. Fertig, 1988.

Bérenger, J. 1990. *Histoire de l'Empire des Habsbourg.* Paris: Fayard. Paris. English translation: *A history of the Habsburg empire.* 2 vols. New York: Longman, 1994–1997.

Bernard, C. 1865. *Introduction a l'étude de la médicine expérimentale.* Paris: J. B. Ballière et fils. English translation: *An introduction to the study of experimental medicine.* New York: Dover Publications, 1957.

Berndt, O. 1897. *Zahl im Kriege: statistische Daten aus der neueren Kriegsgeschichte in graphischer Darstellung.* Vienna: G. Freytag.

Berville, S. A., and J.-F. Barrière. 1823. *Mémoires sur les journées de septembre 1792.* Paris.

Bezanson, A. 1951. *Prices and inflation during the American Revolution: Pennsylvania, 1770–1790.* Philadelphia: University of Pennsylvania Press.

Birch, A. H. 1977. *Political integration and disintegration in the British Isles.* London: Allen and Unwin.

Black, J. 1998. *War and the world.* New Haven: Yale University Press.

Bloch, M. 1928. Pour une histoire comparée des sociétés européennes. *Revue de Synthèse Historique* 46, 15–50. Reprinted in: *Mélanges Historiques* (1963), 16–40. An English translation appeared under the title "Toward a comparative history of European societies," in *Enterprise and secular change,* edited by F. C. Lane and J. C. Riemersma. Homewood, Ill.: R. D. Irwin, 1953.

——— 1974 [1949]. *Apologie pour l'histoire ou métier d'historien.* Paris: Armand Colin. English translation: *The historian's craft.* New York: Knopf, 1953.

Bluche, F. 1986. *Septembre 1792: logiques d'un massacre.* Paris: Robert Laffont.

Bluche, F., and S. Rials. 1989. *Les révolutions françaises.* Paris: Fayard.

Blumenson, M. 1968. *La Sicile, débarquement surprise.* Verviers, Belgium: Marabout.

Bodart, G. 1908. *Militär-historisches Kriegs-Lexikon (1618–1905).* Vienna: Stern.

Boelcke, W. A. 1985. *Die Kosten von Hitler's Krieg: Kriegsfinanzierung und finanzielles Kriegserbe in Deutschland, 1933–1948.* Paderborn: Ferdinand Schöningh.

Borczuk, A. 1972. Contribution à l'étude des grèves de 1919 et de 1920 en France. Ph.D. thesis. Paris.

Borderie, A. de la. 1975 [1884]. *La révolte du papier timbré advenue en Bretagne en 1675.* Paris: Union Générale d'Edition.

Bourgain, L. 1890. *Etudes sur les biens ecclésiastiques pendant la Révolution.* Paris: Louis Vivès.

Bouthoul, G. 1970. *Traité de polémologie: sociologie des guerres.* Paris: Payot.

Boysson, R. de. 1907. *Le clergé périgourdin pendant la persécution révolutionnaire.* Paris: Picard.

Braudel, F. 1967. *Civilisation matérielle et capitalisme (XVe–XVIIIe siècle).* Paris: Armand Colin. English translation: *Capitalism and material life, 1400–1800.* New York: Harper and Row, 1973.

Brown, D. M. 1955. *Nationalism in Japan.* Berkeley: University of California Press.

Bujac, E. 1896. *La guerre sino-japonaise.* Paris: Charles Lavauzelle.

Bunge, M. 1996. *Finding philosophy in the social sciences.* New Haven: Yale University Press.

——— 1998. *Social science under debate: a philosophical perspective.* Toronto: University of Toronto Press.

Burke, P. 1992. *History and social theory.* Ithaca, N.Y.: Cornell University Press.

Burne, J., ed. 1989. *Chronicle of the world.* New York: Longman.

Burton, R. G. 1914. *Napoleon's invasion of Russia.* London: George Allen and Co..

Bywater, H. C. 1925. *The Great Pacific war: a history of the American-Japanese campaign.* Boston: Houghton Mifflin Co.

Cagan, P. 1956. The monetary dynamics of hyperinflation. In *Studies in the quantitative theory of money,* edited by M. Friedman. Chicago: Chicago University Press. Reprinted in: *Major inflations in history,* edited by F. H. Capie. London: Edward Elgar, 1991.

Cahen, L., and M. Braure. 1960. *L'évolution politique de l'Angleterre moderne.* Paris: Albin Michel.

Calhoon, R. M. 1973. *The Loyalists in Revolutionary America, 1760–1781.* New York: Harcourt Brace Jovanovich.

Campbell, J. 1990. *La seconde guerre mondiale.* Paris: Reader Digest.

Carron, P. 1935. *Les massacres de septembre.* Paris: Maison du Livre Français.

Carruth, G., ed. 1993. *The encyclopedia of world facts and dates.* New York: Harper and Collins.

Carsten, F. L. 1959. *Princes and parliaments in Germany from the fifteenth to the eighteenth century.* Oxford: Clarendon Press.

Castellan, G. 1967. *La vie quotidienne en Serbie au temps de l'indépendance, 1815–1839.* Paris: Hachette.

Chaliand, G., and J.-P. Raynau. 1993. *Atlas des empires de Babylone à la Russie soviétique.* Paris: Payot.

Chamberlin, W. H. 1936, 1939. *Japan over Asia.* Boston: Little, Brown and Co.

Channing, E. 1908. *A history of the United States.* Vol. 2: *A century of colonial history.* New York: Macmillan.

Chaunu, P. 1978. *Histoire quantitative, histoire sérielle.* Paris: Armand Colin.

Cheruel, A. 1882. *Histoire de France sous le ministère de Mazarin (1651–1661).* Vol. 2. Paris: Hachette.

Childers, E. 1920. *La terreur militaire en Irlande.* Paris: Gabriel Beauchesne. Translated from: *Military rule in Ireland: a series of eight articles contributed to the Daily News.* Dublin: Talbot Press, 1920.

Chirot, D. 1983. Sociology and history: a review essay. *Historical Methods* 16, 3, 121–123.

Chitwood, O. P. 1961 [1931]. *A history of colonial America.* New York: Harper and Brothers.

Choko, I. 1932. *The necessary war between America and Japan* (in Japanese). Tokyo.

Chou, S.-H. 1963. *The Chinese inflation.* New York: Columbia University Press.

Chrétien, J.-P. 1970. Une révolte au Burundi en 1934. *Annales Economies, Sociétés, Civilisations* 25, 5, 1678–1717.

Churchill, W. S. 1925. *La crise mondiale.* Vol. 1: *1911–1914.* Paris: Payot. Translated from: *The World Crisis.* 4 vols. New York: Scribner.

———— 1928. *La crise mondiale.* Vol. 2: *1915.* Payot. Paris. Translated from: The *World Crisis.* 4 vols. New York: Scribner, 1928.

———— 1930. *La crise mondiale.* Vol. 3: *1916–1918.* Paris: Payot. Translated from: *The World Crisis.* 4 vols. New York: Scribner, 1928.

———— 1950. *The Second World War.* Vol. 3: *The Grand Alliance.* London: Cassel.

———— 1965. *La deuxième guerre mondiale.* Vol. 6: *La grande alliance.* Paris: Cercle du Bibliophile. Translated from: *The Second World War.* New York: Bantam Books, 1949.

Clammer, D. 1973. *The Zulu war.* New York: St. Martin's Press.

Clarke, H. B. 1906. *Modern Spain.* Cambridge: Cambridge University Press.

Clausewitz, K. von. 1900. *La campagne de 1812 en Russie.* Paris: Librairie Militaire. English translation: *The campaign of 1812 in Russia.* Westport, Conn.: Greenwood Press, 1977.

———— 1972. *La campagne de 1815 en France.* Paris: Librairie Militaire Chapelot.

———— 1976. *On war.* Princeton: Princeton University Press. Translated from the German: *Vom Kriege* (1836).

Clayton, A. 1993. Emergencies and disorder in the European empires after 1945. *Journal of Imperial and Commonwealth History* 21, 3, 129–147.

———— 1994. *The wars of French decolonization.* London: Longman.

Clément, P. 1859. *Etudes financières et d'économie sociale.* Paris: E. Dentu.

Clodfelter, M. 1992. *Warfare and armed conflicts: a statistical reference to casualty and other figures, 1618–1991.* Vol. 1: *1618–1899;* Vol. 2: *1900–1991.* Jefferson, N.C.: McFarland and Co.

———— 1995. *Vietnam in military statistitics: a history of the Indochina wars, 1772–1991.* Jefferson, N.C.: McFarland and Co.

Clutterbuck, R. 1973. *Riot and revolution in Singapore and Malaya, 1945–1963.* London: Faber and Faber.

Collection complète des mémoires relatifs à l'histoire de France depuis le règne de Philippe-Auguste jusqu'au commencement du 17e siècle. 47 vols. Published between 1819 and 1825 by M. Petitot. Paris: Foucault.

Collection des mémoires relatifs à l'histoire de France depuis l'avènement de Henri IV jusqu'à la paix de Paris conclue en 1763. Volumes 48–51, and with the same title, volumes 1–78, published between 1824 and 1829. Paris: Foucault.

Collier, G. E., T. E. Skidmore, and H. Blakemore. 1992. *The Cambridge Encyclopedia of Latin America and the Caribbean.* Cambridge: Cambridge University Press.

Collinson, P. *The Church of England.* Sussex Tapes.

Colomb, P., J. F. Maurice, and F. N. Maude. 1893. *The great war of 189–: a forecast.* London: William Heinemann.

Commission d'enquête américaine sur la situation de l'Irlande. 1921. Premier rapport. Paris: La Démocratie.

Connor, W. 1994. *Ethnonationalism: the quest for understanding.* Princeton: Princeton University Press.

Constant, G. 1930. *La réforme en Angleterre.* Vol. 1: *Le schisme anglican: Henri VIII (1509–1547).* Paris: Perrin.

Conte, A. 1991. *Joffre.* Paris: Olivier Orban.

Cook, C., and J. Stevenson. 1978. *The atlas of modern warfare.* London: Weidenfeld and Nicholson.

Costello, J. 1981. *La guerre du Pacifique.* Paris: Pygmalion. Translation of: *The Pacific war.* London: Collins, 1981.

Coupland, R. 1954. *Welsh and Scottish nationalism.* London: Collins.

Courty-Valentin, M.-R. 1981. Les grèves de 1947 en France. Ph.D. thesis. Institut d'Etudes Politiques. Paris.

Coville, A. 1902. *Histoire de France.* Vol. 4: *Les premiers Valois et la guerre de cent ans (1338–1422).* Under the direction of E. Lavisse. Paris: Hachette.

Crommelin. 1799. *Histoire secrète de l'espionnnage pendant la Révolution.* Vol. 2. Francfort.

Crook, W. H. 1931. *The general strike: a study of labor's tragic weapon in theory and practice.* Chapel Hill: University of North Carolina Press.

Crouch, C. 1993. *Industrial relations and European state traditions.* Oxford: Clarendon Press.

Crummey, D., ed. 1986. *Banditry, rebellion, and social protest in Africa.* London: James Correy.

Damé, F. 1900. *Histoire de la Roumanie contemporaine depuis l'avènement des princes indigènes jusqu'à nos jours (1822–1900).* Paris: Félix Alcan.

Daniel-Rops, H. 1958. *Histoire de l'Eglise: l'Eglise des temps classiques—L'ère des grands craquements.* Paris: Fayard. English translation: *The Church in the eighteenth century.* New York: Dutton, 1964.

Davidson, B. 1972. *L'Angola au coeur des tempêtes.* Paris: François Maspéro.

Davin, L. E. 1949. *Les finances de 1939 à 1945: l'Allemagne.* Paris: Génin.

Daws, G. 1968. *Shoal of time: a history of the Hawaiian Islands.* New York: Macmillan.

Dawson, W. H. 1919. *The German empire (1867–1914) and the unity movement.* London: George Allen and Unwin.

Debo, A. 1970. *A history of the Indians of the United States.* Norman: University of Oklahoma Press.

Delaunes, P. 1969. *Les libérations de l'Amérique latine.* Lausanne: Editions Rencontre.

Demelas, M. D., and Y. Saint-Geours. 1987. *En Amérique au temps de Bolivar, 1809–1830.* Paris: Hachette.

Denlinger, S., and C. B. Gary. 1936. *War in the Pacific: a study of navies, peoples, and battle problems.* New York: R. M. McBride.

Deprez, R. 1963. *La Grande Grève: décembre 1960–janvier 1961.* Brussells: Editions de la Fondation J. Jacquemotte.

Descartes, R. 1965 [1637]. *Discourse on method, optics, geometry and meteorology.* Indianapolis: Bobbs-Merill Co.

Deschamps, H. 1965. *Histoire de Madagascar.* Paris: Berger-Levrault.

Desmond, C. 1970. *The discarded people.* London: Penguin Books.

des Odoards, F. 1797. *Histoire philosophique de la Révolution de France.* Vol. 1. Paris.

Deutsch, K. W. 1966 [1953]. *Nationalism and social communication.* Cambridge: MIT Press.

———— 1979. *Tides among nations.* New York: Free Press.

Deventer, M. L. van. 1870. *Cinquante années de l'histoire fédérale de l'Allemagne: étude historique et politique.* Brussells: Mucquart.

Deygas, F.-J. 1932. *L'armée d'Orient dans la guerre mondiale (1915–1919).* Paris: Payot.

Dogan, M., and D. Pelassy. 1984. *How to compare nations: studies in comparative politics.* Chatham, N.J.: Chatham House.

Dogan, M., et al., eds. 1994. *Comparing nations: concepts, strategies, substance.* Oxford: Blackwell. Oxford.

Doherty, J. E., and Hickey, D. J. 1989. *A chronology of Irish history since 1500.* Dublin: Gill and Macmillan.

Donaldson, G. 1971. *Scotland.* Vol. 3: *James V to James VII.* Edinburgh: Oliver and Boyd.

Doubnov, S. 1933. *Histoire du peuple juif.* Paris. English translation (from the Russian): *An outline of Jewish history.* 3 vols. New York: Maisel, 1925.

Dousset-Leenhardt, R. 1976. *Terre natale, terre d'exil.* Paris: Maisonneuve et Larose.

Doyle, W. 1980. *Origins of the French Revolution.* Oxford: Oxford University Press. French translation: *Des origines de la Révolution française.* Paris: Calmann-Lévy.

Drame, S., C. Gonfalone, J. A. Miller, and B. Roehner. 1991. *Un siècle de commerce du blé en France, 1825–1913.* Paris: Economica.

Dreyfus, F.-G. 1970. *Histoire des Allemagnes.* Paris: Armand Colin.

Droz, B., and E. Lever. 1982. *Histoire de la guerre d'Algérie.* Paris: Seuil.

Ducatenzeiler, G. 1980. *Syndicats et politique en Argentine.* Montreal: Presses de l'Université de Montreal.

Dulphy, A. 1992. *Histoire de l'Espagne.* Paris: Hatier.

Dumont, G.-H. 1977. *Histoire de la Belgique.* Paris: Hachette.

Dunnigan, J. F. 1993. *How to make war.* New York: William Morrow and Co.

Durand, R. 1992. *Histoire du Portugal.* Paris: Hatier.

Durkheim, E. 1951 [1897]. *Suicide, a study in sociology.* Glencoe, Ill.: Free Press. Translation of: *Le suicide.* Paris: F. Alcan.

Ebbinghaus, G., and J. Visser. 1997. *The development of trade unions in Western Europe, 1945–1995: a data handbook.* Frankfurt: Campus Verlag.

Edwards, L. P. 1970 [1927]. *The natural history of revolution.* Chicago: University of Chicago Press.

Edwards, R. D. 1981. *An atlas of Irish history.* London: Methuen.

Egret, J. 1962. *La Pré-Révolution.* Paris: Presses Universitaires de France.

Einzig, P. 1934. *Germany's default: the economics of Hitlerism.* London: Macmillan and Co.

Ellis, J. 1993. *The World War II data book.* New York: Aurum Press.

Engels, F. 1976. *Le rôle de la violence dans l'histoire.* Paris. Editions Sociales.

Engerand, F. 1918. *Le secret de la frontière, 1815–1871–1914.* Paris: Editions Bossard.

Entwicklung, Plannung, and Durchführung operative Ideen im Ersten and Zweiten Weltkrieg. 1989. Bonn: E. S. Mittler and Sohn.

Europa World Yearbook. London: Europa Publication Limited.

Eyck, E. 1954. *Geschichte der Weimarer Republik.* Vol. 1: *Vom Zuzammenbruch des Kaisertums bis zur Wahl Hindenburgs.* Stuttgart: Eugen Reutsch Verlag.

Fama, E. F. 1965. The behavior of stock-market prices. *Journal of Business* 38, 34–105.

Féaux, V. 1963. *Cinq semaines de lutte sociale: la grève de l'hiver 1960–1961.* Brussells: Editions de l'Institut de Sociologie de l'Université Libre de Bruxelles.

Ferguson, J. H. 1963. *The revolutions of Latin America.* London: Thames and Hudson.

Fezensac, R.A.P.J. de Montesquiou, duc de. 1970. *The Russian campaign.* Athens: University of Georgia Press.

Firth, C. H. 1902. *Cromwell's army: A history of the English soldier during the Civil Wars, the Commonwealth and the Protectorate.* London: Methuen and Co.

——— 1953. *Oliver Cromwell and the rule of Puritans in England.* London: Oxford University Press.

Fischer, D. H. 1989. *Albion's seed: four British folkways in America.* Oxford: Oxford University Press.

——— 1994. *Paul Revere's ride.* New York: Oxford University Press.

Fisk, R. 1975. *The point of no return: the strike which broke the British in Ulster.* London: André Deutsch.

Fitzmaurice, J. 1985. *Quebec and Canada: past, present, future.* London: Hurst and Co.

Fitzpatrick, E. H. 1909. *The coming conflict of nations, or the Japanese-American war.* Springfield, Ill.: H. W. Rokker.

Flora, P., F. Kraus, and W. Pfenning. 1983, 1987. *State, economy, and society in Western Europe, 1815–1975: a data handbook in two volumes.* London: Macmillan.

Fogel, R. W. 1964. *Railroads and American growth.* Baltimore: Johns Hopkins Press.

Forrest, A. 1975. *Society and politics in revolutionary Bordeaux.* Oxford: Oxford University Press.

Franzosi, R. 1995. *Puzzle of strikes.* Cambridge: Cambridge University Press.

French, D. 1990. *The British way in warfare, 1688–2000.* London: Unwin Hyman.

Friedman, G., and M. Lebard. 1991. *The coming war with Japan.* New York: St. Martin's Press.

Friedman, M. 1953. *Essays in positive economics.* Chicago: University of Chicago Press.

Garnier, C.-M. 1939. *Eire: histoire d'Irlande.* Paris: Aubier.

Garnier, J.-P. 1973. *La fin de l'Empire ottoman.* Paris: Plon.

Gash, N. 1953. *Politics in the age of Peel: a study in the technique of parliamentary representation, 1830–1850.* London: Longmans, Green and Co.

Gaulle, C. de. 1934. *Vers l'armée de métier.* Paris: Berger-Levrault. English translation: *The army of the future.* Philadelphia: Lippincott, 1941.

———— 1935. Comment faire une armée de métier? *Revue hebdomadaire,* June 1.

———— 1945. *Trois études, suivies du mémorandum du 26 janvier 1940.* Paris: Berger-Levrault.

———— 1954. *Mémoires de guerre.* Vol. 1. Paris: Plon. English translation: *War memoirs.* 5 vols. New York: Viking Press, 1955–1960.

———— 1972 [1924]. *La discorde chez l'ennemi.* Paris: Plon.

Gershoy, L. 1966. *L'Europe des princes éclairés.* Paris: Fayard. French translation of: *From despotism to revolution, 1763–1789.* New York: Harper, 1957.

Gibson, R. H., and M. Prendergast. 1932. *Histoire de la guerre sous-marine, 1914–1918.* Paris: Payot.

Gilbert, M. 1966. *British history atlas: 1870 to the present day.* London: Weidenfeld and Nicolson.

Gilje, P. A. 1996. *Rioting in America.* Bloomington: Indiana University Press.

Godechot, J. 1963. *Les révolutions de 1848.* Paris: Presses Universitaires de France.

———— 1965. *La prise de la Bastille.* Paris: Gallimard. English translation: *The taking of the Bastille, July 14th 1789.* London: Faber, 1970.

———— 1971. *Histoire de l'Italie moderne.* Vol. 1: *Le Risorgimento, 1770–1870.* Paris: Hachette.

———— 1986. *La Révolution française dans le Midi toulousain.* Privat: Toulouse.

Goetz-Girey, R. 1965. *Le mouvement des grèves en France, 1919–1962.* Paris: Sirey.

Goldstone, J. A. 1982. The comparative and historical study of revolutions. *Annual Reviews in Sociology* 8, 187–207.

———— 1991. *Revolution and rebellion in the early modern world.* Berkeley: University of California Press.

———— 1997. Methodological issues in comparative macrosociology. In *Methodological issues in comparative social science,* edited by L. Mjöset et al. Comparative Social Research, vol. 16. Greenwich, Conn.: JAI Press.

———— 1998. Initial conditions, general laws, path-dependence, and explanation in historical sociology. *American Journal of Sociology* 104: 829–845.

Goldstone, J. A., J. R. Gurr, and F. Moshiri, eds. 1991. *Revolutions of the late twentieth century.* Boulder: Westview Press.

Graham, F. D. 1930. *Exchange, prices, and production in hyper-inflation Germany, 1920–1923.* Princeton: Princeton University Press.

Graham, R. 1994. *Independence in Latin America: a comparative approach.* New York: McGraw-Hill.

Grand Larousse Encyclopédique. 1963. 10 vols. Paris: Larousse.

Granger, C. W. J. 1969. Investigating causal relations by econometric models and cross-spectral methods. *Econometrica* 37, 3, 424–438.

———— 1991. Reducing self-interest and improving the relevance of economic research. Paper presented at the ninth International Congress of Logic, Methodology, and Philosophy of Science. Uppsala.

Granier de Cassagnac, M. A. 1860. *Histoire des Girondins et des massacres de septembre, d'après les documents officiels et inédits accompagnés de plusieurs facsimilés.* Paris: Dentu.

Gravereau, J. 1988. *Le Japon.* Paris: Imprimerie Nationale. Paris.

Gray, R. 1990. *Chronicle of the First World War.* Vol. 1: *1914–1916.* New York: Facts on File.

Grégoire, L.-J. 1989. *Le Zimbabwe.* Paris: L'Harmattan.

Guerdan, R. 1981. *Histoire de Genève.* Paris: Mazarine.

Guiffan, J. 1992. *Histoire de l'Irlande.* Paris: Hatier.

Guizot, F. 1854. *Histoire de la Révolution d'Angleterre.* Vol. 2: *La République et Cromwell (1649–1658).* Paris: Didier.

Gwynn, D. 1928. *The struggle for Catholic emancipation (1750–1829).* London: Longmans, Green and Co.

Haimson, L. D. H., and C. Tilly, eds. 1989. *Strikes, wars, and revolutions in an international perspective: strike waves in the late nineteenth and twentieth century.* Cambridge: Cambridge University Press.

Hall, J. R. 1992. Where history and sociology meet: forms of discourse and sociohistorical inquiry. *Sociological Theory* 10, 2, 164–193.

———— 1999. *Cultures of inquiry.* Cambridge: Cambridge University Press.

Hall, J. R., and P. Schuyler. 1998. Apostasy, apocalypse, and religious violence: an exploratory comparison of Peoples Temple, the Branch Davidians, and the Solar Temple. In *The politics of religious apostasy,* edited by D. G. Bromley. Westport, Conn.: Praeger.

Hallgarten, G. 1961. *Histoire des dictatures de l'antiquité à nos jours.* Paris: Payot.

Hamblin, R. L., R. B. Jacobsen, and J. L. L. Miller. 1973. *A mathematical theory of social change.* New York: John Wiley.

Hamscher, A. N. 1976. *The Parlement of Paris after the Fronde, 1653–1673.* Pittsburgh: University of Pittsburgh Press.

Haski, P. 1987. *L'Afrique blanche.* Paris: Seuil.

Hatin, E. 1965 [1860]. *Bibliographie historique et critique de la presse périodique française précédée d'un essai historique et statistique sur la naissance et les progrès de la presse périodique dans les Deux Mondes.* Paris: Editions Anthropos.

Hechter, M. 1975. *Internal colonialism: The Celtic fringe in British national development, 1536–1966.* London: Routledge and Kegan Paul.

———— 1994. The role of values in rational choice theory. *Rationality and Society* 6, 318–333.

———— 1997. Sociological rational choice theory. *Annual Reviews in Sociology* 23, 191–214.

Heinig, K. 1962. *Le prix des guerres.* Paris: Gallimard.

Helfferich, K. 1989. *Russie et Japon: les finances des belligérants.* Paris: Guillaumin.

Helle, A. E. 1992. *Histoire du Danemark.* Paris: Hatier.

Hergenroether, J. 1880. *Histoire de l'Eglise.* Vol. 5. Paris: Delhomme et Briguet.

Hesse, M. 1966. *Models and analogies in science.* Notre Dame: University of Notre Dame.

Hibbert, C. 1978. *The Great Mutiny: India 1857.* New York: Viking Press.

Hickey, D. J., and Doherty, J. E. 1980. *A dictionary of Irish history since 1800.* Dublin: Gill and Macmillan.

Hillegas, H. C. 1899. *Oom Paul's people: a narrative of the British-Boer troubles in South Africa with a history of the Boers, the country, and its institutions.* New York: D. Appleton.

Hilpert, A. 1911. Die Sequestration des geistlichen Güter in den kursächsischen Landkreisen Meiszen, Vogtland und Sachsen, 1531–1543. Ph.D. thesis (Leipzig). Druckerei Neupert.

Historical Statistics of the United States. 1975. Washington, D.C.: U.S. Department of Commerce.

Hochschild, A. 1991. *The mirror at midnight: a journey to the heart of South Africa.* London: Collins.

Hoffman, R. J. S. 1933. *Great Britain and the German trade rivalry, 1875–1914.* Philadelphia: University of Pennsylvania Press.

————, ed. 1994. *Two thousand years of warfare.* Danbury, Conn.: Grolier.

Holsti, K. J. 1991. *Peace and war: armed conflicts and international order, 1648–1989.* Cambridge: Cambridge University Press.

Holsti, O. R., P. J. Hopmann, and J. D. Sullivan. 1973. *Unity and disintegration in international alliances: comparative studies.* New York: John Wiley.

Horn, N., and Tilly, C. 1986. Catalogs of contention in Britain, 1758–1834. Working paper no. 32. Center for Studies of Social Change. New York.

Howard, G. E. 1905. *Preliminaries of the Revolution, 1763–1775*. New York: Harper and Brothers.

Huber, E. R. 1988. *Deutsche Verfassungsgeschichte seit 1789*. Vol. 3: *Bismark und das Reich*. Stuttgart: Kohlhammer Verlag.

Hugo, V. 1997. *Miserables*. New York: Knopf.

Hundred-Year Statistics of the Japanese Economy. 1966. Tokyo: Statistics Department of the Bank of Japan.

Huston, J. A. 1989. *Guns and butter, powder and rice: U.S. Army logistics in the Korean War*. Selinsgrove, Pa.: Susquehanna University Press.

Huxley, A. 1959. A case of voluntary ignorance. In *Collected essays*. New York: Harper.

Ienaga, S. 1968. *Japan's last war: World War II and the Japanese, 1931–1945*. Canberra: Australian National University Press.

Ikezaki, C. 1932. *La guerre Japano-Américaine indispensable* [The necessary war between Japan and the United States] (in Japanese). Tokyo.

Ishimaru, T. 1933. *The inevitable war between Britain and Japan* (in Japanese). Tokyo. English translation: *Japan must fight Britain*. New York: Telegraph Press, 1936.

———— *The next world war*. London: Hurst and Blackett.

Jackson, T. A. 1973 [1947]. *Ireland her own: an outline of the Irish struggle of national freedom and independence*. Berlin: Seven Seas.

Jacob, F. 1970. *La logique du vivant: une histoire de l'hérédité*. Paris: Gallimard. English translation: *The logic of life: a history of heredity*. New York: Pantheon Books, 1973.

James, C. L. R. 1985 [1938]. *Negro revolt*. London: Race Today Publications.

Janssen, J. 1892. *L'Allemagne et la Réforme: l'Allemagne depuis la fin de la révolution sociale jusqu'à la paix d'Augsbourg (1525–1555)*. Paris: Plon.

Jaszi, O. 1929. *The dissolution of the Habsburg monarchy*. Chicago: University of Chicago Press.

Jenkins, J. R. G. 1986. *Jura separatism in Switzerland*. Oxford: Clarendon Press.

Jomini, A. H. de. 1838. *Précis de l'art de la guerre*. Brussells: J. B. Petit. English translation: *The art of war*. Westport, Conn.: Greenwood Press, 1971.

Jonard, N. 1965. *La vie quotidienne à Venise au XVIIIe siècle*. Paris: Hachette.

Jonquière, A. de la. 1881. *Histoire de l'Empire ottoman depuis les origines jusqu'au traité de Berlin*. Paris: Hachette.

Jourgniac de Saint-Méard, F. 1792. *Mon agonie de trente huit heures ou récit qui m'est arrivé, de ce que j'ai vu et entendu pendant ma détention dans la prison de l'Abbaye Saint-Germain depuis le 22 août jusqu'au 4 septembre*. Paris: Desenne.

Julien, C.-A. 1964. *Histoire de l'Algérie contemporaine*. Vol. 1: *La conquête et les débuts de la colonisation, 1827–1871*. Paris: Presses Universitaires de France.

———— 1972 [1952]. *L'Afrique du Nord en marche: nationalismes musulmans et souveraineté française*. Paris: Julliard.

Karnes, T. L. 1961. *The failure of Union: Central America, 1824–1960*. Chapel Hill: University of North Carolina.

Karp, W. 1979. *The politics of war: the story of two wars which altered forever the political life in the American Republic*. New York: Harper and Row.

Kee, R. 1972. *The green flag: the turbulent history of the Irish national movement*. New York: Delacorte Press.

Keesing's contemporary archives, 1931–1986 (continued by *Keesing's record of world events*). London: Keesing's Limited.

Keesing's record of world events. Annual. London: Longman. Subsequently: Castermill Publishing, N.J.

Keller, H. R. 1934. *The dictionary of dates*. New York: Macmillan.

Kelley, A. C., and J. G. Williamson. 1974. *Lessons from Japanese development: an analytical economic history*. Chicago: University of Chicago Press.

Kendall, M., A. Stuart, and J. K. Ord. 1987. *Kendall's advanced theory of statistics*. London: Charles Griffin.

Khong, Y. F. 1992. *Analogies at war: Korea, Munich, Dien Bien Phu and the Vietnam decisions of 1965*. Princeton: Princeton University Press.

Kindermann, R., and Snell, J. L. 1980. *Markov random fields and their applications*. Providence, R.I.: American Mathematical Society.

Kindleberger, C. P. 1978. *Manias, panics, and crashes*. New York: Basic Books.

King, G., R. Keohane, and S. Verba. 1994. *Designing social inquiry: scientific inference in qualitative research*. Princeton: Princeton University Press.

Kiser, E., and M. Hechter. 1998. The debate on historical sociology: rational choice theory and its critics. *American Journal of Sociology* 104: 785–816.

Knowles, D. 1959. *Bare ruined choirs: the dissolution of the English monasteries*. Cambridge: Cambridge University Press.

Knowles, K. G. J. C. 1952. *Strikes: a study in industrial conflict with special reference to British experience between 1911 and 1947*. Oxford: Blackwell.

Kodansha Encyclopedia of Japan. 1983. Tokyo.

Kossmann, E. H. 1954. *La Fronde*. Leiden: Universitaires Pers Leiden.

Koul, G. L. 1972. *Kashmir then and now*. Srinagar: Chronicle Publishing House.

Kravchenko, V. A. 1980 [1950]. *J'ai choisi la liberté! La vie publique et privée d'un haut fonctionnaire soviétique*. Paris: Olivier Orban.

Kühn, H.-M. 1966. *Die Einziehung des Geistlichen Gutes im Albertinischen Sachsen, 1539–1553*. Cologne: Bohlau.

Kull, I. S., and N. M. Kull. 1952. *A short chronology of American history, 1492–1950*. New Brunswick, N.J.: Rutgers University Press.

Kurian, G. T. 1994. *Datapedia of the United States*. Lanham, Md.: Bernam Press.

Kuznets, S. 1956. *Quantitative aspects of the economic growth of nations*. Chicago: University of Chicago Press.

Labatut, J.-P. 1978. *Les noblesses européennes de la fin du XVe siècle à la fin du XVIIIe siècle.* Paris: Presses Universitaires de France.

Lacour-Gayet, R. 1970. *Histoire de l'Afrique du Sud.* Paris: Fayard.

———— 1976. *Histoire des Etats-Unis.* Vol. 1: *Des origines jusqu'à la fin de la guerre civile.* Paris: Fayard.

Lacretelle, C. 1801. *Précis historique de la Révolution française.* Paris: Treuttel et Wurtz.

Laitin, D. D. 1998. *Identity in formation: the Russian-speaking populations in the near abroad.* Ithaca, N.Y.: Cornell University Press.

Lallement, M. 1996. *Sociologie des relations professionnelles.* Paris: La Découverte.

Lambelin, R. 1922. *L'Egypte et l'Angleterre vers l'indépendance: de Mohammed Ali au roi Fouad.* Paris: Grasset.

Langer, W. L., ed. 1968. *An encyclopedia of world history, ancient, medieval and modern, chronologically arranged.* Boston: Houghton Mifflin.

Laursen, K., and J. Pedersen. 1964. *The German inflation, 1918–1923.* Amsterdam: North Holland.

Lavisse, E. 1905. *Histoire de France.* Vol. 7: *Louis XIV, la Fronde, le Roi, Colbert (1643–1685).* Paris: Hachette.

Lea, H. 1909. *The valor of ignorance.* New York: Harper and Brothers.

Lecarpentier, G. 1908. *La vente des biens ecclésiastiques pendant la Révolution française.* Paris: Alcan.

Lecky, W. E. H. 1892. *A history of England in the eighteenth century.* Vol. 4. London: Longmans, Green and Co.

Lemonnier, H. 1926 [1911]. *Histoire de France illustrée depuis les origines jusqu'à la Révolution.* Vol. 5, part 1. Published under the direction of E. Lavisse. Paris: Hachette.

Le Roy Ladurie, E. 1966. *Les paysans du Languedoc.* Paris: SEVPEN. English translation: *The peasants of Languedoc.* Urbana: University of Illinois Press, 1974.

Lieberson, S. 1985. *Making it count: the improvement of social research and theory.* Berkeley: University of California Press.

———— 1991. Small N's and big conclusions: an examination of the reasoning in comparative studies based on a small number of N's. *Social Forces* 70, 307–320.

———— 1992. Einstein, Renoir, and Greeley: some thoughts about evidence in sociology. 1991 Presidential Address. *American Sociological Review* 57, 1–15.

———— 1994. More on the uneasy case for using Mill-type methods in small-N comparative studies. *Social Forces* 72, 1225–1237.

Liesner, T. 1989. *One hundred years of economic statistics.* London: Facts on File.

Lindsey, A. 1942. *The Pullman strike: the story of a unique experiment and of a great labor upheaval.* Chicago: University of Chicago Press.

Lingard, J. 1829. *A history of England from the first invasion by the Romans.* Vols. 11 and 12: *1660–1673.* London: Baldwin and Cradock.

Lloyd, C. 1993. *The structures of history.* Oxford: Blackwell.

Lorris, P.-G. 1961. *La Fronde.* Paris: Albin Michel.

Lustik, I. S. 1993. *Unsettled states, disputed lands: Britain and Ireland, France and Algeria, Israel and the West Bank–Gaza.* Ithaca, N.Y.: Cornell University Press.

Luther, M. 1522. *De votis monasticis.* Basel: Adam Petri.

Lynn, J. A., ed. 1990. *Tools of war: Instruments, ideas, and institution of warfare, 1445–1871.* Urbana: University of Illinois Press.

———, ed. 1993. *Feeding Mars: Logistics in Western warfare from the Middle Ages to the present.* Boulder: Westview Press.

Lynn, J. A. 1997. *Giant of the Grand Siècle: the French army, 1610–1715.* Cambridge: Cambridge University Press.

Mabelis, A. A. 1979. Wood ant wars: the relationship between aggression and predation in the red wood ant (Formica Polyctena Först). *Netherlands Journal of Zoology* 29, 4, 451–627.

Macaulay, T. B. 1989. *Histoire d'Angleterre depuis l'avènement de Jacques II (1685) jusqu'à la mort de Guilllaume III (1702).* Paris: Robert Laffont. Translation of: *The history of England from the accession of James II.* London: Longman, Green, Longman, and Roberts, 1861.

MacDermott, M. 1962. *A history of Bulgaria, 1393–1885.* London: George Allen and Unwin.

Macek, J. 1984. *Histoire de la Bohême des origines à 1918.* Paris: Fayard.

Main, I. G. 1978. *Vibrations and waves in physics.* Cambridge: Cambridge University Press.

Major, J. R. 1954. The third estate in the Estates General of Pontoise, 1561. *Speculum,* April, 460–476.

Malcolm, N. 1998. *Kosovo: a short history.* New York: New York University Press.

Mangold, T., and J. Pennycate. 1987. *Tunnel warfare.* Toronto: Bantam Books.

Mankiw, N. G. 1992. *Macroeconomics.* New York: Worth Publishers.

Mantran, R., ed. 1989. *Histoire de l'Empire Ottoman.* Paris: Fayard.

Marchand, J. 1985. *La propagande de l'apartheid.* Paris: Editions Karthala.

Mariéjol, J. H. 1904. *Histoire de France.* Vol. 6: *La Réforme et la Ligue: L'Edit de Nantes (1559–1598).* Under the direction of E. Lavisse. Paris: Hachette.

Marion, M. 1976 [1929]. *Dictionnaire des institutions de la France aux XVIIe et XVIIIe siècles.* Paris: Picard.

Markoff, J. 1994. *The great wave of democracy in historical perspective.* Ithaca, N.Y.: Cornell University Press.

——— 1996a. *Waves of democracy: Social movements and political change.* Thousand Oaks, Calif.: Pim Forge Press.

——— 1996b. *The abolition of feudalism: peasants, lords, and legislators in the French Revolution.* University Park, Pa.: Pennsylvania State University Press.

Martin, J. 1987. *L'empire renaissant, 1789–1871.* Paris: Denoël. Paris.

——— 1990. *L'empire triomphant, 1871–1936.* Vol. 2: *Maghreb, Indochine, Madagascar.* Paris: Denoël.

Marx, K., and F. Engels. 1959. *The first Indian war of independence, 1857–1859.* Moscow: Foreign Language Publishing House.

——— 1971. *Ireland and the Irish question.* Moscow: Progress Publishers.

Marx, R. 1971. *L'Angleterre des révolutions.* Paris: Armand Colin.

Maton de la Varenne (P.A.L.). 1794. *Les crimes de Marat et des autres égorgeurs* [The crimes of Marat and other cutthroats], *ou Ma Résurrection où l'on trouve non seulement la preuve que Marat et divers autres scélérats,* [Marat and other scoundrels], *membres des autorités politiques, ont provoqué tous les massacres de prisonniers, mais encore des matériaux précieux pour l'histoire de la Révolution française.* Reprinted in *Histoire particulière des évènements qui ont eu lieu en France pendant les mois de juin, juillet, août, et de septembre 1792 et qui ont opéré la chute du trône royal.* Paris, 1806.

Maurice, B. 1840. *Histoire politique et anecdotique des prisons de la Seine contenant des renseignements entièrement inédits sur la période révolutionnaire.* Paris: Guillaumin.

May, E. R. 1973. *"Lessons" of the past: the use and misuse of history in American foreign policy.* New York: Oxford University Press.

Mayer, W., F. Metzger, and J. Wilhelmi. 1985. *Schwarz-Weiss-Rot in Afrika: Die Deutschen Kolonien, 1883–1918.* Puchheim: Idea.

Mayeur, J.-M., C. Pietri, A. Vauchez, and M. Venard. 1990. *Histoire du christianisme.* Vol. 6: *Un temps d'épreuves, 1274–1449.* Desclée. Paris: Fayard.

Mémoires du XXe siècle. 9 vols. Paris: Bordas.

Merrit, R. L. 1966. *Symbols of American community, 1735–1775.* New Haven: Yale University Press

Messenger, C. 1989. *World War II: chronological atlas.* London: Bloomsbury.

Metcalf, G. 1965. *Royal government and political conflict in Jamaica, 1729–1783.* London: Longmans.

Meyer, J. 1973. *Noblesse et pouvoir dans l'Europe d'ancien régime.* Paris: Hachette.

Michel, H. 1968. *La seconde guerre mondiale.* 2 vols. Paris: Presses Universitaires de France. English translation: *The Second World War.* New York: Praeger, 1975.

Michelsen, W. 1928. *La guerre sous-marine (1914–1918).* Paris: Payot.

Milioukov, P., C. Seignobos, and L. Eisenmann. 1933. *Histoire de la Russie.* Vol. 3: *Réformes, réactions, révolutions, 1855–1932.* Paris: Librairie Ernest Leroux.

Mitchell, B. R. 1971. *Abstract of British historical statistics.* Cambridge: Cambridge University Press.

——— 1978. *European historical statistics, 1750–1970.* London: Macmillan.

——— 1982. *International historical statistics: Africa and Asia.* New York: New York University Press.

——— 1983. *International historical statistics: the Americas and Australasia.* London: Macmillan.

Mjöset, L., et al., eds. 1997. *Methodological issues in comparative social science.* Comparative Social Research, vol. 16. Greenwich, Conn.: JAI Press.

Mohan, A. 1992. The historical roots of the Kashmir conflict. *Studies in Conflict and Terrorism* 15, 283–308.

Mollat, M., and P. Wolff. 1970. *Ongles bleus, Jacques et Ciompi: les révolutions populaires en Europe aux XIVe et XVe siècle.* Paris: Calmann Lévy. Paris.

Molleville, B. de. 1802. *Histoire de la Révolution de France.* Vol. 9. Paris: Guiguet.

Molnar, M. 1996. *Histoire de la Hongrie.* Paris: Hatier.

Monkkonen, E. H., ed. 1994. *Engaging the past: the uses of history across the social sciences.* Durham, N.C.: Duke University Press.

Montagnon, A. 1974. *Les guerres de Vendée, 1793–1832.* Paris: Librairie Académique Perrin.

Montagnon, P. 1992. *La grande histoire de la seconde guerre mondiale.* 10 vols. Paris: Pygmalion.

Montgaillard, Abbé de. 1827. *Histoire de France.* Paris.

Moreau, E. de, P. Jourda, and P. Janelle. 1950. *Histoire de l'Eglise depuis les origines jusqu'à nos jours.* Vol. 16. *La crise religieuse du XVIe siècle.* Paris: Bloud and Gay.

Morison, S. E. 1969 [1930]. *The growth of the American republic.* Oxford: Oxford University Press.

Morley, J. W. 1957. *The Japanese thrust into Siberia.* New York: Columbia University Press.

Morris, N. 1995. *Puerto Rico: culture, politics, and identity.* Westport, Conn.: Praeger.

Morris, P. 1992. *Histoire du Royaume-Uni.* Paris: Hatier.

Mortimer-Ternaux, M. 1863. *Histoire de la Terreur, 1792–1794, d'après des documents authentiques et inédits.* Vol. 3. Paris: Michel.

Mourre, M. 1978. *Dictionnaire encyclopédique d'histoire.* 8 vols. Paris: Bordas.

Mousnier, R. 1967. *Fureurs paysannes: Les paysans dans les révoltes du XVIIe siècle (France, Russie, Chine).* Paris: Calmann-Lévy. English translation: *Peasant uprisings in seventeenth-century France, Russia, and China.* New York: Harper and Row, 1970.

Mousson-Lestang, J.-P. 1995. *Histoire de la Suède.* Paris: Hatier.

Muzzey, D. S. 1921. *Histoire des Etats-Unis d'Amérique.* Paris: Librairie Larousse. Translation of: *American history.* Boston: Ginn and Co., 1911.

Neustadt, R. E., and E. R. May. 1986. *Thinking in time: the uses of history for decision makers.* New York: Free Press.

Nicolas, J., ed. 1985. *Mouvements populaires et conscience sociale aux 14 et 15e siècles.* Paris: Maloine.

Niox, General G.-L. 1906. *La guerre russo-japonaise.* Paris: Librairie Delagrave.

Norwich, J. J. 1986. *Histoire de Venise.* Paris: Payot. Translation of: *A history of Venice.* London: Penguin Books, 1977.

Nouvelle histoire de la Suisse et des Suisses. 1982–1983. 2 vols. Paris: Payot.

O'Neill, R. J. 1969. *General Giap, politician and strategist.* New York: Praeger.

Organski, A. F. K., and J. Kugler. 1980. *The war ledger.* Chicago: University of Chicago Press.

Pagonis, W. G., and J. L. Cruikshank. 1992. *Moving mountains: lessons in leadership and logistics from the Gulf War.* Boston: Harvard Business School Press.

Pakenham, T. 1979. *The Boer War.* New York: Random House.

Palmer, A. 1967. *Napoleon in Russia.* London: Andre Deutsch.

Palmer, A., and V. Palmer. 1992. *The chronology of British history.* London: Century.

Palmer, R. R. 1959. *The age of democratic revolution: a political history of Europe and America, 1760–1800.* Princeton: Princeton University Press.

Pareto, V. 1917. *Traité de sociologie générale.* Lausanne: Payot. English translation: *The mind and society.* New York: Harcourt, Brace and Co., 1935.

Parillo, M. 1993. *The Japanese merchant marine in World War II.* Annapolis: Naval Institute Press.

Parzen, E. 1960. *Modern probability theory and its applications.* New York: John Wiley.

Passant, E. J. 1960. *A short history of Germany, 1815–1945.* Cambridge: Cambridge University Press.

Patrick, A. 1972. *The men of the First French Republic: political alignments in the National Convention of 1792.* Baltimore: Johns Hopkins University Press.

Peillard, L. 1970. *Histoire de la guerre sous-marine, 1939–1945.* Paris: Robert Laffont.

Penson, T. H. 1909. The Swedish general strike. *Economic Journal* 19 (December): 602–609.

Perrot, M. 1973. *Les ouvriers en grève, 1871–1890.* 2 vols. Paris: Mouton.

Picot, G. 1872–1888. *Histoire des Etats Généraux.* 5 vols. Paris: Hachette.

Pillorget, R. 1975. *Les mouvements insurrectionnels de Provence entre 1576 et 1715.* Paris: Editions A. Pedone.

——— 1977. Les problèmes du maintien de l'ordre public en France entre 1774 et 1789. *L'Information Historique* 1, 114–119.

Pitkin, W. B. 1921. *Must we fight Japan?* New York: Century Company.

Plaatje, S. T. 1982 [1916]. *Native life in South Africa.* Johannesburg: Ravan Press.

Platzky, L., and C. Walker. 1985. *The surplus people: forced removals in South Africa.* Johannesburg: Ravan Press.

Poidevin, R. 1972. *L'Allemagne de Guillaume II à Hindenburg, 1900–1933.* Paris: Edition Richelieu.

Ponelis, F. 1993. *The development of Afrikaans.* Frankfurt: Peter Lang.

Porter, B. 1994. *War and the rise of the state.* New York: Free Press.

Pratt, J. W. 1925. *Expansionists of 1812.* New York: Macmillan.

Price, D. J. S. 1963. *Little science, big science.* New York: Columbia University Press. French translation of: *Science and suprascience.* Paris: Fayard, 1972.

Prudhomme, L. 1796–1797. *Histoire générale et impartiale des erreurs, des fautes et des crimes commis pendant la Révolution française à dater du 24 août 1787.* 6 vols. Paris.

Quid. 1997. Edited by D. Frémy and M. Frémy. Paris: Robert Laffont.

Ragin, C. C. 1987. *The comparative method: moving beyond qualitative and quantitative strategies.* Los Angeles: University of California Press.

———— 1997. Turning the tables: how case-oriented research challenges variable-oriented research. In *Methodological issues in comparative social science,* edited by L. Mjöset et al. Comparative Social Research, vol. 16. Greenwich, Conn.: JAI Press.

Rahmat, A. 1933. Contribution à l'étude du conflit hindou-musulman. Thesis. Paris: Paul Geuthner.

Ranger, T. O. 1968. Connexions between "primary resistance" movements and modern mass nationalism in East and Central Africa. I, II. *Journal of African History* 9, 3–4, 437–453, 631–641.

Rashevsky, N. 1968. *Looking at history through mathematics.* Cambridge: MIT Press.

Rathery, E. J. B. 1845. *Histoire des Etats généraux.* Paris: De Cosse et Delamotte.

Reid, J. M. 1971. *Scotland's progress: the survival of a nation.* London: Eyre and Spottiswoode.

Requien, M. 1934. *Le problème de la population du Japon.* Paris: Paul Geuthner.

Richardson, L. F. 1960. *Statistics of deadly quarrels.* Pittsburgh: Boxwood Press.

Robertson, J. 1962. *Dieppe: the shame and the glory.* London: Hutchinson.

Robichon, J. 1965. *Jour J en Afrique (8 novembre 1942).* Paris: Robert Laffont.

Roehner, B. 1982. Order transmission in large hierarchical organizations. *International Journal of Systems Science* 13, 5, 531–546.

———— 1993. Les logiques de l'histoire. Preprint. LPTHE-University of Paris 7.

———— 1995. *Theory of markets.* Berlin: Springer-Verlag.

———— 1997a. The comparative way in economics: a reappraisal. *Economie Appliquée* 50, 4, 7–32.

———— 1997b. Jesuits and the state: a comparative study of their expulsions (1520–1990). *Religion* 27, 165–182.

———— 1997c. Spatial and historical determinants of separatism and integration. *Swiss Journal of Sociology* 23, 1, 25–59.

———— 1999. Spatial analysis of real estate price bubbles: Paris, 1984–1993. *Regional Science and Urban Economics* 29, 78–88.

———— 2001. *Hidden collective factors in speculative trading.* Berlin: Springer-Verlag.

Roehner, B. M., and D. Sornette. 1998. The sharp peak–flat trough pattern and critical speculation. *European Physical Journal* B 4, 387–399.

———— 1999: Analysis of the phenomenon of speculative trading and one of its basic manifestations: postage stamp bubbles. *International Journal of Modern Physics* C 10, 6, 1099–1116.

Romier, L. 1924. *Catholiques et huguenots à la cour de Charles IX*. Paris: Perrin.

Rotberg, R. I. 1965. *The rise of nationalism in Central Africa: the making of Malawi and Zambia, 1873–1964*. Cambridge: Harvard University Press.

Roy, J. 1963. *La bataille de Dien Bien Phu*. Paris: Julliard. English translation: *The battle of Dienbienphu*. New York: Harper and Row, 1965.

Rudé, G. 1959. *The crowd in the French Revolution*. Oxford: Clarendon Press.

———— 1964. *The crowd in history: a study of popular disturbances in France and England, 1730–1848*. New York: John Wiley.

Ruedy, J. 1992. *Modern Algeria: the origins and development of a nation*. Bloomington: Indiana University Press.

Rule, J. B. 1997. *Theory and progress in social science*. Cambridge: Cambridge University Press.

Sainsbury, K. 1976. *The North African landings, 1942: a strategic decision*. London: Davis Poynter.

Sampson, A. 1960. *Common sense about Africa*. London: Victor Gollancz.

Samuelson, P. A. 1949. The Le Chatelier principle in linear programming. In *The collected scientific papers of Paul A. Samuelson*, edited by Joseph E. Stiglitz, vol. 1, 638–650. Cambridge: MIT Press, 1966– .

———— 1960. An extension of the Le Chatelier principle. *Econometrica* 368–379.

The Sceptred Isle. 1996. Vol. 6. BBC Audiocassette.

Scherer, A. 1980. *La réunion*. Paris: Presses Universitaires de France.

Schwartz, R. D. 1994. *Circle of protest: political ritual in the Tibetan uprising*. London: Hurst and Company.

Scott, F. D. 1977. *Sweden: the nation's history*. Minneapolis: University of Minnesota Press.

Segur, Général-Comte de. 1910. *La campagne de Russie: mémoires*. Paris: Nelson.

Serant, P. 1964. *Les vaincus de la Libération: l'épuration en Europe occidentale à la fin de la seconde guerre mondiale*. Paris: Robert Laffont.

Serman, W. 1986. *La Commune de Paris*. Paris: Fayard.

Seuffert, G. K. L. 1857. *Statistik des Getreide und Viktualien Handels im Königreich Bayern mit Berücksichtigung des Auslandes*. Munich: Weisz.

Shorter, E., and C. Tilly. 1974. *Strikes in France, 1830–1968*. Cambridge: Cambridge University Press.

Silver, B. J., G. Arrighi, and M. Dubofsky. 1995. Labor unrest in the world economy, 1870–1990. *Review of the Fernand Braudel Center* (Binghampton).

Simon, H. 1959. Theories of decision-making in economics and behavorial science. *American Economic Review* 49, 3, 253–283.

Singer, J. D., and M. Small. 1972. *The wages of war, 1816–1965: a statistical handbook*. New York: John Wiley.

Skendi, S. 1967. *The Albanian national awakening, 1878–1912*. Princeton: Princeton University Press.

Skocpol, T., ed. 1984. *Vision and method in historical sociology.* Cambridge: Cambridge University Press.

Smith, W. W., Jr. 1996. *Tibetan nation: a history of Tibetan nationalism and Sino-Tibetan relations.* Boulder: Westview Press.

Snooks, G. D. 1996. *The dynamic society: exploring the sources of global change.* London: Routledge.

────── 1997. *The ephemeral civilization: exploding the myth of social evolution.* London: Routledge.

────── 1998. *The laws of history.* London: Routledge.

Soboul, A. 1989. *Dictionnaire historique de la Révolution française.* Paris: Presses Universitaires de France.

Songeon, G. 1913. *Histoire de la Bulgarie depuis les origines jusqu'à nos jours.* Paris: Nouvelle Librairie Nationale.

Soria, G. 1987. *Grande histoire de la Révolution française.* 3 vols. Paris: Bordas.

Sorokin, P. A. 1937. *Social and cultural dynamics.* 3 vols. New York: American Book Company.

Soule, G. 1934. *The coming American revolution.* London: Routledge.

Spielmans, J. V. 1944. Strike profiles. *Journal of Political Economy* 52, 319–339.

Spindler, A. 1933. *La guerre sous-marine.* Vol. 1: *Les préliminaires.* Paris: Payot.

The Statesman's Year-Book. London: Macmillan.

Stein, E. 1959. *Histoire du Bas-Empire.* Vol. 1: *De l'Etat romain à l'Etat byzantin.* Paris: Desclée de Brouwer.

Steinmo, S., K. Thelen, and F. Longstreth, eds. 1992. *Structuring politics: historical institutionalism in comparative analysis.* Cambridge: Cambridge University Press.

Stephenson, N. W. 1921. *Texas and the Mexican War.* New Haven: Yale University Press.

Stinchombe, A. L. 1978. *Theoretical methods in social history.* New York: Academic Press.

Stourm, R. 1885. *Les finances de l'Ancien Régime et de la Révolution: origines du système financier actuel.* 2 vols. Paris: Guillaumin.

Summers, L. H. 1991. The scientific illusion in empirical macroeconomics. *Scandinavian Journal of Economics* 93, 2, 129–148.

Sumner, B. H. 1951. *Peter the Great and the emergence of Russia.* London: English Universities Press.

Svanström, R., and Palmstierna, C. F. 1944. *Histoire de la Suède.* Paris: Stock.

Symons, J. 1957. *The general strike: a historical portrait.* London: Cresset Press. London.

Szekfu, J. 1945. *Etat et nation.* Paris: Presses Universitaires de France.

Tackett, T. 1997. *Becoming a revolutionary: the deputies of the French National Assembly and the emergence of a revolutionary culture (1789–1790).* Princeton: Princeton University Press.

Tainter, J. A. 1988. *The collapse of complex societies.* Cambridge: Cambridge University Press.

Tanin, O., and E. Yohan. 1936. *When Japan goes to war.* New York: Vanguard Press.

Tapie, V.-L. 1969. *Monarchie et peuples du Danube.* Paris: Fayard.

Tarrow, S. 1995. Cycles of collective action: between movements of madness and the repertoire of contention. In *Repertoires and cycles of collective action,* edited by Mark Traugott. Durham, N.C.: Duke University Press. Originally appeared in *Social Science History* 17, 2–3.

Térestchenko, S. 1931. *La guerre navale russo-japonaise.* Paris: Payot.

Teulières, A. 1978. *La guerre du Vietnam, 1945–1975.* Paris: Editions Lavauzelle.

Theal, G. M. 1910. *History of South Africa since September 1795.* London: Swan Sonnenschein.

Thernstrom, S., ed. 1980. *Harvard Encyclopedia of American ethnic groups.* Cambridge: Harvard University Press.

Thomson, R. W. 1968. *Le jour J: "Ils débarquent."* Verviers, Belgium: Marabout.

Tilly, C. 1981. *As sociology meets history.* New York: Academic Press.

——— 1985. *Big structures, large processes, huge comparisons.* New York: Russell Sage.

——— 1986. *The contentious French.* Cambridge: Harvard University Press. French translation: *La France conteste de 1600 à nos jours.* Paris: Fayard, 1986.

——— 1992. How to detect, describe, and explain repertoires of contention. Working paper no. 150. Center for Studies of Social Change, New York.

——— 1993. *European revolutions, 1492–1992.* Oxford: Blackwell.

——— 1995. *Popular contention in Great Britain, 1758–1834.* Cambridge: Harvard University Press.

——— 1997. Means and ends of comparison in macrosociology. In *Methodological issues in comparative social science,* edited by L. Mjöset et al. Comparative Social Research, vol. 16. Greenwich, Conn.: JAI Press.

Tilly, L. A. 1992. The decline and disappearance of the classical food riot in France. Working paper no. 147. Center for Studies of Social Change, New York.

Times Atlas of World History. 1989. London: Times Books.

Tindall, P. E. N. 1987. *A history of Central Africa.* New York: Praeger.

Tocqueville, A. de. 1958. *Voyages en Angleterre, Irlande, Suisse et Algérie.* Vol. V-2 of the *Collected Works.* Paris: Gallimard. English translation: *Journeys to England and Ireland.* London: Faber and Faber, 1958.

Tolstoy, L. 1966. *War and peace.* New York: W. W. Norton.

Toussaint, A. 1971. *Histoire de l'île Maurice.* Paris: Presses Universitaires de France.

Toynbee, A. J. 1987. *A study of history.* Abridged edition. 2 vols. Oxford: Oxford University Press.

Traugott, M. 1995. Barricades as repertoire: continuities and discontinuities in the history of French contention. In *Repertoires and cycles of collective action,* edited by Mark Traugott. Durham, N.C.: Duke University Press. Originally appeared in *Social Science History* 17, 2–3.

———, ed. 1995. *Repertoires and cycles of collective action.* Durham, N.C.: Duke University Press.

Tulard, J. 1962. *Histoire de la Crète.* Paris: Presses Universitaires de France.

Tullock, G. 1971. The paradox of revolution. *Public Choice* 1, 89–99.

Van Creveld, M. 1995 [1977]. *Supplying war: logistics from Wallenstein to Patton.* Cambridge: Cambridge University Press.

——— 1989. *Technology and war: from 2000 B.C. to the present.* New York: Free Press.

——— 1998. *La transformation de la guerre.* Paris: Editions du Rocher. Translation of: *The transformation of war.* New York: Free Press, 1991.

Vandervelde, E., L. de Brouckère, and L. Vandermissen. 1914. *La grève générale en Belgique.* Paris: Félix Alcan.

Van Tyne, C. H. 1905. *The American Revolution, 1776–1783.* New York: Harper and Brothers.

Vaugeois, D., and J. Lacoursière, eds. 1969. *Canada-Québec: synthèse historique.* Québec: Editions du Renouveau Pédagogique.

Vaussard, M. 1972 [1950]. *Histoire de l'Italie moderne.* Vol. 2: *1870–1970.* Paris: Hachette.

Vernon, R. 1983. *Two hungry giants.* Cambridge: Harvard University Press.

Veyne, P. 1976. *L'inventaire des différences: leçon inaugurale au Collège de France.* Paris: Seuil.

——— 1984. *Writing history: essay in epistemology.* Middletown, Conn.: Wesleyan University Press. Translation of: *Comment on écrit l'histoire: essai d'épistémologie.* Paris: Seuil, 1971.

Vincent, B. 1898. *Haydn's dictionary of dates and universal information relating to all ages and nations.* London: Ward, Lock and Co.

Von Neumann, J., and O. Morgenstern. 1953. *Theory of games and economic behavior.* Princeton: Princeton University Press.

Voogd, C. de. 1992. *Histoire des Pays-Bas.* Paris: Hatier.

Vuilleumier, M., F. Kohler, E. Ballif, M. Cerutti, and B. Chevalley. 1977. *La grève générale de 1918 en Suisse.* Geneva: Editions Grounauer.

Wagemann, E. 1941. *D'où vient tout cet argent?* Paris: Plon.

Wagenheim, O. J. de. 1985. *Puerto Rico's revolt for independence.* Boulder: Westview Press.

Walker, R. 1990. *Struggle without end.* London: Penguin Books.

Wall, M. 1961. *The Penal Laws, 1691–1760.* Dundalk, Ireland: Dungalgan Press.

Wallach, J. L. 1986. *The dogma of the battle of annihilation: the theories of Clausewitz and Schlieffen and their impact on the German conduct of the world wars.* Westport, Conn.: Greenwood Press.

Wallerstein, I. 1974. *The modern world-system.* 3 vols. New York: Academic Press.

Walter, G. 1963. *La révolution anglaise, 1641–1660.* Paris: A. Michel.

Webb, S. B. 1989. *Hyperinflation and stabilization in Weimar Germany.* Oxford: Oxford University Press.

Welsh, D. 1991. *La guerre du Vietnam.* Paris: Presses de la Cité. Translation of: *The history of the Vietnam War.* London: Hamlyn, 1981.

Westrich, S. A. 1972. *The Ormée of Bordeaux: a revolution during the Fronde.* Baltimore: John Hopkins University Press.

Whitelocke, B. 1963. Memories of the English affairs from the beginning of the reign of Charles I to the happy restoration of King Charles II. In *La Révolution anglaise, 1641–1660,* edited by G. Walter. Paris: Albin Michel, 1963.

Wieczynski, J.-L., ed. 1988. *The modern encyclopedia of Russian, Soviet, and Eurasian history.* Gulf Breeze, Fla.: Academic International Press.

Wilkenfeld, J., M. Brecher, and S. Moser. 1988. *Crises in the twentieth century.* Oxford: Pergamon Press.

Williams, D. 1961. *A short history of modern Wales: 1485 to the present day.* London: John Murray.

Williams, M. W. 1916. *Anglo-American isthmian diplomacy.* Washington, D.C.: American Historical Association.

Williamson, J. G. 1980. Greasing the wheels of sputtering export engines: midwestern grains and American growth. *Explorations in Economic History* 17, 189–217.

——— 1985. *Did British capitalism breed inequality?* Boston: Allen and Unwin.

——— 1990. The impact of the Corn Laws just prior to repeal. *Explorations in Economic History* 27, 123–156.

Wolf, E. 1969. *Peasant wars of the twentieth century.* New York. French translation: *Les guerres paysanes du XXe siècle.* Paris: François Maspero, 1974.

Wolff, D. W. 1913. *Die Säkularisierung und Verwendung des Stifts- und Klostergüter in Hessen-Kassel unter Philipp dem Grozsmütigen und Wilhelm IV.* Gotha: Friedrich Andreas Perthes.

Woodhouse, C. M. 1968. *The story of modern Greece.* London: Faber and Faber.

World Directory of Minorities. 1989. Edited by the Minority Rights Group. London.

Woytinski, W. 1926. *Die Welt in Zahlen.* Vol. 2: *Die Arbeit.* Berlin: Rudolf Mosse.

Wright, J. K. 1932. *Atlas of the historical geography of the United States.* Washington, D.C.: Carnegie Institution.

Wright, Q. 1942. *A study of war.* Chicago: University of Chicago Press.

Yergin, D. 1991. *The prize: the epic quest for oil, money, and power.* New York: Simon and Schuster.

Zambrano, R., and C. Tilly. 1992. BRIT SPSS/PC system files. Working paper no. 154. Center for Studies of Social Change, New York.

Zannettaci-Stephanopoli, E. 1938. L'insurrection de 1916 dans l'arrondissement de Batna: ses causes et ses enseignements. University of Paris report. Paris.

Zeitschrift des Königlische Statistische Bureau Bayern. 1896.

Zellner, A. 1988. Causality and causality laws in economics. *Journal of Econometrics* 39, 7–21.

Zinn, H. 1990. *A people's history of the United States.* New York: Harper Perennial.

Zipf, G. K. 1972 [1949]. *Human behavior and the principle of least effort.* New York: Hafner Publishing Company.

Zischka, A. 1935. *Le Japon dans le monde: l'expansion nippone 1854–1934.* Paris: Payot.

Zolberg, A. R. 1972. Moments of madness. *Politics and Society* 2, 183–207.

Zweig, S. 1933. *Marie Antoinette: the portrait of an average woman.* New York: Viking Press.

Index